CHINA'S
UNFINISHED
ECONOMIC
REVOLUTION

CHINA'S
UNFINISHED
ECONOMIC
REVOLUTION

Nicholas R. Lardy

BROOKINGS INSTITUTION PRESS
WASHINGTON, D.C.

Library of Congress Cataloging-in-Publication data

Lardy, Nicholas R.
    China's unfinished economic revolution / Nicholas R. Lardy.
    p. cm.
  Includes bibliographical references and index.
  ISBN 0-8157-5134-6 (alk. paper)
  ISBN 0-8157-5133-8 (pbk. : alk. paper)
  1. China--Economic conditions--1976- 2. China--Economic
policy--1976- 3. Banks and banking--China. 4. Finance--China. I.
Title.
  HC427.92 .L373 1998
  338.951--ddc21

                      98-19667
                        CIP

9 8 7 6 5 4

Typeset in Palatino

Composition by Oakland Street Publishing
Arlington, Virginia

Printed by R.R. Donnelley & Sons Co.
Harrisonburg, Virginia

Foreword

NICHOLAS R. Lardy, in assessing China's economic transition, argues that reform has done little to improve the allocation and use of China's capital. For the past two decades state-owned banks have channeled a large share of sharply rising household savings into unreformed, money-losing enterprises, resulting in a dramatic rise in the debt of enterprises to banks. Chinese enterprises now have debt-to-equity ratios that are among the highest in the world. At the same time, banks have accrued enormous liabilities to households, which have entrusted them with nearly all their financial savings. Because most of the banks' borrowers are no longer paying interest on their loans, several of China's largest financial institutions are insolvent. To avoid a domestic banking crisis, Lardy says that China must recapitalize and restructure its domestic banking system and end the long-standing practice of making lending decisions on political rather than economic criteria.

China's financial system shares certain characteristics with the Asian countries engulfed in the financial crisis of 1997, including an overly rapid expansion of credit, a bank-dominated financial system, weak central bank regulation and supervision of commercial banks, and a massive buildup of nonperforming loans. *China's Unfinished Economic Revolution* analyzes the factors that so far have allowed China to escape the region's financial calamity, including the absence of capital account convertibility of the Chinese currency.

Lardy cautions, however, that China's respite from the Asian financial crisis is temporary. Unless reforms can reverse the buildup of nonperforming loans to state-owned enterprises, the drain of poor lending decisions will reduce economic growth, meaning slower job creation and heightened potential for social unrest. Furthermore, financial reforms are a prerequisite to opening up China's banking market to increased participation by foreign banks, a step the international community sees as essential to China's participation in the World Trade Organization.

This book benefited from comments and criticism offered by participants in manuscript review meetings convened in late 1997 and early 1998 in Beijing, Hong Kong, New York, and Washington, D.C. A special thanks is due to Wu Jinglian who organized the Beijing meeting under the auspices of the State Council Development Research Center; David Dodwell and Victor Fung of the Hong Kong Forum for arranging the Hong Kong meeting; and Jerome Cohen, director of Asian Studies at the Council on Foreign Relations, who organized the meeting in New York.

At Brookings Theresa Walker edited the manuscript, Niclas Ericsson and Scott Kennedy provided research assistance, and Bridget Butkevich and Maya Dragicevic verified the factual content. Princeton Editorial Associates proofread the book, and Bruce Tracy prepared the index.

Brookings is grateful to the Rockefeller Brothers Fund, the Henry Luce Foundation, the John D. and Catherine T. MacArthur Foundation, and the Arthur Ross Foundation for the financial support provided for this project.

The views expressed in this volume are those of the author and should not be ascribed to the organizations whose assistance is acknowledged above or to the trustees, officers, or other staff members of the Brookings Institution.

Michael H. Armacost
President

June 1998
Washington, D.C.

Contents

Tables

CHINA'S
UNFINISHED
ECONOMIC
REVOLUTION

1

China's Economic Reform Strategy

CHINA'S gradual approach to economic reform appears to offer critical advantages compared with the much more rapid economic transitions initiated in the early 1990s in several states of eastern Europe and in parts of the former Soviet Union. In contrast to a period of sharply declining real output in these states, China's reform generated record rates of positive economic growth from the outset. Unlike the transition in Russia, where inflation accelerated dramatically, China has held average annual inflation to a single-digit level, despite two sharp upward spikes, since economic reform began in the late 1970s. Moreover, economic growth in China, especially in the early years of reform, was shared broadly among all regions and segments of society.[1] The precipitous decline in poverty in the first seven years of economic reform was especially dramatic. In 1978, 270 million individuals, or 28 percent of China's total population, lived below the poverty line. By 1985 that number fell to 97 million, less than 10 percent of the population.[2] These early successes, minimizing the number of individuals, economic sectors, and geographic regions that lost economic ground, allowed China's reformers to build a solid coalition of support for ever more far-reaching reforms.[3] By contrast, in Russia the combination of a disintegrating social safety net and declining real output have inflicted sharply lower living standards on large segments of the population, even as a small class of nouveau riche Russians enjoys ostentatious lifestyles.

Similarly, China's reforms facilitated its progress toward integra-

1

tion into the world economy. By the early 1990s China's share of world trade had quadrupled compared with the prereform period, and it regularly was the recipient of more foreign direct investment than any other transition or developing country. Indeed in 1993, when these inflows exceeded those into all developed economies as well, China was the recipient of more foreign direct investment than any other country in the world. Moreover, it was the first transition economy to be awarded an investment grade rating for its sovereign debt in international capital markets and has sold far more debt and equity in these markets than any other transition economy.[4]

Because of this pattern of contrasting economic performance, students of transition economies have debated intensely the questions of the optimal pace and sequence of economic reforms. China eschewed the conventional recommended combination of rapid privatization, overnight price reform, and the immediate dismantling of trade barriers. Although a variety of new forms of ownership have flourished, de facto privatization of small state-owned firms did not get under way until the mid-1990s and few, if any, medium and large state-owned firms have been fully privatized.[5]

Relative prices in China for the most part have converged to world levels, but this process was extremely gradual. The state ended controls on many agricultural prices first and then, by the mid-1980s, introduced a two-tier pricing strategy for most industrial goods.[6] Under this system planned output continued to be distributed at prices fixed by the state, whereas supply and demand in the market determined the price of above-plan output. Market prices provided firms appropriate information on the relative scarcity of both inputs and outputs, creating the possibility of efficiency-enhancing adjustments of production technology and output mix. Planned output was provided to privileged end-users at fixed prices that typically were below-market levels, mitigating bureaucratic resistance to this form of price reform. This dual track approach increased efficiency without creating any economic losers.[7] Since the planning authorities tended not to raise planned output levels over time, by the mid-1990s the share of output distributed at below-market prices had shrunk dramatically, paving the way for the elimination of fixed prices in favor of a single market price for most industrial goods. Opening the economy to foreign trade was similarly gradual and was a key part of the process by which relative domestic prices converged to world levels.[8]

As a result, China's stunning combination of rapid economic growth, relative price stability, broadly shared real income gains, and increased participation in international goods and financial markets has led some to argue that a more gradual approach to economic reform leads to superior economic performance in transition economies.[9]

Although not denying the success of China's strategy, others have argued that its initial conditions were unique and that the more gradual Chinese approach was not a viable option for the countries of eastern Europe or the former Soviet Union.[10] China, most importantly, was far more dependent on agriculture as a source of employment and output than were the countries of Central Europe or the former Soviet Union. Moreover, because of their rapid political transformations, new leaders in these latter countries were able to work for more far-reaching transformations of economic institutions. Rather than trying to preserve the primacy of state-owned firms, for example, they were able to try more radical reforms, such as the voucher privatization approach of the Czech Republic.

Overlooked in this debate is the economic cost of postponing, until almost the end of the second decade of reform, fundamental transformation of China's state-owned enterprises. Initially, of course, China lacked the legal, institutional, and governance structures that are required to support an economic system based predominantly on private ownership. Thus, early and rapid privatization of state-owned firms could not have been expected to improve economic efficiency. Instead China undertook other liberalizing measures that facilitated the extraordinarily rapid growth of nonstate industry, particularly township and village enterprises. As a result, the share of output produced in the state-owned sector of the economy has fallen dramatically since reform began. This decline is the basis for the characterization of China's economic reform as "growing out of the plan."

Upon closer examination, however, a more complex and nuanced picture appears. Between 1978 and 1994 employment in state-owned firms increased by 40 million. Even though employment levels then stabilized, the sector continued to absorb a disproportionately large share of investment resources. This long-term expansion of employment and ongoing rapid expansion of fixed assets in the state-owned sector seems not to be part of a process of restructuring, in which unprofitable firms shrink or go out of business while profitable firms expand and entrepreneurs create new firms to exploit emerging opportunities. Output of state-owned firms has grown much more slowly than that of nonstate firms. Exit of unprofitable state firms through bankruptcy or merger, however, continues to be relatively infrequent, even though the share of state manufacturing firms incurring financial losses has increased almost continuously since the mid-1980s. Unwilling to tolerate the level of urban unemployment that would accompany the widespread bankruptcy of loss-making firms, the state assumed the burden of subsidizing growing losses through fiscal subsidies and, increasingly, through so-called policy loans from the state-owned banking system. Since the late 1980s these direct and indirect subsidies absorbed 10 percent or more of gross domestic product every year.[11] In short, the strategy of preventing the emergence of economic losers was accomplished largely by deferring industrial restructuring, a process financed by the buildup of huge financial liabilities on the part of Chinese firms.

This strategy of gradualistic economic reform has created three economic trends that appear to be unsustainable over the long run. First, state-owned enterprises are becoming ever more indebted, particularly to banks. These firms increasingly borrow not only to finance the purchase of new equipment or other productive assets but also to finance the purchase of inputs used in production, to pay their wage bills, to provide a broad range of social services to their workers, and, in some cases, even to meet their pension and tax obligations. In short, on average they are not able to cover their total costs with the income they receive from the sales of their products.[12] In addition to their massive indebtedness to banks, these firms also have built up huge unfunded pension liabilities, unpaid tax liabilities, and interenterprise arrears.[13] For the average state-owned enterprise the sum of bank debt, unpaid taxes, unfunded pension liabilities, and net indebtedness to nonstate firms far exceeds the value of its assets. As a result, many state-owned firms already are insolvent and more seem headed in that direction.

Second, state-owned banks and other financial institutions are extending loans at what appears to be a pace that will not be economically sustainable. Loans outstanding relative to gross domestic product have almost doubled since reform began and by year-end 1997 were equal to total output. In a market economy an increase in the size of the financial sector, as measured by assets (mostly loans) relative to real output, can indicate financial deepening, which is usually considered positive for economic growth. For several reasons, however, the rise in the ratio of loans to gross domestic output in China appears to be greater than can be explained by the increasing demand for money to finance transactions and investment. First, the rapid rise in loans relative to output has led to an unusually rapid expansion of the money supply. As a result the ratio of money to gross domestic product in China by 1996 had reached 110 percent, about three times the average of developing economies and one of the highest levels in the world.[14] Second, and more important, a rising and now large share of bank loans are nonperforming.[15] Given the modest amount of their own capital and their tiny loan-loss reserves, after taking into account the magnitude of nonperforming loans, by Western accounting standards several of China's major banks already are insolvent.[16] Since households continue to add enormous amounts of funds to their savings accounts, these banks remain liquid and a financial crisis has been avoided. But this is not sustainable in the long run.

Third, government revenues declined by two-thirds relative to output between 1978 and 1995.[17] As a result, during the reform era the state increasingly has been unable to finance normal government expenditures from the budget. Although the official budget deficit has been modest, and in recent years financed entirely through the sale of treasury bonds, the broader public sector nonfinancial deficit by the mid-1990s had been running at an unsustainable level of over 10 percent of gross domestic output for almost a decade.[18]

These three problems are closely interrelated. Declining tax revenues relative to the size of the economy have led the government to force excessive social obligations on state-owned firms. One of the reasons enterprises have borrowed such large sums is that they are obligated to provide a broad range of social services that should be financed from the government budget. They also are required to keep an excessive number of workers on their payrolls in order to meet the political objective of maintaining low levels of open unemployment in urban areas. These pressures contribute to the declining financial performance of state-owned enterprises, many of which are unable to service their debt. This, in turn, is a major contributor to the insolvency of large parts of the banking system.

These interrelationships also mean that a strategy of focusing sequentially on the problems of banking, state-owned enterprises, and taxes is not likely to be effective. The banks cannot operate on fully commercial terms until the behavior of their principal borrowers fundamentally changes. But many potentially profitable enterprises will find it difficult to improve their financial performance and deal with banks on a normal commercial basis until the state relieves them of the obligation of providing a broad range of social services and of employing more workers than economically are necessary. The state will not be able to finance either these social expenditures or the needed recapitalization of the banking system from the budget until a fundamental reform of tax policy and tax administration increases government revenues relative to output.

Thus Beijing's reformers have developed a strategy that offers a coordinated and simultaneous attack on all three of these areas. The State Council in late 1993 approved a far-reaching blueprint for banking and financial reform that took as its objective the commercialization of the banking system. The Chinese Communist Party, at the Third Plenum of the Fourteenth Party Congress in 1993, endorsed an equally far-reaching proposal to change the structure of governance of state-owned enterprises by converting them to modern share-holding companies. And in 1994 China instituted a major tax reform designed to reverse the long-term trend of declining tax revenues relative to output. These three broad initiatives were followed by many additional specific laws and regulations. Some of them, such as the Central Bank Law and the Commercial Bank Law, laid out the concrete steps through which commercialization of the banking system or other of the three objectives would be achieved. Others, notably new accounting laws, were central to achieving all three objectives.

This book analyzes the banking and financial system primarily as a means of understanding the magnitude of the reform challenges China now confronts. Its evaluation of the strategy that China has adopted to address simultaneously the three problems just summarized focuses primarily on finance. Its evaluation of enterprise and tax reform is much more selective.

The Public Sector Deficit

The most convenient way of measuring the consequences of deferring reform in the state-owned sector of the economy is the nonfinancial public sector deficit or public sector borrowing requirement. This provides a broad measure of the extent to which the annual resource requirements of the state, including not only government agencies and institutions but also state-owned industrial and commercial enterprises, exceed current budgetary revenues.[19] It includes not only borrowing to finance the government's budget deficit, that is, the sale of government bonds to the public and borrowing by the treasury from the central bank, but also the sale by state-owned enterprises of bonds and stocks to the public and net public sector borrowing from the banking system. The latter item, which is far and away the largest, is simply the increase in borrowing by state-owned firms from banks less any increase in their deposits in the banking system.

The public sector deficit is important for several reasons. First, a high public sector deficit is "a key factor underlying inflationary pressures in the economy."[20] The macroeconomic fluctuations of the reform period can be traced at least in part to the high public sector deficit, which has contributed to a growth of the money supply far in excess of the real growth of the economy.

Second, a high public sector deficit reduces the flow of savings available to finance nonstate investment. As discussed in chapter 3, state-owned firms receive the lion's share of bank lending, leaving nonstate firms with little direct access to bank credit. Instead they rely more on informal credit markets, the reinvestment of profits, and, in some cases, funds supplied by state-owned firms with which they have close economic ties, to finance their growth. That has meant that nonstate firms to date have played only a marginal role in more capital-intensive industries characterized by significant economies of scale in production. The start-up costs of such firms exceed the capacity of informal credit markets and reinvested profits. And state-owned firms are not interested in extending so much indirect credit that they might create new competition in their core businesses. As a result, unlike more labor-intensive manufacturing, where many new nonstate firms now provide competition to existing state-owned firms, capital-intensive manufacturing remains the domain of large state-owned firms. As will be discussed in chapter 2, limited competition from the nonstate sector is one reason the economic performance of many state-owned firms has lagged.

Third, since a significant portion of the borrowing by state firms from banks is nonrecoverable, over time the public sector deficit accumulates, reducing the net worth of government assets below the level they would otherwise attain. In China the value of internal debt, that is, the stock of government bonds outstanding, is still quite small. But the stock of government bonds is a substantial understatement of total public sector debt. As long as the Chinese government, like most governments, provides an implicit guarantee of the value of deposits placed in the banking system by the public, a broader definition of internal debt, inclusive of nonrecoverable lending of state banks, is a more appropriate measure of the state's domestic debt.[21]

The present rate of buildup of public sector debt, both implicit and explicit, is not sustainable over the long run. Since lending is growing far more rapidly than output and, at least through 1997, the share of this lending that is nonperforming has been steadily increasing, implicit government debt as a share of output has been rising. In addition, explicit government debt also has risen, although it is much smaller in size. As the total stock of government debt rises, eventually investors will lose confidence in the ability of the government to finance its expenditures on a noninflationary basis over the long term. When this occurs they will demand an ever higher rate of interest on government bonds to compensate them for this anticipated increase in inflation. Thus the interest cost of financing the explicit debt will balloon. And, as the government's implicit debt rises, savers eventually will lose confidence in the credibility of the government's implicit guarantee of their deposits and withdraw their savings from the banking system, creating the potential for a domestic banking crisis.

Explaining China's Rapid Growth

If China's reforms have been flawed, as reflected in large ongoing quasi-fiscal deficits that are accumulating to form a public sector debt that is expanding more rapidly than output, how has China been able to grow so rapidly? And why has inflation on average been so low, when conventional economic analysis suggests that China's large public sector deficit should have led to much more rapid price increases? Put alternatively, why has China's leadership initiated a difficult restructuring of the state-owned sector that already has increased urban unemployment dramatically, at least on a transitory basis, when China is at or near the top of the world economic growth leagues and its inflation performance is better than many other transition economies?

Measurement of the pace of Chinese growth and a full explanation of its causes lie well beyond the scope of this study. Several important points, however, need to be borne in mind. First, official data overstate the rate of growth during the reform period.[22] This exaggeration appears to arise primarily because of the procedures that the State Statistical Bureau uses to deflate output measured in current prices in order to be able to express the rate of growth of gross domestic product in real terms. The problem is that the deflators used show a much lower rate of price inflation than alternative measures of price inflation.[23] One study suggests this problem is acute in collectively owned manufacturing firms, where official data are estimated to overstate the growth by about a third.[24] Since collectively owned firms produce a large share of manufactured goods, adjusting for this overstatement would result in a substantial downward revision in the rate of growth of manufactured goods output in the reform era.[25] The World Bank has applied alternative deflators to the consumption and investment components of gross domestic product and concluded that the official data may overstate the real rate of growth by about 1.3 percentage points a year for the period 1986 through 1995.[26]

Although considerable uncertainty remains, Chinese official data may overstate the average annual rate of growth of output by 1 to 2 percentage points. Thus any assessment of the success of China's reform strategy needs to begin by recognizing that real growth between 1978 and 1996 may have been as low as 7.9 percent a year, rather than the 9.9 percent official figure.

Second, while this would still make China one of the five most rapidly growing economies in the world over this period, most of its growth can be explained simply by "capital accumulation supported by an extraordinarily high savings rate that has come to depend increasingly on China's thrifty households."[27] The World Bank estimates that two-thirds of the growth of output between 1985 and 1994 can be accounted for by capital formation. The average rate of investment has risen significantly during the reform period. Most of this investment has been financed by domestic savings, which increased from 35 percent of gross domestic product in 1979 to 44 percent in 1994.[28] As will be discussed, in the absence of more far-reaching reform of the financial system, it is not clear whether these exceptionally high rates of savings can be sustained over the longer run.

Third, productivity improvements account for the balance of

growth not explained by factor accumulation. However, a large portion of this growth is explained by the reallocation of labor and other factors of production from low to high productivity sectors, rather than an improvement in productivity within each sector. The World Bank estimates that simply moving large numbers of workers from agriculture to manufacturing, and to a lesser extent to services, accounts for 1.5 percentage points a year of China's growth since output per worker in the latter sectors is greater than in agriculture.[29] But, as the World Bank points out, "The potential for productivity gains from reallocating labor from agriculture to other sectors will diminish as surplus labor in agriculture is reduced."[30]

Long-term productivity gains in any economy are the result of improvements in productivity within each sector, rather than the result of reallocation of factors among sectors. Here China's record is somewhat ambiguous. According to two World Bank studies, improvements in productivity within each sector accounted for about one-fourth of annual growth.[31] But this number is calculated as a residual in an estimate that relies entirely on official Chinese data on economic growth. If one uses an alternative estimate of economic growth that is from 1 to 2 percentage points below the official figure, the estimated contribution of total factor productivity growth to economic output could be much smaller, perhaps a percentage point a year, only about one-tenth of annual growth.[32] In short, while China's economic growth has been rapid, official data overstate its pace. Most of the growth is explained by high rates of savings and investment and the reallocation of factors of production from low to high productivity sectors rather than improvements in productivity within each sector.

Sustaining future economic growth will depend increasingly on financial and related reforms that will lead to improved efficiency in the allocation and use of capital. Financial and enterprise reforms also are needed to sustain the high rate of savings that has been so important in achieving high growth in the reform era. By the mid-1980s Chinese households had emerged as the principal source of savings in the Chinese economy. Yet the central bank's controls on interest rates meant that the average real rate of return on household savings was relatively low. Households effectively are taxed in the form of below-market interest rates so that borrowers, mostly state-owned firms, can get access to funds at more favorable rates. Some countries with bank-dominated financial systems, such as Japan, have been able to sustain high household savings rates, even when real interest rates paid on savings are not very attractive.[33] However, the absence of significant competition from capital markets in such systems typically has led to inefficiency in the allocation of funds and a low rate of return on bank capital.

Chinese banks, of course, will be unable to offer very attractive rates of return to savers until they are allowed and are able to develop the capacity to lend on a much more selective basis than has been the case to date. That, in turn, implies a restructured enterprise sector, particularly the exit of firms that are not financially capable of paying market-determined rates of interest on their borrowing. Should the savings rate decline because these reforms are not undertaken and banks are unable to offer more attractive returns to depositors, China's rate of growth could fall significantly, even if total factor productivity performance improves.

Finally, without further financial and enterprise reform, inflation on average is likely to be higher in the future than it has been to date. The reason is that the first decade and a half of reform was characterized by an increase in both the demand for cash and in the rate of savings. These developments allowed the government to run large public sector deficits with lower inflationary consequences than would be expected. However, this situation will not continue indefinitely. Thus, without further reforms that bring down the public sector deficit, inflationary pressure is likely to become more severe in the future.

During the reform era the government has issued increasing amounts of currency, a phenomena called seignorage, adding directly to tax revenues, thus reducing the government deficit.[34] The demand for cash increased rapidly in the first decade and a half of reform because of increasing monetization of the economy, rapidly rising real household income, and the absence of a modern payments system. The first factor is perhaps the most obvious. In the prereform era economic self-sufficiency in China was quite high, especially in the countryside. Mao Zedong repressed most rural marketing during the Cultural Revolution so that peasant households were almost entirely self-sufficient. They were rewarded for their labor on communally run farms largely in the form of grain, which was raised collectively. Households grew their own vegetables on small private plots and relied on traditional handicraft techniques to produce many of the nonagricultural products they required. Per capita annual cash income from collective rural production on the eve of reform was only RMB (*renminbi*) 13, the equivalent of two U.S. pennies a day.[35] Cash income was used to purchase salt, kerosene, and a few other basic commodities that could not be produced locally by households in rural communities.

When agricultural reform began the Chinese Communist Party abandoned the ideology of self-sufficiency. Rural markets expanded dramatically in number and in the magnitude of transactions.[36] Households were given long-term leases to what previously were communal lands and they began to specialize in growing the crops that were best suited to local agronomic conditions, selling them on the market and using the income to purchase other products.[37] Increasing specialization meant commercial transactions grew even more rapidly than rural output, generating a huge increase in the demand for cash.

This underlying cause of the increasing demand for currency was enhanced by rapidly rising real incomes in both rural and urban areas. As incomes rose, so did transactions related to consumption. Thus the demand for cash rose as well.

Rising demand for currency also was reinforced by China's lack of a modern payments system. As discussed in chapter 3, until quite recently banks have provided households with neither checking accounts nor credit cards to make payments. Households have been forced to rely almost exclusively on cash as a means of payment. Workers in industry and service trades also are paid in cash, for the most part, further reinforcing the tendency for urban households to use cash in virtually all of their purchases. Banks do provide savings accounts for households, but the inconvenience of going frequently to the bank and the absence of alternative payment mechanisms means that households hold huge amounts of cash. Indeed the ratio of currency in circulation to gross domestic product in China is extraordinarily high by international standards. In the mid-1990s, for example, it was about 6.5 times the ratio in the United States, where payment systems are especially well developed.[38]

The central government has benefited from the rapid growth in the demand for cash since the central bank issues the currency. As discussed in chapter 4, since holders of currency receive no interest, cash is an ideal liability for a central bank. In effect currency is an

Table 1-1. Net Issue of Currency, 1978–97

Year	Amount of currency issued RMB millions	Percent of GDP
1978	1,660	0.5
1980	7,850	1.7
1984	26,230	3.7
1985	19,570	2.2
1986	23,060	2.3
1987	23,610	2.0
1988	67,950	4.6
1989	21,000	1.2
1990	30,040	1.6
1991	53,340	2.5
1992	115,820	4.3
1993	152,870	4.4
1994	142,390	3.1
1995	59,680	1.0
1996	91,660	1.4
1997	133,561	1.8

Sources: State Statistical Bureau, *China Statistical Yearbook 1995* (Beijing: China Statistical Publishing House, 1995), p. 574; *Statistical Yearbook 1996*, p. 616; and "Materials on Chinese Financial Statistics in 1997," *Jinrong shibao* (Financial News), January 23, 1998, p. 2.

interest-free loan to the government on the part of those that hold the currency. Thus, at least in the short run, issuing currency is similar to collecting taxes.

The amounts of currency issued rose rapidly once the effects of reform began to be felt in the economy (table 1-1). The amount of currency issued as early as 1980 was 1.7 percent of gross domestic product, more than three times the level of 1978. The amount in the years 1984 through 1997 averaged more than 2.5 percent of gross domestic product. If the demand for cash had not been rising so rapidly, the government would have had to reduce its expenditures proportionately or would have run larger deficits, thus putting more upward pressure on prices than was actually observed.

Already, as shown in table 1-1, the demand for increased cash began to rise more slowly beginning in the mid-1990s. The annual additions to currency in circulation peaked in 1993 at RMB 153 billion, an amount equivalent to 4.4 percent of gross domestic product that year. But in the three years starting in 1995 the increase averaged well under 2 percent of gross domestic product.

The decline in seignorage in the mid-1990s reflects at least three factors, two of which suggest a continued slower expansion of currency in the future. First, the central bank exercised increasing monetary constraint as part of its program of reducing the rate of price inflation, which peaked at more than 20 percent in 1993. Second, the monetization of the economy may now be largely complete, making the underlying growth of the economy the principal source of increased demand for cash to finance transactions.[39] Third, the introduction of modern payment systems may be slowing the growth in the demand for currency. In recent years banks have begun to provide checking accounts and to issue debit cards to households in large urban centers. Employers in some urban areas have begun to offer direct deposit of wages into worker bank accounts. Even if these are still too rare to have already influenced the demand for cash, as direct deposit of wages and modern means of payments become more common, the demand for cash by urban households is likely to shrink relative to real output of the economy. They can be expected to hold a larger portion of their net worth in bank deposits and other financial assets and less in the form of currency, thus shrinking the rate of growth of currency in circulation. The resulting reduction in seignorage will place pressure on the central government which, in effect, has relied on the issuance of cash to finance a significant portion of its expenditures. This reinforces the need for further reforms of China's tax system, discussed in chapter 4. Without these reforms China may run larger budget deficits, which will contribute to greater upward pressure on prices.

This upward pressure on prices will be reinforced by the likely trend in the savings rate. The rise in the national savings rate made it easier for the government to finance the large public sector deficits of the last decade. An increasing rate of household savings, mobilized almost entirely through the banking system, was the most important factor contributing to the rising national savings rate. Household savings as a percent of gross domestic product rose from about 2 percent in 1978 to 22 percent by 1994, more than offsetting the decline in government savings that occurred over the same period.[40] Since household savings rates are already very high by international standards, however, it is unlikely that the savings rate will rise further. That will make it more difficult to finance the large public sector deficit and the continued buildup of the stock of public sector debt, both implicit and explicit, reinforcing the upward pressure on prices that likely will result from decreased seignorage.

Banking in China's Economic Transition

Measured by economic growth, expanding foreign trade, and massive capital inflows, China is clearly among the most successful of the transition economies. China has not yet, however, solved fundamental problems of declining tax revenues relative to output, deteriorating financial performance of state-owned enterprises, and the increasing fragility of the banking system.

As already suggested, since these problems are closely intertwined, China's reform strategy addresses all three simultaneously. Yet this book focuses more on banking than on the other topics for three reasons. The first is relative ease of measurement. Declining financial performance of state-owned enterprises and the fiscal decline of the state ultimately are reflected in the growing public sector deficit. Since this deficit is financed through loans, it has a direct effect on the banking and financial system. Although, as shown in chapter 3, financial and banking statistics are subject to numerous shortcomings, they are more tractable than some of the data emerging from the enterprise sector, which provide a somewhat uncertain basis for assessing the success of reform in the state-owned portion of the economy.

Second, the most pressing stimulus within China for reform of state-owned enterprises and the fiscal system now comes from the deteriorating condition of the financial system. The collapse of several small financial institutions in the mid-1990s in China and the emergence of a major banking and financial crisis in Asia in 1997 have increased substantially the sense of urgency of financial reform at the highest levels of China's leadership. For example, banking and financial reform was a major focus of discussion at the National People's Congress in the spring of 1997 and at a major financial work conference in November 1997. Thus a better understanding of the financial sector is key to evaluating the impetus for the overall economic reform process. And the failure of the strategy to solve the problems of China's unfinished economic reform likely would be reflected first and most starkly in the financial system.

Finally, while China's banking and finance system has been studied less extensively than the enterprise sector and the fiscal system, it is central to the ultimate goal of economic reform—improving the efficiency of resource allocation within the domestic economy.[41] China's economic reform was not stimulated by economic stagnation. Economic growth in the two decades leading up to the reform era averaged about 4 percent a year in real terms, a stark contrast with the economic stagnation or even absolute decline that had set in in many other centrally planned economies.[42] Rather, the impetus for reform was declining economic efficiency and an imbalanced pattern of growth. In the First Five-Year Plan (1953–57) China grew at an annual rate of about 8 percent, fueled by a rate of investment of about 25 percent. But in the years before reform the investment rate was significantly higher, averaging somewhat over 30 percent, while, as already noted, the growth rate was much lower. Moreover, by 1976 agricultural production on a per capita basis had stagnated for two decades, because individual incentives were weak and because economic planning discriminated against the farm sector. Stagnant levels of food consumption and the combination of ever slower growth with ever rising rates of investment clearly were not politically or economically sustainable. Thus Deng Xiaoping began the process of economic reform, ultimately in order to raise economic efficiency.

The role of banks in achieving this objective is paramount simply because China has a financial system that is heavily dominated by banks. Their share of financial intermediation is almost nine-tenths, a ratio exceeding that found in almost all other Asian countries. The only region of the world where banks account for such a large share of the assets of the entire financial system is Latin America.[43]

The challenge China faces in reforming its banking system in certain respects exceeds that of most other emerging markets, where banking crises have occurred with increasing frequency in the past two decades.[44] In part this is because virtually all banks in China are state owned. Empirical evidence suggests that a high degree of state ownership of banks, or substantial government involvement in allocating credit extended by nominally private banks, is a chief cause of banking crises. A high degree of state ownership is not only associated with poor lending decisions but also frequently is accompanied by overstaffing, overdevelopment of branch networks, and other practices that contribute to relatively high operating costs. As discussed in chapter 3, these are prominent features of China's banking system.

The challenge China faces in reforming its banking system is more severe in part because its central bank is a relatively new institution. By the time the People's Bank of China was established in the mid-1980s the volume of loans outstanding by the financial system was already quite high. In the ensuing years the central bank has not gained sufficient independence and, equally important, it has not yet been able to develop the capacity to supervise effectively the emerging commercial banking system. This problem is compounded by weaknesses of China's financial accounting systems and disclosure practices.

China's economic reform, judged from the perspective of the financial system, is only half complete. China has abandoned the heavy reliance on budgetary financing of investment that was characteristic of the prereform era. Investment, particularly in the state sector, is now financed primarily through banks.[45] But these institutions are state owned and embedded in a financial system that impedes the efficient allocation of capital. The new system, moreover, has the additional shortcoming that it involves the buildup of enormous liabilities to households, the source of the savings that the banks channel to state-owned firms. However inefficient the allocation of resources was in the prereform system, at least investment through the budget was financed from current tax revenue and involved no accumulation of liabilities to households in the form of savings deposits in state banks.

If China fails to complete the transformation of its banking system, the consequences are predictable. The intermediation of funds between savers and investors by banks likely would continue to be marked by the inefficiencies already evident. As the contributions to economic growth of various once-for-all factors wind down, one would expect the rate of growth of the economy to slow. That trend would be reinforced by the increasing physical constraints to growth that are evident—environmental deterioration, the challenge of sustaining an adequate rate of growth of agricultural output, and growing infrastructure shortages. Unless resources are used more efficiently in industry and commerce, it is difficult to foresee where China will find the resources to overcome these physical constraints to growth. An inefficient banking system also would impede the development of stock and bond markets which, as per capita output rises and appropriate regulatory structures are developed, normally come to play an important supplementary role in the allocation of resources. The continued fragility of the banking system would limit the ability of the People's Bank, through the more active use of interest rate policy, to dampen the marked fluctuations in economic activity that have characterized the reform era. Ultimately, the failure to transform the banking system could undermine the high rate of household savings that has provided most of the fuel for China's high rate of economic growth.

The international consequences of China's failure to complete the transformation of its banking system are also predictable. A sound banking system is a prerequisite for moving to convertibility on capital account transactions. This factor underlies the reluctance of government officials to declare an unduly optimistic target date for achieving full convertibility of the domestic currency. Until China's banking system has been restructured and placed on a sound financial foundation, foreign financial institutions will be forced to continue to operate under the many severe restrictions placed on them by the People's Bank. That means that China will fall short of meeting the expectation of the international community that China provide national treatment of foreign banks and nonbank financial institutions. This expectation is likely to be reflected in any protocol governing China's accession to the World Trade Organization.

The Asian financial crisis of 1997 underlines the challenge that China faces in completing its economic transition. China, like countries in the region undergoing financial crises, has had an extremely rapid growth of bank lending, much of it driven by politics and connections rather than hard-nosed credit assessment. As a consequence, the growth of credit has been accompanied by an even more rapid deterioration in the quality of bank assets. China's acknowledged, if imperfectly measured, share of nonperforming loans at year-end 1997 was well above the share of nonperforming loans reported in Southeast Asian countries and in Korea just before the onset of their financial crises.

China's leaders have learned the lessons of Asia's financial crisis and are moving aggressively to accelerate domestic economic reforms. Premier Zhu Rongji has publicly declared that the problems of the state-owned enterprises, as well as those within the banking sector, will be resolved within three years.[46] These efforts focus on privatizing and restructuring state-owned enterprises and commercializaton of the banking system. It is recognized that the latter will ultimately require a large-scale recapitalization, which will entail substantial fiscal costs. A significant start on this process has already been announced.

If these measures are successful they will lift China to a new stage of economic reform, providing solutions that have eluded the leadership for two full decades. Success would make it more likely that China would restore its competitive position in Asia through reforms that would increase productivity via internally generated efficiencies, rather than through a competitive devaluation of its domestic currency. That would contribute significantly to the recovery from the Asian financial crisis. It would also undoubtedly smooth the way for China's eventual accession to the World Trade Organization. Finally, it would provide a striking contrast with Japan, which has seemed unable to contribute significantly to a solution to the Asian financial crisis. For all these reasons the successful implementation of the reform of banks and enterprises would confirm China's ascendancy not only in Asia but also on the world economic stage.

If reforms are not successful, China could yet become engulfed in the Asian financial crisis. Most obviously, the failure of reforms likely would push China onto a slower growth path, which, in turn, would expose dramatically the underlying weakness of its banking system. An ensuing loss of public confidence in the banking system could set off a demand for a large-scale withdrawal of funds from banks, a demand that could only be met by the central bank serving as a lender of last resort. But the resulting large increase in the money supply could set off an inflationary spiral that likely would lead to a collapse of credit and thus a major recession. It also would be highly adverse for maintaining China's high rate of savings.

Less obviously, China remains vulnerable to the Asian financial crisis through Hong Kong. Hong Kong is doubly exposed to China, both through substantial cross-border lending of its banks and because its economic growth is almost entirely dependent on its entrepôt role. The failure of China's domestic banking and enterprise reforms would not only reduce China's growth but also its foreign trade, which would adversely affect Hong Kong's real economic growth and perhaps the performance of Hong Kong banks. The result could be an attack on the Hong Kong currency that is so threatening that China might feel compelled to make good on its pledge to contribute its own foreign exchange reserves to defend the Hong Kong dollar. That could weaken the ability of the Chinese authorities to maintain the value of the renminbi. Ultimately, because capital flight from China might increase and China might find it difficult to roll over short-term external debt, the authorities might be forced to devalue the renminbi, setting off another downward leg in the Asian financial crisis.

China's leaders thus face a profoundly difficult task. The external environment makes the need for accelerated domestic economic reform increasingly clear. But the short-term domestic social and political costs will be substantial. Unlike earlier stages of reform, the current stage will reduce the incomes of a significant portion of the population, at least on a transitory basis. Already high rates of unemployment are likely to rise further before the efficiency gains of accelerated reform lead to increased rates of job creation, creating unprecedented potential for social unrest.

2

The State-Owned
Enterprise Problem

THE STATE sector is the core of the challenge faced by China's reformers.[1] Its large size alone means that any reform that does not improve the financial performance of the state-owned sector ultimately will fail. On the eve of reform the state dominated economic resource allocation. Moreover, the problem of long-run declining efficiency in the use of resources, a major stimulus for undertaking reform, was most acute in the state sector. The sources of inefficiency can be traced to factors that were deeply embedded in an economic planning system that developed in the prereform era.

Although reformers recognized the challenge, social, political, and institutional constraints, particularly the absence of both property rights and a tradition of rule of law, precluded them from initiating a direct assault on state ownership via a program of privatization. Rather they pursued a twofold strategy that preserved state ownership as a major feature of the institutional landscape. The first part of the strategy was gradually to restructure incentives faced by enterprise managers and enhance the role of the market. The second part was to allow the relatively unconstrained growth of what the Chinese call the nonstate sector—urban collectives, rural township and village enterprises, private firms, and foreign-funded enterprises.

One difficulty this gradualistic approach creates is that it is difficult to measure the progress of reform. In the absence of a rapid increase in the role of the market in the allocation of goods, labor, and capital, changes in financial performance of enterprises do not neces-

21

sarily reflect underlying changes in economic efficiency. Even simple yardsticks commonly used in analysis of other transition economies, such as progress in the privatization of state-owned companies, are not relevant. Given this problem, researchers have devoted considerable effort to measure directly the trends in factor productivity.

Following a very brief summary of the stages of reform, this chapter examines two fundamental questions. The first is simply whether or not the size of the state sector, relative to the rest of the economy, has shrunk so dramatically that the question of whether or not reforms have led to increased productivity of state firms has become largely irrelevant. The conclusion is that although the relative contribution to output of the state sector has shrunk dramatically, state firms remain a disproportionally large employer and claimant of society's scarce investment resources. Thus the second question is the extent to which the economic performance of the state sector has improved. The tentative conclusion is that reforms to date have failed in large portions of the state-owned sector and that their ultimate success will depend on the willingness of the Chinese Communist Party to embrace privatization.

The Stages of Reform

The priority accorded to reform in the state-owned sector confirms the view that there was an early widespread recognition within the Chinese leadership that reform could not be limited to agriculture. Although rural reforms initially captured much of the attention of external observers, the Chinese Communist Party launched a major effort from the outset of reform in 1979 to reinvigorate the state-owned sector.[2] This initial stage focused on increasing the operational autonomy accorded to enterprise managers, largely by allowing them greatly increased authority over the allocation of their profits. Profit retention, the key policy in this first phase of reform, was widely adopted in state firms in 1979–80. Some profits were used to finance increased investments, but enterprise managers also were able, for the first time, to pay bonuses to workers. These quickly became a significant source of wage growth.

Although these steps were a promising beginning, two shortcomings undermined them. First, price reform in those early years was limited, resulting in persistent distortions. Second, several efforts to force enterprises to pay interest on their fixed and working capital failed.[3] Without these changes there was little reason to expect that increased enterprise autonomy would improve the efficiency of resource allocation and utilization, particularly of capital.

A second phase of enterprise reform emerged in the mid-1980s. The key new policy instrument was long-term contracts between enterprises and their bureaucratic superiors spelling out deliveries of profits and taxes as well as other financial targets.[4] The emphasis on financial variables was a distinct break from traditional economic planning, which had relied primarily on physical output targets to both guide and judge enterprise performance. Contracts were designed to provided better incentives for improving the financial performance of enterprises by limiting the ability of higher bureaucratic levels to rachet up, on an annual basis, the requirement to remit profits. Thus under long-term contracts enterprise managers who were able to increase profitability consistently over time were assured of the ability to retain these incremental profits. The second phase also included provisions that further enhanced the autonomy of managers, a policy initiated in the first phase of reform, and introduced substantial price flexibility for output produced above planned levels.

Although the second-phase reforms constituted a consistent reform package and greatly enhanced the role of the market, they also had important shortcomings.[5] They fell short of establishing a system of uniform market-determined prices. That meant some enterprises continued to lose money largely because of externally imposed price controls. In turn, that made it impossible for the state to impose hard budget constraints on enterprises via bankruptcy of money-losing enterprises. Thus China's bankruptcy law, passed after much debate in 1986, was rarely applied. Second, the negotiation of financial contracts on an enterprise-by-enterprise basis precluded the development of a modern tax system with uniform rates applied universally and impartially. Finally, the dual-track price system created enormous incentives for corruption—merely transferring a good from within plan to outside plan could raise its price by 50 to 100 percent or even more.

The third stage of reform of state-owned enterprises began in 1993 when the Third Plenum of the Fourteenth Chinese Communist Party

Congress endorsed the creation of a modern enterprise system.[6] The key features of this initiative were its approval of the development of diversified forms of ownership, which would compete on equal terms in the marketplace, and the introduction of a framework for modern corporate governance of state-owned firms. In the words of one specialist, this reform "is undoubtedly the most ambitious plan for China's reform since the launching of reform in 1978 and may well prove to be a watershed in China's modern economic history."[7] The Fifteenth Communist Party Congress in the fall of 1997 approved a broadening and an acceleration of this initiative. Most small state-owned companies effectively are being privatized by converting them into various forms of nonstate and noncollective ownership, especially stock cooperative companies.[8] Large and medium enterprises are being converted into limited liability or shareholding companies.

The ownership reforms for medium and large state-owned enterprises center on two objectives. The first is their transformation into limited liability companies under the Company Law, which was passed by the Standing Committee of the National People's Congress within a few weeks after the close of the party plenum in 1993.[9] The objective of the law is to separate government and business functions and to create incentive structures that ensure that firm managers act in a manner consistent with the interests of the firm's owners. The Company Law allows for the establishment of corporations as distinct legal entities, separate from their owners (shareholders), "with a clear definition of and accounting for its own assets and liabilities."[10] Second, it introduces the idea of limited liability for shareholders. Third, it calls for the establishment of boards of directors, elected by shareholders, responsible for hiring the managers of the firm and evaluating their performance. Finally, the law provides for transferability of ownership shares. In Harry Broadman's words these are the four structural attributes of the modern corporation.

The second broad objective is to optimize the capital structure of medium and large state-owned enterprises by lowering their debts and raising their asset-to-liability ratios. This program involves reduced rates of taxation on profits, accelerated rates of depreciation on fixed assets, and reduced interest rates on loans made available to finance a share of enterprise tax liabilities.[11]

Have these three stages of reform been successful in shrinking the relative size of the state sector or increasing its economic efficiency?

The Size of the State Sector

At the outset of reform the state dominated the nonagricultural portions of the Chinese economy. This domination was reflected in the high share of output produced in state-owned firms, the large share of urban employment in the state sector, the disproportionately large share of fixed assets owned by state firms, and the large role of the state budget in allocating resources within the Chinese economy.

State domination was most obvious in manufacturing, where on the eve of reform fully four-fifths of output was produced in state-owned firms.[12] These firms employed about 30 million workers, more than two-thirds of all industrial employees.[13] Although state-owned industrial enterprises accounted for only about one-fourth of all industrial enterprises, they owned the vast majority of the machinery, equipment, and other physical assets employed in manufacturing.[14]

State domination was also evident in construction, transportation, and other services. In 1980 three-quarters of all construction workers in urban areas worked for state-owned firms and by value these firms built almost four-fifths of all projects.[15] State-owned transport enterprises, mostly under the direct control of the Ministry of Railroads and the Ministry of Communications, were responsible for almost all transport of goods by rail, road, and water.[16] In retail trade state domination was particularly strong. Although state-owned retailing units accounted for only a third of all retail stores and shops and employed just over half of all retail workers, state-owned units accounted for more than 90 percent of the value of all retail sales as reform was getting under way in 1978.[17]

Finally, the dominant role of the state was reflected in the large share of output allocated through the state budget. On the eve of reform budgetary expenditures were equal to almost a third of the economy's output.[18] This proportion is low in comparison with advanced industrialized countries where transfer payments loom large in government expenditures. It is quite high, however, in comparison with other low-income countries primarily because in the late 1970s most investment in fixed and working capital in China was financed through the budget.

Many analyses of China's economic reform strategy have focused on the dynamic role of the nonstate sector, particularly township and village manufacturing enterprises that have grown so rapidly. The relatively slow growth of state-owned firms in industry has led to a reduction in the share of output they produce, from about four-fifths at the outset of reform to about one-third by 1995.[19] Because state-owned firms are more likely to be controlled by or at least influenced by planners either in Beijing or at the local level, whereas nonstate firms appear to be more entrepreneurial, the rapid growth of the non-state sector has led Barry Naughton to characterize China's reform process as growing out of the plan.[20]

However, focusing on the declining share of manufactured goods produced in state-owned factories in certain respects overstates the extent to which the role of the state has declined during the reform process. First, the decline in the role of the state is more modest in the service sector than in manufacturing. In construction, for example, by value state-owned firms in 1995 continued to be responsible for more than three-fifths of all building projects in urban areas, a relatively small decline from their share in 1980.[21] Similarly, even though there has been a dramatic increase in the number of collective and private wholesale and retail establishments, in 1995 state-owned firms still were responsible for two-thirds of the combined value of wholesale and retail sales.[22] Telecommunications and long-distance transport remain almost entirely within the domain of state ownership.

Second, even within manufacturing, focusing on the declining share of output produced in state-owned firms obscures the continued importance of the state sector, both as a major source of employment and as the recipient of a disproportionately large share of investment resources. Moreover, even though the share of output produced by state-owned firms has declined dramatically on average, there remain many important industries where state-owned firms have yet to feel much competitive pressure from nonstate firms.

Employment

As shown in table 2-1, employment in the state sector soared by almost 40 million, or more than 50 percent, between 1977 and 1993 and then stabilized at just over 110 million. State sector employment rose so briskly that the share of the urban sector labor force employed by the state declined only moderately, from 78 percent in 1978 to 70 percent by 1992 and then to 65 percent by the end of 1995. And the decline since 1992 is somewhat overstated since most of it is because of the reclassi-

Table 2-1. State Sector Employment, 1977–96

Year	Millions of workers	Percent of urban labor force
1977	71.96	79
1978	74.51	78
1979	76.93	77
1980	80.19	76
1981	83.72	76
1982	86.30	76
1983	87.71	75
1984	86.37	71
1985	89.90	70
1986	93.33	70
1987	96.54	70
1988	99.84	70
1989	101.08	70
1990	103.46	70
1991	106.64	70
1992	108.89	70
1993	109.20	68
1994	112.14	67
1995	112.61	65
1996[a]	112.44	...

Sources: State Statistical Bureau, *Statistical Yearbook of China 1993* (Beijing: China Statistical Publishing House, 1993), p. 97; *China Statistical Yearbook 1995*, p. 84; *Statistical Yearbook 1996*, pp. 87, 90; and *Statistical Yearbook 1997*, p. 93.

a. Because of a change in the definition of urban, the percent of the urban labor force that can be calculated for 1996 is not comparable with that for earlier years.

fication of state-owned enterprises into what are called corporatized or shareholding firms. In most cases the state remains the dominant shareholder in these firms after the conversion, and there appears to be only modest initial change in corporate governance.[23]

This is not to underestimate the dramatic transformation of the labor force that has been under way for more than a decade. According to official statistics the share of the work force employed in agriculture has declined from 71 percent in 1978 to only 51 percent in 1996. As a result, the number of persons employed in agriculture peaked in 1992 at 383 million and has since declined in absolute terms.[24] In large part this change occurred because of the growing importance of jobs in the nonstate sector, particularly in township and village enterprises where employment expanded by more than 100 million between 1978 and 1995.[25] Private sector employment has also increased by almost 62 million by year-end 1996.[26]

But this structural transformation of the labor force occurred primarily in rural areas. In urban areas the state accounted for half of the new jobs created between 1978 and 1995. More than twice as many new jobs were created in the state sector than in private enterprises and proprietorships combined.[27]

Most of the increase in state sector employment came in manufacturing, where employment shot up by more than 9 million. But state employment in banking and insurance, commerce, construction, public utilities, and other activities also rose. The number of government and party bureaucrats soared by almost 150 percent. State employment fell in absolute terms only in agriculture, largely owing to a shrinkage in employment on state farms.

Investment

Table 2-2 shows the broad allocation of investment resources throughout the economy to alternative forms of ownership. For the years through 1992 it shows the allocation among state, collective, and individual forms of ownership. These data show that collective and individual investment jumped sharply in the early 1980s, largely reflecting stepped-up investment in collective industries and in individually owned housing in rural areas. But in the following decade little change occurred in the share of investment in state-owned units, and the share of investment in collective units rose at the expense of individual investment. However, these data do not take into account the more diverse forms of ownership that emerged in the 1980s.

Belatedly, beginning in 1993, the State Statistical Bureau adjusted its classification system for reporting investment to take into account the growing importance of new forms of ownership, particularly foreign-funded and shareholding firms.[28] The more disaggregated data published beginning in 1993 suggests that the seeming constancy of the share of investment in state firms through 1993 disguises the growing share of investment in foreign-funded firms and the emergence of the new category of shareholding firms. If one accepts the view that joint ventures and wholly foreign-owned firms are quite

Table 2-2. The Allocation of Investment in Fixed Assets, 1980–96

Percent

Year	State	Foreign-Funded	Shareholding	Collective	Individual
1980	82	...	...	5	13
1981	69	...	...	12	19
1982	69	...	...	14	17
1983	67	...	...	11	23
1984	65	...	...	13	22
1985	66	...	...	13	21
1986	66	...	...	13	22
1987	63	...	...	15	22
1988	61	...	...	16	23
1989	61	...	...	14	25
1990	66	...	...	12	22
1991	66	...	...	13	21
1992	67	...	...	17	16
1993	61	6	2	18	12
1994	57	10	3	18	12
1995	54	11	4	16	13
1996	53	12	5	16	14

Sources: State Statistical Bureau, *A Statistical Survey of China 1991* (Beijing: China Statistical Publishing House, 1991), p. 19; *Statistical Survey 1994*, p. 27; State Statistical Bureau, *Statistical Yearbook of China 1993*, p. 145; *China Statistical Yearbook 1995*, p. 137; *Statistical Yearbook 1996*, pp. 22–23, 139; and *Statistical Yearbook 1997*, p. 32.

Note: Investment in fixed assets is the broadest measure of fixed investment in China. It includes investment in capital construction as well as investment in technical updating and transformation. It is inclusive of investment from all sources of finance including budgetary funds, bank loans, foreign funds, and retained earnings and other "self-raised" funds. Individual investment includes household investment in agriculture and in housing. The data on foreign-funded enterprises are the sum of what the Chinese separately report as foreign funded and overseas Chinese investment. It is inclusive of both joint ventures and wholly foreign-owned investment projects. Data on investment by jointly operated units (investments undertaken jointly by enterprises of different forms of ownership or jointly by enterprises and institutions, such as universities) and investment by other economic units are not included for years 1993 and after. In 1996 these two categories accounted for 0.6 percent and 0.7 percent, respectively, of total investment in fixed assets.

distinct from state-owned enterprises but that shareholding companies are not, the share of investment in all state-owned firms fell by about one-seventh, from 69 percent in 1981 to 58 percent in 1996.[29]

The modest decline in the annual allocation of investment resources to state-owned companies is confirmed in data on the ownership of the entire stock of productive assets. In 1995 two-thirds of all assets were controlled by state-owned firms.[30]

In industry the share of assets owned by state firms fell to 53.7 percent in 1995, compared with their 74.6 percent share a decade earlier. But this decline is only about one-half of the proportionate shrinkage in the share of industrial output produced in state-owned enterprises over the same period.[31] The inescapable implication is that the relative efficiency of state-owned firms in the use of capital has declined significantly over time.

Competition

The most important potential stimulus to improvements in productivity at the firm level is competition. In many industries, ranging from textiles and apparel to electronics and computers, the domination of state-owned firms has receded rapidly. Yet in some industries state-owned firms as late as the mid-1990s faced only modest competitive pressure from nonstate companies. In the mid-1990s state firms produced 91 percent of all electric power, 91 percent of all coal, 95 percent of all petroleum, 79 percent of metallurgical products, and 77 percent of all chemicals.[32] Of course, the state continues to own the rail system, which continues to be the dominant mode of long-distance transportation, most of the water-borne transport capacity, and all telecommunications operating companies.[33]

The lack of competition in manufacturing more generally is confirmed by the relatively low rates of capacity utilization in many branches of Chinese industry in the mid-1990s. A major census of Chinese industry revealed that for more than 900 major industrial products the rate of capacity utilization in 1995 was below 60 percent. Rates in some products were extraordinarily low, particularly when one takes into account that the years leading up to the census were ones of rapid economic growth, not recession in which one would expect utilization rates to have been depressed. For photographic film the rate was 13.3 percent; movie film, 25.5 percent; air conditioners between 30 and 40 percent; telephone sets, 51.4 percent; color televisions, 46.1 percent; machine tools, less than 40 percent; copper smelting and pressing, 50 percent; chemical products and chemical fibers, 50 to 60 percent; large- and medium-sized tractors, 60.6 percent; and final products produced from rolled steel, 62.0 percent.[34] These low rates suggest massive overinvestment in capacity across a broad range of products. This overinvestment almost certainly raises production costs for many firms to a level where loss-making is almost inevitable. Yet the absence of exit of a significant number of firms from these industries suggests that there is little competition. This result is explained primarily by the availability of credit on very soft terms, the role of local government and party officials in preserving local enterprises, and the inability of banks and other financial institutions to impose either restructuring or exit on firms that are unable to amortize their debts.

In short, the evidence does not really support the view that the state manufacturing and commercial sector is withering away rapidly. State-owned firms continue to loom large in employment and investment and continue to produce a dominant share of output in many critical industries and services. Have state-owned firms become more efficient under the reforms summarized briefly at the outset of this chapter? The evidence I examine to answer this question includes total factor productivity studies as well as a variety of financial indicators.

Factor Productivity

The importance of understanding trends in total factor productivity is attested to by the dozens of published studies on the topic.[35] Factor productivity studies compare the growth of inputs relative to the growth of output, both measured in constant prices. The basic idea of total factor productivity growth is straightforward. If output expands more rapidly than inputs used in the production process, total factor productivity is rising. Complexity arises from a variety of methodological issues. Initially, these studies used a very simple methodology, comparing the growth of output with the growth of capital and labor, the latter aggregated by appropriate weights. Subsequently, the methodologies became more complex. Researchers included intermediate inputs, as well as capital and labor, when measuring the growth of inputs. This was an important improvement since the earlier methodology would have overestimated productivity growth if, for example, firms had increasingly substituted purchased intermediate inputs for either labor or capital. Some researchers attempted to exclude labor and capital used to provide social services to employees when calculating the productivity of state-owned enterprises. Finally, procedures for stripping out the influence of price changes also became more complex. Not only did researchers use improved measures to deflate output to remove the bias introduced by rising prices, they also introduced separate deflators for capital and intermediate inputs.

Despite the increasing methodological sophistication, no consensus has emerged on whether the numerous reform initiatives summarized at the outset of this chapter have led to increases in total factor productivity in the state-owned sector. Initially, most researchers reported that productivity continued to stagnate, as in the prereform era. Subsequently, other authors, utilizing a different price index to deflate the cost of capital, argued that productivity had turned up significantly in response to reforms. But others failed to confirm these findings and argued that productivity stagnated or even declined in the reform era.

Subsequently the authors that most consistently presented evidence of improved factor productivity modified their earlier findings in several important respects. First, they revised their estimates of total factor productivity growth for state-owned industry from an earlier estimate of a range of 5.2 to 5.9 percent a year for the years 1978–85 to 2.24 percent a year for 1980–84.[36] Although the time coverage is not precisely the same, this is a substantial downward revision. Second, they reported that improvements in factor productivity in state firms slowed markedly after 1988. The estimate for 1988–92 is 1.58 percent a year compared with estimates of 2.24 percent for 1980–84 and 3.68 percent for 1984–88. Although part of the decline may be due to cyclical factors, the authors also judge that financial factors such as preferential access to loans and negative real interest rates on such borrowings "encouraged many SOE managers to make unwise investment decisions during the later 1980s and early 1990s . . . that may have contributed to a reduction in the growth of TFP (total factor productivity) observed in China's state industries."[37] Third, they revised downward dramatically their estimate of total factor productivity growth in collective industry so that it is now less than 1 percentage point higher than the estimate for state-owned industry. Previously, the differential had been much greater.

Even if an empirical consensus on productivity had emerged, however, this would not settle the question of the success of reforms in the state-owned sector for two reasons. First, it has long been understood that total factor productivity is an imperfect reflection of the underlying variable we want to measure—the ability of firms to increase output through improvements in technology. The reason is that improved total factor productivity can be due to improvements in x-efficiency or to technological progress. The former occurs when firms operating below their production frontier are able to move closer to the frontier, which represents the maximum level of output that can be obtained in the short run with existing inputs and levels of technology. Gains of this type, frequently called improvements in static efficiency, are important, especially for countries in the early stages of economic growth. But, since they will eventually be exhausted, they cannot be the source of improvements in total factor productivity over the long run. That depends on the second factor, technical change. In short, given the distortions that prevailed in the prereform economy, it would not be surprising if reforms led initially to growing total factor productivity. If these measured gains arose from improvements in x-efficiency, rather than underlying technical change, this rise in productivity would tell us little about the long-term success of reform.

Second, and equally important, the success of reform of state-owned enterprises depends on converting gains in productivity to improved financial performance. If firms are able to raise total factor productivity through improvements in technology, but either poorly defined property rights mean that the managers can siphon off most of the gains or declining budgetary revenues lead local leaders to require enterprise managers to use them to finance health, education, and other social expenditures, reforms ultimately will not succeed. More generally, even if enterprise managers are not corrupt but are required to maintain higher levels of employment than would prevail in a competitive environment or if they have any significant motives other than profit, total factor productivity becomes a "questionable measure of SOE performance. . . . [Under these conditions] higher productivity may lead to lower profits."[38] It is therefore essential to consider the financial performance of state-owned firms.

Financial Performance

Most measures suggest that the financial performance of state-owned enterprises has declined dramatically during the reform period. These measures include the rate of return on assets of state enterprises, the percent of state firms that are incurring financial losses, and the magnitude of fiscal subsidies provided to state-owned firms. Each of these measures provides an indicator based on annual financial data, sometimes called financial flows. These data, since they are readily available, have received the most attention. This study introduces systematic data derived from the balance sheets of state-owned firms, which provide data on the stocks of liabilities and assets. Analysis of these data provides more definitive support for the view that the financial performance of state firms has deteriorated over the course of reform.

Profitability

The profits of state-owned industrial firms fell from almost 7 percent of gross domestic product in 1987 to only 2 percent by 1994.[39] In the first quarter of 1996 the state-owned sector as a whole, for the first time ever, was actually in the red; the losses of money-losing enterprises exceeded the profits of other firms.[40] For all of 1996 the state industrial sector was barely in the black with profits as a percent of gross domestic product of under 1 percent.[41] One might suspect that a major explanation for this dramatic decline in profits as a share of total output is simply that the state-owned sector contributes an ever-diminishing share of gross domestic product. The reality is that most of the decline in profits, at least through 1994, occurred because of a dramatic reduction in the rate of return on investments of state enterprises. In 1987 the return was 15 percent whereas by 1994 it had fallen to about 5 percent.[42]

Incidence of loss-making

One of the reasons the rate of return on investment by state-owned firms as a group has declined is that the share of these enterprises operating at a loss has risen over time. Table 2-3 summarizes Chinese data on losses for two categories of state-owned industrial firms—those practicing independent financial accounting and those considered to be under the state budget.[43] Since enterprises under the budget are a subset of enterprises with independent financial accounting, the two data series are generally quite similar.

As shown by the data in table 2-3, the share of loss-making state-owned industrial firms initially fell in the early years of reform,

Table 2-3. State-Owned Industrial Enterprise Losses, 1978–97

Year	Enterprises with independent accounting		Enterprises with independent accounting under the budget	
	Enterprises losing money (percent)	Losses (RMB billions)	Enterprises losing money (percent)	Losses (RMB billions)
1978	n.a.	4.2	23.9	4.4
1979	n.a.	3.6	23.4	3.7
1980	19.2	3.4	22.4	3.2
1981	22.9	4.6	27.7	4.2
1982	20.8	4.8	25.1	4.3
1983	12.8	3.2	14.6	2.9
1984	10.2	2.7	10.5	2.3
1985	9.6	3.2	9.6	2.7
1986	13.1	5.4	13.4	4.7
1987	13.0	6.1	12.8	5.1
1988	10.9	8.2	10.7	7.1
1989	16.0	18.0	15.9	12.8
1990	27.6	34.9	30.3	27.9
1991	25.8	36.7	28.0	30.0
1992	23.4	36.9	22.7	30.0
1993	30.3	45.3	29.8	29.0
1994	n.a.	48.3	n.a.	33.5
1995	n.a.	64.0	44.0	40.9
1996	n.a.	79.1	n.a.	53.0
1997	n.a.	74.4	n.a.	n.a.

Sources: Finance Yearbook of China Compilation Committee, *Finance Yearbook of China* (Beijing: Chinese Financial Magazine Society Publishers, 1994), p. 438. Zhongguo Xinwen She (China News Service), "State-Owned Enterprises Reform Not Path to Privatization," March 14, 1996, in Foreign Broadcast Information Service, 96-052, *Daily Report: China*, March 15, 1996, p. 24. (Hereafter, FBIS, *China*.) *Economic Note* (Beijing: World Bank Resident Mission, July-August 1997), p. 8. State Statistical Bureau, *China Statistical Yearbook 1996*, p. 429, *Statistical Yearbook 1997*, p. 439; Zheng Jie, "State Enterprise Reform Must Accomplish Five Strategic Tasks," *Jingji Ribao* (Economic Daily), June 5, 1995, in FBIS, *China*, 95-148, August 2, 1995, pp. 31–32; and Xinhua (New China News Agency), "Statistical Communiqué of the PRC State Statistics Bureau on National Economic and Social Development in 1997," March 4, 1998, in FBIS, *China*, 98–071, March 12, 1998.

reaching a low of less than 10 percent in 1985. Subsequently, however, the share of loss-making firms has risen steadily, reaching an all-time high by the mid-1990s. By 1996 the absolute level of enterprise losses also reached a record high of almost RMB 80 billion.

Initially it was believed that a large share of enterprise losses could be explained by distortions in the price system that required some enterprises to sell a large share of their output at state-controlled prices that were far below those prevailing on the market. Thus financial losses were not necessarily considered an indication of economic inefficiency and were expected to disappear as price controls were eliminated.

This explanation is roughly consistent with the declining share of loss-making enterprises and the decline in the monetary value of losses in the first half of the 1980s, when more and more product prices were liberalized. However, it is not consistent with the rising share of loss-making enterprises and the twenty-five-fold increase in the magnitude of these losses between 1985 and 1996, when price liberalization accelerated.

Loss-making is not confined to state-owned industrial firms. In 1997 the total losses of all industrial enterprises practicing independent financial accounting were RMB 134.1 billion, implying that nonstate firms incurred losses of RMB 59.7 billion.[44] Between 1985 and 1997 nonstate firms have accounted for a rising share of the financial losses of all industrial enterprises. In 1985 their losses, RMB 0.8 billion, accounted for only a fifth of the total. In 1997 their share was over two-fifths.[45] These data are consistent with the low rates of capacity utilization and associated loss-making discussed earlier. Several of the products for which capacity utilization is quite low are produced predominantly by nonstate firms.

Fiscal subsidies

Table 2-4 shows data on fiscal subsidies to loss-making enterprises that are often cited in the literature on Chinese economic reform. The scope of these data is both broader and narrower than those in table 2-3. It is broader since it is not restricted to manufacturing firms but includes state-owned commercial firms as well. But it is narrower since not all financial losses are offset by fiscal subsidies. Table 2-4 shows that subsidies flowing through the state budget rose from about RMB 32 billion in 1986 to a peak of RMB 60 billion in 1989 and then declined dramatically to RMB 34 billion in 1996.

The numbers in tables 2-3 and 2-4 are sometimes used to support the view that China's state-owned firms are not a significant impediment to further reform, and the Chinese strategy of gradualism,

Table 2-4. Fiscal Subsidies to Loss-Making State-Owned Enterprises, 1985–96

Year	RMB billions	Percent of budget expenditures	Percent of gross domestic product
1985	50.7	25	5.7
1986	32.5	15	3.2
1987	37.6	17	3.1
1988	44.6	18	3.0
1989	59.9	21	3.5
1990	57.9	19	3.1
1991	51.0	15	2.4
1992	44.5	12	1.7
1993	41.1	9	1.2
1994	36.6	6	0.8
1995	32.8	5	0.6
1996	33.7	4	0.5

Sources: *China Statistical Yearbook 1997*, pp. 42, 235, 239; and *Communiqué of the State Statistical Bureau of the People's Republic of China and the Third National Industrial Census Office on the Third National Industrial Census* (Beijing: State Statistical Publishing House, February 1997), p. 22.

sketched out in chapter 1, continues to be sound. State-owned manufacturing firms may incur rising losses, but even the record RMB 80 billion in 1996 represented only 1.2 percent of gross domestic product that year. Fiscal subsidies to all loss-making state-owned enterprises peaked at 3.5 percent of gross domestic product in 1989 but have fallen since to only 0.5 percent. These relatively modest numbers suggest that state-owned firms are not imposing much of a burden on the economy, and that this burden could be borne almost indefinitely with little real penalty in terms of efficiency and ultimately economic growth.

Moreover, it is sometimes argued that the increasing share of enterprises losing money is misleading since most of the money-losing firms are small.[46] If money-losing firms on average are small in size, any needed restructuring in industry should be relatively painless. The share of employment and assets of small firms is also small, so workers and machinery could be redeployed to more productive uses with modest social costs.

Both these views are mistaken, in large part because the data in tables 2-3 and 2-4 present only a partial picture of the financial performance of state-owned firms. This is most obvious with respect to the data on fiscal subsidies. The simple fact is that most enterprise losses are no longer covered by grants from the state budget but by loans from state banks. As the government has sought to finance its budget deficit increasingly from the sale of bonds, rather than simply borrowing from the central bank (that is, printing money), the Ministry of Finance has been under growing pressure to reduce the explicit budget deficit. Since 1994 the entire government deficit has been financed by the sale of bonds. As the option of borrowing from the central bank was reduced and then foreclosed, the Ministry of Finance simply reduced subsidies to loss-making state enterprises, forcing these institutions to borrow from state-owned banks rather than relying on funds channeled through the budget in order to stay in business.

The data on financial losses of state-owned firms in table 2-3 are probably understated significantly, primarily because most state firms do not pay interest on their outstanding loans but rather roll over their loans periodically, increasing the principal of each new loan by at least as much as the interest that was due on the maturing loan. The bank then does not disburse the increase in the value of the loan attributable to the previous year's interest but keeps it and records it as interest income.[47] This practice is particularly prevalent for working capital loans, which account for a very large share of total bank lending. Since enterprises traditionally relied primarily on cash rather than accrual accounting in compiling their profit and loss statements, they did not include the increase in their debt attributable to the capitalization of their interest payment obligations as an element in their expenses. Obviously these firms have overstated their income relative to their expenditures. Thus, both the share of enterprises losing money and the amount of losses may be far higher than the numbers in table 2-3 indicate.

This assessment is consistent with Chinese estimates of the financial difficulties enterprises face as a consequence of their heavy indebtedness to banks. According to Zhou Tianyong, a member of the Economics Department of the Central Party School, as of the end of 1994 state-owned enterprises would have needed to write off RMB 1,215 billion in loans to state banks in order to reduce their indebtedness to a level at which they could pay interest on their debt at then-current levels of profitability.[48] That figure, which is equal to one-quarter of gross domestic product in 1994, is several times the cumulative financial losses through 1994 reflected in table 2-3.[49] That disparity suggests the financial losses shown in table 2-3 represent only the tip of the iceberg.

Moreover, while it is true that most of the state firms that report losing money are small, this does not imply that the challenge of further reforms is modest.[50] Among state-owned industrial enterprises practicing independent accounting, only about one-fifth are classified as medium and large scale.[51] Thus even though loss-making large and medium firms compose a small share of the total universe of loss-making state firms, they represent a significant share of the total number of large and medium firms. In 1995, for example, one-third of all medium and large firms were operating at a loss.[52] The incidence of loss-making was virtually identical in the two size categories. Moreover, medium- and large-scale firms have borrowed disproportionately large amounts from the state banks that they are unable to amortize at their current levels of profitability. Thus four-fifths of the borrowing of state-owned enterprises that needed to be written off in 1994 in order to reduce the debt to a level at which enterprises could make the interest payments was the debt of medium- and large-scale enterprises.[53] Thus even if small firms could be restructured and returned to profitability, such measures would not address the problem of the massive cumulative borrowing by larger firms that do not have sufficient cash flow to pay interest on their outstanding debt and, as discussed greater detail in chapter 3, threaten the financial viability of the entire banking system.

Liability-to-Asset Ratios

Whatever its cause, the declining profitability of state-owned enterprises has reduced the share of fixed investment of state enterprises financed with after-tax, retained profits. By 1994 the share was down to one-fifth compared with about three-fifths in 1987.[54] By 1996 the share was even lower, one-tenth.[55] Thus enterprises have become ever more dependent on banks, rather than their own retained earnings, both as a means to finance fixed investment and as a source of working capital. The deterioration of the balance sheets of state-owned enterprises is reflected clearly in the changes in the ratio of financial liabilities to assets. In addition, in the reform era state-owned enterprises have accumulated substantial financial liabilities that are not included in their balance sheets and thus not reflected in the official data on liability-to-asset ratios. Of these, unfunded pension liabilities are far and away the most significant.

As shown in table 2-5, at the outset of reform, financial liabilities of state-owned industrial firms were only 11 percent of the value of their assets. This figure, which is far below the average for industrial firms in market economies, is not surprising. It simply reflects the fact that during the planning era state-owned firms remitted most of their profits to the state treasury and, in return, received state budgetary grants to finance most of their fixed investment and to meet a significant portion of their working capital needs. These budgetary grants did not have to be repaid. Since enterprises had little need to borrow from banks, financial liabilities were quite modest.

After reforms began, these arrangements of the planned era were scrapped. Starting in 1983, budget financing of working capital for state-owned firms was drastically curtailed, and in late 1984 the authorities announced that the budget also would no longer provide financing for fixed-asset investment.[56] Thus state-owned enterprises began to borrow more heavily from banks. By 1988 their liabilities, mostly bank loans, reached a value equal to almost half their assets.[57] This ratio is roughly comparable to that typically found in market economies.

Rather than stabilizing, however, the ratio of liabilities to assets continued to rise after 1988. Data for state-owned industrial firms for the years from 1989 through 1992 are not available but, as shown in table 2-5, liabilities relative to assets for all state-owned firms rose continuously throughout those years. By 1993 the liabilities of state-owned industrial firms were the equivalent of two-thirds of the value of their assets and in 1994 the ratio reached four-fifths. By the end of 1995 the ratio for all state-owned firms reached an all-time high of 85 percent.[58]

The official data in table 2-5 significantly understate the liability-to-asset ratio of state firms, particularly for more recent years. This stems from the understatement of liabilities and the overstatement of assets. Liabilities are understated because, according to Chinese sources that analyze enterprise assets and liabilities, they do not take into account interenterprise debt, which the Chinese refer to as triangular debt.[59] These are unpaid bills that accumulate rapidly when the central

Table 2-5. Liabilities of State-Owned Enterprises, 1978–95

Percent of assets

Year[a]	All SOEs	Industrial SOEs
1978	n.a.	11
1980	n.a.	19
1988	n.a.	45
1989	55	n.a.
1990	58	n.a.
1991	61	n.a.
1992	62	n.a.
1993	72	68
1994	75	79
1995	85	n.a.

Sources: Barry Naughton, *Growing Out of the Plan: Chinese Economic Reform 1978–1993* (Cambridge University Press, 1995), p. 264; Zhang Jin, "Concerned Officials of the State Restructuring Commission State Debt Restructuring of State-Owned Economy Is Imperative," *Jingji cankao bao* (Economic Reference News), October 31, 1996, p. 3, in FBIS, *China*, 97-028, October 31, 1996; Guo Shuqing, "Restructuring of State Assets and the Repayment of Social Insurance Debts," unpublished manuscript, 1995, p. 2. Wang Lihong, "Pilot Measures in 50 Cities Yield Results: Trial Project Targets Debt," *China Daily Business Weekly*, October 7, 1996, p. 1; A Ming, "State-Owned Enterprises: How to Confront the Debt Ratio?" *Jinrong shibao* (Financial News), October 7, 1995, p. 1; and Liu Kaiyun, "The Difficult Problem and the Choice in the Commercialization of the Specialized Banks," a paper presented at the 1996 Guangzhou Conference on Financial and Enterprise Reform, p. 2.

n.a. Not available.

a. The data for different years in this table appear to be compiled on the same methodology and thus are comparable. In 1995, a new methodology was introduced that placed the ratio of liabilities to assets for all state-owned enterprises at 65.9 percent. Gao Shangquan, "Innovation of the State Enterprise System and Development of the Capital Market," *Jingji cankao bao* (Economic Reference News), September 30, 1997, pp. 1, 2, in FBIS, *China*, 97-325, November 21, 1997. The new methodology differs primarily in the valuation of land of state-owned enterprises. Data for earlier years have not been restated to be consistent with this new methodology.

authorities restrict the growth of credit. When firms are unable to borrow enough to pay for their inputs, for example, they frequently simply postpone paying their suppliers. To the extent the triangular debt phenomenon exists among state-owned firms, it does not affect the net liabilities of the sector as a whole since one firm's liability is another firm's asset. State firms, however, have a significant net indebtedness to nonstate firms, suggesting that it is easier for state-owned firms to refuse to pay nonstate firms than vice versa. At year-end 1994 this debt amounted to RMB 440 billion, about two-thirds of all interenterprise debt. Taking this figure into account increases the liability-to-asset ratio of state-owned firms from 75 to 83 percent.

Compounding the understatement of liabilities, data on enterprise assets appear to be overstated. First, observers have long noted that depreciation rates used by Chinese firms are too low.[60] Thus the depreciated value of plant and equipment, the single largest component of enterprise assets, is overstated. Second, many enterprises hold large inventories of finished goods that they value at full price when in at least some cases the goods may not be saleable.[61] The failure to value inventories at their likely market value results in an overstatement of the value of working capital, the other main component of enterprise assets.

All these factors—excluding net triangular debt to nonstate firms in liabilities, overvaluing plant and equipment, and carrying unsold inventories at their full price—result in an understatement of the liability:asset ratio for state-owned enterprises as a group. Moreover, the understatement probably has increased over time, because both inventories and triangular debt grew rapidly in the years up to the mid-1990s.

The ratio of working capital that is composed of borrowed funds is even higher than the overall liability-to-asset ratio of state firms—97 percent in 1995.[62] In short state-owned firms are so poorly capitalized that, besides inventories and accounts receivable, they have virtually no working capital other than funds they have borrowed from banks.

These national figures obscure important regional variation. Perhaps the most extremely indebted state-owned enterprises are located in China's industrial heartland—the northeast. In Liaoning, historically China's most industrialized province, at the end of 1992 the average liability-to-asset ratio for the province's 392 medium and large industrial enterprises was 190 percent, about three times the national average.[63] Because the average ratio was so far above the 100 percent critical level differentiating solvent from insolvent firms, it seems likely that virtually all of the medium and large state-owned firms in the province were insolvent. The situation in Heilongjiang Province was also unfavorable. In one of the province's fourteen districts the liability-to-asset ratio in 1994 was 86.1 percent, more than 11 percentage points greater than the national average. And nonperforming loans as a share of outstanding loans in the region at the end of October 1995 exceeded 55 percent, two and one-half times the national average.[64]

There are three implications of an average liability-to-asset ratio of 85 percent. First, a significant portion of Chinese state-owned firms are insolvent, that is, the value of their liabilities exceeds the value of their assets. Even in 1994, when the liability-to-asset ratio for state-owned industrial enterprises was 10 percentage points below the level of 1995, liabilities exceeded assets for more than one-fourth of the enterprises and liabilities were equal to assets in an additional one-fifth of all enterprises.[65] In short, without even taking into account net debt to nonstate firms, unfunded pension liabilities, or overstatement of assets, half of all state-owned enterprises were at or beyond the brink of insolvency. They remained in operation only because of generous access to additional bank loans.

Second, the continuous rise in the ratio of liabilities to assets suggests that many firms operate continuously at a loss; their output is worth less than the cost of all of the labor and other inputs required to manufacture it. Their liabilities rise relative to their assets because borrowed funds are not used to finance fixed investment but are also used to pay wages and taxes and to finance growing inventories of unsold, and all too frequently unsaleable, goods.[66] This problem, which Ronald McKinnon identifies as value-subtracting firms, was important throughout eastern Europe and the Soviet Union in the prereform era.[67]

Third, enterprises in China are so highly leveraged that an economic slowdown could create liquidity problems for banks. An asset-to-liability ratio of 85 percent is the equivalent of a debt-to-equity ratio of well over 500 percent. Thus the average state-owned firm in 1995 was even more highly leveraged than Korean chaebol, which are notorious for their high gearing ratios of 300 to 400 percent.[68] One shortcoming of such a high debt-to-equity ratio is that in an economic downturn the earnings of these firms could easily fall below the level necessary simply to pay interest on their heavy debts, subjecting them to the possibility of bankruptcy if their lenders are unwilling to roll over their loans.

Unfunded Pension Liabilities

Besides the rapid expansion of liabilities to banks, state-owned enterprises also have accumulated large, unfunded pension liabilities during the reform period. The World Bank estimates that implicit pension debt in the mid-1990s was equal to about 50 percent of China's gross domestic product.[69] Implicit pension debt is measured by the present value of benefits that state enterprises would have to pay to current pensioners and to current workers on the assumption that the pension system was terminated when the estimate was made.[70] It makes no allowance for the higher levels of pension benefits that current workers in state-owned firms would be eligible for by virtue of the additional years they will work, on average, before they retire. Thus the estimate of implicit pension debt understates the magnitude of unfunded pension liabilities.[71]

The World Bank characterizes China's situation as a "pension crisis in the state-owned enterprise sector."[72] But this is not a hypothetical distant future problem, like that of the U.S. social security system in which revenue currently exceeds outlays by $65 billion a year. That annual surplus will more than double over the next decade. Estimated annual pension expenditures will not exceed revenues until 2018. Because of the buildup of the surplus in the intervening years, however, without any changes the U.S. system would not be insolvent until 2030.[73] In contrast with an insolvency that is three decades away, the World Bank describes China as facing an "urgent and immediate problem."[74]

China's high level of implicit pension debt results from a combination of several factors. First, China's pension system is financed strictly on a pay-as-you-go basis, meaning that payments to current retirees are financed almost entirely from the current pension contributions made both by enterprises and workers. Moreover, the World Bank estimates that the reserves of the pension system in the mid-1990s were only RMB 30 billion. That was only 0.6 percent of GDP and less than a third of the pension payments made to retirees in 1994.[75] As a result China's system compares unfavorably with the U.S. social security system, which also operates on a pay-as-you-go basis but which had accumulated reserves of U.S.$496 billion or 6.8 percent of U.S. gross domestic product in 1995.[76]

Second, the number of retirees relative to active workers covered by China's pension system has soared since reform began. Only 3 million retirees were collecting pensions in 1978. By 1995 that number exceeded 30 million, ten times as many. At the outset of reform there were thirty workers contributing to the pension system for each retiree but by 1995 there were fewer than five.[77]

Third, by international standards, China's pension system replaces a high percent of preretirement income. Cash pensions and in-kind payments replace the equivalent of 80 to 90 percent of total preretirement compensation, substantially more than the 40 to 60 percent replacement rates that prevail in most countries.[78]

Fourth, China's retirement age is relatively young, age sixty for men and age fifty-five for women. These ages were set in 1951 when the system was established and the average life expectancy was fifty years. They have not been adjusted upward, despite the fact that life expectancy is now seventy-one years. The average worker retiring today will live an additional sixteen years, far longer than a worker retiring in the 1950s.[79]

Finally, although there are regional variations, pensions generally are indexed to wages rather than prices, meaning that pensioners share the increasing prosperity of current workers at the cost of a more rapidly rising pension burden on enterprises and current workers. In normal times, when wages rise more rapidly than prices, this approach means that pensioners are more than protected from rising prices. By contrast social security payments in the United States are indexed, perhaps imperfectly, to prices. In some countries, such as Switzerland, pension indexation is based on the average of price and wage inflation.[80] Given China's rapid growth of real wages in recent years, indexing pensions to wages has dramatically increased the pension burden.

China's current pension system appears unsustainable. Because of the rapid aging of the population, the number of workers per retiree will continue to fall. As a result the contribution rate has risen and, unless the system is modified, will continue to rise. When the system was established in 1951, there were more than 400 workers for each retiree, and enterprise contributions to pensions equal to 3 percent of the wage bill were more than sufficient to fund the very generous pension system established at that time.[81] By 1994 the average pension contribution rate was 23.5 percent of the wages or eight times the ratio prevailing in the 1950s. Enterprises paid 20.8 percent, and workers paid in an additional 2.7 percent of their wages. The combined rate was twice the rate of payroll taxes prevailing in developing countries, close to twice the 12.4 percent rate prevailing in the United States, and much higher than the 16.5 percent rate in Japan, and 18.6 percent in Germany.[82] Among transition economies Hungary has a pension contribution rate exceeding China's, 30.5 percent. It too faces a pension crisis.[83]

Without changes to the system a Chinese research group estimated that the contribution rate necessary to sustain the present pension system will rise to 39.27 percent in 2033. More elaborate models underlying World Bank estimates show the contribution rate must rise as high as 46 percent. Although this estimate, one of nine alternative scenarios, assumes the greatest degree of continuity with the current system, it incorporates two critical assumptions that hold down the required increase in the contribution rate. First, it assumes that pension indexation in the future is tied to an average of price and wage increases, rather than to wages alone, as in the current system. Second, it assumes that the rate of growth of the economy and thus the rate of growth of real wages will decline dramatically over time from 6.4 percent in 1990–94 to 5 percent in the years 2000–10, 4 percent for 2011–30, and 3 percent thereafter.[84]

The World Bank concludes that drastic changes are needed. It recommends reducing pension costs through a combination of an increase in the age of retirement, a reduction in the rate of wage replacement, and less generous indexing of pensions. Thus the pay-as-you-go part of the pension system would provide a replacement rate of only about one-fourth of preretirement compensation, far less than the 80 to 90 percent at present, and would be indexed to prices rather than wages. Besides the pay-as-you-go system, there would be a two-tier system of fully funded individual pension accounts. The first tier of this new system would be funded by mandatory contributions of workers and enterprises. Under certain assumptions concerning the rate of return on investments, income generated by the individual pension accounts would replace about 35 percent of wages. Thus the combined pension from the modified traditional system and the mandatory fully funded individual accounts would replace 60 percent of preretirement wages. Finally, the World Bank recommends a second tier of fully funded individual accounts financed entirely by voluntary contributions by workers alone. The fully funded individual accounts borrow features from retirement systems in Chile and Singapore.

Under the recommended plan, the old pay-as-you-go system would be terminated at the outset, necessitating separate financing of the pensions of current retirees and the accrued pension rights of current workers who have been contributing under the present system, that is, the implicit pension debt outstanding at the time of termination.[85] This is what happened in Chile in 1981 when the pay-as-you-go public pension fund was terminated and replaced with mandatory defined contribution pension funds, similar to 401K plans in the United States. The World Bank recommends that the pensions of current workers and the accrued pension rights of current workers be financed by pledging the housing and land use rights of state-owned enterprises, which they calculate to be sufficient to finance the implicit pension debt.[86]

The urgency of the pension situation is evident in the fact that many state-owned enterprises, particularly those that are running at a loss or have stopped production, have negotiated to delay making pension contributions or have simply stopped making such contributions. A limited amount of pension pooling at the municipal and provincial level may provide for pension payments for retirees from those enterprises that are no longer contributing, but anecdotal evidence suggests that these payments are partial or in some cases have been suspended entirely. In some cases enterprises are financing pension payments by borrowing from state banks.

Explanations

Why have financial indicators of enterprise performance, particularly asset-to-liability ratios, deteriorated so badly when factor productivity studies are less conclusive, with a few suggesting improvement in the efficiency of resource use? Are there explanations for declining financial performance that are consistent with stagnating or even rising total factor productivity?

Erosion of Abnormal Profits

Barry Naughton has argued that the declining profitability of state-owned firms is the natural result of the rapid expansion of non-state firms, which erodes the monopoly power of state firms.[87] At the outset of reform, profitability was high, at 25 percent. It varied widely by sector, however, with higher rates in light industries, which relied primarily on agricultural inputs and much-below-average rates in sectors producing heavy industrial goods. Liberalization naturally attracted new firms, mostly nonstate, in high profit sectors. On Naughton's calculation by the end of the 1980s average profitability fell to 17 percent, largely because the entry of new firms reduced profits in light manufacturing. Thus a convergence in profitability rates across sectors occurred. In short, the reduction in profits was owed to increasing competition, not declining efficiency.

But increasing competition appears to be only a partial explanation of the convergence in profitability across sectors and the decline in the average profit rate. First, it is difficult to separate out the effects of price reform from those of increased competition. High profits in light manufacturing, which were dependent on agricultural raw materials, reflected the state's long-time policy of taxing the agricultural and raw-material-producing sectors indirectly through unfavorable terms of trade.[88] When the state in the early stages of reform raised prices it paid to farmers for agricultural products and then subsequently increasingly allowed agricultural prices to be set in the market, it was inevitable that profit rates in the food processing, textile, and garment industries would fall. Furthermore, profitability declined dramatically even in some industrial sectors where there was only limited entry by nonstate firms. For example, profitability declined by a third in electric power and by more than nine-tenths in petroleum and natural gas extraction. These are sectors where there has been virtually no entry by nonstate firms. That suggests that price reform has been a key contributor to convergence in profit rates across sectors.

Second, the average rate of profitability of state-owned industrial firms has continued to plummet since 1989, the end year in Naughton's calculations. By 1996 the average profit rate had fallen to 6.5 percent, less than half the level of 1989.[89] Expressed as a return on all the assets reflected on the balance sheet of state enterprises, profitability in 1996 was only 5.2 percent, which is low by international standards.[90]

Accounting and Tax Reforms

A second possible explanation of the increase in reported losses since 1993, shown in table 2-3, is the introduction of more modern accounting rules, which began to take effect in July 1993, and tax reforms that were instituted beginning in 1994.[91] In particular, the adoption of accrual accounting may have led to a more accurate accounting of interest expenditures which, as discussed earlier, would not be recorded by firms using cash-based accounting. If this is a significant factor, it would mean that profits in earlier years were overstated and that the currently low level of return on assets of state-owned industrial assets is a longer-term problem than the analysis above of data on financial losses suggests.

Tax reforms initiated in 1994 could have had a similar effect. The reforms introduced a more uniformly applied value-added tax, reducing the ability of firms to negotiate their tax payments. That presumably gave enterprise managers a stronger incentive to lower their reported profits, a possible outcome in China's weak accounting environment.

Excessive Wage Payments

Another possible explanation of declining profitability and rising liability-to-asset ratios is too rapid growth of real wages. When wages grow more rapidly than labor productivity, profitability is likely to decline. Although official data show wage growth in the state sector lagging behind the growth of labor productivity between 1978 and 1990, these data appear to understate the growth of total compensation, that is, wages plus various subsidies and in-kind benefits. The growth of total compensation has outstripped the growth of labor productivity, contributing to a decline in profitability.[92]

Since 1990 this trend has worsened, with nominal wage growth to 1996 of 175 percent, outstripping the 110 percent increase in the general consumer price index in urban areas.[93] Thus the real wage increased 30 percent, before taking into account the increased value of housing and other benefits.

One reason for excessive wage payments may be insider control. With insider control, managers may ignore the interests of the owners of the firm and pay workers too much, especially bonuses. The state attempted to alleviate this problem by imposing sharply progressive taxes on bonus payments exceeding specified limits. In 1984, for example, the state fixed the tax rate at a peak of 300 percent on bonuses exceeding six months' standard wages.[94] This system was not very successful and later was replaced by a scheme tying the total wage bill of each enterprise to pretax profits or other indicators of enterprise productivity.

The continued existence of regulations specifying various constraints on the wage bill of an enterprise suggests that excessive wage payments remain a problem. In a market economy the combination of competitive labor markets and managers acting on behalf of the owners of firms would make such regulations superfluous.

Excess Employees

Besides providing a broad range of specific social services, state-owned firms have long been required to employ redundant workers as part of the government's ill-founded strategy to maintain full employment in urban areas. Although the 1988 law on state-owned enterprises gave managers the right to hire and fire workers, many firms still have excess employees.[95] A World Bank survey of 142 enterprises in 1994, for example, found 60 percent of the firms had redundant workers exceeding 10 percent of their labor force. One-third of the firms reported labor redundancy exceeding 20 percent.[96] Chinese estimates of redundant labor cover a broad range, but the consensus seems to be from about one-fifth to one-quarter.[97] As already noted, if enterprise managers are prevented from pursuing profit maximization, higher productivity may be accompanied by lower profits.

Excessive Social Expenditures

Growing social expenditures, which in most economies would be financed through the state budget, may also have contributed to the declining financial performance of state-owned firms. Although a comprehensive study of this topic lies well beyond the scope of this book, some important indicators of this burden should be noted. Annual construction of residential housing owned by state-owned units rose by half, from 116 million square meters in 1985 to 177 million square meters in 1995. Their share of newly constructed urban housing over the same period declined only moderately, from 62 percent in 1985 to 47 percent in 1995.[98] In short, state-owned units continue to have the responsibility for building almost half of all new housing provided for urban residents. In some cities progress has been reported in selling enterprise housing to workers. But even when this has been done, all too frequently the prices have been set at artificially low levels. When housing is sold below cost, enterprises are still burdened by having to pay interest on the loans taken out to finance the initial construction. More commonly, workers pay rent that does not even cover the cost of maintaining the buildings.

Besides being burdened by the need to provide subsidized housing for most of their workers, state-owned enterprises shoulder substantial costs for education and health. In the mid-1990s they operated more than 18,000 schools with an enrollment of 6.1 million students. Enterprises employed a total of 600,000 teachers and other staff to teach in and manage these institutions. Hospitals built and run by state firms accounted for one-third of all hospital beds in China![99] A World Bank survey in 1994 showed that enterprise social burdens absorbed 7.6 percent of the sales revenue of the 67 profitable firms in the sample.[100] This growing burden of social expenditures could have pushed some enterprises into the red even if they had successfully adopted technical improvements that increased factor productivity.

Asset Stripping

A final possible explanation of deteriorating financial performance of state-owned firms is asset stripping, the illegal transformation of state assets to nonstate ownership. Given the uncertainty of property rights, managers of some state-owned firms have moved assets of state-owned firms into new nonstate enterprises, leaving the original state-owned firm only as the holder of liabilities. Subsequently the original firm may declare bankruptcy and default on its outstanding financial obligations, notably loans from banks. These cases are referred to as "false bankruptcies." Alternatively the managers of state-owned enterprises lease or contract out the use of the assets to workers. But the lease payments or profits transferred back to the state firm may be so small that the latter cannot amortize the loans that it took out to finance the original purchase of the equipment.

State-owned enterprises also engage in practices that at least temporarily may raise their liability-to-asset ratios even if they do not necessarily involve permanent asset stripping. State-owned firms frequently use their preferential access to loans from state banks to acquire funds that are then re-lent to nonstate enterprises at substantially higher interest rates.[101] These borrowed funds are likely to be recorded as a liability on the balance sheet of the enterprise. Since the on-lending to nonstate enterprises is illegal, it probably is not recorded on the asset side of the balance sheet, thereby leading to an overstatement of liabilities relative to assets. Similarly some firms transfer funds to their workers who then deposit them in personal savings accounts.[102] This apparently is a not uncommon scheme enterprises use to conceal income and avoid taxes.[103] Even if the funds are eventually returned to the firm, in the short run the practice may result in an understatement of the firm's assets.

Chinese estimates suggest that this drain of state assets through these mechanisms, as well as blatant theft, has been growing. For the years 1987 through 1992 the State Economic and Trade Commission of the State Council estimated the state lost RMB 230 billion in assets drained away from state-owned enterprises, a loss of about RMB 33 billion annually.[104] A later estimate by a researcher in the Policy Research Office of the State Council placed cumulative losses between 1990 and 1995 at more than RMB 300 billion or more than RMB 50 billion annually.[105] Concern over the problem has become so severe that in early 1997 the State Council established a leading group led by Vice Premier Zhu Rongji to investigate the extent of asset stripping and make recommendations to end this problem.[106]

Conclusion

The evidence on whether total factor productivity of state-owned firms is rising is inconclusive. Different researchers report diametrically opposed results. Even those who believe total factor productivity growth has accelerated in the reform era report widely varying empirical results as their methodologies are refined.

The financial performance of enterprises, however, appears to have deteriorated during the past twenty years. The rise in liabilities relative to assets of state-owned firms, reaching an average of 85 percent in 1995, is perhaps the most conclusive evidence.

The alternative explanations of declining financial performance, outlined above, point to a common underlying cause—the lack of a fundamental change in ownership and in corporate governance. The lesson from other transition economies is that without formal programs of privatization that vest secure ownership rights in the hands of new private owners, "Assets and earnings in [the] . . . state sector tend to be increasingly diverted into private hands after the private economy becomes legitimate."[107] In China enterprise managers too often are able to ignore the interests of the state in favor of the interests of managers and workers. In particular, they are likely to maximize wages, bonuses, benefits in kind for workers, managerial emoluments, and retained funds, including depreciation and social welfare funds, rather than maximizing profits.[108] Since wages are not determined by a competitive labor market but are set by firms, managers can overpay workers. Similarly firms have every incentive to overinvest. Because the firm can avoid paying interest or repaying the principal or because in some years the nominal interest rate is less than the rate of inflation, the real cost of capital to state firms is very low or even negative. But depreciation of machinery and equipment is treated as a deduction from pretax profits. The state has sought, without much success, to limit overinvestment and payment of excess wages by intervening to limit capital spending and by taxing excess wage payments.

Given the environment in which they operate, especially the availability of explicit and implicit subsidies to cover losses, it is perhaps not surprising that so many firms report negative profits. But some of these firms may be operating efficiently and making economic profits.[109]

The solution is obviously to impose hard budget constraints on firms; introduce measures that further enhance the role of the market in wage determination; promote labor mobility by making pensions portable and separating employment from the provision of subsidized housing and a broad range of social services; and ensure that managers act on behalf of the owners of the firm. Given the evidence from the first two decades of reform, the latter almost certainly will have to include widespread privatization of state-owned firms.

Is the enterprise reform program, endorsed by both the Third Plenum of the Fourteenth Party Congress in the fall of 1993 and by the full Fifteenth Party Congress in the fall of 1997, adequate to deal with the substantial challenge that enterprise reform presents? The answer will be known only over time, but the record is mixed.

Progress has been most rapid in the conversion of small state-owned firms. In many provinces by the end of 1996 more than half of all small state-owned enterprises at the county level had been transformed, most commonly to stock cooperative companies, where shares are sold mostly to employees. Some of these firms, in turn, have been transformed into limited liability companies, often after managers bought a controlling number of shares.[110]

The economics of these transformations are most interesting. Since many of these firms have a very small net worth, the transfer price of equity is very low or even zero. Thus the real cost of employees' acquiring shares in these firms is the assumption of the firms' debts to banks and other liabilities.

It is too soon to say whether this ownership transformation will lead to an increase in profitability and eventually to a reduction in the nonperforming loans outstanding to small state-owned firms. Initially most small state-owned enterprises had liability-to-asset ratios even higher than medium and large firms. After they became stock cooperative companies, some firms, however, were able to issue new shares, resulting in an increase in their equity and thus a lower debt-to-equity ratio. That improves the prospect that they can become profitable and make interest payments on their borrowing, thus improving the financial position of banks and other lenders.

One problem apparent almost from the outset of the transformation of small, state-owned firms is that some workers were forced to buy shares as a condition of continued employment. The Ministry of Labor issued a nationwide circular in mid-February 1998 stipulating that purchases of shares by workers must be voluntary and that state enterprises should not use improper means to force such purchases upon employees.[111] The state appears to want to avoid a situation in which workers are forced to buy shares in enterprises that continue to lose money and eventually go bankrupt. Workers might well expect the state to compensate them for their lost savings in such a situation.

The transformation of medium and large state-owned enterprises evinces several shortcomings. First, in contrast to the rapid transformation of small firms, the conversion of medium and large state-owned enterprises into limited liability shareholding companies has been somewhat slower. By year-end 1996, 36,000 state-owned firms had adopted the limited liability form of ownership laid out in the 1993 Company Law.[112] Of this number, only 9,200 had sold shares to the public, making them limited liability stock companies.[113] Thus of approximately 300,000 state-owned enterprises, only 3 percent had become limited liability stock companies. One obstacle to faster progress in corporatization is that the Company Law specifies that the articles of association required to establish a firm under the corporate form of ownership identify the investor or investors in the company as well as the magnitude and form of their investment. Competing claimants, including government bureaus and ministries, frequently can not reach a consensus as to who is the investor in the firm. This is a particularly difficult problem for firms with relatively large liabilities. "Everybody wants the valuable assets, but nobody wants the liabilities."[114]

Second, there is little evidence of significant changes in the governance of the medium and large state-owned firms that have converted to limited liability shareholding ownership. There appear to be several reasons. First, many of the state-owned enterprises that are being "corporatized" have chosen to become wholly state-owned companies. For example, almost all of the 100 firms selected by the State Council in 1994 to spearhead the corporatization experiment have opted to convert to wholly state-owned companies.[115] This legal organizational form, which is provided for in the Company Law, embodies the fewest changes from the rules governing state-owned enterprises.[116] For example, since there is only a single owner, there is no provision for shareholder meetings. Thus the members of the board of directors of wholly state-owned limited liability companies are not elected but are appointed. The powers of these boards are severely truncated, compared to the boards of limited liability shareholding companies that are not wholly state-owned. For example, they have no power to make or approve mergers, break-ups, dissolutions, increases or decreases in a firm's capital, or the issuance of bonds. The authority to make these decisions is all reserved for "an organization authorized by the state."[117]

Another reason that there appears to be little change in the governance of corporatized firms is that their boards of directors are dominated by insiders, that is, the senior managers of the firm. A recent World Bank study of enterprise reform reported "In every case examined for this study, the majority of members of the boards of directors and the senior executives are one and the same. There is no real distinction."[118] The result is insider-dominated firms, a form of governance that has weaknesses that are readily apparent in Russia and some other transition economies. Among these weaknesses are "asset stripping, poor investment decisions, decapitalization through excessive wage increases, and increases in other private benefits."[119]

One reason for insider domination is that through the end of 1996 less than 6 percent of those companies that had reorganized into limited liability shareholding companies were listed.[120] In market economies poor firm management and financial performance are typically reflected in a declining share price. That market signal frequently leads to a takeover by a stronger, more efficient firm. But when shareholding firms are not publicly listed, capital markets are unable to provide this monitoring function and poor managers and insider-dominated boards are less likely to be replaced.

Finally, even when corporatized enterprises are publicly listed, individual shareholders "seem to have little, if any, influence on management."[121] In part this is because only a small portion of the shares of listed companies are available to the public.[122] The majority shareholders almost always are traditional line ministries at the national level or industrial bureaus at the provincial and municipal level.[123] In a few cases they are newly established state asset management institutions. These institutional shareholders "are generally not organized in such a way to marshal sufficient information, experience and skill to assess effectively an enterprise's performance."[124] There are no institutional investors, such as pension funds, insurance companies, or mutual funds, that might exercise influence on corporate governance on behalf of individual shareholders.

Beyond the failure of this reform to lead to significant changes in corporate governance, the third main shortcoming of the enterprise reform program introduced since 1993 is that government and business functions have not been separated when firms become limited liability shareholding companies. Transformed firms continue to bear the responsibility for providing a broad range of social services that should be financed from the government budget or paid for directly by workers.

The fourth shortcoming of the enterprise reform program initiated in 1993 is that labor mobility and the role of the market in determining wages in the medium and large state-owned enterprises remains limited. This, in turn, reflects generally slow progress in divesting individual enterprises of the responsibility for providing unemployment insurance, old-age pensions, and health care to their workers.

Fifth, institutional constraints have limited the ability of medium and large corporatized firms to develop a more balanced capital structure that depends less on debt and more on permanent equity financing. In part that is because so few companies are qualified and approved to raise funds through public listing of shares. If more companies had listed, they would have been able to reduce their bank debt and thus reduce their operating costs.

There are two other reasons medium and large state-owned firms have not been able to develop more balanced capital structures. First, although there have been many mergers, some differ significantly from those in market economies. Some of the largest mergers have not been voluntary but rather were orchestrated by the state.[125] Moreover, the nominally acquiring firm has to assume all of the liabilities of the firm it takes over. The only reduction in the acquiring firm's cost basis is that it is not required to pay interest on the liabilities to banks of the firm it acquires for two to three years.[126] All too often "a good company is forced to take over a bad one, to save it. But the final outcome is that both are doomed."[127] China needs to move to a system of voluntary mergers at market-determined prices that allows for deleveraging of the firm being acquired.

Another reason that more balanced capital structures are not likely to emerge is that the resources that the government has allocated to finance the write-offs of bad debts to facilitate mergers and takeovers of unprofitable firms, and thus improve the capital structure of the 1,000 large state-owned enterprises that are to form the core of the new modern enterprise system, are too small. The state has allocated a total of RMB 500 billion for the enterprise reform program during the Ninth Five-Year Plan (1996–2000). But most of these funds, RMB 280 billion, are to finance investment in technical renovations of these firms and another RMB 160 billion to cover worker redundancy payments. The amounts initially allocated to write off debts, RMB 20 billion in 1996 and an additional 30 billion in 1997, were inadequate.[128] Thus direct debt reduction was modest.

Moreover, some of these resources were provided in a way that appears to undermine incentives for improved enterprise performance. Firms in the program benefited from a reduction in their income tax rate from 33 to 15 percent; a dispensation to pay only 40 to 60 percent of this reduced tax obligation from their own funds, while borrowing the rest from banks at a special subsidized interest rate; and an increase in their allowable annual depreciation rate from 3 to 5 percent.[129]

Since there was no specified time frame for phasing out most of these new subsidies, the reforms represented a softening rather than a firming up of the budget constraint under which state-owned firms operate. A much larger initial write-off of accumulated nonperforming loans, combined with a hard budget constraint going forward, is more likely to lead to improved enterprise performance.[130]

What have been the consequences of an ever-growing but financially deteriorating state-owned sector for the banking system? This topic is discussed in chapter 3.

3

The Evolving Banking System

T HE PRIMARY role of banks and other financial institutions in a market economy is to serve as an intermediary between savers and investors and to facilitate payments between economic units. Banks fulfill their intermediary function by taking deposits and lending funds to investors. Individuals, in theory, could provide their funds directly to entrepreneurs starting new businesses or to established firms that wished to expand. In practice at least four drawbacks exist to such direct investments, all of which banks can overcome, at least in part. First, the scale of many investment projects is sufficiently large that it requires the pooling of funds of many small savers. Banks provide an efficient mechanism for pooling, obviating the need for firms to raise funds directly from a large number of savers. Second, some savers may want their funds back relatively soon while investors' projects are typically long term. Banks can take short-term deposits from a large number of individuals and lend some of them long term and still stand ready to meet the demand for withdrawals on the part of some depositors. Third, savers may regard placing all their funds in a single or small number of investments as too risky. Banks, by lending to a broad range of projects, perform the function of diversifying the risk faced by savers. Finally, through the accumulation of experience in evaluating large numbers of borrowers, banks are better able than individuals to identify the most promising projects. Thus banks can be more successful than individual savers in allocating funds to the highest rate of return.

Banks also provide discipline in the market. Their lending practices can ensure that high-quality borrowers not only have access to

59

funds, but that they are provided a lower cost of funds and they can force lower quality borrowers and projects to pay a premium for funds received. Once funds are lent they monitor the borrower to ensure that the use of funds is consistent with the loan contract. Most important, they can force borrowers who fail to amortize their loans on a timely basis either to restructure their businesses in order to survive or to exit. This disciplinary function of banks is all too frequently overlooked.

Capital markets can also perform these intermediary and disciplinary functions. In practice, as discussed in chapter 1, banks play the dominant role in intermediating between savers and investors in the early stages of economic development. Bond and equity markets tend to develop later. China is no exception to this pattern.

Not only were there no capital markets in prereform China, but banks, for two reasons, did not serve as intermediaries between savers and investors.[1] First, household savings, the source of bank deposits in developing market economies, were extraordinarily small.[2] In the years just prior to reform the annual additions to household financial savings were equal to only about 0.5 percent of gross national product. As economic reform got under way in 1978, the entire cumulative stock of household savings was only RMB 21.06 billion or about 6 percent of that year's gross national product.[3] China had sustained an average rate of national savings of more than 25 percent since the 1950s. But this high rate of savings was mobilized almost entirely within the government sector.[4] The principal source of government funds was the profits of state-owned enterprises that were surrendered, almost in their entirety, to the Ministry of Finance.

Second, investment was financed predominantly from interest-free budgetary grants and, to a lesser degree, from the retained profits of enterprises.[5] The budget was even the source of much of the working capital of state-owned enterprises.[6] Banks made few loans to state-owned firms to finance their investment in fixed assets and concentrated their lending on providing a portion of the working capital needs of state industrial and commercial enterprises. Township and village enterprises and other nonstate firms were already important on the eve of reform. But they typically were financed initially by pooled savings of their workers, often supplemented with support of county and lower-level governments. These firms expanded largely by reinvesting their profits. In these circumstances, the intermediary role of banks was quite circumscribed and their disciplinary role nonexistent. The limited role of banks also was reflected in the simple institutional structure of the financial sector. On the eve of reform China nominally had three banks—the People's Bank of China, the Bank of China, and the Construction Bank of China—and a network of rural credit cooperatives.[7] The Bank of China was not an independent entity, however, but was subordinate to the People's Bank. Moreover, its role was limited primarily to handling foreign exchange and international payments. Its domestic currency business was almost entirely with a handful of state foreign trading companies. The Construction Bank was a bank only in name. It operated as a subsidiary of the Ministry of Finance and its role, since its creation in October 1954, was simply to disburse fixed investment funds for projects that were incorporated in the state economic plan and financed through the state budget.[8] The primary role of rural credit cooperatives was to mobilize deposits from the population. They engaged in relatively little lending.[9]

The People's Bank of China, with a vast network of over 15,000 branches, subbranches, and offices, dominated China's financial landscape.[10] It controlled almost four-fifths of all deposits in banks and credit cooperatives and was the source of 93 percent of all loans by financial institutions.[11] The People's Bank simultaneously served as China's central bank, regulating the money supply, fixing interest rates, managing the state's holdings of foreign exchange, and supervising and controlling all other financial institutions. In short, China had a monobank system typical of centrally planned economies in which one bank operated simultaneously as both the central bank and the sole commercial bank.[12]

Institutional Transformation

As reform unfolded, China's financial system grew more complex. A new array of banks and nonbank financial institutions emerged. These institutions initially competed with existing banks to only a very limited degree. Their capital was quite small. Moreover, interest rates were set centrally and, with few exceptions, were uniform across all institutions, limiting the scope of competition among financial institutions. It was clear immediately, however, that as these new institutions grew, particularly as they were allowed to expand the number of branches they could operate, they would compete head-to-head with the existing banks. Because these new institutions, for the most part, were not required to extend loans to money-losing state-owned enterprises, their financial condition was stronger and they were in a better position to provide more efficient intermediation between savers and borrowers. Thus, over time, they had the potential to play a key role in solving the fundamental problem of the prereform Chinese economy identified in chapter 1—the growing inefficiency in the allocation of capital.

The first steps in the institutional transformation of the financial sector were quite modest. The Agricultural Bank of China, which focuses on deposit and lending activity in rural areas, was reestablished in February 1979 as a separate bank.[13] This move reflected the priority that the Chinese Communist Party assigned to agriculture in the initial stage of economic reform and its assessment that an infusion of funds was central to reviving growth in the farm sector. Agricultural Bank lending more than doubled between 1977, the eve of reform, and 1981.[14] By the mid-1990s it was China's fourth largest bank, as measured by assets.[15]

In March 1979 the State Council elevated the administrative status of the Bank of China by separating it from the People's Bank and making it an economic entity directly subordinate to the State Council.[16] More important, at the same time the State Council vastly expanded the bank's authorized business scope, primarily to support China's economic opening to the outside world. For example, it was authorized to sell bonds on international markets. It grew quite rapidly and by the mid-1990s was China's second largest bank, again as measured by assets.[17]

The role and status of the Construction Bank was enhanced. In October 1979 it was removed from the administrative control of the Ministry of Finance and elevated to an organization subordinate directly to the State Council, placing it on the same administrative level as China's other banks.[18] In 1980, for the first time, it also began to accept deposits and to engage in lending to support investment projects, rather than simply acting as a pass-through for government budgetary funds. Between 1979 and 1985 it extended loans in excess of RMB 10,000 million in support of almost 2,000 investment projects.[19]

Some of the institutional changes in the financial system were in response to China's increasing participation in the international economy, particularly its entry into the World Bank and the International Monetary Fund in 1980. The China Investment Bank was formally created in December 1981 to serve as the institution to control the disbursement of project funds provided to China by the World Bank.[20] After China became a member of the Asian Development Bank in 1986, the China Investment Bank assumed the same responsibility for the disbursement of loans from that institution. It not only disbursed foreign currency loans to finance imports of technology and capital goods, but it also disbursed domestic currency loans to finance the local counterpart component of foreign-funded projects.[21] Given this specialized function, the bank remained quite small in the early years of its existence.

In 1994, however, the central bank approved the conversion of the China Investment Bank into a commercial bank, allowing it to take deposits from the public for the first time and to engage in a broader range of banking activities. Although it remains a separate legal entity, the bank began to operate as a subsidiary of the Construction Bank. The State Administration of Exchange Control also authorized it to engage in a broader range of foreign exchange business.[22] Its assets began to expand rapidly, growing by 47 percent and 18 percent in 1994 and 1995, respectively.[23] The conversion to operate on commercial principles has put some pressure on the bank to control costs, and in 1995 China Investment Bank reduced the number of its branches by half, from 32 to 16.

Other, far more significant, institutional changes occurred starting in the mid-1980s. A number of new banks and an array of nonbank financial institutions were created. But the single most important change was the decision of the State Council in September 1983 to create a central bank.[24] Institutionally this was accomplished by simply designating the People's Bank of China as the central bank and establishing the Industrial and Commercial Bank to take over the deposit-taking and lending functions of the People's Bank. Although the central bank came into existence formally on January 1, 1984, it assumed normal central bank functions only gradually.[25]

Beginning in 1985 the People's Bank became responsible for issuing currency, managing credit, setting interest rates, and supervising China's foreign exchange business. It set reserve requirements for the specialized banks, promulgated credit targets, and adjusted the flow of funds across banks in different locales. Reflecting the People's Bank's growing role, the State Council in November 1985 incorporated the lending activities of the Construction Bank within the unified state credit plan, subject to the approval of the central bank. Before that time the Construction Bank was not subject to reserve requirements and was not allowed to borrow from the People's Bank.[26]

The People's Bank also assumed the supervisory and regulatory roles usually associated with central banks. In May 1985 the People's Bank established a Department of Examination and Supervision. In January 1986 the State Council issued a formal regulation establishing the legal basis for central bank supervision of specialized banks and rural credit cooperatives, as well as other emerging financial institutions, such as trust and investment companies and urban credit cooperatives.[27]

The vast branch network of the People's Bank was reorganized to form the Industrial and Commercial Bank of China that, upon its formal creation on January 1, 1984, immediately became China's largest financial institution. At the end of 1985, the Bank's first full year of operation, it accounted for fully half of all bank lending.[28] Its staff of more than 405,000 was distributed over a geographically far-flung network consisting of more than 21,500 branches, subbranches, business offices, and deposit taking (savings) stations.[29] Despite the creation of a number of new banks in the 1980s, in the mid-1990s the Industrial and Commercial Bank continued to be far and away China's largest financial institution. By the end of 1995 its branches and other offices had grown by three-quarters to number more than 37,000 and its staff had increased by one-fourth to exceed 560,000. More important, between 1986 and 1995 its assets grew more than sevenfold to reach RMB 3.1 trillion, more than half again as large as China's next largest bank.[30]

The other significant development starting in the mid-1980s, besides the creation of a central bank, was the gradual introduction of competition into the financial system. This was accomplished in two different ways.

First, the separate business scope of the four major banks gradually diminished. From their inception these banks were known as specialized banks because they operated in well-defined, nonoverlapping types of business. Lending to support agricultural production as well as rural industrial and commercial enterprises was the exclusive domain of the Agricultural Bank of China; state-owned commercial and industrial enterprises borrowed from the Industrial and Commercial Bank; and the Construction Bank was the principal source of funds for new investment projects. In the 1980s these banks continued to dominate their traditional markets, but they gradually began to face competition, at least at the margin.

The best example of increasing competition may be foreign exchange business. Initially the Bank of China had the sole monopoly to carry out all types of foreign exchange business. But in 1985 this situation began to change when the other specialized banks were permitted to conduct foreign exchange business at their branches in the three special economic zones, which had been established on the southeast coast in 1980.[31] But subsequently the State Administration of Exchange Control gradually allowed more and more branches of the specialized banks in other locations, as well as nonbank financial institutions, to enter the foreign exchange business.[32] In 1987, for example, 33 new approvals were granted, bringing the total number to 58 branch banks and 78 trust and investment companies.[33] By the end of 1992 more than 1,000 branch banks and 145 nonbank financial institutions had been licensed to carry out foreign exchange business.[34] Thus the Bank of China lost its monopoly on offering deposits and loans denominated in foreign currencies and settlement of foreign trade transactions, as well as other types of foreign exchange business. By 1996, for example, the bank's share of the market in foreign trade settlement had fallen to two-fifths.[35]

The state also increased competition by allowing the entry of new financial institutions. Beginning in the mid-1980s, China created a number of new commercial banks and a range of nonbank financial institutions. The new commercial banks include several that are explicitly national in character, as well as a number that are more regionally focused. They are almost all joint stock banks, but the pattern of ownership of the shares of these new institutions varies widely and has evolved over time. As of the late-1990s the state has allowed only one bank, the Shenzhen Development Bank, to list its shares on a stock exchange and only one, Minsheng Bank, is described by the Chinese as private.

National Commercial Banks

China established two major national level comprehensive banks in the mid-1980s—the Bank of Communications and the China International Trust and Investment Company (CITIC) Industrial Bank.[36] They are national since they are not subject to any geographic restrictions on where they can establish branches, although the central bank must approve the expansion of their branch networks. And, unlike the existing specialized banks, these new institutions are not restricted in their business scope. Thus they are described as comprehensive. For example, they were authorized from the outset to conduct foreign exchange business.

The Bank of Communications is a joint stock bank. Initially half of the shares were held by the central bank on behalf of the state.[37] Most of the rest of the shares were owned by local governments and state enterprises, although in theory up to 10 percent of the shares can be owned by individuals.[38] The bank pioneered the use of modern banking methods in China. For example, in 1993 it was the first to begin implementing asset-to-liability ratio management. That meant that the quantity of loans that it could make was limited primarily by the quantity of deposits that it could attract, rather than by the loan quotas that were handed down by the central bank to each of the large state-owned banks.[39] As a result it was largely exempt from the state credit plan.

More important, unlike China's specialized banks, the Bank of Communications from the outset was not required to undertake directed lending on behalf of the state. Rather it has been able to make its lending decisions primarily on commercial considerations. Thus the quality of its loan portfolio appears relatively high and perhaps could be considered the best of all of China's larger banks. This is reflected in a relatively small share of nonperforming loans, a relatively high rate of capital adequacy, somewhat higher loan loss reserves relative to assets, and a comparatively high rate of return on assets.[40] By the mid-1990s it was the second largest of the banks created since the beginning of reform, with assets more than one-fourth of those of the Agricultural Bank of China, the smallest of the four specialized banks.[41]

The CITIC Industrial Bank is the banking arm of the CITIC Group. It has developed a substantial domestic and foreign currency business, the latter based in part on the authority of the bank to raise funds abroad to help finance enterprises affiliated with CITIC. Because of its more focused character it has developed a smaller branch network than the Bank of Communications. Its assets, by the mid-1990s, were less than one-fourth of those of the Bank of Communications.[42]

Besides these two major national commercial banks, there are three smaller national comprehensive banks—the Everbright Bank, the Huaxia Bank, and the Minsheng Bank. The first two initially were affiliated closely with a single industrial group, similar to the CITIC Industrial Bank. In the case of the Everbright and Huaxia Banks these close affiliations were the source of a variety of lending irregularities that led the central bank in the mid-1990s to reorganize both banks. Both reorganizations were accompanied by a substantial injection of new capital. In the case of Huaxia, the injection appears to have amounted to a bank rescue.

Everbright Bank, which opened in August 1992, initially was wholly owned by the China Everbright (Group) Co. It is a national bank and by the mid-1990s had nine branches. It engages in a broad range of businesses including renminbi lending, foreign exchange, financial leasing, and, until mid-1996, securities trading.[43] The People's Bank in April 1995 approved the bank's application to convert to a joint stock form of ownership. The conversion was accompanied by an expansion of the bank's capital by RMB 2.4 billion, via the sale of 1.37 billion new shares to other enterprise groups, foreign-invested enterprises, and collective enterprises. The Everbright Group retained a 51 percent majority ownership of the bank.[44] In an important development the Asian Development Bank took a minority ownership of about 3.3 percent, making the ADB the bank's third largest shareholder.[45] The investment of U.S.$20 million by the Asian Development Bank was approved by the bank's board in January 1997. This is the first time the People's Bank has allowed a foreign financial institution to acquire a partial ownership of a Chinese bank.[46]

Huaxia Bank, which is headquartered in Beijing, also was formed in 1992. At its founding it was owned entirely by the Capital Iron and Steel (Group) Co., whose main asset is the Capital Iron and Steel Works, commonly called Shougang (Capital Steel), an abbreviation of its full Chinese name (Shoudu gangtie gongsi). Capital Steel is one of China's largest producers of steel and steel products with well over 200,000 employees. In the 1990s the group expanded rapidly into a broad range of businesses, including shipping, mining, and electronics, as well as banking. Shougang Group also controls several publicly listed Hong Kong companies (so-called red chips), most sharing the name Concord, that are used in part as vehicles for raising funds abroad. By the mid-1990s Shougang (Group) was one of China's largest conglomerates as measured by assets or by pretax profits. Huaxia Bank also grew exceptionally rapidly. For example, its assets grew by 65 percent in 1994 and then more than doubled in 1995.[47] In retrospect this extraordinarily rapid growth appears to have been accompanied by a substantial deterioration of asset quality and a number of lending irregularities.[48]

Beginning in March 1995 Huaxia Bank was converted from a private fiefdom of Shougang (Group) into a joint stock commercial bank with more than thirty large companies as shareholders.[49] This reorganization followed by one month the "retirement" of Zhou Guanwu, the chairman of the Shougang Group. Zhou's retirement appears to have been precipitated by the arrest of his son Zhou Beifang, the head of the Hong Kong-based Shougang Concord International Enterprises, on charges of economic crimes.[50] Not only did the People's Bank initiate the process of terminating Shougang's sole ownership of Huaxia within weeks of Zhou's arrest in February 1995, the Shougang Group reportedly also was forced to terminate some its activities not related to its core steel business.[51]

Shougang's financial mismanagement of Huaxia is suggested by two factors. First, although Shougang remained the largest shareholder after Huaxia's reorganization, retaining one-fifth of the bank's shares, other large firms gained significant stakes in the bank's ownership. Three large industrial corporations, the Shandong Electric Power Company, the Yuxi Red Pagoda Tobacco Group, and the Shandong Lianda Group bought 16, 14, and 12 percent, respectively, of the bank's shares.[52] These three large shareholders, which were selected by the Central Bank, collectively have a stake in the Huaxia Bank that is over twice that of Shougang. As a result Shougang, even though it remains the largest single shareholder, is no longer able to run the bank as its private fiefdom.[53]

Second, the transformation of Huaxia's ownership structure was accompanied by a substantial injection of capital. The new owners did not buy shares of the bank business from Shougang but injected capital that resulted in the bank's registered capital increasing from

RMB 1 billion to RMB 2.5 billion.[54] In the mid-1990s, in addition to seven offices in Beijing, the bank had branches only in Nanjing in Jiangsu Province and Hangzhou in Zhejiang Province but planned to expand its presence by opening branches in east, south, and northeast China.

China's first private shareholding bank, the China Minsheng Bank, was approved by the State Council and the People's Bank of China in 1995, and its headquarters in Beijing opened for business in early 1996. Organized under the aegis of the All-China Federation of Industry and Commerce, its specific purpose is to lend to small businesses in both the collective and private sectors. The bank's initial 59 shareholders, almost entirely nonstate enterprises, are members of the Federation. The bank is authorized to engage in both domestic and international business. By year-end 1996 the number of shareholders had grown to 2,000 and total assets stood at more than RMB 8 billion.[55] The bank's chairman, Jing Shuping, has set a goal of Minsheng becoming one of China's biggest banks within ten years. But achieving this objective depends critically on the pace at which the central bank approves additional branch banks and, more generally, the pace of financial liberalization.[56] Minsheng is notable in that it is the only bank in China that has hired an internationally recognized accounting firm to audit its financial statements. Perhaps this is being done to reassure its depositors that although it is not state owned and thus enjoys no implicit government guarantee of its deposits, it is a sound institution. It also may be intended to pave the way for a listing of the bank's stock, either on the B share domestic market or abroad. In late 1996 the International Finance Corporation, a member of the World Bank Group, indicated its interest in purchasing a minority ownership of Minsheng Bank. However, as of early 1998 this purchase was still pending.[57]

Regional Commercial Banks

Besides the five national banks just discussed, China in the mid-1980s and again in the mid-1990s approved the establishment of a number of regional banks. These include the Guangdong Development Bank (approved 1988), the Shenzhen Development Bank (1987), Merchants Bank (1987), the Fujian Industrial Bank (1988), the Shanghai Pudong Development Bank (1988), the Yantai

Housing Savings Bank in Shandong Province (1987), the Bengbu Housing Savings Bank in Anhui Province (1987), and the Hainan Development Bank (1995). Also in the mid-1990s China began to convert its urban credit cooperatives to urban cooperative banks.

Although they are all commercial banks, these regional banks are diverse in their ownership arrangements, size, and geographic scope of business.[58] At least through 1997 the Shenzhen Development Bank was the only listed bank. Its shares are traded on the Shenzhen stock market. Moreover, unlike some joint stock financial institutions, such as the Bank of Communications, whose shares are owned predominantly by the central bank on behalf of the central government and by local governments, two-thirds of the shares of the Shenzhen Development Bank are held by individual investors. Shenzhen Municipality and the Guangdong Provincial government, however, are both major shareholders. Merchants Bank initially was wholly owned by the Guangdong-based Merchant Group. But in October 1989 it became a shareholding bank with a total of seven shareholders. In June 1994 the number of shareholders expanded to ninety-three. These expansions were accompanied by a substantial increase in paid-in capital.[59]

The housing banks were established as experiments to help facilitate the transfer of ownership of housing from enterprises to occupants. These housing savings banks have grown quite slowly, however, in part because of their peculiar structure. They do not take deposits from the public but rather depend on funds deposited by manufacturing and commercial firms. By year-end 1995 the total assets of the Yantai Housing Savings bank were only RMB 3.55 billion and it had extended mortgages of only RMB 17.03 million to a total of 1,500 households.[60] The Bengbu Housing Savings Bank was even smaller.

The geographic scope of these five smaller institutions also varies. Although these banks are classified by the Chinese as regional, some of them have established a significant network of branches outside their home bases. The best example may be Merchants Bank, which is headquartered in Shenzhen. Although its formal registered name is Merchants Bank, it is commonly called China Merchants Bank, implying a franchise far beyond Shenzhen. Indeed, by 1995 it had established a network of 107 branches, subbranches, and banking offices in north, northeast, northwest, southwest, and east China.[61]

Similarly, the Shanghai Pudong Development Bank is well on the way to establishing a national business network. By late 1995, it already had offices in Hangzhou and Nanjing, the capitals of neighboring Zhejiang and Jiangsu Provinces, respectively, as well as in Beijing. By September 1997 its Beijing office had been converted to a branch and the bank had branches or subbranches in seven other cities and planned to open additional branches in Guangzhou and Chongqing, as well as four additional subbranches in Jiangsu and Zhejiang, before the end of the year.[62] At the other extreme, the housing and savings banks have been able to build up only small branch networks within their named cities.

Nonbank Financial Institutions

In the mid-1980s several new types of nonbank financial intermediaries began to emerge and flourish. These included urban credit cooperatives, trust and investment companies, finance companies associated with enterprise groups, financial leasing companies, securities companies, and credit rating companies. Nonbank financial institutions generally engage in a fairly broad range of lending activities. With the exception of credit cooperatives, however, they do not take deposits from individuals. Rather, deposits of institutions and firms, as well as borrowing on the interbank market, are their main sources of funding. The form of ownership of nonbank financial institutions varies from the shareholding structure of urban credit cooperatives to ownership by state-owned entities, such as banks, which initially owned many trust and investment companies, or enterprise groups, which own finance companies.

Urban Credit Cooperatives

Although the first urban credit cooperative was established on an experimental basis in Henan Province in 1979, the central bank did not formally authorize these new shareholding financial institutions until July 1986.[63] After that date credit cooperatives expanded rapidly in most large and medium cities and in economically more developed counties as well. By the end of 1987 there were more than 1,600 urban credit cooperatives and by 1994 more than 5,200.[64] Their lending activity expanded at a similarly rapid pace. By year-end 1994 total lending exceeded RMB 130 billion, more than sixty-five times the RMB 1.95 billion in loans outstanding at the end of 1986.[65]

The creation of this vast network of urban credit cooperatives with such a rapidly expanding loan portfolio is somewhat surprising, given that the Industrial and Commercial Bank already had a dense network of offices throughout China's urban areas. However, urban credit cooperatives were able to compete with existing state banks by providing better services to depositors, mostly individuals and non-state enterprises rather than state-owned firms. And, on the lending side, they found a good market among collective and private firms whose needs were not being met by the existing state banks in urban areas, which lent overwhelmingly to state-owned firms.

The cooperatives' service of an overlooked market is reflected in the pattern of their lending. At year-end 1995 more than half their loans outstanding were to collective firms and another 8 percent was to private firms. Indeed, although state banks dwarfed the urban credit co-ops in total lending, loans outstanding to private firms by urban credit cooperatives were almost five times those of state-owned banks.[66]

Beginning in the mid-1990s networks of urban credit cooperatives in some cities began to consolidate and emerge as full-fledged commercial banks. Initially the State Council authorized existing co-ops in five cities—Beijing, Shanghai, Shenzhen, Shijiazhuang, and Tianjin—to merge to form urban cooperative banks to serve small and medium private and commercial firms more effectively.[67] The Beijing Urban Cooperative Bank, formed from the merger of ninety local urban credit cooperatives, opened in early 1996. Like other urban cooperative banks, it is organized as a joint stock company with urban enterprises, residents, and local governments as shareholders. Its initial registered capital was RMB 1.50 billion.[68]

The largest of the new cooperative banks is the Shanghai City United Bank, organized in late 1995 through the consolidation of more than one hundred local urban credit cooperative offices in the city. Its initial capital was RMB 1.6 billion, contributed 30 percent by individual shareholders, 30 percent by enterprises, and 40 percent by the Shanghai municipality and its districts. In the first nine months of operation the new bank's assets expanded by half to reach RMB 43.5 billion.[69]

By the end of 1996 more than eighteen urban cooperative banks had opened for business and the central bank had approved the creation of another fifteen.[70] These institutions were well on the way to becoming a general urban phenomenon. Formal cooperation among these new banks began in May 1996 when they established a clearinghouse involving city united banks in various municipalities.

Trust and Investment Companies

The most important category of nonbank financial institutions, after the rural credit cooperatives, is trust and investment companies. Trust and investment companies are of two broad types. The first are internationally oriented, of which the best known is the China International Trust and Investment Company (CITIC), the parent of the CITIC Industrial Bank. It was chartered by the State Council in 1979 and, through its authority to raise funds on international capital markets, quickly assumed a major role in China's opening to the outside world.[71] Other international trust and investment companies were established beginning in 1980 by provincial governments in Shandong, Liaoning, and Guangdong, by major municipalities such as Guangzhou, Xian, and Dalian, as well as by smaller cities such as Changjiang in Sichuan Province.[72]

The second type is domestically oriented trust and investment companies, specializing in long-term investments financed by funds provided by shareholders or from the sale of bonds. The People's Bank of China initially authorized separate trust departments of state-owned banks to undertake trust activities in 1980.[73] But in 1986 the central bank required state banks to shift their trust businesses to separate companies that were subject to more stringent regulation.[74] At the same time a large number of trust and investment companies sprang up that were not affiliated with banks.[75] Most were under the sponsorship of provincial or local governments. In 1988 the number of trust and investment companies reached an all-time high of 745.

The assets of the trust and investment companies grew rapidly after 1985, expanding from RMB 29.3 billion at year-end 1986 to RMB 458.6 billion by the end of 1995.[76] As a result of this rapid growth, the assets of these institutions as a share of the total assets of all Chinese financial institutions more than doubled from 1.7 percent in 1986 to 3.5 percent in 1995.[77] Their relative asset growth slowed in the mid-1990s, however, as the People's Bank sought to exercise greater supervision over trust and investment companies, in the process closing a large number of these institutions.[78]

One small but important trust and investment company is the China Trust and Investment Corporation for Foreign Economic Relations and Trade. Established in September 1987, this institution's role is to manage the concessionary government-to-government loans China receives from most industrial countries. Although administratively subordinate to the Ministry of Foreign Trade and Economic Cooperation, the corporation is subject to the financial supervision of the People's Bank.[79] By far the largest source of these funds is Japan, through its Overseas Economic Cooperation Fund. By 1994 the OECF had committed three yen loan packages to China totaling ¥1,610 billion.[80] At the end of 1994 Japan committed an additional ¥580 billion in OECF loans for the first half of the fourth yen loan package, covering the fiscal years 1996–98.[81]

Finance Companies

A third type of nonbank financial institution is finance companies, which also were created beginning in 1987 following a green light from the State Council. They most commonly are formed by industrial or commercial conglomerates, which the Chinese call groups. Finance companies carry out financial transactions among firms within a single group. By the end of 1987 seven such companies had been established. For example, the China Heavy Truck Group Finance Corporation, with total assets of RMB 1 billion in 1992, took deposits from and made loans to member enterprises as well as participating in the interbank market.[82] Other well-known finance companies dating from this period include the Xidian Group Finance Company, founded February 1988, and the Dongfeng Motor Group Finance Company, established July 1987.

The Dongfeng Finance Company is the finance arm of the Number Two Automobile Group, based in Wuhan, Hubei Province. The group, known formally as the Dongfeng Automobile Industry Group, was formed in 1981 and by 1987 was composed of 198 enterprises that were spread over almost all of China's provinces. It ranks among the top ten state-owned enterprises. The Finance Company's initial share capital, contributed by just over half of the firms in the group, stood at RMB 28 million. Profits in 1987 were RMB 262,000, of which RMB 131,000 was paid out as dividends to the shareholding companies. Working capital loans at year-end 1987, all to members of the group, stood at RMB 41.38 million while loans for fixed investment were RMB 1.81 million.[83] Several years later total loans had grown eightfold to reach RMB 331 million.[84]

By the end of November 1996 there were sixty-nine finance companies with assets totaling RMB 109.7 billion.[85] Most of these finance companies were affiliated with large industrial groups, which controlled more than one-quarter of the fixed assets of state-owned companies.[86] Although their assets have grown rapidly, under the terms of the Commercial Bank Law the People's Bank of China still restricts the scope of these finance companies. Like finance companies in most other countries, they are not licensed as banks and thus are not allowed to take deposits from the public or from firms that are not members of the underlying group. They are not allowed to borrow from the central bank or establish branch networks. And, as of 1998, none had been authorized to raise funds abroad.

Financial Leasing Companies

Financial leasing companies were first created in the early 1980s as part of China's early opening to the outside world. These early leasing companies, of which China Oriental Leasing Company was the first, were joint ventures in which the foreign partner was usually a Japanese, German, French, or Italian bank. By 1985 at least thirty-two joint venture leasing companies were operating.[87] Leasing companies provided a mechanism for Chinese firms to acquire foreign capital goods, as part of a strategy of technical upgrading and modernization. Rather than taking ownership and paying outright for these capital goods, however, Chinese firms simply made lease payments.[88]

Beginning in 1986 purely domestic leasing companies were first created. By the end of 1987 five such companies had been established.[89] One example is the China Electronics Leasing Corporation, established in December 1986 by the China Electronic Import-Export Company and the Bank of China Trust and Consultancy Corporation. It serves as a nonbank financial intermediary providing banking, leasing, and foreign trade services for enterprises in the machinery and electronics industry. In 1991 it broke into the ranks of the five hundred largest service companies in China, becoming

China's third largest leasing company.[90] By the end of 1994 the number of domestic financial leasing companies had expanded to fourteen and the total value of leases in force had reached $4 billion.[91]

Securities and Credit Rating Companies

Securities firms were first established beginning September 1987.[92] Initially these firms were restricted to carrying out over-the-counter transactions in stocks and in government bonds. But these firms grew rapidly in anticipation of the official opening of the Shanghai and Shenzhen stock exchanges in December 1990 and July 1991, respectively. By the end of 1991 there were 59 securities firms, with 300 affiliates, and over 30,000 employees.[93] As stock markets expanded the number of securities companies continued to grow, reaching 97 by midyear 1996.[94]

Credit rating companies were first established in four cities beginning in August 1987.[95] They provide ratings for enterprise development bonds and commercial paper issued by enterprises. Their growth has paralleled that of securities markets and securities companies.

The Growth of Lending

The expanding role of financial institutions in the reform period is reflected in the dramatic growth of total lending. Total loans outstanding by all types of financial institutions, shown in table 3-1, grew from RMB 190 billion in 1978 to RMB 7.4 trillion at the end of 1998. Loans outstanding as a percent of gross domestic product almost doubled between 1978, when they stood at just over 50 percent, and 1997, when they were 100 percent.

The expanding role of financial institutions and the declining role of the budget, discussed in chapter 1, also is reflected in the relative magnitude of the resources allocated through financial institutions and the state budget, respectively. The annual increase in loans outstanding now exceeds the combined annual fiscal revenues of all levels of government combined by an increasing margin. In 1979 government budgetary expenditures of RMB 127 billion were almost seven times the increase in loans.[96] Only thirteen years later in 1992, the increase in loans of RMB 498 billion surpassed for the first time annual government expenditures of RMB 439 billion.[97] By 1996 the RMB 1.1 trillion increase in loans outstanding was more than a third larger than total government fiscal expenditures of RMB 791 billion.[98]

Moreover, the lending data in table 3-1 understate the growth of credit extended during the reform period because banks and other financial institutions have an incentive to extend credit in forms they can avoid reporting as loans. Their goal is to avoid being in violation of lending quotas jointly established by the State Planning Commission and the People's Bank of China. These quotas only restrict the volume of loans and do not cover credit extended through repurchase agreements, trust transactions, and certain other transactions. Since these latter types of businesses did not exist in the late 1970s, the data in table 3-1 understate the long-term growth of credit.

Banks do not report their discounting and repurchase of bills of exchange and other financial assets as loans. Rather these are reported as separate, well-identified items on the balance sheets of banks. Discounting of bills of exchange is a transaction in which banks advance funds to enterprises in exchange for a pledge of receivables. Enterprises short of working capital, for example, borrow funds from banks rather than waiting to receive payment for goods they have sold. The bank receives the right to the funds ultimately to be paid by the final purchaser of the goods. The bank profits from the transaction by buying bills of exchange at a discount to their face value, giving rise to the name discounting to describe these transactions. Repurchase of financial assets is credit extended by banks in exchange for government bonds or other financial assets owned by enterprises. These transactions grew dramatically over time. For example, the Bank of China had extended RMB 7.0 billion in credit via these transactions at year-end 1988. By 1995 the amount outstanding was RMB 40.6 billion. The bank's purchases of various types of securities from customers grew at the same pace but were much larger, RMB 142 billion, at year-end 1995.[99]

The second type of credit not included in the data on lending in table 3-1 is trust loans (*xintuo daikuan*), entrusted loans (*weituo daikuan*), and funds extended by the bank acting as an agent.[100] Trust funds are provided to a bank or financial institution that the bank agrees to manage in accordance with goals stipulated in a trust agreement. Entrusted deposits, however, as well as agency business (*daili*

Table 3-1. Loans by Financial Institutions, 1978–97

RMB billions

Year[a]	Total	Banks	Rural credit co-ops	Urban credit co-ops	Trust and investment companies	Finance companies
1978	(190)	185	5	0	n.a.	0
1979	(209)	204	5	*	n.a.	0
1980	(249)	241	8	*	n.a.	0
1981	(296)	286	10	*	n.a.	0
1982	(330)	318	12	*	n.a.	0
1983	(375)	359	16	*	n.a.	0
1984	(512)	477	35	*	n.a.	0
1985	(631)	591	40	*	n.a.	0
1986	(840)	759	57	2	22	0
1987	(1,030)	903	77	6	44	n.a.
1988	1,222	1,055	91	13	66	n.a.
1989	1,436	1,241	109	20	65	n.a.
1990	1,768	1,517	141	25	89	n.a.
1991	2,134	1,804	181	32	121	n.a.
1992	2,632	2,162	245	49	183	14
1993	3,294	2,681	314	78	205	16
1994	4,081	3,305	417	132	203	23
1995	5,039	4,045	523	193	241	37
1996	6,116	4,907	636	274	234	63
1997	7,491	n.a.	n.a.	n.a.	n.a.	n.a.

Sources: *Almanac of China's Finance and Banking 1988* (Beijing: China Financial Publishing House, 1988), pp. 54–55, 58–59, *Almanac 1990*, p. 52; *Almanac 1992*, p. 548; *Almanac 1993*, pp. 437–38, 457; People's Bank of China, *China Financial Outlook '94* (Beijing: China Financial Publishing House, 1994), p. 92; *Financial Outlook '95*, p. 94; *Financial Outlook '96*, p. 94. State Statistical Bureau, *A Statistical Survey of China 1994* (Beijing: China Statistical Publishing House, 1994), p. 41; "Materials on Chinese Financial Statistics for the Fourth Quarter of 1996," *Jinrong shibao* (Financial News), January 21, 1997, p. 1; "Materials on Chinese Financial Statistics for 1997," *Jinrong shibao*, January 23, 1998, p. 2, and Jin Rong, "Achievements of Financial Adjustment Are Outstanding: The Financial Situation Is a Healthy Equilibrium," *Jinrong shibao*, January 23, 1998, p. 1.

n.a. Not available

( ) Estimated as the sum of the separate components.

* Believed negligible.

a. Values are amounts outstanding at the end of each period. The 1996 figure for total lending was subsequently revised to RMB 6,421 billion. The 1996 and 1997 data on urban credit cooperatives are inclusive of the lending by urban cooperative banks that have been created from the merger of credit cooperatives in many cities. There appear to be no published consolidated data for the lending activities of urban credit cooperatives and trust and investment companies before 1986 and for finance companies before 1992. However,

Table 3-1. (continued)

total lending by all financial institutions from 1978 through 1987 must have been very close to the sum of the components for which data are available. Although a single experimental urban credit cooperative was established in 1979, neither urban credit cooperatives nor domestic finance companies were created in significant numbers until the mid-1980s. The trust and investment companies created in the late 1970s and early 1980s were internationally focused and did little domestic currency business. Domestically oriented trust and investment companies were first established in 1986. Finance companies were first authorized in 1987. In a few years the sum of the components differs slightly from the total, because of a rounding error or because the data on total lending and the components of the total are taken from sources published in different years with more recent sources presumably reflecting slight revisions in the data. The reported totals for 1988–91 appear to be exclusive of lending by finance companies, but these omitted amounts obviously were quite small.

yewu), are funds provided to a bank or other financial institution for a specific purpose. The financial institution is simply a conduit to disburse the funds and collect the income associated with the investment.

Total trust lending of the four major banks is quite large. In 1990 and 1992 these loans totaled about RMB 345 billion and RMB 490 billion, respectively, equal to almost one-fourth of the regular lending activity reported by these institutions. The growth of various types of trust assets of the four major banks rose more slowly than their regular lending after 1993. By 1995 all types of trust lending stood at RMB 550 billion, the equivalent of one-seventh of their regularly reported lending.[101] The decline in the relative share of trust lending of the main banks presumably reflects the efforts of the People's Bank to separate trust business from banking business in the mid-1990s.

The third method banks use to hide credit extended to enterprises is simply to record loans as "other assets" in their balance sheets. The extent to which this occurs is difficult to judge but its potential has grown significantly over time. "Other assets" of the four major banks in the late 1980s were quite small. In 1989 they stood at RMB 27.6 billion, a little over 1 percent of the total assets of these banks. By year-end 1996 "other assets" stood at RMB 290 billion, 3 percent of assets.[102]

In summary, the data on loans in table 3-1 significantly understate the long-term growth of credit. Thus banks and other financial institutions have become even more important than these numbers suggest in the intermediation of funds in the reform period.

The rapid growth of lending in the reform era has been accompanied by an increased role for newly created financial institutions, particularly nonbank financial intermediaries. By the end of 1996 lending by credit cooperatives, trust and investment companies, and finance companies reached RMB 1.2 trillion or one-fifth of total lending by financial institutions of all types. This was a dramatic transformation compared to the eve of reform, when the trust and investment and finance companies did not even exist and credit cooperative lending stood at only RMB 5 billion, less than 3 percent of total lending.

Despite the increased competition resulting from the proliferation of new nonbank financial institutions, banks continue to dominate lending activity, accounting for four-fifths of all outstanding loans at the end of 1996. Moreover, despite the creation of a number of new banks, domination of China's financial sector by the four specialized banks eroded only gradually. Between 1986 and 1995 their share of total financial assets shrank only by a modest 10.2 percentage points, from 71.2 percent to 61.0 percent. Much of this decline was due to the increasing role of the newly created state-owned policy banks, rather than the increased lending of the somewhat more commercially oriented banks created since the mid-1980s.[103] In some regions, however, the transformation was more rapid than these national data suggest. By 1994, for example, the market share of the big four state banks in the Shenzhen Special Economic Zone and in Guangdong Province had fallen to about 50 percent.[104] That reflected the rapid expansion of new regional banks such as the Shenzhen Development Bank, Guangdong Development Bank, and Merchants Bank. Although small on a national scale, they quickly became large players in south China. This is no doubt largely because they took deposits from and lent primarily to the rapidly developing nonstate firms in the region.

The continued domination of China's financial landscape by the specialized banks is not surprising. The Industrial and Commercial Bank was very large at its creation since it took over the branch network and all of the deposits and loans of the People's Bank. Since then it has continued to expand from this large initial base. Similarly, the Bank of China, as it was allowed to increase its domestic currency lending, rapidly expanded its branch network in order to increase its deposit-taking capacity. As a result, China's four major banks are huge, even by international standards. At year-end 1996 the Industrial and Commercial Bank of China was the world's fifth largest bank, as measured by assets. The Bank of China and the Construction Bank were the world's twenty-fourth and thirty-first largest banks, respectively. Even the Agricultural Bank, the smallest of China's four major banks, ranked forty-seventh on a worldwide basis.[105]

Although the volume of lending increased dramatically and the mix of lenders began to change during the first decade and a half of economic reform, there was little change in the mix of borrowers, particularly from state banks. State banks continued to lend predominantly to state-owned enterprises. Indeed, the degree to which the financial system, the specialized banks in particular, simultaneously relies on households for deposits and directs its lending to the enterprise sector is extraordinary.

China's financial system provides few financial services to depositors beyond maintaining their savings accounts. Basic retail banking services, such as checking accounts for households, are rare, even in China's largest cities where higher household incomes have created a demand for more banking services. Checking accounts were first offered in Shanghai in the mid-1980s but never caught on, in part because of slow check clearing procedures. Retail businesses had to wait many days for checks presented by their customers to clear. Rather than bear the risk that some checks would not be honored by banks because of insufficient funds in the accounts on which they were drawn, merchants required customers to wait for their checks to clear. Only then could they return to the retail establishment, claim their goods, and take them home. China's major banks began to offer personal checking accounts on an "experimental basis" in Beijing only in 1996.[106]

Consumer credit is extremely limited. Each of the four specialized banks and the Bank of Communications offer what appear to be credit cards. But for two reasons these cards provide little credit to households. First, most of the cards have been issued to firms, which use them as a means of payment.[107] Firms holding corporate MasterCards can use them to make payments to other firms using wireless technology rather than paper checks, which can take weeks to clear. Firms send electronic payment messages via cellular phone to a dish farm and then via the MasterCard transducer to a substation in Shanghai and then to MasterCard's supercomputer in Singapore, which clears the payments among firms. MasterCard has captured so much of this business that its transaction volume in China, U.S.$71 billion in 1995, is second only to the United States.[108]

Second, almost all the cards issued to households are debit rather than credit cards, meaning that the cost of goods and services purchased by the cardholder is deducted from funds already placed in designated accounts.[109]

The first attempted provision of credit for automobile purchases began in July 1996, when the Construction Bank announced it would begin offering financing for firms and individual business executives purchasing Jetta sedans manufactured by a joint venture between the First Automobile Works and Volkswagen in Changchun, Jilin Province.[110] The central government almost immediately sought to halt this initiative, however, apparently fearing the resulting credit either would add to inflationary pressure or divert funds from traditional borrowers.[111]

Banks introduced home mortgage lending in the early 1990s, but the sums extended through the mid-1990s were minuscule, relative to total bank lending and to household savings deposits. The Industrial and Commercial Bank, for example, in 1991 began to offer mortgage loans of up to 70 percent of the value of a home purchase repayable over ten years. But at year-end 1996 the bank's total mortgage lending stood at RMB 4.2 billion, only 0.3 percent of its total loan portfolio.[112] The bank's mortgage loans outstanding were less than 0.5 percent of the RMB 906.5 billion in household savings on deposit at the bank.[113] In China's largest city, Shanghai, the mortgage business did not get started until 1992. The biggest provider of funds there is the China Construction Bank, with RMB 2 billion in mortgages outstanding at year-end 1995.[114] The Industrial and Commercial Bank did not begin offering home mortgages in Shanghai until February 1996.

The central bank in 1997 sought to regularize mortgage lending procedures as part of a broader program to encourage urban residents to purchase residences, but the terms do not suggest that mortgage lending will grow rapidly. For example, banks will lend only 70 percent of the value, meaning that a 30 percent down payment is required. Moreover, state banks are restricted to lend only to purchase of residences built with public housing funds and are not allowed to lend to finance the purchase of higher quality privately built residences.[115]

In short, China's state banks offer few loans or other financial services to consumers. Credit cards, home mortgages, and car loans are in their infancy. Bank loans to individual consumers for other purposes are nonexistent.

Most lending by state banks is to state-owned enterprises. At the end of 1995, the outstanding borrowing of state-owned enterprises from banks stood at RMB 3.36 trillion, 83 percent of all bank loans outstanding.[116] Bank lending for fixed investment is even more focused on state-owned firms. For example, more than 90 percent of the lending for fixed investment from 1980 through 1995 by the Industrial and Commercial Bank of China was to state-owned firms.[117]

The continued dominance of lending activity by the four largest state-owned banks and the continued concentration of lending to state-owned firms suggests that the central problem that plagued China in the prereform era—inefficient allocation of capital—persists. Since 1993 China has embraced the concept of converting its banks to operate on commercial principles. But the continued importance of policy lending as a share of total lending activity, the continued reliance on allocation of funds through the credit plan rather than through the market, continued state controls on interest rates, and a variety of quantitative measures of the performance of China's financial institutions all suggest that only limited progress appears to have been made toward achieving this objective.

Policy Lending

The banks have extended a significant portion of the increasing volume of credit in the reform period at the behest of the governmental authorities at the central and local level rather than as a result of normal commercial bank decisionmaking. These administratively allocated funds are referred to as "policy loans" (*zhengce daikuan*) or "relending" (*zai daikuan*). In Western terminology these are commonly called directed credit programs. In short the banks, particularly the specialized banks, are required to support government objectives ranging from the expansion of priority sectors, usually referred to as "pillar industries," to underwriting loss-making state-owned enterprises. Unfortunately, there is no uniform definition of policy lending and no time series data specifically identified as policy lending. Several alternative proxies for policy lending are explored below.

Table 3-2. Borrowing and Lending of the Specialized Banks, 1986–95

Year	Borrowing from central bank[a] (RMB billions)	Total lending[a] (RMB billions)	Borrowing from central bank as a percent of total lending
1986	268.2	811.1	33.1
1987	275.65	976.5	28.2
1988	336.12	1,024.6	32.8
1989	416.33	1,206.4	34.5
1990	508.29	1,476.0	34.4
1991	590.56	1,759.5	33.5
1992	670.99	2,108.2	31.8
1993	961.26	2,587.0	37.2
1994	697.23	3,282.8	21.2
1995	680.23	3,908.0	17.4

Sources: *Almanac of China's Finance and Banking 1989*, p. 106; *Almanac 1990*, p. 53; *Almanac 1991*, pp. 120–23; *Almanac 1992*, p. 522; *Almanac 1993*, pp. 387, 397; *Almanac 1996*, pp. 472–73; and People's Bank of China, *China Financial Outlook '94*, pp. 89–90.

a. The amounts for borrowing and lending are the amounts outstanding at the end of each year.

One possible though partially flawed measure of policy lending is the flow of loans from the central bank to financial institutions, primarily the specialized banks. These funds are earmarked to finance specific projects identified by the State Planning Commission, giving rise to the Chinese term "relending" to describe loans made with these funds. These loans are clearly policy loans because they are both directed and financed by the central government. Total central bank lending grew from RMB 225 billion in 1985 to RMB 1,151 billion by the end of 1995.[118] If this definition is used, about one-fifth of loans outstanding from all financial institutions at year-end 1995 were policy loans, down from about one-third in 1985.[119]

Through 1993 the vast majority of central bank funds extended to support policy loans was extended to the four largest banks, although by the early 1990s some went to other banks and some even to nonbank financial institutions. For example, at the end of 1993 of total central bank lending outstanding of RMB 989.85 billion to financial institutions, RMB 962.57 billion had been extended to banks and RMB 27.28 billion to nonbank financial institutions.[120] The specialized banks received RMB 961.26 billion, more than 97 percent of the total amount extended to all financial institutions.

The magnitude of central bank loans to the specialized banks, as reflected in table 3-2, grew from RMB 268.2 billion in 1985 to over RMB 960 billion by 1993 and then fell to RMB 680 billion at year-end 1995 as policy lending began to be channeled through newly created policy banks created in 1994. On average, until the growth of lending from the central bank was curtailed as part of the government's anti-inflationary policy in 1994 and new directed lending began to flow through the policy banks, these loans from the central bank financed roughly one-third of the total lending of the four specialized banks. By this measure, at least through 1993 one-third of specialized bank lending could be said to be relending or policy lending.[121]

The degree of dependence on central bank funds to support lending varied widely among the specialized banks. At year-end 1991 the Bank of China was most dependent on borrowing from the central bank, using this source of funds to finance 53 percent of its total RMB loan portfolio. The Agricultural Bank was next most dependent, receiving 38 percent from that source. The Construction Bank and the Industrial and Commercial Bank were least dependent at 28 and 27 percent, respectively.[122]

Chinese banks also extend loans at the "request" of local party and government officials to support their favorite projects. In many cases these projects have not been approved by the central government authorities and thus no central bank funds have been provided for relending. Banks finance these loans from deposits taken from the public, rather than from earmarked funds provided by the central bank. Since banks are unable to subject these loans to normal commercial criteria and since prospects for the repayment of these loans is uncertain at best, they should also be regarded as policy loans.

One indicator of the magnitude of policy loans financed from deposits can be derived from a Chinese paper reporting on total policy lending by each of the four specialized Chinese banks at year-end 1991. This paper placed policy lending as a percent of total lending as follows: Bank of China, 67 percent; Agricultural Bank, 51.2 percent, Construction Bank, 58 percent; and Industrial and Commercial Bank, 25 percent.[123] A comparison of these numbers with those reported in the penultimate paragraph suggests that the share of policy lending financed by borrowing from the central bank was about one-half in the case of the Construction Bank. In other words, this bank appears to have financed a little over half of its policy lending from deposits, as opposed to borrowing from the central bank. At the other end of the spectrum the Industrial and Commercial Bank in 1991 apparently was able to finance all of its policy lending by borrowing from the central bank. The Bank of China and the Agricultural Bank were intermediate cases with about one-fifth and one-fourth, respectively, of their policy lending financed by deposits.

On this second, broader, definition policy lending of the four banks as a group constituted 42 percent of all lending at year-end 1991. About four-fifths of this lending was financed by borrowing from the central bank and the remaining fifth was financed from deposits.

Another indicator of the large magnitude and pervasive influence of policy lending has been the effect of credit quotas on the regional distribution of lending.[124] The State Planning Commission, working in conjunction with the central bank, has imposed an annual credit plan on financial institutions. The aggregate lending quota was set partly in response to underlying macroeconomic conditions. However, it was built from the bottom up, starting with the borrowing needs of specific new investment projects and of the largest state-owned firms in specific cities. These needs, as well as some allowance for general lending, were aggregated into regional lending plans. The sum of these regional lending requirements was then adjusted in light of overall macroeconomic conditions to reach a national credit plan. The final national credit plan then was broken down into a lending quota for each province and municipality with provincial-level administrative status. The People's Bank allocated an annual credit quota to each of the head offices of the major banks. Each bank's head office then assigned lending quotas to each of its provincial-level branches. In the case of Shanghai and Shenzhen the central bank allocated the quota to the central bank office in each of the two cities and it, in turn, allocated credit quotas to each of the specialized banks and other banks and financial institutions in the municipality that were included in the credit plan. The municipal branches of these institutions further disaggregated their individual lending quotas to their subbranches.[125]

The credit quotas in each region were established to meet concrete policy objectives, independent of the ability of branch banks in each region to finance the lending target from local deposits. Bank branches in rapidly growing regions where a low lending quota was

Table 3-3. Loan-to-Deposit Ratios in Selected Provinces, 1988–93

Region	1988	1989	1990	1991	1992	1993
Jilin	1.88	1.88	2.01	1.99	1.86	1.89
Inner Mongolia	1.50	1.56	1.61	1.59	1.50	1.59
Heilongjiang	1.56	1.51	1.49	1.48	1.37	1.45
Fujian	1.23	1.18	1.07	0.96	0.88	0.95
Zhejiang	1.26	1.19	1.05	0.97	0.93	0.92
Guangdong	1.34	1.26	1.12	0.94	0.76	0.82

Source: Table A-2.

imposed were heavily constrained in their lending relative to the rapid growth of deposits generated by fast economic growth. These bank branches had interest income from lending that was insufficient to pay interest to their depositors. Thus these branches looked for alternative uses of their funds in order to avoid a potentially dramatic squeeze on their profits. Since the People's Bank pays interest on reserves placed on deposit, the most obvious solution to the problem was to maintain large excess reserves in the central bank.[126]

However, branch banks in slower growing regions that were assigned a high lending quota likely had insufficient local deposits to finance their lending. Branches in these regions deposited only the minimum amount of reserves required by central bank regulations and depended on the central bank to lend them additional funds to offset any shortfall in available funds. One source of these funds for the central bank was the excess reserves placed on deposit by branch banks in regions that had lending quotas that were quite low relative to their deposits. Thus the linkage between the credit plan and central bank lending to the specialized banks was quite close.[127]

The result of this interaction between the volume of deposits, which was determined by underlying economic activity, and the volume of lending, which largely was determined by policy, was a huge variation in loan-to-deposit ratios among China's provinces. Table 3-3 shows these ratios for six provinces for the years 1988 through 1993. The table includes the three provinces with the highest ratios and the three provinces with the lowest ratios.[128] Jilin Province, with the highest loan-to-deposit ratio, was able to sustain between 40 and 145 percent more loans per unit of deposits than was Guangdong Province, which had the lowest ratio. Inner Mongolia and Heilongjiang were the two provinces with the next highest loan-to-deposit ratios. Though not quite as advantaged as Jilin, their loan-to-deposit ratios were regularly from one-fifth more to up to twice the ratio prevailing in Guangdong.

The degree to which the central bank redistributed loanable funds across regions appears to have risen between 1988 and 1993. Jilin, the province with the highest loan-to-deposit ratio, was able to make 40 percent more loans per unit of deposits in 1988 than Guangdong, the province with the lowest ratio. But by 1993 the Jilin ratio had risen to 130 percent more than Guangdong. In short, to meet its policy lending objectives the central bank had to increase the extent of its intervention over time, redirecting even more funds interregionally.

One method for measuring the consequences of this interregional redistributive process is to compare the actual volume of loans made by bank branches in each province with the hypothetical pattern that would have prevailed if the loan-to-deposit ratio for branch banks in each province was equal to the national average. Branches in provinces with high ratios in effect were able to make what might be called "excess loans," that is a greater volume of loans than would have prevailed under the hypothetical case of equal loan-to-deposit ratios. Bank branches in provinces with low ratios experienced "loan shortfalls," that is, they were constrained to make fewer loans than would have been possible in the hypothetical case.[129]

This measure also reveals the highly redistributive character of the regional credit quotas. By the end of 1993 the loans outstanding from the branch banks in the three provinces in the northeast—Liaoning, Jilin, and Heilongjiang—were more than RMB 80 billion greater than they would have been had banks in the northeast been required to maintain the same loan-to-deposit ratio as the national average. On an annual basis the "excess loans" reached as much as RMB 8.5 billion in Heilongjiang in 1993, an amount equal to almost 8 percent of provincial gross domestic product that year. For Jilin the absolute amounts of annual "excess loans" were smaller, but since the economic output of the province was a small fraction of that in Heilongjiang the "excess loans" were a much higher share of provincial gross domestic output. The value of annual "excess loans" reached a peak of more than 18 percent of provincial output in 1990 and averaged fully 12 percent over the five-year period.

The greatest loan shortfalls occurred in Guangdong. On average in

1989–93 the annual increase in loans outstanding by branch banks in the province was RMB 14 billion less than it would have been if branch banks in the province had been able to extend the same volume of loans relative to deposits as the national average. The loan shortfall averaged 7.5 percent of provincial product over the five-year period.

The most powerful variable explaining the regional variation in the loan-to-deposit ratio is the share of industrial output produced by state-owned firms in each region.[130] The larger the share of industrial output produced by state-owned firms in a province, the higher is the loan-to-deposit ratio of branch banks in the province and the greater is the relative magnitude of "excess loans." Inversely, the smaller the share of output produced in state-owned firms in a province, the lower is the loan-to-deposit ratio of branch banks in the province and the greater is the relative magnitude of "loan shortfalls."

The provinces where branch banks were most constrained by loan quotas—Fujian, Zhejiang, and Guangdong Provinces—in 1993 ranked the third lowest, the lowest, and the fourth lowest, respectively, among all of China's provinces in terms of the share of industrial output produced by state-owned firms. Branch banks in Jilin, Inner Mongolia, and Heilongjiang Provinces, however, were most dependent on borrowing from the central bank to finance their relatively high lending quotas. In each of these provinces a significantly above-average share of manufactured goods is produced in state-owned firms.

Other regions with relatively high concentrations of state-owned manufacturing firms include Guizhou, Yunnan, Shaanxi, Gansu, Qinghai, Ningxia, and Xinjiang. Branch banks in each of these seven provincial level units, except Yunnan, had very high loan-to-deposit ratios, resulting in "excess loans." Because these provinces are relatively small in terms of population and economic output, the magnitude of annual "excess loans" by branch banks was only occasionally more than a few hundred million RMB. But relative to gross domestic product in these provinces, the magnitude of these "excess loans" was sometimes quite high. In the most extreme case of Qinghai, excess loans averaged a little over RMB 800 million annually, an amount equivalent to over 10 percent of the province's average annual gross domestic output in the five years 1989 through 1993.

Significantly, the effect of the lending quotas imposed by the State

Planning Commission and the People's Bank of China was to reallocate loan funds away from regions of relatively high economic growth to regions of relatively low economic growth. Guangdong, Zhejiang, and Fujian were the fastest, second fastest, and fourth fastest growing provinces during the 1985–94 decade. The three provinces, however, with the highest loan-to-deposit ratios all grew at rates below the national average. Indeed, Heilongjiang was China's slowest growing province during 1985–94.[131]

At an even more general level one could argue that since interest rates on loans in the reform period have been held at below-market clearing levels, virtually all lending by financial institutions is policy lending. Artificially low lending rates have ensured a condition of permanent excess demand for loans, requiring administrative allocation of the limited funds available. This distortion is particularly obvious during periods of inflation, when lending rates have been adjusted upward only modestly, leading to sharply negative interest rates in real terms. For example, at the peaks of inflation in 1989 and 1993, prices of producer goods, which includes both industrial raw materials as well as machinery and equipment, rose by 19 and 24 percent, respectively.[132] But the highest interest rate enterprises had to pay to borrow working capital funds, which might be used to finance the purchase of industrial raw materials, was only 11.34 percent and 10.98 percent in the corresponding years.[133] In these years of peak inflation, the interest rate charged on loans for fixed investment, which would have been used to finance the purchase of machinery and equipment, was 3 to 4 percentage points higher than the interest rate for working capital loans. But it was still well below the rate of producer goods price inflation. The resulting highly negative real interest rates for loans, both for working capital and for fixed investment, created excess demand for loans.

The structure of authority in the Chinese banking system would have made it difficult to limit political intervention in loan allocation, even in the absence of excess demand. But chronic excess demand for loans reinforced the tendency for lending to be based on local political considerations and corruption. China's central bank is an immense institution with branches in every provincial level administrative unit and offices in all larger cities as well as most counties. Especially before the imposition of then Vice-Premier Zhu Rongji's sixteen-point austerity program in mid-1993, the provincial branches of the central bank responded primarily to provincial level political leaders rather than central bank headquarters in Beijing. This was not surprising since the control of appointments of the top officials in each provincial branch of the central bank was largely in the hands of provincial party officials rather than in the hands of the central bank headquarters in Beijing. In turn, the provincial branches of the four specialized banks, and to a lesser degree even other banks, were responsive primarily to the policies emanating from the provincial branches of the central bank rather than their own head offices in Beijing. This structure maximized the possibility that loan decisions within each province would be in response to local political pressure and even corruption.

The distortion of controlled interest rates is also reflected in the low real interest rates paid to depositors, particularly during inflationary periods. Deposit rates in general fell far behind price rises during periods of inflation. In the early 1980s, when inflation as measured by the retail price index was in the very low single digits, the interest rate paid on sight deposits, 2.88 percent, was roughly equal to inflation. But, when consumer prices rose by an average of 18 percent in both 1988 and 1989, the banks continued to pay only 2.88 percent interest on sight deposits, leaving savers with a highly negative real rate of return.

The same phenomenon occurred again in the mid-1990s. Retail prices rose 22 percent in 1994, but the banks paid only 3.15 percent interest on sight deposits. During periods of accelerating price inflation, savers chose to shift some of their funds into longer-term deposits that paid more favorable interest rates. However, because of their need for liquidity, households kept a substantial portion of their savings in the form of sight deposits. In 1994, for example, they kept just over one-fifth of their savings in sight deposits. The highly negative real return households earned on these funds can be thought of as a tax on liquidity, the proceeds of which allowed the banks to provide an implicit subsidy to borrowers, who received loans on unusually favorable terms.

The large share of total lending accounted for by policy lending, the role of the central bank in reallocating loanable funds from regions of high to low growth, and continued reliance on administered interest rates all suggest an environment in which financial institutions were unable to allocate funds efficiently. This is borne out by the analysis below, which suggests that the financial strength of banks has been eroded significantly by poor lending decisions during the reform era.

Bank Strength

The strength of banks and other financial institutions is generally measured by the ratio of capital (the banks' "own" funds as opposed to funds placed on deposit by households and firms) to assets (loans and so on); the size of reserves held relative to the quality of outstanding loans; profitability; and the margins between lending and deposit rates. All of these measures confirm the view that the first two decades of economic transition have left China's financial institutions, particularly three of its four largest state-owned banks, in a precarious position.

Bank Capital

In general bank capital is composed of core capital, including permanent shareholder's equity (paid-in capital) and publicly disclosed reserves derived from retained earnings or other surpluses, and supplementary capital, including undisclosed reserves. In China, since the government is the only shareholder of the largest banks, it was the initial source of capital. This capital is usually identified in the balance sheets of banks as paid-in capital.

Bank capital serves two functions. First, it "provides a cushion against unusual losses." Second, "it promotes better governance" of banks. Because their own capital is at risk, bank owners (shareholders in the case of private banks) have an incentive to appoint good managers and elect good directors who will "not put the bank's solvency in danger."[134]

The paid-in capital of China's four largest state-owned banks has been declining relative to bank assets and now is surprisingly small. Between 1985 and 1996 their assets grew almost six times more rapidly than their paid-in capital. Thus, as reflected in the data in table 3-4, relative to their assets, the paid-in capital of these banks actually fell by five-sixths, from 12.1 percent in 1985 to 2.2 percent in 1996.

Table 3-4. Paid-In Capital of the Specialized Banks, 1985–96

Year	RMB billions	Percent of total assets
1985	77.78	12.1
1986	n.a.	11.7
1987	n.a.	9.5
1988	91.44	9.4
1989	94.36	8.8
1990	102.26	7.8
1991	113.64	7.2
1992	131.30	7.5
1993	154.33	4.7
1994	183.11	2.6
1995	198.35	2.5
1996	209.67	2.2

Sources: *Almanac of China's Finance and Banking 1986*, p. II-28; *Almanac 1996*, pp. 472–73; People's Bank of China, *China Financial Outlook '94*, pp. 89–90; and Zhou Wenjie and Wang Jianxin, "A Discussion of Central Bank Supervision of Bank Asset Risk," *Zhongguo jinrong* (Chinese Banking), no. 10 (October, 1994), p. 29. The 1996 data are from the annual 1996 reports of the specialized banks.

n.a. Not available.

In addition to their paid-in capital, state banks also have retained profits and other surpluses that, when added to paid-in capital, constitute net worth or total capital. The ratio of net worth to total assets thus provides an alternative, broader definition of the adequacy of capital. On this definition the capital of banks has fallen, almost as dramatically. In 1985 the net worth of the four specialized banks stood at RMB 84.8 billion, or 13.2 percent of assets.[135] By year-end 1996 net worth had risen to RMB 285.97 billion but was only 3.1 percent of assets.[136]

As part of the strategy formally adopted by the State Council in 1993 of converting specialized banks to commercial banks, the People's Bank early in 1994 notified banks that they would have to comply with the capital adequacy standards of the Basle Committee on Banking Regulations and Supervisory Practice.[137] The Basle guidelines require the core capital (called tier-one capital) of a bank to be a minimum of 4 percent of its risk-adjusted assets and its total capital or net worth to be a minimum of 8 percent of its risk-adjusted assets.[138] Some thirty-five countries follow the Basle capital standards, and almost all countries follow a Basle-like risk-weighted

Table 3-5. Capital Adequacy of China's Specialized Banks, 1988–94

Percent

Year	Industrial and Commercial Bank	Agricultural Bank	Bank of China	Construction Bank
1988	6.81	n.a.	5.59	11.17
1989	5.45	n.a.	7.20	9.75
1990	5.48	7.49	6.72	8.72
1991	5.35	6.41	6.69	7.40
1992	5.13	5.50	6.31	6.32
1993	6.57	4.10	5.35	4.79
1994	5.70	6.95	7.37	4.31

Source: *Just How Bad Really Are the Chinese Banks?* (Hong Kong: W. I. Carr, October 1995), p. 3.

n.a. Not available.

Note: The numbers shown are calculated on a risk-weighted basis.

approach to measuring capital adequacy, even if they don't follow the 8 percent standard. A few countries have set a higher standard. For example, regulators in Argentina and Singapore require banks to maintain capital equal to 12 percent of their risk-weighted assets.[139]

One independent estimate of the risk-weighted capital adequacy of China's major state-owned banks is shown in table 3-5. Through 1994 all of China's specialized banks fell short of meeting the Basle capital adequacy standard.[140] Moreover, with the exception of the Bank of China, the second largest of the specialized banks, the capital adequacy of these institutions has been falling since the late 1980s. The precipitous decline in the capital adequacy of the Construction Bank is particularly conspicuous.

Given the relatively weak capital positions of China's main banks in 1994 when the Basle standard was adopted, the goal was to come into compliance with the 8 percent capital adequacy standard gradually by the end of 1996, largely through the growth of retained earnings and increasing provisions for nonperforming loans.[141] Some local branches of the People's Bank set a faster pace for the banks operating in their jurisdictions. For example, banks in Shenzhen were to reach 4 percent capital adequacy by June 1994, 6 percent by June 1995, and 8 percent by December 1995, a year ahead of the national standard.[142]

However, declining capital adequacy is unlikely to be reversed without an injection of new capital into the specialized banks.[143]

Since the state has not provided significant fresh capital to the specialized banks in recent years, the main source of additions to capital has been retained profit. But profitability of the four specialized banks declined sharply in the early 1990s (see discussion below). In the case of China's biggest bank, pre-tax profits in 1994 were only RMB 4.24 billion. After paying income taxes and meeting certain other obligations that are financed from profits, the bank was left with only RMB 1.654 billion to add to its own capital.[144] That represented an increase of less than 2 percent in the bank's capital. On the other hand, the bank's assets in the same year rose by fully one-third, making a sharp decline in capital adequacy inevitable.[145] Simply to maintain its already low level of capital adequacy the bank would have had to add almost RMB 30 billion to its capital, an amount more than seventeen times greater than the profit that the bank was able to add to capital!

China's major banks are even weaker than most official data suggest. First, and most important, their capital is very substantially overstated since large quantities of bad debt are carried on bank balance sheets as assets. Normally, the write-off of such bad debt would be offset by a reduction of loan loss reserves. But these reserves are far too small to serve this purpose. The nonperforming loans that several of China's four largest banks ultimately will have to write off almost certainly exceed the combined value of their reserves and their own capital. On a realistic accounting, these banks' capital adequacy is negative, and they are insolvent.

Second, certain investments that these banks have made in trust and investment companies, securities firms, and other subsidiary financial institutions have not been deducted from the capital of the parent banks prior to calculating capital adequacy, as is required by the Basle standards.[146] These subsidiary institutions, in turn, have made investments in real estate, securities, and other speculative ventures. Thus they have assumed risks that would not necessarily be expected for banks. Most of the financial institutions that have failed in China in recent years have been trust and investment companies, confirming the risky nature of these firms.[147]

Third, China's risk weighting system diverges significantly from the Basle standards.[148] In several asset categories Chinese banks apply weights according to criteria that are substantially less stringent than those specified in the Basle agreement, resulting in an overstatement of capital adequacy.[149] This fact alone led Moody's Investors Service, a leading international independent credit rating agency, to conclude that the capital adequacy ratios published by China's specialized banks are "meaningless."[150]

Finally, the riskiness of the portfolio of bank loans is underestimated since the lending of the four largest state-owned banks is concentrated heavily on state-owned industrial and commercial enterprises. As noted in chapter 2, a surprisingly large share of these enterprises are losing money, and many may not be economically viable in a fully marketized economy. Moreover, state banks are heavily exposed to a few very large borrowers.[151] The Industrial and Commercial Bank, for example, has extended particularly large loans to the Anshan Iron and Steel Corporation, the Beijing-Kowloon Railroad, and the First Auto Works in Changchun.[152] The risk-weighting scheme currently in use does not reflect the additional risk arising from this high degree of loan concentration.

In most countries bank regulators strictly limit loan concentration to ensure that the bankruptcy of either the single largest borrower or a small number of very large borrowers does not undermine the solvency of a bank. A Basle committee survey in the mid-1990s found that in two-thirds of emerging market economies, regulators do not allow any bank to lend to a single customer an amount exceeding 25 percent of the bank's own capital.[153]

Beginning in 1994 China also sought to reduce the risk arising from loan concentration by limiting the lending of any bank to a single borrower to an amount no more than 15 percent of the bank's own capital.[154] This restriction was tightened and made a matter of law in 1995 when the maximum ratio was reduced to 10 percent in article 39 of the Commercial Bank Law.[155] Thus China's legal lending concentration standard is tougher than that of most emerging economies. Unfortunately, China's banks do not disclose any quantitative information on loan concentration so it is impossible to judge the extent to which they are in compliance with this new prudential rule.

Loan Loss Reserves

Loan loss reserves are a critical tool for maintaining the solvency of banks. In most banking systems there are two types of loan loss reserves. First, there are reserves against loans that already have been classified as nonperforming. In most countries regulators require banks to set aside provisions for nonperforming loans within a very short period of time to facilitate, if eventually necessary, the complete write-off of the loans without endangering the bank's capital.[156] Second, there are general loan loss reserves that are not ascribed to particular assets. Under the rules of the Basle committee, reserves in the second category are included in tier-two bank capital.

China falls short of meeting international standards with respect to loan loss reserves in two fundamental respects. First, China makes no differentiation between loan loss reserves in the two categories just discussed. Chinese banks are required to make provision for nonperforming loans. But the quantity of such provisions is linked to the volume of total loans outstanding, not to the magnitude of classified loans. Thus banks do not have to increase their loan loss provisions as their loan portfolios decline in quality. It therefore becomes more likely that loan loss reserves will be inadequate to meet their intended function of preserving the solvency of banks. Compounding this error, Chinese banks appear to count all reserves as part of their tier-two capital.

Second, reserves for nonperforming loans set aside by the four major specialized banks are best described as minuscule. In part this is because of the conflicting interests of the People's Bank of China and the Ministry of Finance. One of the central bank's chief objectives is to preserve the integrity of the banking system, which implies that banks be required to make adequate provisions for nonperforming loans.

Adequate provisioning would directly reduce, if not entirely eliminate, however, the income taxes banks must pay to the Ministry of Finance. Thus the Ministry of Finance is interested in limiting the amount of bank profit set aside to cover loan loss reserves so that tax payments are not reduced.[157] Interestingly, the regulations that specify the portion of assets that banks should set aside to cover loan losses are issued by the Ministry of Finance, not the People's Bank of China. The system the ministry laid down in 1991, for example, called upon the banks to set aside reserves for nonperforming loans equal to 0.6 percent of their loans outstanding.[158] Later this target reportedly was revised to require banks to gradually increase their reserves, reaching 1.0 percent of their loans outstanding by year-end 1997.[159]

Table 3-6. Construction Bank of China Loan Loss Provisions and Reserves, 1988–96

	Annual provisions		Cumulative reserves	
Year	RMB millions	Percent of new loans	RMB millions	Percent of loans outstanding
1988	161	.73	161	.13
1989	46	.16	203	.14
1990	45	.15	239	.12
1991	87	.15	309	.12
1992	1,161	1.36	526	.15
1993	n.a.	n.a.	1,021	.22
1994	n.a.	n.a.	3,713	.67
1995	n.a.	n.a.	4,977	.64
1996	n.a.	n.a.	5,809	.58

Source: *Almanac of China's Finance and Banking 1989*, p. 92; *Almanac 1993*, pp. 401, 405; *Almanac 1995*, p. 518; *Almanac 1996*, p. 473; Moody's Investors Service, *The People's Construction Bank of China* (New York, April 1995), p. 11; and China Construction Bank, *Annual Report 1996* (Beijing, 1997), p. 24.

Information on the actual amounts set aside for nonperforming loans by China's four specialized banks has increased somewhat in recent years but still is sparse. All available data, however, support the view that reserves for nonperforming loans are very inadequate. The largest of the four banks, the Industrial and Commercial Bank of China, did not report setting aside provisions for bad loans until 1994. In that year it reported reserves for bad loans of RMB 6.173 billion, an amount just under 0.5 percent of its loan portfolio and only 0.2 percent of its total assets.[160]

The Construction Bank was the first to publish data on both annual loan loss provisions and cumulative loan loss reserves. These data are reflected in table 3-6. The Construction Bank first reported provisions for nonperforming loans in 1988, when its total loan portfolio stood at RMB 121 billion. After an initial provision of RMB 161 million, which was equal to about 0.7 percent of new loans made that year and 0.1 percent of the bank's total loan portfolio, annual provisions dropped sharply. In 1989–91 annual provisions averaged only 0.15 percent of new loans. Provisions increased sharply in 1992, apparently largely to facilitate the write-off of almost RMB 1 billion in bad loans in that year.[161] The bank discontinued publishing data

Table 3-7. Agricultural Bank of China Loan Loss Reserves, 1989–96

Year	RMB millions	As a percent of loans outstanding
1989	300	.10
1990	200	.05
1991	300	.07
1992	500	.09
1993	200	.03
1994	2,798	.48
1995	4,318	.62
1996	4,191	.47

Source: *Almanac of China's Finance and Banking 1993*, p. 399; *Almanac 1992*, p. 519; *Almanac 1994*, p. 510; *Almanac 1995*, p. 517; *Almanac 1996*, p. 472; and Agricultural Bank of China, *Annual Report 1996* (Beijing, 1997), p. 30.

on provisions in 1993, so it is not possible to estimate the magnitude of loans written off after 1992. The Construction Bank continued to publish data on its cumulative loan loss reserves, which at the end of 1993 stood at only a little over RMB 1 billion. Reserves jumped sharply to reach almost RMB 6 billion by year-end 1996, presumably reflecting the effort of the bank to come into compliance with the 1.0 percent standard by year end-1997. But RMB 6 billion was still less than 0.6 percent of loans outstanding that year and less than 0.3 percent of total assets. The inadequacy of these reserves will become clear when the magnitude of nonperforming loans of the major banks is considered later in this chapter.

Less complete loan loss reserve data for the Agricultural Bank of China confirm the parlous state of the loan loss reserves of state-owned banks. As shown in table 3-7, reserves of the Agricultural Bank in the late 1980s and early 1990s never exceeded 0.1 percent of loans outstanding. Moreover, over time loan loss reserves fell sharply relative to loans outstanding, reaching only 0.03 percent of the bank's portfolio of outstanding loans at the end of 1993. Only after 1993, when there was a sharp increase in reserves, was this trend reversed. Even at the highest level of 1995, however, reserves of RMB 4.3 billion were only 0.6 percent of outstanding loans. Reserves declined in 1996 to RMB 4.1 billion, less than 0.5 percent of outstanding loans.[162] Again this amount pales when compared with the 22 percent of loans of China's four major banks that are reported as nonperforming.[163]

Table 3-8. Pre-Tax Profits of China's Specialized Banks, 1985–96

Year	RMB millions	Return on assets (percent)
1985	13,103	1.4
1986	15,823	1.3
1987	20,416	1.4
1988	20,545	1.1
1989	25,950	1.1
1990	25,496	0.9
1991	30,699	0.9
1992	32,304	0.7
1993	23,354	0.4
1994	20,264	0.3
1995	25,558	0.3
1996	26,900	0.3

Sources: *Almanac of China's Finance and Banking 1991*, pp. 120–22, 128–29; *Almanac 1992*, p. 524–26; *Almanac 1994*, pp. 510, 516, 517; *Almanac 1995*, pp. 524–25; *Almanac 1996*, pp. 482–84; and Moody's Investors Service, *The People's Construction Bank of China* (New York, April 1995), p. 13. For the Construction Bank, the given profit for 1985–88 is post-tax; pre-tax profit is calculated as taxes minus 5 percent of interest income plus post-tax profit. The 1996 data are from specialized banks' 1996 annual reports.

Note: Reported pre-tax profits are profits prior to paying income taxes, which are levied at a 55 percent rate. However, banks treat business taxes of 5 percent of gross interest income, as well as some business tax surtaxes, as an above the line, operating expense. Thus reported pre-tax profits understate profits prior to all taxes.

Profitability

Chinese banks reported earning robust profits through the early 1990s. Table 3-8 shows that pre-tax profits reported by the four specialized banks more than doubled from RMB 13 billion in 1985 to a peak of over RMB 32 billion in 1992. However, absolute profits then fell by more than one-third over the next two years before recovering modestly in 1995 and 1996. More significant than absolute profits is profitability, which can be measured by return on assets or by return on capital. The analysis of profitability presented below relies on return on assets, which is calculated as pre-tax profits divided by total assets.[164]

Profitability of China's four specialized banks as a group was relatively stable at about 1.4 percent in 1985–87 but has fallen sharply since then. Over the four years from 1993 through 1996, return on assets averaged only one-fourth the average level of 1985–87. This simply reflects the fact that while loans (the principal asset of banks) expanded rapidly, profits grew much more slowly. This is an almost certain indicator of declining loan quality or a sharp increase in the banks' cost of loanable funds relative to interest rates they charge borrowers.[165] As will be discussed below, both of these factors appear to have contributed to declining profitability in the 1990s.

The reported profitability of Chinese banks compared reasonably well with major international banks in the mid-1980s. However, by the mid-1990s their returns were well below banks of comparable size in most market economies. Chinese banks in the mid-1990s looked good only in comparison with large Japanese banks that, as they began to write off significant portions of their portfolios of nonperforming loans, for the first time ever reported financial losses and thus negative returns on assets. In the fiscal year ending in March 1996 the twenty largest Japanese banks reported combined net losses of U.S.$14 billion, making it "the worst year in Japanese banking history."[166]

The profitability of China's largest bank, the Industrial and Commercial Bank, is particularly weak in comparison with banks in countries other than Japan. In 1995 its return on assets was only 0.42 percent.[167] A comparison with the Hongkong and Shanghai Bank, widely regarded as one of the best managed banks in the world, is illuminating. The two banks are very similar in asset size, but the rate of return on assets of HSBC Holdings, 1.62 percent, was four times that of the Industrial and Commercial Bank of China. The Industrial and Commercial Bank compares even less favorably with Citicorp, the parent of New York-based Citibank. In 1995, before the merger of Chase Manhattan Bank and Chemical Bank, Citibank was the largest U.S. bank, as measured by assets. However, Citibank's rate of return on assets was 2.18 percent, more than five times that of the Industrial and Commercial Bank.

Moreover, for at least six reasons the financial health of China's major banking institutions is almost certainly worse than the reported Chinese numbers on bank profitability shown in table 3-8 suggest. The first, and most important, reason is that interest income is overstated. This occurs because of the practices of capitalizing interest payments and accruing interest on nonperforming loans. Put simply, many borrowers are not able or willing to pay interest on their outstanding loans. Capitalization occurs when banks respond to this situation by "lending" the necessary funds to the borrower and recording these funds as interest income received from the borrower. For most working capital loans this is done on an annual basis, when the underlying loan is rolled over. In short, each year the principal of the loan increases by at least the amount of the interest due. The borrower turns over the interest payment to the bank. The bank reports the payment as income, inflating its profits in the process.[168] This practice frequently is referred to as "evergreening."[169]

Evergreening is particularly likely to result in an overstatement of the profits of China's specialized banks because their income derives overwhelmingly from interest on loans outstanding. For the Industrial and Commercial Bank, for example, interest income amounted to 97 percent of total income in the early 1990s. Only the Bank of China had significant noninterest income from commissions and other sources, but interest earnings still constituted 85 percent of the bank's income.[170]

Until it was made illegal, savings and loans in the United States also followed the practice of capitalizing interest payments, concealing for years the insolvency of many of their borrowers. The resulting delay in addressing the financial problems of savings and loans greatly increased the ultimate cost of the savings and loan crisis in the late 1980s and early 1990s.

The second practice, accrual of interest on nonperforming loans, occurs when banks simply add the unpaid interest to the principal of the loan without officially extending a new loan. Accrual of interest, like capitalization of interest, results in an overstatement of bank income since the accrued interest is treated as income, as if it had actually been paid by the borrower.

There is little doubt that capitalizing of interest and interest accrual are widespread. As chapter 2 discussed, a large portion of all borrowers are losing money and are unable to meet their interest obligations to banks from their own funds. In 1996, for example, interest due on loans of state-owned enterprises was RMB 468 billion, of which only RMB 134.2 billion was actually paid.[171] However, banks are required to accrue interest on nonperforming loans for three years.[172] The pervasiveness of accrual and capitalization can be inferred by examining the magnitude of interest income reported by the specialized banks. For each of the banks, reported interest income is almost equal to the magnitude of its loan portfolio times an estimate of the average interest rate prevailing on loans.[173] In short, the financial statements of the banks imply that the vast majority of their borrowers are paying interest in full. As a result, it appears that a very large share of the interest income reported by banks is accrued interest or originates with the capitalization of interest when loans are rolled over.[174]

The People's Bank appears to be well aware of the potential negative consequences of capitalization and accrual of interest and has attempted to limit these practices. For example, in 1995 the Central Bank explicitly forbade extensions on loans of less than one year and limited the length of extensions allowed on longer-term loans.[175] If this new rule was followed, the practice of capitalizing interest payments would be reduced significantly. The second reason that the profitability of China's specialized banks is vastly exaggerated is because, as already analyzed, they have made inadequate provisions for nonperforming loans. Since provisions should be a deduction from income, inadequate provisioning results in an overstatement of pre-tax income. If the banks had made additional annual provisions as small as 1 percent of their new loans, their pre-tax earnings and their rate of return on assets would have been reduced by 10 percent in 1991 and 1992. But, because loans rose while profits shrank, by 1995 provisions of 1 percent would have reduced pre-tax profits and the rate of return on assets by one-fourth.[176] Third, since China has no deposit insurance scheme, financial institutions pay no insurance premiums.[177] Since under normal accounting procedures these premiums would be a deduction from earnings, they would directly reduce reported profits. In Japan, where falling stock and land prices weakened the banking system in the first half of the 1990s, the Ministry of Finance in late 1995 raised annual deposit insurance contributions sixfold, from 0.012 percent to 0.084 percent of deposits. This increase was expected to absorb 8 percent of the net earnings of Japanese banks.[178] In developed countries with sound banking systems, contributions to deposit insurance are much lower. In the United States, for example, the Federal Deposit Insurance Corporation in 1995 cut premiums to zero for well-capitalized commercial banks. But a few weaker banks paid premiums as much as 0.27 percent of deposits.[179] If China's four specialized banks had made contributions of only 0.2 percent of their deposits in 1994, that would have absorbed 18 percent of their reported pre-tax profits.[180] But by 1995, since deposits had grown much more rapidly than profits, the same deposit insurance premium rate would have absorbed one-third of reported profits.[181]

Fourth, in periods of accelerating inflation the formal annual profit and loss statements of Chinese banks appear to significantly understate the cost of retaining existing deposits and attracting new deposits. This stems from the practice of paying interest on time deposits at the end of the period when deposits mature.[182] For example, when an individual deposits RMB 100 in a regular savings account from which the money can be withdrawn at any time, a so-called sight deposit, the bank pays interest annually and records the payment as an interest expense each year. However, if the individual deposits the funds in a five-year certificate, the bank pays no interest until the deposit matures. If the annual interest rate is 10 percent, the depositor will be paid RMB 150 at the end of five years.[183] When banks used cash-based accounting, they would not record the interest cost until the end of the fifth year, when it is actually paid.[184]

The widespread use of cash accounting results in an understatement of interest expense when inflation accelerates because depositors shift to longer-term deposits. Households lengthen the maturity structure of their savings for two reasons. First, because time deposits even as short as three or six months pay much higher rates of interest than sight deposits, households allocate less of their savings to sight deposits and more to time deposits as inflation begins to rise. That shift alone increases the cost of funds to banks. Second, as will be documented below, in periods of rising inflation depositors shift their time deposits increasingly into the longer-term three, five and eight-year deposits on which the banks pay interest that is tied to the rate of inflation. The perverse effect of this transformation of the maturity structure of savings is that just when the real cost of funds to the banks is rising sharply, their reported cost declines because an increasing share of their higher interest payment obligations is shifted into future years.

The fifth reason that data on profits published by China's large state-owned banks overstate their financial performance is that these institutions have made investments in securities firms, trust and investment companies, and other subsidiary financial institutions. With the exception of the Bank of China, however, the specialized banks do not report their earnings on a consolidated basis. If their subsidiaries are losing money, these losses are not reflected in the profits that the banks report, contrary to generally accepted international accounting principles. As already noted, many of these institutions engage in risky businesses and have lost money. A number have even been forced into liquidation.

These risks were recognized to be sufficiently large that in 1995 the State Council endorsed a recommendation of the central bank directing China's four major state-owned banks to disaffiliate themselves from their trust and investment companies.[185] By the end of 1995 the Industrial and Commercial Bank and the Construction Bank of China had disaffiliated themselves from fifty-nine of their eighty-nine subsidiary trust and investment companies.[186] This incomplete separation and the absence of any reported progress on the part of the Bank of China and the Agricultural Bank of China in winding up their investments in their trust and investment subsidiaries presumably reflects the difficulty all of these institutions have had in retrieving the capital that their affiliated trust and investment companies have committed to real estate development and other illiquid investments.[187]

Sixth, the recovery in the level of absolute profits the four largest banks reported in 1995 largely reflects an injection of funds from the central government to offset part of the increased interest expenditures banks incurred as a result of the reintroduction of the value-guarantee savings program in 1994. The details of the transfer of funds from the Ministry of Finance to the banks have not been disclosed, but one Hong Kong source suggested that the Ministry of Finance had pledged to cover 70 percent of the extra interest expenditures associated with the program.[188]

Information for two banks suggests that the recovery of profits in 1995 was due entirely to these injections. The vice president of the Agricultural Bank of China, in reporting a tripling of the bank's profits to RMB 3 billion in 1995, noted that the profit figure included "value preservation subsidies."[189] These transfers were treated as current income and thus raised reported profits by an amount equal to the transfer.[190] The message of the president of the Construction Bank in the bank's 1995 annual report explicitly acknowledged that although the bank's profits were only RMB 3.38 billion, "deposit index subsidies" received from the treasury allowed the bank to report total pretax profits of RMB 6.3 billion.[191] If the subsidies provided to the other three main state banks were similar to the RMB 2.92 billion received by the Construction Bank, the reported profits of the four specialized banks in 1995, net of such subsidies, would have been approximately one-half of the RMB 25 billion level shown in table 3-8.[192] It can be concluded that the underlying profits of these banks, net of subsidies received to offset higher interest expenses associated with the value preservation deposit scheme, fell sharply in 1995.[193]

In sum, it seems almost certain that on generally accepted accounting principles, China's four largest banks as a group lost a great amount of money in 1995. Simply taking into account the transfers from the Ministry of Finance that were treated as income and making modest provisions for nonperforming loans and deposit insurance more than accounts for reported profits! Based on the situation in 1996, evergreening and accrual of interest on nonperforming loans to state-owned firms resulted in an overstatement of interest income by as much as RMB 210 billion in 1995.[194] That is roughly eight times the reported profits of the group as a whole. It is not possible to adjust income to take into account the effects of the failure to report income on a consolidated basis or the possible understatement of interest expenses resulting from the continued use of cash accounting on the part of some branch banks. Even if many borrowers had paid the interest on their loans, there is little doubt, however, that China's largest banks as a group would have been operating heavily in the red in 1995.

Margins

Given the shortcomings just discussed of reported data on bank profits, it is useful to examine the spread between deposit and lending rates as a means of judging the underlying profitability of Chinese banks. This analysis of interest rate margins suggests that for certain critical intervals in the reform era, the interest rate environment for Chinese banks was so adverse that they probably would have suffered financial losses even if they had restricted their lending to blue chip companies. Thus their profitability would have been negative and their capital would have eroded, even if all their borrowers made their principal and interest payments in full and on time.

The source of this problem was the state's policy for dealing with the threat of disintermediation during periods of accelerating inflation. During periods of accelerating inflation, real interest rates for savers turned negative, in turn leading to an abrupt decline in the inflow of savings into Chinese banks. From the second quarter of 1992 through the middle of 1993, for example, the rate of growth of deposits by households and enterprises plummeted.[195]

For central policymakers, declines in the inflow of savings into the banking system set off alarm bells for two reasons. First, if households actually took the next step and began to withdraw their savings, it could trigger a banking crisis. For example, in 1989 the banks were highly leveraged with outstanding loans equal to 138 percent of deposits.[196] In the face of a demand for significant withdrawals, they would have to recall loans from their borrowers, borrow even more funds from the central bank, or close their doors. The first of these alternatives was unlikely to be successful, given the financial condition of many of their borrowers. The second alternative ultimately would contribute to even greater inflation, but at least in the short run would probably be politically preferable to refusing to honor household requests for withdrawals. However, it would fail in the long run, since accelerating inflation would simply stimulate households to increase their withdrawals, hastening the arrival of a banking crisis.

Second, even in the absence of significant withdrawals of savings deposits, the abrupt decline in inflows of funds threatened to curtail the ability of banks to continue to expand their lending to state-owned enterprises in a relatively noninflationary manner. As discussed in chapter 1, the large inflows of household savings into the banks had made possible the combination of a relatively high rate of growth of broad money with a relatively low average rate of inflation throughout the 1980s.

In short, from the policymakers' perspective it was imperative to continue to attract funds from savers during periods of inflation. To accomplish this goal, the state raised interest rates paid on deposits, ending a period of decades in which interest rates paid on savings were relatively stable. The adjustments of rates paid on sight and selected time deposits are shown in table 3-9. From September 1988 through the end of 1997, the central bank adjusted rates on most time deposits eleven times, increasing them when inflation picked up and decreasing them when inflation was brought under greater control.

For example, as inflation accelerated, the central bank raised the interest rate banks paid on one-year time deposits by just over 4 percentage points in 1988 and early 1989 and then, as inflation deceler-

Table 3-9. Select Deposit and Lending Interest Rates, 1985–97

	Deposit rates[a]					Lending rates[a]	
						Working capital loans	Capital construction loans
Date	Sight deposits	Time deposits				1 yr.	3–5 yrs.
		3 mos.[b]	1 yr.	3 yrs.	8 yrs.[c]		
April 1, 1985	2.88[d]	...	6.84	7.92	9.00	7.92	6.48
August 1, 1985	2.88	...	7.20	8.28	10.44	7.92	9.36
Sept. 1, 1988	2.88	...	8.64	9.72	12.42	9.00	10.80
Feb. 1, 1989	2.88	7.56	11.34	13.14	17.64	11.34	14.40
April 15, 1990[e]	2.88	5.30	10.08	11.88	16.20	10.08	11.52
August 21, 1990	2.16	4.32	8.64	10.08	13.68	9.36	10.80
April 21, 1991	1.80	3.24	7.56	8.28	10.08	8.64	9.54
Dec. 31, 1992	1.80	3.24	7.56	8.28	10.08	8.64	9.54
May 15, 1993	2.16	4.86	9.18	10.28	14.58	9.36	12.06
July 11, 1993	3.15	6.66	10.98	12.24	17.10	10.98	13.86
Jan. 1, 1995	3.15	6.66	10.98	12.24	17.10	10.98	14.58
July 1, 1995	3.15	6.66	10.98	12.24	17.10	12.06	15.12
May 1, 1996	2.97	4.86	9.18	10.80	...	10.98	14.94
August 23, 1996	1.98	3.33	7.47	8.28	...	10.08	11.70
Oct. 23, 1997	1.71	2.88	5.67	6.21	...	8.64	9.90

Sources: People's Bank of China Research and Statistics Department, *China Financial Statistics 1952–1987* (Beijing: China Financial Publishing House, 1988), pp. 145, 149. *Almanac of China's Finance and Banking 1986*, p. II-41; *Almanac 1988*, pp. 117, 119; *Almanac 1989*, p. 151; *Almanac 1990*, pp. 168, 171, 454; *Almanac 1991*, p. 84; *Almanac 1992*, pp. 507, 509; *Almanac 1993*, pp. 387–89; *Almanac 1994*, pp. 492–94; "Financial Institutions Interest Rates on Loans Will Be Raised from Today," *Jinrong shibao* (Financial News), January 1, 1995, p. 1; Wang Baoqing, "Interest Rates on Loans Will be Raised Starting July 1," *Jinrong shibao*, July 1, 1995, p. 1, "Starting Today Deposit and Loan Interest Rates of Financial Institutions Will Be Lower," *Jinrong shibao*, May 1, 1996, p. 1, "From Today Deposit and Loan Interest Rates Will Be Adjusted," *Jinrong shibao*, August 23, 1996, p. 1; and "Table on the Adjusted Interest Rates on Loans and Deposits of Financial Organizations," *Renmin ribao* (People's Daily), October 23, 1997, p. 1.

a. Rates given are a small fraction of those on offer. The sources give a full range of available deposit and lending rates.

b. Three-month time deposits were first offered beginning February 1, 1989.

c. Eight-year fixed deposits were first available April 1, 1982, and were eliminated after April 31, 1996.

d. The sight deposit rate had been in effect continuously since July 1, 1980.

e. Lending rates changed on March 21, 1990.

ated, it reduced the rate by about 3.8 percentage points in 1990 and 1991.

In addition, at times of rapid inflation the People's Bank instituted so called value-guarantee deposits, which were designed to insulate longer-term deposits from inflation. The interest rate that savers earned on value-guarantee deposits was equal to the base rate of interest plus an interest rate subsidy. The subsidy, which was not announced until deposits were maturing, was calculated so that the total nominal interest rate paid offset inflation, leaving the depositor with at least a zero rate of real return regardless of how high prices rose after the deposit was made.[197] This program was first instituted beginning on September 10, 1988.[198] Formally it continued until December 1991.[199] However, when the inflation rate again rose sharply in 1993, the central bank reinstated the value-guarantee subsidy program beginning July 11, 1993. The program lasted until April 1996 when it was ended for new deposits.[200]

The effect of this program on the nominal interest rate that banks paid to hold and attract deposits was considerable. For example, banks paid depositors 8.28 percent a year on three-year time deposits beginning in 1987, when prices as measured by the retail price index rose 7.3 percent.[201] But, as inflation accelerated, banks were forced to raise the base interest rate by 4.86 percentage points and also to pay supplementary interest under the value-guarantee program. These supplements began at 7.28 percent in the final quarter of 1988 and peaked at 13.64 percent in the third quarter of 1989. Similarly, as inflation accelerated again in 1993, the banks had to raise the basic interest paid on three-year deposits by 3.96 percentage points and offer supplements that peaked at 13.24 percent in December 1995.

These adjustments raised the marginal cost of funds to banks enormously.[202] Because of the way interest payments were calculated, in the first inflationary period the marginal cost of funds to banks as inflation accelerated after 1987 rose by 19.22 percentage points, reaching a peak of 28.58 percent in the third quarter of 1989.[203] By the time of the second inflationary period the central bank had changed the method of calculating the rates so the marginal cost of funds went up by a smaller amount.[204] Nonetheless the marginal cost of funds peaked at 23.68 percent, a 13.24 percentage point increase compared to the cost of funds in the early 1990s when inflation was low and no indexing was in effect.[205]

Although the state partially insulated savers from the effect of inflation by indexing deposits of three years or more, the central bank raised lending rates upward by much more modest amounts. For example, the People's Bank raised the rates they required banks to charge on one-year working capital loans by only 3.44 and 3.42 percentage points as inflation accelerated in 1988–89 and 1993–95, respectively. The state was unwilling to raise rates more because of the weak financial position of many state-owned enterprises. As discussed in chapter 2, a large number were operating with significant financial losses. Raising interest rates on their borrowing would simply push more enterprises into the red.

The combination of sharply rising deposit rates and relatively stable lending rates in periods of accelerating inflation put enormous pressure on bank interest rate margins. But Chinese banks do not provide information on the average cost of their deposits and the average interest rate charged on loans. As noted, however, because banks use cash-basis accounting, their profit and loss statements understate significantly their growing interest payment obligations during periods of rapidly rising prices. Examining published data on interest income and interest expenditure is not necessarily a reliable basis for estimating trends in interest rate margins. As a result, the changing spread between lending and deposit rates and the resulting squeeze on interest margins must be estimated indirectly. The critical variable in this estimate is the extent to which Chinese households and enterprises lengthen the average maturity of their savings in response to rising inflation.

The answer is that Chinese savers significantly adjust the maturity structure of their savings to mitigate the adverse effect of rising inflation on the real rate of return on their savings. As inflation rises, they reduce the share of savings allocated to sight deposits and place a larger share of their savings in time deposits, which are effectively certificates of deposit. These pay significantly higher rates of interest than sight deposits. For example, as shown in table 3-9, the lowest interest rate the banks paid on time deposits in 1989 was 7.56 percent for three-month deposits, almost three times the rate paid on sight deposits.

Furthermore, as inflation rises households allocate a larger portion of their time deposits to longer-term maturities, which pay higher interest rates. As shown in table 3-9, in the case of the longest maturity, eight years, the annual interest rate in 1989 was 17.64 percent, more than six times the rate paid on sight deposits. Finally, when the state offers "value-guarantee deposits," households move large amounts of funds into these accounts.

This changing maturity structure of savings was evident in two periods of high inflation during the reform period, from 1988 to 1990 and from 1993 through April 1996. For example, in 1987, when retail price inflation was a relatively low 7.3 percent, savers allocated almost one-fourth of their increased savings to sight deposits, which paid the lowest interest rate, 2.88 percent. In short, in part because they valued liquidity, depositors were willing to accept a negative real rate of return on one-fourth of their savings.[206]

As inflation accelerated in the late 1980s, however, savers significantly reduced the portion of their savings allocated to sight deposits. By 1989, when annual retail price inflation soared to 17.8 percent, households allocated the entire increment of savings into longer, fixed-term time deposits.[207] Not only did banks pay higher rates on time deposits than on sight deposits, but time deposit rates also were adjusted upward as inflation rose in 1988 and 1989 while the rate paid on sight deposits remained fixed at 2.88 percent. Moreover, for the longer maturities, indexing of the interest rate to the rate of inflation was introduced in September 1988.

As inflation subsequently fell in response to tight monetary policy, the trend was reversed.[208] By 1992 when inflation, as measured by the retail price index, dropped to 5.2 percent, savers allocated a relatively high one-third of their incremental savings to sight deposits, which at the time earned simple interest of only 1.80 percent annually.

One bank, the Bank of China, has reported more disaggregated data on the structure of its savings deposits, which grew extraordinarily rapidly after 1987 as the bank expanded its branch network to be able to attract deposits to finance its increasing renminbi lending activity.[209] For the years 1989 through 1993 the Bank of China has reported not only the breakdown of total domestic currency savings into sight and time deposits, but also the magnitude of value-guarantee deposits. In 1988 total savings deposits more than tripled and value-guarantee deposits, which were available only during the last four months of the year, accounted for more than one-fifth of total deposits and one-third of the increase in deposits that year. As inflation stayed high in 1989, the composition of the bank's deposits continued to shift toward indexed deposits. By the end of 1989 value-guarantee savings accounted for fully one-third of the bank's savings deposits and two-fifths of the increase in total savings deposits that year. Subsequently, as the inflation rate fell sharply, the share of deposits in value-guarantee accounts declined, to 27 percent in 1990 and then 11 percent in 1992.[210]

What is the effect of these substantial changes in the maturity structure of savings deposits on the interest rate margins of the banks? For the Bank of China the estimated average cost of domestic currency funds in the form of savings accounts rose from 6.7 percent in 1987 to a peak of 15.3 percent in the third quarter of 1989. The average cost of funds for 1989 as a whole was only slightly less, 14.8 percent, more than double the level of the preinflation year of 1987.[211] However, the average interest rate that the Bank of China charged on its domestic currency loans rose by less than half, from 8.1 percent in 1987 to 11.6 percent in 1989.[212] Thus, on average, in 1989 the Bank of China suffered a negative spread of 3.2 percentage points between its average lending rate and its average deposit rate on savings accounts. That was a dramatic change from 1987 when the bank's average spread was a positive 1.4 percentage points.

To calculate whether or not the Bank of China actually lost money in 1989 on its domestic currency deposit taking and lending activity in 1989 is more complex than simply looking at the negative interest rate margin. First, in 1989 the bank had deposits from enterprises that exceeded those from households. Enterprises could shift their funds from sight deposits to longer-term deposits and earn the same higher interest rates as households. They valued liquidity more highly than households, however, and shifted the maturity structure of their deposits less than households did in response to accelerating inflation. Thus the bank's overall cost of funds rose less rapidly than estimated above.[213]

Second, the Bank of China, like the other specialized banks, borrowed money from the People's Bank to finance part of its policy lending. Particularly during periods of accelerating inflation, this was a much cheaper source of funds than attracting deposits from households. In 1989 the central bank charged only 10.44 percent interest on its loans to banks, one-third less than the estimated average cost of household deposits.[214] As noted earlier in this chapter, in

1991 the Bank of China was the most dependent of the specialized banks on this kind of borrowing to finance its loan portfolio. The same was true in 1989 when the Bank of China's borrowings from the central bank stood at RMB 96 billion, an amount one-third larger than its deposits from households and enterprises combined and equivalent to 60 percent of its total lending portfolio.[215]

Third, one needs to examine the noninterest expenditures that the bank must defray from its margins. In 1989 the Bank reported total noninterest outlays for wages and other expenditures of RMB 4.3 billion, an amount equal to 1.7 percent of its total loan portfolio, including foreign currency denominated lending.[216]

Taking into account the relative importance of funds from households, enterprises, and the central bank, the estimated cost of funds to the Bank of China in 1989 was 9.7 percent, only 1.9 percentage points less than the average interest charged to its borrowers. Since the bank's noninterest costs of doing business were equal to 1.6 percent of loans, the spread between the bank's total costs and total interest earnings can be estimated to have been a very thin 0.3 percentage points.[217] Thus for every RMB 100 in loans outstanding, the bank's profits were only RMB 0.3. Based on a total domestic currency loan portfolio of RMB 160 billion, the bank's profits on its domestic currency lending must have been only RMB 480 million.

The discrepancy between this estimate and the bank's reported 1989 pre-tax profit of RMB 5.1 billion is due to three factors. First, the bank had RMB 3.9 billion in noninterest earnings which were not taken into account in the estimate immediately above, which was based on the negative spread between total interest costs and total interest earnings on domestic currency lending. Second, the bank presumably achieved a positive spread on its foreign currency denominated lending, which accounted for about one-third of its loan portfolio in 1989.[218] Finally, the bank substantially underreported its cost of funds, for reasons outlined in the analysis of bank profitability earlier in this chapter, and thus overstated its profits. The conclusion is that the true profit of the Bank of China must have been RMB 4.38 billion plus profits on foreign currency lending but was probably less than its reported profits of RMB 5.1 billion.

The interest rate fundamentals at the three other specialized banks in 1989, on average, were significantly less favorable than those faced by the Bank of China for three reasons. First, the Industrial and

Commercial Bank and the Agricultural Bank of China were much more dependent on household deposits and much less dependent on enterprise deposits than was the Bank of China. Since households adjust the maturity structure of their deposits much more rapidly than enterprises in the face of accelerating inflation, the cost of funds to these banks must have risen more rapidly than at the Bank of China.[219]

Second, the other specialized banks all were much less dependent on funds borrowed relatively cheaply from the People's Bank of China to finance their lending. Industrial and Commercial Bank relending of central bank funds in 1989 accounted for only 30 percent of its loan portfolio, half the share of the Bank of China.[220] At the Construction Bank of China the share was even lower, only 17 percent.[221]

Finally, compared to the other large state-owned banks, the Bank of China had the advantage that a much higher portion of its lending was denominated in foreign currency where margins were much higher than in domestic currency business. Not only were there significant positive spreads on foreign currency lending, these spreads were not subject to rapid erosion when domestic inflation rose. This was because foreign currency deposits were not eligible for indexing and because dollar-denominated lending was all based on relatively short-term floating rates, giving the banks an opportunity to raise their lending rates if the cost of funds rose.[222] The cost of foreign currency deposits actually declined over the same period that the cost of domestic currency deposits was rising dramatically.[223] As a result, most of the profits of the Bank of China were generated from its foreign currency business.[224]

Thus, properly measured, three of the large specialized banks almost certainly incurred substantial losses on their domestic currency deposit taking and lending activities in 1989.

The second round of inflation occurred in 1993–95, with the annual retail price index peaking at 21.7 percent in 1994. Again depositors shifted their funds into longer-term accounts, including value-guarantee deposits, which the state reintroduced in July 1993.[225] In 1994 and 1995 households again allocated a growing share of their incremental savings to fixed-term deposits.[226] As a result of this shift in the maturity structure of deposits, the cost of funds to the banks again rose dramatically.[227] Since lending rates were adjusted upward only fractionally, banks' margins again were squeezed. The extra interest cost to the banks of indexing of longer-term savings deposits was RMB 25 billion in 1995.[228] At least one Chinese author admitted that three of China's four specialized banks, all but the Bank of China, lost money in 1994.[229]

In conclusion, all available evidence suggests that the financial strength of three of China's four largest state-owned banks has deteriorated significantly in the reform period and that they are now financially quite fragile. Their own capital falls short of the Basle standard by an increasing margin; loan loss reserves while increasing through 1995 fell in 1996 and are extraordinarily low, especially in light of the large share of outstanding loans that have been extended for policy purposes; profitability, even as overstated, has declined sharply; and bank margins have been squeezed dramatically in two recent periods of high inflation. The financial strength of banks also needs to be measured against the magnitude of nonperforming loans.

Nonperforming Loans

Information on nonperforming loans, especially of the specialized banks, is even more limited than that on policy lending. Again this partly reflects the historical evolution of China's financial system. In the 1980s there appears to have been little or no effort to classify bank loans by their quality. This was perhaps not surprising when enterprise bankruptcy was unheard of, loans routinely were rolled over, and the financial soundness of borrowers was largely unknown to lenders.

Even after the Chinese Communist Party began to articulate the goal of encouraging the largest state-owned banks to operate on commercial principles, the system of classifying loans and writing off bad debt emerged slowly. Before 1994 each of the major banks had its own system and standards for classifying nonperforming loans. In any case these procedures were virtually meaningless since the central bank dictated that the specialized banks could classify no more than 2 percent of all their loans as "bad debt," that is, the volume of loans not recoverable from the proceeds from bankruptcy and liquidation; no more than 5 percent as "problem loans," meaning loans on which interest is still being paid but for which principal repayments are more than three years past due; and a maximum of 8 percent as "of concern," meaning borrowers were more than one year behind on principal repayments.[230] In short, there were ceilings on the portion of loans that could be classified, irrespective of the actual quality of a bank's loan portfolio.

China's loan classification system, set forth formally by the People's Bank in 1995, is quite simple.[231] Classified loans are of three types. The first, "past due loans" (*yuqi daikuan*), includes loans not repaid when due or not repaid after the due date has been extended.[232] The next most severely impaired category is "doubtful loans" (*daizhi daikuan*). These are loans that have been past due two years or more or loans that have been extended to a borrower who has suspended production or whose project is no longer being developed. Finally, there is "bad debt" (*daizhang daikuan*), the value of loans that have not been repaid after the borrower has been declared bankrupt and gone through liquidation.

Although this system has a certain symmetry with the three-tier classification schemes used in some countries, it is worth noting that for four reasons this scheme generally is far more lenient than those prevailing in the most modern banking systems. First, regulators in developed countries require that reserves be established primarily based on risk assessment rather than payment status. Thus banks can be required to provision for some risky loans, even if the borrower is in full compliance with the terms of the loan. For example, after the emergence of the Korean and Southeast Asian financial crisis in 1997, major international banks added hundreds of millions of dollars to their provisions for bad debts against loans to the region, even though the borrowers were current on their payments of interest and principal. These banks took these charges against their earnings based on an assessment that the declining value of the Korean won, Thai baht, and so forth would make it difficult for the borrowers to remain current on their payments.[233]

Second, compared with international standards, Chinese banks are allowed to delay classifying loans as nonperforming. This is both because the specified time periods during which delay of repayment is allowed are longer and because in China classification of loans is generally tied to failure to repay principal rather than interest.[234] In most countries regulators follow the Guidelines of the Basle Committee for Bank Supervision and require banks to classify any loan on which either an interest or principal payment is past due for as short a time as 90 or 180 days.[235] By contrast, in China loan classification is not only generally tied to repayment of principal, many loans are "bullet loans" on which no repayment of principal is required until the end of the loan term. Thus many loans in China would not be classified as past due until repayment of principal was delayed beyond the due date or the extended due date of the loan. That means that a five-year bullet loan that had been extended by the maximum allowed three years could not be classified as past due until eight years after the loan was taken out. By contrast, in many countries a five-year loan could be classified as past due as soon as 180 days after it was taken out if the loan called for quarterly interest payments and the first payment was missed.

The contrast is even greater in the categories of doubtful and bad loans. In international practice a loan is classified as bad when any interest payment is overdue by 180 days or more, whereas in China this step is not taken until the borrower has declared bankruptcy and has gone through liquidation.

The third reason China's loan classification scheme is more lenient is that in most developed countries when a bank classifies any loan, it simultaneously classifies the entire amount of all loans outstanding to that particular borrower.[236] The presumption, based on the principle of risk assessment, is that if a borrower is out of compliance with the repayment terms of one loan, the borrower likely soon will be out of compliance on all other loans as well.[237] Since Chinese banks classify loans exclusively on the basis of the payment status of loans, they diverge from this practice in two respects. First, they consider each loan separately. If a borrower falls behind in repayments on one loan, any other loans to that borrower would not be classified until such time as they became past due. Second, Chinese banks classify only the portion of the loan or payment that is past due. For example, if a loan requires annual repayments of principal in equal amounts over a five-year period and the borrower misses the first repayment, only the amount of that specific required repayment would be classified as past due. If the borrower misses subsequent repayments, they would be added to the quantity of past due loans over the next four years, as the payments were missed. Standard practice elsewhere, since it is based on risk assessment, would be to classify the entire loan once the first payment was past due. Thus Chinese data on classified loans are based on a methodology that is more lenient than standard international practice. The approach used by Chinese banks results in a serious understatement of the speed at which the quality of a loan portfolio is deteriorating when loan quality is falling.

Fourth, the practice of delaying the complete write-off of loans not repaid from the proceeds of the liquidation of a borrower is unprecedented in economies in which banks are solvent. Before 1988 the specialized banks were not allowed to write off any bad loans without specific approval from the State Council.[238] After China began to implement its bankruptcy law in 1988, a handful of firms were liquidated each year.[239] But the banks had little authority to write off loans they had extended to enterprises that were liquidated. Local and provincial branches of the People's Bank had the authority to approve write-offs of up to RMB 50,000 and RMB 100,000, respectively. But the banks could not write off loans over RMB 100,000 without the specific approval of the State Council.[240] Beginning in 1992 the banks could write off loans of up to a half billion yuan, but larger amounts still required approval of the State Council.

The result appears to be that banks are required to keep on their books many loans to borrowers that have been liquidated. This conclusion is borne out by examining data on reported write-offs and write-offs that can be deduced from data reported on loan loss reserves and provisioning. These data all point to the same conclusion—the magnitude of bad debt that banks have written off is tiny. As noted earlier, the Construction Bank appears to have written off almost RMB 1 billion in bad debt in 1992. The Bank of China reported write-offs of RMB 3.6 billion, RMB 1.7 billion, and RMB 1.6 billion in 1993, 1994, and 1995, respectively. That was an average of only 0.16 percent of assets annually.[241] These extremely modest write-offs suggest that state-owned banks hold large quantities of nonperforming loans that are carried on their balance sheets as assets. The extent of this problem in China is indicated by the loans made to rural communes that were still carried on bank balance sheets as assets in the late 1980s, more than a decade after the original borrowing institutions had been disbanded as part of the rural reforms of the late 1970s.[242]

Numerous statements have been made in the Chinese press on the problem of nonperforming loans. Many of them, unfortunately, are not very precise and do not disaggregate the total amount into the three different categories. There is a huge difference between loans that are overdue, on which there may be some ultimate recovery by the bank, and "bad debt," which represents loans on which there is no possibility of recovering anything from the borrower. For example, Zhao Haikuan, the secretary general of the Chinese Monetary Society in mid-December 1994 stated that the bad debts of Chinese banks totaled RMB 1 trillion.[243] One example of an authoritative and detailed statement on nonperforming loans, made by the deputy director of the Planning and Information Department of the Industrial and Commercial Bank of China in early 1996, revealed that past due loans, doubtful loans, and bad debt constituted 12, 8, and 2 percent, respectively, of the combined value of the loan portfolios of the four largest state-owned banks at year-end 1995.[244] Thus, on average, classified loans were approaching one-fourth of the loan portfolios of these banks. Since the loans outstanding of these four institutions at year-end 1995 stood at RMB 3.9 trillion, classified loans can be estimated as RMB 860 billion.[245] Of these RMB 469 billion were past due, RMB 313 billion were doubtful, and RMB 78 billion were bad debts.

These numbers suggest that China's four major banks as a group have a negative net worth and thus are insolvent. The total net worth of these banks at year-end 1995, including paid-in capital, surpluses, and retained profits, stood at only RMB 269 billion.[246] Deducting the value of bad debt, which is loans that have not been repaid from the liquidation proceeds of firms that have completed the bankruptcy process, the net worth of these institutions would be only RMB 191 billion. If the ultimate recovery rate on the remaining classified loans is less than three-quarters, the magnitude of loans to be written off would exceed the remaining net worth of these banks. Based on international experience with banking crises and the low recovery rate on outstanding loans that Chinese banks have achieved when enterprises go through bankruptcy and liquidation, it is extremely unlikely that the ultimate recovery rate on China's past due and doubtful loans will even approach three-quarters.[247]

Moreover, several factors suggest this analysis underestimates the financial problems faced by the largest Chinese banks. First, bank accounting and auditing practices have severe shortcomings. Until the mid-1990s none of China's major banks was subject to external audits. Even as late as 1996 the Bank of China's annual report contains a one-sentence statement of the bank's own board of supervisors asserting that the figures reported are "genuine and correct" rather than any report of an independent external auditor.[248] The annual reports of the other three large banks do include statements from audit firms. But since the underlying financial information on which these audits is based does not comply with generally accepted accounting principles, the audits are not likely to reveal accurately the quality of the loan portfolios of these banks. Moody's has expressed "doubts as to the efficacy" of the audits of the Construction Bank, for example.[249]

Second, banks have other nonperforming assets besides loans. These nonperforming assets are not included in reporting on non-performing loans. These other assets include investments in and credit extended to subsidiary financial institutions, as well as various types of trust transactions. Most of the banks' loans to nonbank financial intermediaries are extended through the interbank market and reported in the banks' balance sheets as interbank transactions rather than loans. Because of the risky nature of the activities undertaken by trust and investment companies, the central bank in 1993 issued regulations denying trust and investment companies access to the interbank market. Although trust and investment company borrowing on the interbank market fell by one-fifth that year, from RMB 67 billion to RMB 55 billion, the central bank appears to have been unable to enforce the regulation in the long term. Trust and investment company interbank borrowing dropped by only RMB 1 billion in 1994 and then jumped 20 percent to RMB 65 billion.[250]

In addition, as discussed earlier, by year-end 1995 China's largest banks had extended RMB 550 billion in trust and entrusted loans that form part of the assets of these banks. However, for some purposes these are not considered loans. For example, banks are not required to set aside reserves for nonperforming trust lending and trust assets are given a very low weight when calculating capital adequacy, meaning banks hold very little capital against trust assets. Moreover, it seems unlikely that nonperforming trust assets are included in the estimate of nonperforming loans discussed above.

This treatment of trust assets arises because in principle the provider of trust, entrusted, or agency funds bears the risk of loans and investments undertaken with the funds. If the project fails or the objectives of the trust are not met, the loss is borne by the provider of the funds. The bank would not bear any of the losses from such failed transactions since it would be absolved from the need to return the funds to their provider. Because there would be equal reductions in both assets and liabilities, the bank's balance sheet would be unaffected by the failure of trust or entrusted lending activity. This is especially clear in the case of entrusted and agency funds.

In practice Chinese banks may bear the risk of a significant portion of their trust and entrusted loans. It appears that banks actually approach firms with funds on deposit and ask whether their deposits can be used to finance loans for projects in which the firm has no interest. This is much more likely to occur during periods of credit tightening, since neither trust nor entrusted loans are included within the centrally fixed credit plan. Thus banks can continue to make trust and entrusted loans after their regular lending quotas have been exhausted. If projects financed with these solicited trust or entrusted deposits fail, however, it is unlikely that the firms supplying the funds will be willing to absorb the losses. These firms would argue that since the banks coerced them into supplying the funds and because the funds were lent for projects in which they had no direct or indirect interest, they should not bear any of the losses. Thus the banks ultimately may bear the risk, meaning any write-offs would have to be financed from the bank's own capital rather than by writing off the liability to the nominal supplier of the loan funds. Since the volume of trust and entrusted loans has grown rapidly during the reform era, the issue of who bears the credit risk is of more than academic interest.

The data on nonperforming loans, because they exclude interbank and trust lending as well as credit that is concealed in their balance sheets as "other items," may understate significantly the total nonperforming assets of China's largest banks.

Other authoritative statements show that the magnitude of nonperforming loans of China's largest banks was increasing in the mid-1990s. For example, just before he became governor of the central bank in June of 1995, Dai Xianglong revealed that the share of the combined loan portfolios of China's four largest banks that was nonperforming had been "rising by 2 percentage points per annum in recent years."[251] This assessment was confirmed by a more detailed statement of a staff member of the headquarters of the Industrial and Commercial Bank of China. He placed the share of past due loans, doubtful loans, and bad debt of the four largest state-owned banks at year-end 1994 at 11.3 percent, 7.7 percent, and 1.3 percent of the total loans outstanding by these banks.[252] The sum of these numbers, 20.4 percent, is 2 percentage points less than the year-end 1995 data. The share of nonperforming loans of the Agricultural Development Bank, the largest of the three new policy banks created in 1994, is rising even more rapidly, from 20 percent at year-end 1995, 26 percent at year-end 1996, and 27 percent by February 1997.[253] This rising share of nonperforming loans poses a major challenge for restoring the financial health of China's banks, a subject taken up in chapter 4.

Not all banks are in the increasingly fragile financial condition characteristic of several of China's largest banks. The Bank of Communications, reestablished in 1987, perhaps provides an example among the banks created in the reform era. Although it has grown extremely rapidly, at least through 1994 it was better able to maintain the quality of its loan portfolio and, as a result, its financial performance was superior to that of the four big banks. For example, although assets of the Industrial and Commercial Bank are almost nine times those of the Bank of Communications, its pre-tax profits in 1995 were only just over twice as large.[254] As a result, the profitability of the Bank of Communications, as measured by the pre-tax return on assets, was almost four times that of the Industrial and Commercial Bank.

The rapid growth of the capital of the Communications Bank also differentiates it from the major state-owned banks. The paid-in capital of the bank grew from RMB 2 billion when it began operations in 1987 to more than RMB 11 billion at year-end 1995. Moreover, because of its high profitability and its policy of retaining profits rather than paying dividends to shareholders, its retained surplus and undistributed profits at year-end 1995 exceeded RMB 9 billion compared with only RMB 600 million in 1987. This boosted the bank's total net worth at year-end 1995 to more than RMB 20 billion.[255]

Although the bank's loans have grown rapidly, this expansion of its capital has allowed the Bank of Communications to maintain levels of capital adequacy significantly higher than China's specialized banks. For example, even at the all-time low levels of year end-1994, the ratio of capital to total assets of the Bank of Communications was 5.6 percent, two-thirds higher than the average of China's four largest banks. Moreover, the risk-weighted capital adequacy of the Bank of Communications is in excess of the 8 percent level stipulated by the Basle committee.[256]

Table 3-10. Bank of Communications Loan Quality, 1991–94

Percent of total loans

Type of classified loan	1991	1992	1993	1994[a]
Past due	4.27	3.32	4.19	5.14
Doubtful	1.96	1.27	n.a.	1.36
Bad debt	0.10	0.07	0.28	0.37
Total	6.33	4.66	n.a.	6.87

Sources: *Almanac of China's Finance and Banking 1993*, p. 95; *Almanac 1994*, p. 88; and Jiang Xinghua, "Asset Liability Management Enters a New Stage," *Jinrong shibao* (Financial News), September 12, 1995, p. 1.

a. The Bank of Communications discontinued publishing information on the quality of its loan portfolio for the years after 1994.

The relatively high quality of the bank's loan portfolio is reflected not only in the relatively high return on assets and well-above average capital adequacy, but also in its low ratio of classified loans. As table 3-10 shows, the bank's total classified loans in 1994 stood at less than 7 percent. This is substantially less than the reported ratio of 22 percent for China's major state-owned banks as a group. Equally important, nonperforming loans as a share of the Bank of Communications total loan portfolio shows only a modest upward trend between 1991 and 1994, and the share of loans in the most impaired category remained well under 0.5 percent.[257]

Bank of Communications loan loss reserves, though still inadequate, are larger relative to its assets than those of the four largest state banks. At year-end 1995 loan loss reserves stood at RMB 1.768 billion and were equal to 0.5 percent of assets. That was a third higher than the ratio for the Industrial and Commercial Bank.[258] Unlike the four large specialized banks, the Bank of Communications also maintains reserves for investment risk associated with its long-term investments. It also sets aside additional reserves to offset possible losses in its accounts receivable. The combined amounts of these additional reserves stood at RMB 383 million and RMB 489 million at year-end 1994 and 1995, respectively. Reserves for investment risk were equal to 0.2 and 0.3 percent of the bank's long-term investments, and allowances for losses on receivables were the equivalent of 10.8 percent and 6.1 percent of the bank's receivables, in 1994 and 1995, respectively.[259]

Among the traditional specialized banks, the Bank of China has clearly turned in the best financial performance in recent years. In large part, as discussed earlier, this superior performance occurred because in comparison with the other large state-owned banks, the Bank of China's cost of funds was lower and rose less rapidly during the 1988–89 and 1993–95 inflationary periods. But to a large degree, the bank was able to enhance its performance because its high concentration of foreign currency business, particularly in its growing offshore branch network, gave it greater flexibility than its far more domestically oriented competitors. Most of the bank's profit continues to come from overseas business, but according to Wang Xuebing, the president and chairman of the Bank of China, domestic business has started to make a contribution to the bottom line.[260] The bank's 1996 annual report acknowledges that its nonperforming loans composed 9 percent of its loan portfolio, substantially below the reported 22 percent figure for the four big banks as a group in 1995.[261]

Conclusion

China has only just begun the institutional transformation that will be required to allocate capital more efficiently. It has created a few new commercially oriented banks, such as the Bank of Communications, that are better equipped to meet the needs of a modern economy. But since the state continues to somewhat insulate the specialized banks from competition with these new financial institutions, their catalytic role is less than it might be. This insulation is most evident in the restrictions that the People's Bank has placed on the development of the network of branches and subbranches of the new institutions. At the end of 1994, for example, the central bank had allowed the fourteen new banks to establish 130 branches, 98 subbranches, and 724 organizational structures below the subbranch level.[262] By contrast, the four main state banks at the same time had 174 branches, 9,205 subbranches, and 138,081 organizational structures below the subbranch level.[263] In short, the large existing institutions had a structure of offices more than 150 times larger from which they could both attract deposits and offer financial services. Given the limited geographic mobility of most Chinese and the very underdeveloped state of electronic banking, the four major banks continue to enjoy a near monopoly in the provision of financial services over broad parts of China's landscape.

The state also continues to insulate the specialized banks from competition from international banks. Evidence from eastern Europe suggests that competition from foreign banks provides the most effective stimulus for the transformation of domestic banking systems in transition economies.[264] China has encouraged a large number of foreign banks to operate in China, initially via representative offices and subsequently increasingly via branch banks. By the end of August 1996 China had approved the establishment of 526 representative offices and 126 branches of foreign banking institutions as well as five solely foreign-funded banks, six Sino-foreign joint venture banks, five foreign finance companies, one Sino-foreign joint venture investment bank, and six foreign insurance companies.[265]

Despite these large numbers, the role of foreign financial institutions remains limited for two reasons. First, they remain extremely small. At year-end 1994 the total assets of foreign banks and finance companies were only U.S.$11.84 billion, which was less than 1 percent of the assets of domestic financial institutions.[266] By October 1996 the assets of foreign banks and finance companies had more than doubled to reach U.S.$28 billion, but were still well under 2 percent of the assets of domestic financial institutions.[267]

Comparisons with eastern Europe are instructive. Hungary's strategy for creating a competitive banking sector relies heavily on foreign financial institutions. As a result, the majority of banks are foreign controlled and "the Hungarian banking system has become the most stable in the former Communist bloc."[268] Even in Poland, which in comparison with several other eastern European countries has taken a much more restrictive approach to licensing foreign financial institutions, the role of foreign banks is much larger than in China. At year-end 1994 foreign banks accounted for only 2.3 percent of bank assets.[269] But only two and a half years later 30 percent of the capital in Poland's banking system was foreign owned, giving foreign institutions control of twenty-five of eighty-one existing banks. And plans for the sale to foreigners of minority stakes in two additional large state-owned banks were well advanced.[270]

The second reason the role of foreign financial institutions in China is limited is that they have been quite constrained in the range of services permitted and in the geographic areas in which they are licensed to operate. Foreign banks, for example, have been effectively prevented from conducting RMB business except in the Pudong Development Zone in Shanghai, where the People's Bank licensed nine foreign banks to conduct RMB business beginning in 1997. However, their business scope is extremely limited. They are not allowed to take deposits from or offer loans to Chinese households or Chinese-owned businesses but can carry out RMB business only with wholly foreign-owned and joint venture companies. Foreign insurance firms similarly have been limited by licenses that restrict the types of insurance they can sell and also limit their operations to two cities, Guangzhou and Shanghai. Thus foreign financial institutions have provided only limited competition to Chinese banks and insurance companies.

Evidence of the distortions inherent in the existing system is pervasive. For example, controls on interest rates provide a substantial incentive for the creation of unauthorized banks and other financial institutions. These institutions are able to offer higher interest rates to depositors and meet at least part of the demand for credit by individuals and nonstate firms that has not been met by state banks. The willingness of borrowers from these institutions to pay interest rates far above those charged by state banks shows that these borrowers do not have access to loans from state banks. Additionally, it strongly suggests that many projects with rates of return higher than those typical of many state firms, which do have access to bank lending, go unfunded.[271]

For example, in mid-1995 the authorities closed eighteen unauthorized private banks in Wenzhou, south of Shanghai. These institutions controlled assets of more than RMB 1 billion and offered loans at rates up to half again as high as those charged by state banks.[272] In a similar crackdown in mid-1996 in Hejin, a small city in Shanxi Province, authorities closed nearly one hundred private banks that offered loans, reportedly at rates as much as 16 percent a month.[273] In some cases, such as three finance companies established in Lanxi in Zhejiang Province in 1994 and 1995 and a fund established in Sichuan Province, local government officials and leaders of local offices of the People's Bank were directly involved in the establishment of these institutions and failed to take action when they expanded their business scope by entering directly into banking business. The institutions in Lanxi offered deposits rates 50 percent higher than the officially posted rates and provided loans at rates that were 90 percent over posted rates. The central bank closed these three illegal banks at the end of 1996.[274]

The central bank closure of these unlicensed financial institutions was certainly warranted. Because these institutions were not subject to central bank prudential supervision and probably did not meet capital adequacy requirements, depositors presumably were quite likely to lose their money. One implication of the persistence of institutions that offer unauthorized banking services is that the government's continued control of interest rates is highly distortionary. Below-market deposit rates constitute an indirect tax on savings. Setting lending rates at well below market clearing levels ensures excess demand for loans. Political allocation of credit funds, including corruption, inevitably results. And, as discussed in chapter 2, state-owned firms are highly favored in this process of administrative allocation of credit. A central goal of the process of financial liberalization analyzed in chapter 4 is to reduce the distortions just described, thus improving the allocation of resources within the economy.

4

Creating a Modern Financial System

CHINESE banks, particularly the largest state-owned banks, are handicapped in playing the critical role of allocating capital efficiently. This is not simply because they are poorly capitalized, under-reserved, and only marginally profitable. More important, they face a major challenge in transforming themselves into true commercial banks, a goal that the government has embraced at least in principle since 1993. There are two reasons.

The first is internal. After decades of extending loans largely at the behest of political leaders, the banks have not accumulated sufficient experience in real commercial banking. Credit policy standards remain lax, and personnel lack the appropriate credit training.[1] Even as such skills are being developed, poor financial disclosure by borrowers "will long hinder rational credit assessment."[2] The central bank has sought to address this problem by limiting the practice of firms borrowing simultaneously from several banks and requiring greater financial disclosure by borrowers.[3] Moreover, the central bank has limited regulatory and supervisory capacity and thus is not in a strong position to lead and manage the transition to a commercial banking system.

The second is external. China's highest political authorities have not yet been able to require the banks to operate on fully commercial principles because they are only gradually imposing a restructuring of state-owned firms. In the mid-1990s the response of local political leaders to demonstrations and other actions by workers who had been furloughed from their jobs in state firms sometimes was to require local branches of state banks to extend additional credit so that back wages could be paid and urban unrest defused. Until these banks have the independence to refuse to extend additional credit to failing state firms and can force these firms to exit, it will be difficult for the central bank to require banks to be fully responsible for their own profits and losses. As analyzed later in this chapter, these steps require further evidence of success of the fiscal reforms instituted in 1994.

Despite these internal and external obstacles, if China is to successfully complete its transition to a market economy and sustain a reasonably high rate of economic growth in the future, it must create a modern banking system, one that will meet accepted international accounting standards. The failure to do so will not only mean that the allocation of capital by banks will continue to be inefficient. It will also constrain the development of capital markets, limit the growth of the new domestic banks created since the mid-1980s, require continued indefinite severe limitations on the scope of business of foreign banks operating in China, limit the ability of the government to relax its heavy controls on interest rates, and make it more difficult to adopt monetary policy instruments that might moderate the large macroeconomic fluctuations experienced in the last two decades. Failure to create a modern banking system will make it difficult, if not impossible, to achieve full capital account convertibility of the domestic currency as well as impede the development of a viable pension system.

Efficient Intermediation

As outlined in chapter 1, in market economies financial institutions are not simply passive, responding to underlying changes in the real economy. Efficient financial systems contribute positively to economic growth. They do this through several means. Most obvious is their role in allocating funds to projects with the highest rate of return, thus increasing the marginal productivity of capital.[4] What is less frequently noticed, however, is that more developed financial systems, characterized by lower taxation and regulatory burdens, can allocate resources at lower costs. Thus financial development can reduce the leakage of resources by increasing the proportion of savings funneled to investment. Finally, financial systems can influence the rate of private savings.[5]

Financial systems in transition economies face an additional challenge—intermediating between savers and new forms of economic activity. Even in more market-oriented economies the ability of a financial system to provide funds to private activities, as opposed to simply funneling credit to state enterprises, has been found to be strongly associated with growth, even controlling for the influence of other variables.[6] This is likely to be still more important in transition economies that are undergoing a structural change in the forms of ownership. Even if banks are able to allocate funds more efficiently among traditional borrowers, they are likely to leave higher rate of return projects that might be undertaken by new borrowers operating under new ownership forms significantly underfunded. The potential importance of banks and other financial institutions in allocating funds to new borrowers is particularly important in China since under reform these institutions are the source of finance for an unusually large share of investment projects. But, as already noted, more than four-fifths of bank loans outstanding at the end of 1995 were to state-owned firms, suggesting that Chinese banks have not adequately performed the function of allocating funds to enterprises operating under new forms of ownership.

Capital Markets

Normally, after economic development has proceeded for some time and per capita income has risen significantly and appropriate legal and regulatory structures have been created, markets for equity and corporate bonds come to play an important supplementary role to banks in the allocation of capital.[7] Bonds can be more effective than banks in providing long-term capital for infrastructure and other projects with long gestation periods. For enterprises, equity markets provide an alternative to bank financing, usually geared more to providing short-term funding, thereby allowing enterprises to achieve a more balanced financing structure. Bonds and equities can also offer better returns to long-term savers, helping to maintain high savings rates. Under some institutional arrangements the role of capital markets can be quite large, even exceeding that of banks.[8] Even when capital markets are small, their presence increases competition in financial markets and stimulates banks to allocate capital more efficiently.

A weak banking system and an inefficient state-owned enterprise sector constrain the development of capital markets for at least two reasons. First, capital markets must rely on well-functioning banks to process payments and act as custodians.[9] More important, in China the state cannot allow unfettered competition for funds if banks are fragile. On the one hand, that process would undoubtedly reduce the share of funds flowing to state-owned firms, forcing many of them into bankruptcy, a fate China's political leaders only gradually seem willing to countenance on a wide scale. On the other hand, the increased availability of alternative financial assets for savers likely would lead to a withdrawal of funds from savings accounts, revealing the insolvency of large parts of the banking system and creating the potential for a financial crisis.

In China households have been willing to place most of their savings in the banking system for two reasons. First, the public appears to have confidence in banks. Unlike some other transition economies, China has not suffered widespread bank failures nor has the state confiscated household savings through the inflation tax, as occurred in Russia and most of the other newly independent states. Indeed, to date no licensed financial institution in China that is authorized to take deposits from the public has failed.[10] Confidence in the banking system is so great that households even are willing to place tens of billions of dollars worth of hard currencies in savings accounts in state banks.[11] In other transition economies, households hold most of their hard currency in cash, presumably because they do not trust their domestic banks.

Second, and perhaps more important, the range of alternative financial assets available to households, as reflected in table 4-1, has expanded slowly. At the beginning of the reform era cumulative household financial savings were tiny and, except for cash, the only financial asset available to households was savings accounts in banks and credit cooperatives.[12] Although households now have become the single largest source of savings, the range of financial assets available to households has expanded slowly. For example, the state began to sell treasury and other types of government bonds in 1981. But, because government budget deficits have been relatively small, the total stock of government bonds outstanding at the end of 1995, of which about 75 percent was held by households, was only RMB 330 billion.[13] Besides government bonds, state-owned enterprises

Table 4-1. Composition of Household Financial Assets, Year-end 1978, 1995, 1996

	1978		1995		1996	
Item	RMB billions	Percent	RMB billions	Percent	RMB billions	Percent
Savings deposits	21	50	2,966	77	3,850	77
Cash	21	50	526	14	587	12
Government bonds	0		248	6	320	6
Enterprise bonds	0		19	<1	21	<1
Equities	0		90	2	254	5
Total	42	100	3,849	100	5,032	100

Sources: Yang Jisheng, "The Economic 'Big Triangle' in Perspective," *Jingji cankao bao* (Economic Reference News), August 6, 1997, p. 1, in Foreign Broadcast Information Service, *China*, 97-253, September 10, 1997. *Almanac of China's Finance and Banking 1996* (Beijing: China Financial Publishing House, 1996), pp. 411, 430, 436; *Almanac 1997*, pp. 465, 472; People's Bank of China, *China Financial Outlook '96* (Beijing, 1997), pp. 90, 92; People's Bank of China Research and Statistics Department, *China Financial Statistics 1952–1987* (Beijing: China Financial Publishing House, 1988), pp. 4–5; and Xiao Minjie, "The Stable Development of China's Stock Market," *JETRO China Newsletter* vol. 4, no. 129 (1997), pp. 15–24.

Note: Savings includes deposits in banks, credit cooperatives, and the postal savings system. At the end of the second quarter of 1997 households held RMB 600 billion in currency, or two-thirds of the total RMB 912 billion then in circulation. Cash holdings at year-end 1978, 1995, and 1996 are estimated based on the assumption that the share of total currency in circulation held by households was two-thirds. Households own about three-quarters of government bonds outstanding. Households are assumed to hold all enterprise bonds outstanding. At year-end 1996 in Shanghai, traded A shares plus employee stock of listed companies accounted for 25.8 percent of the value of the shares of listed companies. The balance was held by the state, 43.9 percent; by companies, 27.3 percent; and by foreigners (who hold the foreign currency denominated B shares), 3.0 percent. Estimated total household equity holdings is 25.8 percent of the combined capitalization of the markets in Shanghai and in Shenzhen, in both 1995 and 1996.

and investment companies as well as state-owned financial institutions were authorized to sell bonds beginning in 1986. But the market for these debt instruments developed extremely slowly. At year-end 1995 the combined amount of enterprise bonds and short-term commercial paper outstanding was only RMB 36.4 billion, the combined value of state investment bonds and state investment company bonds was only RMB 29.12 billion, and the value of financial bonds outstanding was RMB 167.52 billion.[14] Investment bonds, financial bonds, and commercial paper, moreover, were sold primarily to institutions and only part of the bonds sold by state-owned enterprises was owned by households. Finally, the Shanghai and Shenzhen stock exchanges opened in 1990 and 1991, respectively. The market value of all 323 listed companies at the end of 1995 was RMB 347.4 billion. Of this amount three-quarters was held by the state, the companies themselves, and foreign investors. Households held only RMB 90 billion in equities at year-end 1995.[15] Finally, households purchased stocks in unlisted companies, most frequently shares in the firms where they were employed.[16]

In contrast to the modest sums held in government bonds, enterprise bonds, and equities, at year-end 1995 households held RMB 3 trillion in savings accounts in banks and credit cooperatives and over RMB 500 billion in currency. The magnitude of alternative financial assets that was available at year-end 1995 was so small that households held more than three-quarters of their financial savings in the form of bank savings deposits.[17] Most of the balance was in cash while the combined share held in the form of government bonds, corporate bonds, and equities was less than 10 percent.

This pattern changed little in 1996. The offering of government bonds hit a new high of RMB 195 billion, the value of new shares sold on the Shanghai and Shenzhen stock exchanges also reached a new high of RMB 34.54 billion, and the value of enterprise bonds sold was RMB 13 billion.[18] However, households allocated a staggering RMB 850 billion to increased bank savings deposits so the proportion of funds allocated to financial assets other than savings accounts in 1996 did not increase significantly when compared with earlier years. As table 4-1 shows, the equity portion of the stock of total household financial assets more than doubled in 1996 to reach 5 percent. However, this increase was mostly because of a huge run-up in 1996 in average share prices on both the Shanghai and Shenzhen stock markets rather than a dramatic increase in the value of the initial offerings of stock and a change in the pattern of allocation of the flows of household savings.[19]

The government in 1996 was able to increase the supply of equities as well as to finance the current government deficit and refinance maturing government debt because of the huge continued flow of household savings into the banking system. As explained in chapter 3, if the state were to allow capital markets to develop rapidly, the magnitude of household savings flowing to the banking system could decline significantly as households increased their holdings of stocks and bonds. Indeed households could even begin to withdraw funds from savings accounts on a net basis if the state allowed capital markets to develop very rapidly. This would curtail the ability of the banks to expand their lending to traditional borrowers and thus threaten the survival of state-owned firms. As a result, the state is likely to continue to constrain the development of capital markets, which would presumably allocate funds largely to nonstate borrowers that are more credit worthy.

New Domestic Banks and Foreign Banks

A similar logic constrains the development of new banks and perhaps an expanded role for foreign banks. Since these institutions begin without the handicap of a large portfolio of nonperforming loans, they will achieve higher profitability than existing large state-owned banks. They can use these higher earnings to offer depositors better services or, if interest rates were deregulated, to offer higher interest rates on savings. In either case the specialized banks would be less competitive. Allowing new domestic banks to expand their franchise rapidly would almost certainly reduce the flow of funds into the existing state banks. That, in turn, would impair their ability to increase their lending to their traditional borrowers, state-owned firms. Thus, until it is able to strengthen state-owned banks, the state probably will constrain the development of new domestic financial institutions.

The authorities may continue to limit the ability of foreign banks to carry out domestic currency business for the same reason. Foreign banks operating in China had long wanted the right to take renminbi deposits and make renminbi-denominated loans. The Chinese Minister of Finance Liu Zhongli, on the occasion of a meeting with U.S. Treasury Secretary Lloyd Bentsen in January 1994, made the first official announcement that China would open domestic currency business to foreign banks.[20] He gave no specific assurances, however, on the timing of this reform and indicated that it would be on an experimental basis. In early 1995 Chen Yuan, the vice governor of the People's Bank of China, said that the central bank had decided to designate Shanghai and Guangzhou as the initial cities in which foreign banks would be allowed to carry out domestic currency business, but on a "small scale."[21] One year later Ma Delun, a central bank spokesman, said that foreign banks would be authorized to conduct renminbi business only in Shanghai, but that a precise timetable had not yet been set. Moreover, Ma revealed the authorities planned two new, severe additional restrictions. First, the experiment was to be limited to foreign banks based in the Pudong Economic Development Zone in Shanghai. At the time foreign banks in Shanghai had no branches in Pudong. They were all located in Shanghai proper, where it made more economic sense to establish branch banks. Banks licensed to carry out domestic currency business were required to move their branches to Pudong as a condition for entering the domestic currency business.[22] Second, foreign banks were not to be allowed to carry out such business with Chinese firms but only with joint venture companies or other foreign-related firms.[23]

When the regulations governing the entry of foreign banks into the domestic currency business finally were promulgated in December 1996, other major constraints emerged. Foreign banks' domestic currency liabilities, primarily deposits, cannot exceed 35 percent of their foreign exchange liabilities.[24] This, of course, means the growth of foreign banks' domestic currency business over the long term will be restricted to the rate of growth of their foreign currency business. A second constraint on foreign banks in China is that they are not able to provide the full range of domestic currency business. For example, although they can accept deposits, make loans, provide guarantees, and invest in Chinese government and other financial bonds, they are not able to enter into the credit card business. Third, as a condition for being able to conduct limited domestic currency business, foreign banks have had to give up their preferential tax rate.[25] Finally, the central bank limited to nine the number of foreign and Sino-foreign joint venture banks initially authorized to conduct renminbi business.[26]

These severe constraints on the geographic and sectoral scope of domestic currency business, the severe limits on the growth of this business, and the limited number of foreign institutions authorized to engage in domestic currency transactions all suggest that Chinese banking authorities are unwilling to allow foreign banks to compete freely with domestic institutions, even in the few major cities where foreign banks want to do business. Foreign banks have and will apply normal commercial criteria in their lending. The Chinese government cannot require them to extend policy loans to insolvent state-owned enterprises, so the quality of their assets will be far higher than that of domestic banks. They therefore can be profitable with a lower spread between lending and deposit rates than can China's large state-owned banks. In a liberalized financial environment they could be expected to offer higher interest rates to depositors and charge lower interest rates to borrowers compared to state-owned banks and still achieve levels of profitability that are beyond the reach of the largest state-owned banks.

Allowing foreign banks to conduct domestic currency business without limit, however, is not likely to set off a massive migration of deposits from domestic to foreign banks. Very few foreign banks operating in China are likely to focus on the retail banking business. Nonetheless, the apprehension of China's state-owned banks has some merit. Foreign financial institutions are likely to target large institutional depositors in a few major urban centers. Moreover, foreign banks would also skim off the most creditworthy large borrowers, leaving the large state-owned banks to serve weaker borrowers. Foreign banks would also capture a significant share of the foreign trade settlement business from state-owned banks. All of these developments would tend to erode the deposit base, cause some deterioration in the quality of the loan portfolios, and depress the profitability of the large state-owned banks.

Decontrol of Interest Rates

Although the People's Bank has begun to liberalize short-term interest rates in the interbank market, it will not be able to free up interest rates on deposits as long as the largest domestic banks and their principal borrowers remain financially fragile. As discussed in chapter 3, the large specialized banks benefit considerably from the People's Bank policy of setting artificially low interest rates on sight deposits. For example, in 1995, when inflation as measured by the consumer price index was 17.1 percent, households received only 3.15 percent interest on their passbook savings accounts while borrowers paid only 10.98 percent interest on one-year working capital loans.[27] Deregulation of interest rates in 1995 certainly would have raised the interest rate on sight deposits to at least the rate of inflation. It also likely would have raised interest rates on one-year working capital loans to about 21 percent.[28] Since household savings in the form of sight deposits during 1995 averaged RMB 530 billion, banks received an implicit subsidy from households of approximately RMB 74 billion.[29] In turn, the banks passed this subsidy on to their borrowers in the form of artificially low interest rates on loans. Thus, while the World Bank has long recommended that the People's Bank introduce greater flexibility in interest rates, it seems unlikely that this will be possible on the deposit side as long as banks are financially weak and dependent on access to very low-cost household deposits.[30]

Decontrolling interest rates on loans is an essential part of a strategy of reducing fluctuations in economic activity and the more general liberalization of interest rates. Over the long run decontrolling deposit rates is probably essential to maintaining the high rates of household savings that have fueled so large a portion of China's economic growth in the reform period. The World Bank cautions that China's savings rate could decline in the future, leading to a lower rate of capital accumulation and thus a lower rate of economic growth.[31] Offering savers consistently positive real rates of return on their bank savings is likely to be a key factor in sustaining high rates of household savings.

Improved Macroeconomic Performance

The insatiable demand of state-owned enterprises for credit lies at the root of China's macroeconomic instability in the reform period. In periods of relative price stability, credit has been readily available to state-owned firms and loans outstanding rise rapidly. Typically this situation is partly because of growing leakages from the credit plan. In 1988, for example, leakages were primarily through a rapid expansion of loans by nonbank financial intermediaries. In 1993 they were intermediated largely through the growth of the interbank market. The resulting increased levels of investment and more rapid growth of the wage bill stimulates inflation, leading eventually to a period of credit tightening as the authorities attempt to rein in inflationary pressures. But tighter credit was not reflected in rising real interest rates on loans. Indeed, since nominal interest rates were adjusted upward slowly during inflationary periods, the real lending rate tended to be falling when the government's credit policy turned contractionary. Thus the government had little choice but to rely on a more intensive use of credit quotas and other administrative controls to restrict the growth of credit.[32]

This is typically reflected in a broadening of the scope of the credit plan to include financial institutions whose lending previously was not subject to direct quantitative control. For example, after inflation began to accelerate in 1988, the People's Bank of China instituted a broader credit plan beginning in March 1989. Practically all lending institutions, including credit cooperatives, trust and investment companies, and other nonbank financial intermediaries were brought under the credit plan.[33] In 1993, ceilings on credit creation, which had been allowed effectively to lapse after inflation was brought under control in 1991, were instituted once again. However, since real interest rates on loans were not adjusted upward and because the demand of many state-owned firms for funds is not very sensitive to the cost of borrowing, the excess demand for funds persists, which "translates into pressures for the PBC to loosen credit."[34]

The central bank recognizes that to moderate these macroeconomic fluctuations more effectively it must shift to greater reliance on indirect instruments of monetary control, especially adjustment of bank liquidity through open market operations and other measures to control excess reserves of banks, in place of relying on direct controls through the credit plan. The central bank set the stage for using open market operations in 1993, when it issued central bank bills to absorb excess liquidity. Although the bank planned to begin genuine open market operations in 1994 it was forced to postpone this initiative, largely because it was unable to allow greater interest rate flexibility.[35] The Central Bank Law of 1995 anticipates a shift to reliance on indirect instruments of monetary policy. Credit quotas are not even listed as a specific monetary policy tool.[36] Movement in this direction was evident in 1997 when the scope of credit quotas was limited to the four largest banks and in 1998 when mandatory credit quotas for even the largest banks were eliminated.[37]

Although the central bank established the framework to shift from credit policy to monetary policy in 1994–96, greater reliance on indirect instruments of monetary control, however, is still in an early stage. The central bank plans to continue to issue quarterly guidance credit plans to influence the lending of the largest banks. Until some experience has accumulated, it will be impossible to judge the significance of the shift from mandatory to guidance planning of bank lending. Ultimately, however, effective use of open market operations will depend on much greater flexibility of interest rates on lending, greater sensitivity of banks to costs, and on further reforms in the enterprise sector that increase the sensitivity of firms to the interest rate charged on loans.

Attaining Capital Account Convertibility

China formally achieved convertibility on current account transactions in December 1996. That means that the renminbi can be readily traded for foreign currency to be used to finance trade and service transactions. The latter includes foreign and joint venture firms acquiring hard currency in order to remit profits abroad as well as domestic firms and financial institutions acquiring hard currency to make scheduled repayments of approved foreign currency loans.

Chinese leaders repeatedly have said their goal is to make the renminbi fully convertible, meaning that Chinese firms and individuals would be able to purchase foreign currency to be used to buy foreign currency denominated financial assets, such as stocks and bonds. No target date, however, has been announced. Since full convertibility would represent a dramatic expansion of the range of financial assets available to Chinese households, it poses the threat of disintermediation and thus could undermine the financial viability of domestic banks. The Chinese authorities well understand that one lesson of the Asian financial crisis of 1997 is that countries with weak banking systems are ill advised to maintain the combination of capital account convertibility and fixed or heavily managed exchange rate systems.

Thus China's move to capital account convertibility must be closely integrated with domestic financial market reforms, particularly strengthening its fragile, undercapitalized banking system. The central bank, furthermore, must relax its heavy regulation of domestic interest rates and allow interest rate liberalization. Unless domestic interest rates are internationally competitive, when capital account convertibility is introduced there will be substantial pressure on the balance of payments and the exchange rate, as well as the potential for disintermediation.[38] For example, if interest rates on foreign financial assets are higher than on domestic assets, Chinese households would sell renminbi to purchase higher yielding foreign assets, resulting in substantial downward pressure on the value of the domestic currency. If the central bank sought to maintain a fixed value of the renminbi by selling U.S. dollars and buying up domestic currency, banks would be subject to disintermediation as households withdrew their domestic currency deposits from banks.

Pension System Reform

The development of a sustainable pension system also depends on the creation of a modern banking system. As discussed in chapter 2, the pension system in place in the first two decades of the reform period was unsustainable since it has required and would continue to require ever-escalating contribution rates. In 1997 the State Council approved a new pension scheme, large parts of which are adopted from recommendations of the World Bank.[39] The bank's proposal, which entails compulsory contribution rates about one-fourth less than current levels, is viable only with "a capital market and financial system that pays a positive real rate of return to long-term savings."[40] In 1993–95 the rates of return on pension balances, which must be invested in a mix of government bonds and bank deposits, were below the inflation rate and thus their value eroded in real terms.[41] The viability of the World Bank's recommended alternative scheme, discussed in chapter 2, depends on rates of return of about 5 percent in real terms.[42] That, in turn, depends on liberalization of interest rates and the further development of the market for long-term (five to ten years) financial assets, such as treasury bonds and certificates of deposit, designed for institutional investors such as pension funds.

Reform Strategy

The creation of a modern banking system is not only essential for improving the efficiency with which capital is allocated, it is also closely tied to improved macroeconomic stability, capital account convertibility, and other important economic policy objectives. What is the reform strategy that is most likely to allow banks and other financial institutions to fulfill their role of allocating capital efficiently, thus paving the way for the achievement of these objectives?

China has initiated coordinated reforms of its financial, enterprise, and fiscal systems. Given the intimate interconnections among these three, the goal is to create a critical mass of concurrent reforms rather than to address these problems sequentially. One group of influential reformers refers to this as an integrated or comprehensive approach to creating a market economy.[43]

Two key reforms were undertaken simultaneously with the financial reform package. The first was a fiscal reform designed to stem and then reverse the long-term decline in tax revenue relative to output and to demarcate more clearly the sources of revenue available to the central government on the one hand, and local governments on the other. The fiscal reform must provide sufficient additional tax revenues to allow the government to relieve state-owned enterprises from their responsibility for providing a broad range of services that in most states are financed through the budget. The magnitude of funds required for this purpose is explored below. Besides the steps already taken, including the establishment of a national tax bureau and making the value added tax the major indirect tax to be shared at a fixed rate between central and local governments, the fiscal reform may also require increased rates of taxation of the nonstate sector, which currently is undertaxed relative to state-owned firms.

The second reform is the imposition of hard budget constraints on enterprises. Until a fundamental change in the behavior of enterprises is well under way it makes little sense to attempt to undertake the rehabilitation of the banking system along the lines outlined below. Banks began to curtail the access of money-losing state-owned enterprises to increased credit after mid-1993. For example, the number of firms that went bankrupt increased and a growing number of firms reported laying off workers. Even more firms, which were unable to increase their borrowing from banks, sent workers home on furlough. These workers retained their access to enterprise housing and sometimes other benefits but received only a small fraction of their normal monetary compensation. Thus while the official unemployment rate in urban areas at year-end 1996 was only 3 percent, according to a mid-1997 survey another 7.2 percent of the urban work force had been sent home from their jobs. That means about 13 million workers were furloughed by mid-1997.[44] Another indicator of the increasing commercial orientation of the largest state-owned banks was that in 1997, for the first time in many years, apparently they did not exhaust their credit quotas. Their authorized loan ceiling for 1997 went up by RMB 800 billion, but by the end of the third quarter the net increase in their loans outstanding was only RMB 400 billion.[45] This was not simply a response to the repeated exhortation to banks that they must improve their profitability, but was also a newly announced policy that the heads of banks that failed to improve their financial performance would be fired.[46]

Despite these significant developments, many enterprises were able to avoid making permanent reductions in the size of their work force, and exit of firms via bankruptcy continued to be relatively infrequent.[47] In some cities furloughed workers who had not been paid for months staged sit-ins to disrupt rail lines in order to attract the attention of higher political authorities. Elsewhere worker actions were even more vigorous. The result in some cases was disappointing, however—local banks were ordered to extend additional loans so that enterprises could pay back wages to minimize what the authorities perceive as a potential threat to social stability.[48] This anecdotal evidence suggests that some state-owed firms are still not subject to hard budgets.

Imposing hard budget constraints on enterprises depends in part on the passage and enforcement of a revised bankruptcy law that would protect the rights of creditors, notably banks. The 1986 Bankruptcy Law in principle provides substantial protection for creditors. Claims of secured creditors, according to Chinese law, are to be paid from bankruptcy assets before any other claims, even before administrative costs and taxes.[49] The position of banks, at least in principle, was strengthened by the passage of the Civil Procedure Law, which took effect in 1991. That law also gave state banks the highest priority for repayment, whether loans were formally secured or not. The Security Law, which took effect in 1995, set forth the legal framework for secured transactions generally.[50] It should have further strengthened the position of banks vis à vis their borrowers, especially those that have not started the bankruptcy process. Under the provisions of the Security Law, banks should be able to seize and sell collateral pledged for a loan if a borrower is in violation of the underlying loan contract.

Despite these growing legal protections, in practice banks in 1995 and 1996 recovered only a very small share of the loans outstanding to firms that went through bankruptcy and liquidation.[51] Not surprisingly, under these circumstances fewer than 2 percent of all bankruptcies in those years were initiated by banks.[52] A revised bankruptcy law, which would strengthen the position of creditors, was drafted several years ago. But its passage has been blocked by the

National People's Congress, reportedly by provincial delegates who fear it would be used to force money-losing firms out of business in their regions.

Moreover, the State Council in the second half of 1996 effectively nullified the legal position of banks in the bankruptcy process by issuing a regulation specifying that the proceeds from the liquidation of bankrupt enterprises should first be allocated to meet pension and social welfare obligations.[53] Only if there are funds left over will banks recover part of the loans extended to these firms. The state clearly should mitigate the social costs of enterprise restructuring. But these costs should be borne by the state budget. Transferring this burden to the banks makes the cost of such mitigation programs less transparent. More important, it delays the process of converting the banks to operate on a fully commercial basis. As long as enterprises finance social programs through their borrowing, the state is unlikely to be able to hold them accountable for their own profits and losses for the simple reason that it will be difficult to determine whether inefficiency or excessive social burdens account for their poor financial performance. In turn, that will make it difficult for the state to make banks accountable for their own financial performance.

Banking reform in all transition economies must be based on the rehabilitation of existing banks, entry of new banks, or some combination thereof. As already shown in chapter 3, China's approach to date emphasizes rehabilitation but also includes the creation of some new banks and other new financial institutions. This is an appropriate mix given China's unusually high ratio of bank deposits to gross domestic product. Relying primarily on new institutions is a more viable strategy in Russia and the other newly independent states, where high inflation so reduced the value of savings deposits that the ratio of deposits to gross domestic product in 1994 was only one-sixth that in China.[54] Relying largely on new institutions in China would inevitably mean the collapse of existing banks, wiping out most of the value of household savings deposits, which at year-end 1997 were RMB 4.6 trillion, the equivalent to well over one-half of gross domestic product.[55] That could create a financial crisis.

The failure of China's largest financial institutions would disrupt the flow of credit and disrupt the payments system, leading to a collapse of economic activity. The failure of major banks also could have long-term negative implications for the household savings rate, which could pose a major problem for any future government. A lower savings rate would mean a lower rate of investment and slower growth, in turn depressing the rate of new job creation, leading to sustained higher levels of unemployment.

Rehabilitation of existing state-owned banks requires both addressing the accumulated stock of nonperforming loans and changing the behavior of both banks and government and party leaders at all levels so that new lending is based on commercial rather than political criteria. There is an inherent conflict in dealing with these two problems since recapitalization of banks and a corresponding write-off of the stock of accumulated nonperforming loans "can undermine bank's incentives to adopt prudent investment criteria by fostering the expectation that, having bailed out troubled banks once, governments would do so again."[56]

Bank Recapitalization

Although recapitalization is the core of any bank rehabilitation strategy, in principle there are several different ways of achieving this objective. These alternative methods have important implications, particularly for those who bear the losses of the banking system. Andrew Sheng argues that in general these losses should be borne, in descending order, by borrowers, private bank shareholders, bank employees, the government, and depositors.[57] The central implication of this advice is that depositors should be protected against losses due to bank failures. There are several ways this could be accomplished.

Banks could sell the collateral underlying their loans. If the market price of the collateral at least equals the value of the loan, the bank can write-off the loan without any use of its own loan loss reserves and with no loss of its own capital. Since the bank's nonperforming assets would be reduced at no expense to the bank's own capital, the financial position of the bank would be improved. The sale of collateral allocates the losses to borrowers, who lose the assets that were pledged to back the original loan.

Alternatively the banks could forgive nonperforming loans outstanding to enterprises in exchange for a share of ownership in the borrowing enterprise. This is commonly called a debt-equity swap.

Since the Basle agreement allows banks to count up to 45 percent of the unrealized gains on marketable securities as part of tier-two capital, such swaps eventually could increase the capital of China's largest banks. Third, banks could sell some of their loans, and the new owner of the loan could swap it for an equity stake in the borrower. Either the second or third method, by diluting the stake of the original enterprise owners, also would allocate the loss to the borrowers.

Fourth, banks could be liquidated, allocating losses to the individuals owning shares in these bank.

Fifth, banks could be given access to the equity markets, so they could sell shares as a means of raising new capital. According to the Basle standard, the value of shares sold on equity markets contributes directly to tier-one capital. Finally, the central government could directly inject fresh capital into the banks. Either of the two latter methods allocates the losses to the government. The sale of equity does so indirectly, since the state would no longer be the sole owner of the banks. The injection of fresh capital allocates the losses directly to the government.

Only the last of these alternatives—a direct government injection of fresh capital—is likely to prove viable as the principal method of recapitalizing China's banks, given their present financial situation. It would appear that the opportunity to allocate the losses to borrowers is extremely limited. Few loans to state-owned firms are backed by collateral, largely precluding the option of seizing the collateral and selling it.[58] Even when loans are collateralized, the uncertainty of the property rights associated with the collateral and the limited nature of secondary markets for machinery, equipment, and other hard assets usually make the sale of collateral infeasible.

Having the banks take an equity ownership in exchange for forgiving loans may be a viable approach to dealing with a few cases of poorly performing borrowers in an otherwise healthy enterprise sector. Once relieved of the obligation to amortize their loans, these few firms may be restored to profitability. If banks exercise effective control and supervision of the firms in which they acquire an equity stake, over time the price of the shares of the firms may rise in the market. Thus the bank ultimately would be able to sell its shares, generating substantial profits that could be added to bank capital.

In China large-scale debt-equity swaps are not likely to prove a viable method for recapitalizing banks for several reasons. First, as seen in chapter 3, the problem is one of a large share of nonperforming loans, not a few isolated borrowers unable to repay their loans. Swaps on a large scale are less feasible since equity stakes in loss-making enterprises won't provide a flow of income to banks with which they can meet their obligation to pay interest to depositors. Moreover, such swaps could not be expected to have a significant positive effect on the balance sheets of banks since the value of an equity stake in a money-losing enterprise would be modest at best. Swaps on a large scale could even undermine public confidence in banks if depositors thought the ultimate guarantor of the viability of their deposits was shifting from the state itself to enterprises, many of which are widely perceived as economically nonviable. The erosion of confidence in the banks would accelerate if it was believed that banks, once they had acquired a direct ownership stake, would be even less likely to impose commercial standards on lending and be more willing to prop up nonperforming firms with additional loans.

Second, only a handful of Chinese companies are publicly listed.[59] The value of unlisted companies is uncertain. The Basle rules are quite specific in allowing banks to count as capital only permanent equity in companies whose shares are traded publicly. Thus even if money-losing enterprises could be turned around after the debt-equity swap had taken place, the capital of banks, at least by international standards, would not automatically be increased through equity ownership.

Third, and equally important, there is little reason to believe that Chinese banks have accumulated the expertise to provide more effective supervision and control of firms than do their current managers. There is little basis for assuming that these firms could be turned around if banks became major shareholders. As a result, even if the companies were publicly traded, it is far from certain that investors would bid up the price of the shares in anticipation of a successful turnaround.

Finally, China's commercial banking law severely limits bank equity ownership of enterprises, indicating that the Chinese authorities do not envisage large-scale debt-equity swaps as part of a solution to the problems of the banking system.[60]

The sale of loans is an even less likely alternative than debt-equity swaps in China's current situation. China lacks the necessary secondary markets for loans, the same limitation that has stymied the application of this approach in Poland, the only transition economy where it has been attempted.[61] In any case, given the very poor quality of the loans Chinese banks presumably would like to sell, it is likely that the discounts would be steep and that banks would recover very little. Thus loan sales in effect allocate losses to banks. But they do not have sufficient capital to absorb such losses.

China cannot allocate losses to private shareholders via bank liquidation for the simple reason that China's banks are state owned. There are no private shareholders to absorb losses. Even if they were privately owned, in their current financial condition—in which the losses to be absorbed are far in excess of the net worth of the banks— liquidation really would mean the allocation of losses to depositors.

The sale of equity shares in existing banks would be feasible only under two conditions. First, China's political authorities would have to be willing to countenance the partial privatization of state-owned banks, which is what the sale of bank shares to the public would represent. There is little concrete evidence that the authorities would support such a move in the near term.[62]

Even if this were not a constraint, the willingness of the public to purchase shares in financial institutions with negative net worth and, if allowance for adequate provisioning was made, negative profits as well, is in doubt. In market economies banks frequently have a franchise value that makes them attractive to other banks or outside investors, even if their financial performance is poor. Since China's four major banks are shielded to some degree from competition, their franchise value might be thought to be particularly high.

However, the franchise value of state-owned banks is likely to be small until their massive overstaffing is ended. Although this move will take time, these steps should be pursued for two reasons. Even after the major banks have been recapitalized, which is the preferred strategy suggested below, they will not be viable institutions, able to compete with new banks, in the long run unless they reduce their extraordinarily high operating costs.[63] Second, if overstaffing and other causes of high operating costs eventually are eliminated so that shares could be sold to the public, the government could use part of the proceeds from partial privatization to retire part of the increase in state debt that will be issued to recapitalize the banks. That would reduce the fiscal burden recapitalization necessarily entails, since it would cut the magnitude of increased interest expenditures. It would not jeopardize bank capital, however, since the transaction would substitute cash for government bonds.

Some have proposed an even more imaginative solution to the nonperforming loan problem of China's state-owned banks. The banks could simply write off the loans that they have made to enterprises that are unable to repay their debts. This reduction in bank assets could be offset on the liability side by confiscating the deposits that other state enterprises have in the banking system. The thinking underlying this approach is that borrowing by state-owned enterprises from state-owned banks and deposits by state-owned firms in state-owned banks simply represent paper transactions within the public sector. Simply canceling these paper transactions would have no effect on the net worth of the state and no effect on households. Heavily indebted enterprises, once unburdened by their cumulative borrowing, in some cases would be restored to profitability. For the banks the result of the cancellations would be a simultaneous equal reduction in both assets and liabilities. Their unchanged capital would then loom larger relative to their assets. Thus they would emerge as better capitalized institutions, possibly capable of operating on commercial principles.

In practice, this approach has been judged "one of the least successful methods" of bank recapitalization.[64] Its shortcomings include lack of transparency, since the scale of losses in the banking system is obscured. More important, it has the very high cost of financially weakening the most successful and economically most viable state-owned firms, that is, those that are large net depositors in the banking system.

This approach of offsetting assets and liabilities is not even feasible when debts and credits are not concentrated within the public sector. "In such circumstances, mere bookkeeping is impossible: recapitalizing the banks can be achieved only by a government injection on the asset side or by default on household deposits on the liability side."[65] Since the net deposits of state enterprises in the banking system are quite small, this approach to recapitalizing the banks is wholly unsuited to the Chinese situation. As already noted, the Chinese banking system is highly dependent on households, which provided almost 60 percent of the deposits in banks at the end of 1995. Moreover, these data almost certainly understate the dependence of the banks on households as a source of deposits. Although 32 percent of the deposits in the banking system at the end of 1995 nominally belonged to enterprises, the ultimate source of virtually all of these funds was borrowing from the banks.[66] At the end of 1995, 95.6 percent of all working capital of state-owned industrial enterprises had been borrowed from banks.[67] Firms borrow the money and keep it in their bank accounts until it is drawn down to pay wages and meet other costs of doing business.[68] On a bank's balance sheet these funds show up as "enterprise deposits." In short, outside of funds of the treasury and other government departments, virtually all funds in the banking system ultimately come from households.

A variant on the bookkeeping approach says that it is not necessary to confiscate the deposits of state enterprises to offset the write-off of nonperforming loans to enterprises and the resulting reduction in the assets of the banks. It might be applicable in China where enterprise deposits in the bank are almost entirely borrowed funds. The state simply could create paper capital, so-called soft money, which it gives to the bank to offset the write-off of the nonperforming loans. It need only add the simple caveat that this "soft money" not be used as the basis for new lending. This canceling of the debts of enterprises would leave households unaffected and also, as long as the banks do not use the newly created paper asset as the basis for new lending, would not contribute to inflation.[69]

The importance of household deposits to the banking system also means that the paper asset offset approach is risky since it could stimulate a major inflationary spiral. Household savings deposits are potential claims on real assets. Even if the banks do not extend new loans based on their new "soft money," a large-scale bank write-off of assets financed by "soft money" might stimulate households to convert some of their financial savings into real goods. The reason is that if bad loans are written off and the banks are not given an asset that yields a real return, households may regard this as a reduction in the state's commitment to preserve the viability of the banking system. It would erode the credibility of the government's implicit 100 percent guarantee of deposits. Thus households would be likely to withdraw part of their savings from the banks. Because the range of other financial assets available for purchase by households is quite limited, households might convert their withdrawn cash mostly into real goods. Since households' cumulative savings deposits at year-end

1995 were equal to more than 50 percent of gross domestic product, even if this conversion to goods was very partial it would stimulate a large, sudden increase in aggregate demand and a resulting large run-up in prices.[70] In short, the plan runs the risk of stimulating accelerating inflation even if the banks do not extend any new loans. In the longer run the public's loss of confidence in the banking system, given the lack of alternative financial assets, also could depress the rate of household saving and thus have unfavorable implications for long-term economic growth as well.

Two additional alternatives to an injection of fresh capital by the state deserve discussion. The first is the gradual recapitalization of banks through reinvestment of their profits. The World Bank's 1996 World Development Report, which focused on the problems of transition economies, is skeptical of the long-term efficacy of using tax revenues to recapitalize banks in transition economies. This view was based in part on the early Hungarian transition experience where "some banks have been recapitalized as many as five times."[71] The World Development Report favors policies that "promote self-help for banks to encourage them to build up their capital base," allowing banks to "grow out of their bad debt problems."[72]

Although this strategy may have merit in other transition economies, it is much less feasible for China. In China, the magnitude of nonperforming loans and thus the size of the required recapitalization (both relative to gross domestic product) are so large that the gradual rebuilding of capital through the reinvestment of profits does not appear viable. The gradualistic approach, sometimes called a flow solution, is feasible in the most mild cases of banking distress, where capital adequacy of problem banks while low is still positive.[73] As already discussed in chapter 3, several of China's major state-owned banks on a proper accounting are insolvent; that is, the value of their liabilities exceeds the value of their assets and their capital adequacy is negative. Moreover, the reported level of profitability of these banks is quite low and almost certainly negative on realistic accounting principles. In short, there are no real profits to be added to capital.

The specific recommendations of the World Development Report for implementing a flow solution—liberalization of interest rates on loans, elimination of quasi-fiscal demands on banks, more realistic provisions for loan losses, and so forth—are essential for China.[74] But they are best regarded as reforms that will allow Chinese banks to maintain their capital adequacy and operate on a commercial basis going forward after recapitalization, rather than steps that could increase profitability by enough for the banks to solve the problems arising from the historical accumulation of bad loans.

Moreover, requiring banks to cure their own solvency problem has risks that are just as, or even more, severe than those associated with recapitalization. For example, it increases the possibility that banks will raise interest rates to attract more deposits. That may allow insolvent banks to avoid temporarily a liquidity crisis but, unless lending rates are raised, it would reduce bank margins and thus profits as well. More likely, banks would increase lending rates by more than deposit rates, in order to increase the spread between the two and thus increase profits. If retained these increased profits would raise bank capital. However, higher lending rates may discourage investment and lead to a lower rate of economic growth. And the flow approach gives banks an incentive to undertake increasingly risky lending at higher interest rates in an attempt to increase profitability.

The experience of the U.S. thrift industry in the 1980s exemplifies the risks of the flow approach to dealing with problem banks. Insolvent thrift institutions were allowed to stay in business in the 1980s, largely because the resources available to the Federal Savings and Loan Insurance Corporation (FSLIC) were grossly inadequate to pay off depositors of the thrifts that should have been liquidated. Instead, FSLIC reduced by two-fifths the minimum net worth ratios required for thrifts to remain in operation and, when this proved inadequate, issued outright exemptions so that thrifts that failed to meet the new lower capital requirements could continue to operate. The U.S. Congress cooperated by eliminating Regulation Q interest rate ceilings on thrift institutions and authorizing "certain capital forbearance measures."[75] Thus in the early 1980s weaker thrifts offered higher interest rates to attract more deposits, often by using brokers of such deposits to get access to funds from outside their traditional regional markets. In an attempt to increase their profitability, in the mid-1980s thrifts abandoned their traditional focus on residential mortgage lending in favor of commercial real estate lending and investments in high-yield junk bonds. In this search for higher earnings that could be used to buttress their weak capital positions, the thrifts moved into unfamiliar assets without fully understanding the greater risks involved.[76]

The attempt to use the flow approach to solve the problems of U.S. thrift institutions was a financial disaster. FSLIC began incurring financial losses in 1984 and, despite additional funding provided by Congress, went bankrupt in 1989. The U.S. Congress was forced to create the Resolution Trust Corporation to handle failing thrifts. The mission of the Resolution Trust Corporation was to close insolvent thrifts and sell off the collateral backing their loans in order to reduce the cost to the government of protecting depositors from financial losses. Since this involved the use of government funds to protect depositors while shutting bankrupt institutions, the establishment of the Resolution Trust Corporation was an admission that the decade-long hope that the thrifts could grow their way back to solvency had failed. The initial estimate of the cost to taxpayers of cleaning up insolvent thrifts was U.S.$60 billion.[77] The ultimate cost to taxpayers, when the Resolution Trust Corporation finally completed its work at the end of 1995, was in excess of U.S.$132 billion.[78]

The second alternative to an injection of fresh capital by the state that deserves discussion is the indirect recapitalization of banks through the sale of equity shares in state-owned companies or through the sale of land use rights and housing of these companies. The program of state-owned enterprise reform endorsed by the Chinese Communist Party at the Fifteenth Party Congress envisages an acceleration of public offerings of state-owned companies, both on domestic stock markets and on the Hong Kong Stock Exchange. By the eve of the Fifteenth Congress, Chinese companies had raised a cumulative total of RMB 256 billion on domestic and overseas stock markets.[79] This is a relatively modest amount. By comparison, between the time the Shanghai and Shenzhen stock markets opened in 1990 and 1991, respectively, and the fall of 1997 the increase in bank loans was RMB 5,300 billion, more than twenty times the value of all new equity issues.[80]

However, if the number of enterprise public offerings could be expanded and a significant portion of the capital raised was used to pay down debt owed to banks, the financial position of banks could be strengthened. Moreover, that also clearly would provide a better capital structure for enterprises. Thus the role of stock markets should expand significantly.

Although this is an attractive option to recapitalize banks, there are two constraints. First, share offerings will have to be limited, for reasons outlined earlier in this chapter. Banks are not in financial condition to withstand a large-scale withdrawal of funds by depositors who wished to shift their financial assets out of savings deposits into stocks. Second, many money-losing enterprises, which are in arrears on their debt to banks, may not be able to issue equity. As noted in chapter 2, under regulations of the Chinese Securities Regulatory Commission, companies must be profitable for three years prior to their initial public offering. Even if this regulation were to be eliminated, it seems unlikely that the public would be willing to invest in state-owned firms with negative profits and, in many cases, negative net worth.

In market economies start-up companies in high technology industries frequently are able to sell shares to the public, despite the fact that they have no earnings and in some cases even very little sales. But the situation of money-losing firms in China differs in at least two fundamental respects. First, these firms are predominantly in heavy manufacturing and industrial processing. Nobody realistically expects any of these firms to be the world's next computer software or telecommunications company that will eventually reward investors in the initial public offering with extraordinarily high returns. A second difference is that while start-up firms may have no earnings, their balance sheets are not stuffed with enormous liabilities in the form of obligations to banks and unfunded pensions. For all these reasons money-losing state-owned enterprises are not likely to be able to raise a significant amount of capital on domestic equity markets.

What about foreign markets? Many observers expect that the Hong Kong market will be a major source of capital for the privatization of China's state-owned sector. Through the end of August 1997 Chinese companies had raised U.S.$13.5 billion on international equity markets. These listings include "H-share" offerings in Hong Kong, "N-share" offerings in New York, and "S-share" offerings in Singapore. In addition, Hong Kong companies that control assets in China, known as "Red Chips," by mid-1997 had raised an additional U.S.$12 billion in share offerings and rights issues, part of which had been injected into China.[81]

The largest ever Red Chip offering, China Telecom (Hong Kong) Limited, raised over U.S.$4 billion in late 1997 in shares sold in Hong Kong and New York. China Telecom, which was not even incorporated until September 1997, was created to become the primary vehicle for the Chinese Ministry of Posts and Telecommunications (MPT) to gain access to international capital markets. At the time of the initial public offering China Telecom's only asset was a controlling ownership interest in the cellular telephone networks of the MPT in Guangdong and Zhejiang Provinces.

Many features of this offering, however, suggest why it is not a model for debt-ridden, money-losing, state-owned enterprises.[82] First, China Telecom (Hong Kong) Limited is highly profitable, in absolute terms and as measured by net income relative to operating revenue.[83] Net income rose from RMB 2.8 billion on operating revenues of RMB 4.59 billion in 1994 to RMB 4.5 billion on operating revenues of RMB 10.4 billion in 1996. Second, the company's balance sheet is quite strong. The net worth of the company rose from RMB 5.0 billion in 1994 to RMB 12.5 billion at year-end 1996 and then to RMB 18.3 billion by May 1997.[84] The company, moreover, has a near monopoly on mobile phone service in Guangdong and Zhejiang, the two provinces in which it operates. The number of subscribers jumped from under 600,000 at year-end 1994 to more than 2.6 million by May 31, 1997, when the company enjoyed a market share of 98.4 percent.

Finally, the MPT has made two critical pledges that vastly enhanced the initial market value of China Telecom. The MPT pledged not to participate, directly or indirectly, in the provision of cellular telecommunications services in Guangdong, Zhejiang, or in any other province in which the company might operate in the future. The company thereby has the ability to maintain an extremely strong market position in two of China's richest and fastest growing provinces and the possibility to expand its franchise to other provinces.[85] The MPT also has pledged that China Telecom will be "the only cellular telecommunications services company operating in mainland China under its control that will be listed on any securities exchange in Hong Kong or outside China."[86] Given the prohibition on foreign ownership of Chinese telecommunications operating companies, that effectively makes China Telecom, a Hong Kong registered company, the only investment vehicle for foreigners who want to invest in the world's third largest and fastest growing cellular telephone market.

The conclusion is that while the listing of Chinese state-owned companies on the Shanghai, Shenzhen, Hong Kong, and other foreign stock markets is likely to accelerate, there is little prospect either that the regulatory authorities will approve the sale of heavily indebted money-losing firms or that there would be a market for such firms if the regulatory requirements were not relevant or could be waived.

What about the sale of land use rights or housing owned by state-owned enterprises? The value of these assets, which the World Bank estimated to be about RMB 5 trillion in 1995, is not usually reflected on the balance sheets of firms, probably because historically there was no market for these assets.[87] But in recent years markets for land use rights and housing have emerged in many parts of China.[88] Could state-owned enterprises use proceeds from the sale of these assets to repay outstanding loans to banks? This seems a particularly attractive option because even money-losing enterprises frequently have extremely valuable land use rights and substantial housing stocks.

Two problems present themselves. First, the banks need to be recapitalized in the short run while the value of land use rights and housing can only be realized over time. The combined value of financial assets of households and firms in 1995 was only about RMB 5 trillion, suggesting that if land use rights and housing were all dumped on the market the proceeds from their sale would be substantially less than RMB 5 trillion.[89] Second, as noted in chapter 2, over time the proceeds from the sale of these assets are estimated by the World Bank to be roughly sufficient to cover the unfunded pension obligations of state enterprises. In short, if the value of the off-balance sheet assets of firms is used to cover the liabilities of these firms to banks, which are on the balance sheet, then some other means must be found to finance the implicit pension debt of state-owned enterprises. Using the property assets to reduce the burden of bank recapitalization would not be a net improvement unless the state is willing to contemplate a wholesale default on its pension obligations to workers.

The upshot is that China's recapitalization of its banks must include a substantial injection of fresh capital.[90] In principle, the cost of this injection could be borne by either the treasury or the central bank. The usual prescription is that when possible the injection of funds into a commercial banking system be financed by a reduction in the net worth of the central bank. This is possible when a country's central bank has high levels of capital, primarily noninterest-bearing monetary liabilities, and significant foreign exchange reserves. When this is not the case, the cost of injecting fresh capital into the banking system must be borne by the treasury.[91]

The ability of the People's Bank of China to absorb the losses of the largest state-owned banks is limited by its own financial weakness, as reflected in both the asset and liability sides of the bank's balance sheet. The principal asset of most central banks is government bonds. These pay a fixed rate of interest and are backed by the full faith and credit of the central government. In contrast, the People's Bank of China holds no significant amount of government bonds. Its chief asset is loans, the vast majority of which were extended initially to the specialized banks and since 1993 increasingly to the new policy banks, particularly the Agricultural Development Bank. From the mid-1980s through 1993 these loans on average constituted more than three-quarters of the central bank's assets. After the tightening of credit that began in 1993, the growth of central bank lending slowed dramatically. At year-end 1996, however, the central bank's loans to financial institutions stood at RMB 1.5 trillion, which was equal to just over half of its assets.[92] Since the ultimate borrowers of the funds the central bank has lent to other financial institutions all too frequently are unable to repay the loans, many of these loans will need to be written off.

The liability side of the People's Bank balance sheet also compares unfavorably with most central banks. The largest liability of central banks traditionally is currency issued. Holders of currency receive no interest, making this an ideal liability for a financial institution. But the single largest liability of the People's Bank, accounting for over one-half of total liabilities, is the required and excess reserves placed by state-owned and commercial banks with the central bank.[93] The central bank pays interest on all of these reserves. By contrast most central banks pay no interest on the reserves they require commercial banks to maintain.[94]

In short, as a consequence of two decades of supporting excess bank lending to the state-owned sector, China's central bank financially is weak. Its single largest holding, accounting for over half of total assets, is of dubious quality and, unlike many other central banks, it pays interest on its principal financial liability. Thus the cost of injecting fresh capital into the large banks is more logically borne by the treasury rather than the central bank.

Based on the analysis of the magnitude of acknowledged nonperforming loans in chapter 3, it is clear that recapitalization of China's banks is far beyond the capacity of the state to finance from current tax revenues. In 1996 the annual revenues accruing to all levels of the Chinese government combined were just under 11 percent of gross domestic product.[95] The government would be unable to allocate more than a small portion of these current revenues to refinance the banks and, in any case, the injection of capital required to restore the banks to solvency far exceeds 11 percent of gross domestic product.

Therefore, China's best option is probably to follow the course pursued by several transition economies in eastern Europe and inject government bonds in an amount equal to the value of the nonperforming loans being written off. This is usually called a bond-bad debt swap. It differs from the proposed injection of paper assets already dismissed in one critical respect—the bonds would be a real asset. Since the bonds would pay interest, an injection of bonds would provide the banks with an income earning asset. Moreover, over a period of time the bonds could be sold on the secondary market, making the value of the injection quite transparent. Thus the injection of bonds would give the banks a measurable asset and an obvious source of income that could be used to pay interest to household savers. As a result the likelihood of a loss of public confidence and resulting run on the banks would be reduced significantly.

What would be the fiscal cost of such an injection? The answer depends only on two variables: the magnitude of the loans to be written off and the interest rate the state would pay on the bonds. Table 4-2 summarizes several alternatives for both variables, assuming recapitalization was based on reported nonperforming loans outstanding at the end of 1995 and had occurred in late 1995 or in 1996. The amounts to be written off range from 17 percent to 35 percent of gross domestic product. The lowest estimate is based on the assumptions that the entire amount of the reported 22 percent of nonperforming loans of the four largest state banks at year-end 1995 has to be written off and that this amount accounts for 90 percent of the nonperforming loans of all financial institutions.[96] The intermediate estimate, in which the required recapitalization is equal to 25 percent of gross domestic product, assumes that in addition to their nonperforming loans the four largest state-owned banks also have other nonperforming assets that need to be written off and that other banks

Table 4-2. Alternative Estimates of the Annual Cost of Bank Recapitalization at Year-End 1995

Percent of gross domestic product

If the annual interest rate is (percent)	*If total recapitalization as a percent of GDP is*		
	17	25	35
10	1.7	2.5	3.5
12	2.0	3.0	4.2
14	2.4	3.5	4.9

Source: See text.

and nonbank financial institutions also have nonperforming loans greater than the relatively small amount implicit in the lowest estimate. The other nonperforming assets of banks may include investments in subsidiary financial institutions, various types of trust transactions, as well as credits disguised on the banks' balance sheets as "other items." The intermediate estimate is consistent with the view that the share of nonperforming loans of nonbank financial institutions, such as trust and investment companies and credit cooperatives, is at least as high as in the largest state banks.[97] The highest alternative estimate, with recapitalization equal to 35 percent of gross domestic product, assumes that the acknowledged portion of nonperforming loans is an underestimate and that financial institutions of all types have significant nonperforming assets other than loans.[98]

The highest estimate is consistent with the pattern of losses in other countries that have experienced systemic banking problems. In such crises "external auditors' estimates of losses are almost always double those of the bank management; bank inspectors' estimates are at least double those of the auditors; and final losses on liquidation are double those estimated by the bank inspectors."[99] The highest alternative, which only increases the estimates of the management of Chinese banks by about three-fifths, certainly cannot be ruled out since, as discussed in chapter 3, none of China's major state-owned banks is subject to credible audits. Furthermore, the procedures Chinese banks use to classify loans are quite lax by international standards. In particular, the combination of a loan classification scheme based entirely on failure to repay principal, rather than the failure to make interest payments, as well as the practices of routinely rolling over loans when they are due and accruing interest on nonperforming loans, almost certainly makes it difficult for lenders to identify with confidence all dodgy loans.

There are potentially substantial costs to succumbing to the natural tendency of reducing the cost of bank recapitalization by underestimating the magnitude of nonperforming loans or by overestimating the amount that ultimately can be recovered from borrowers. The experience of transition economies in eastern Europe suggests the key pitfall of recapitalization is the failure to recapitalize adequately. When recapitalization is inadequate to restore banks to financial health it can erode the credibility of the government's claim that there will be no further bailouts.[100] Partial recapitalizations, as in the Hungarian case, could have undermined the incentive for a change in bank behavior going forward by increasing the possibility of future recapitalizations.

Responsibility for recovery of bad debts can be vested in a single institution, as in the case of the Resolution Trust Corporation in the United States. Or it can be the responsibility of the individual banks, which would retain ownership of the nonperforming loans after they were recapitalized. The latter approach was used in Poland. Debt workout by banks is most effective when "banks have sufficient skills and resources to deal with their problems" and when the restructuring of loans is limited to "case by case resolutions that have little economy-wide impact."[101] Since neither of these conditions applies in China, the preferred approach to bank recapitalization is to fully compensate banks for their nonperforming loans and to move these loans into a centralized asset recovery agency. This agency can concentrate the limited human skills and other resources available for debt recovery in a single institution. Funds that are recovered could be used to buy back a part of the government debt injected into the banks, reducing the ongoing interest cost of the bank recapitalization program.

Estimates of the cost of bank recapitalization in China assume that the state should pay a market-determined rate of interest on bonds placed with the banks and that limitations on the marketability of the bonds be held to a minimum, so as not to impair their value.[102] Anything less than market-determined terms would undermine confidence in the recapitalization. In the middle of 1996 the Ministry of Finance sold a RMB 24.92 billion issue of ten-year treasury bonds that yielded 11.82 percent.[103] Since the interest rate was determined by an auction, it appears that it represented a market rate. Unlike some bonds sold earlier in 1996, for which the Ministry of Finance did not allow secondary trading, there were only the most modest restrictions placed on the marketability of this ten-year bond. Active trading of the bonds on the Shanghai Stock Exchange began on July 12, one month after the placement of the issue was complete.[104] Thus the baseline estimate of the cost of bank recapitalization assumes an interest rate of 12 percent, which can be seen in table 4-2. The higher rate, 14 percent, can be taken as representative of the rate that might have prevailed at the end of 1995, when inflation was higher than at mid-year 1996. The lower rate of 10 percent might be relevant for recapitalization later in 1996 since inflation was moderating during the first part of 1996 and expectations for future inflation presumably were falling.

The combination of the three alternative estimates of the magnitude of loans to be written off and the three alternative estimates of the interest rate that the state would have had to pay on the bonds placed with the banks yields an estimated initial annual fiscal cost to the state of recapitalizing the banks at the end of 1995 of from 1.7 percent to 4.9 percent of gross domestic product. Based on the factors discussed above, the most likely annual cost would have been between 3.0 and 4.2 percent, based on write-offs of from 25 to 35 percent and an interest rate of 12 percent. It is important to remember that this interest is not a one-time expense but must be paid on an ongoing basis. But as the economy grew over time the fixed interest expenditure would decline as a percent of gross domestic product.

These estimates generally are higher than the cost of recapitalizing banks in eastern Europe. The estimated annual interest cost of recapitalizing banks in 1992 as a percent of gross domestic product was 0.6 percent for Poland, 2.1 percent for Hungary, and 2.8 percent for Czechoslovakia. The lower cost in eastern Europe is not due to a smaller portion of nonperforming loans. The estimates assumed that 30 percent of all loans to enterprises would have to be written off, similar to the proportion of likely write-offs in China. Nor is it due to a lower assumed interest rate. Indeed, the assumed interest rates, on average, were somewhat higher in eastern Europe, largely because inflation was higher. The somewhat lower overall estimated cost of recapitalizing banks in eastern Europe is largely because loans outstanding were a much smaller share of gross domestic product than in China. In Poland, for example, they were only about one-fifth of

GDP. Only Czechoslovakia, with a ratio of almost three-quarters, approached the Chinese level.[105]

Fiscal Implications

The fiscal implications of bank recapitalization are greater than the annual allocation of from 3.0 to 4.2 percent of gross domestic product to pay interest on the bonds injected into the banks as part of their recapitalization. A precondition for the ultimate success of the financial reform package is that enterprises be subject to hard budget constraints and that their continued operation depend on their bottom line financial performance. But that, in turn, is a rational approach only if enterprises are absolved of all of their quasi-fiscal expenditures. Thus the state, in evaluating its needs for increased fiscal revenues, must consider not only the annual interest payable on the bonds given to the banks but also the need to finance the portion of social expenditures currently borne by enterprises that should be financed from the government budget. Furthermore, the state also needs to finance its existing explicit government budget deficit. What would these fiscal demands amount to cumulatively and how large a share of these would have to financed from an increase in tax revenues?

The magnitude of social expenditures that are undertaken by enterprises is suggested by World Bank research on enterprise reform. Surveys in 1994 and 1995 showed that the expenditures of state-owned industrial enterprises on social programs averaged 7.6 percent of sales revenues. This is the equivalent of 3.3 percent of gross domestic product.[106] Employees in state-owned industrial enterprises account for only one-third of all state employees. Taking this into account and making certain other crude assumptions, total social expenditures financed by enterprises that should be shifted to fiscal financing might amount to 3.3 percent of gross domestic product.[107]

Finally, the government needs to take into account the need to finance its ongoing budget deficit. As already noted, the explicit annual deficit is relatively small since the banks, through loans to state-owned enterprises, have financed an increasing volume of quasi-fiscal expenditures in recent years. Nonetheless, in 1995 the budget deficit was 1.7 percent of gross domestic product.[108]

The sum of the three items just analyzed is from 8.0 to 9.2 percent of gross domestic product, approaching the 1995 levels of consolidated government expenditure. Almost doubling tax revenues within a short period of time is beyond the fiscal capacity of virtually all states, suggesting that the prospects for implementing the reform program outlined in this chapter are vanishingly small, even if the political leadership was willing to take the risks associated with the underlying industrial restructuring. That conclusion needs to be modified in three respects. First, China's tax share of gross domestic product is well under half that of the average of other developing economies.[109] Thus doubling expenditures undertaken within the scope of the government budget would leave China well within the realm of experience of other emerging markets. The tax reforms China initiated in 1994 have begun to increase government revenues relative to output. Revenues rose slightly relative to output in 1996 and more strongly in 1997, suggesting that the long-term decline in the tax share of gross domestic product that began in 1978 is now being reversed.[110] Improvements in tax administration, particularly increasing taxes on the rather lightly taxed nonstate sector of the economy, could raise tax revenues further relative to gross domestic product.

Second, revenues actually collected by various levels of government are far in excess of the 10 to 11 percent of gross domestic product reflected on the expenditure side of the state budget. A large part of these funds are classified as extrabudgetary revenue and do not come under the system of expenditure control of the Ministry of Finance. Allocation of these extrabudgetary funds is at the discretion of various central government ministries, provincial and local governments, enterprises, and so forth. As recently as 1992 extrabudgetary expenditures exceeded RMB 360 billion, with about RMB 160 billion controlled at the central level and another RMB 200 billion locally. These funds amounted to more than four-fifths of budget expenditures and 15 percent of gross domestic product in 1992.[111] In 1993 extrabudgetary funds dropped by almost RMB 250 billion, largely because depreciation was removed from the category of extrabudgetary funds. These funds, however, continued to accrue to, and be spent by, enterprises. They slipped into the category of extra-extrabudgetary funds, even one more level removed from expenditure controls. In short, the challenge for the central government is not so much to increase revenue collection as to gain control of a portion of the extrabudgetary and extra-extrabudgetary funds that are already being collected.

Third, a portion of the needed increase in fiscal revenues could be financed by selling even more government bonds rather than from an increase in tax revenues. What is the rate at which new debt could be issued, even after the recapitalization of the banks dramatically increased the stock of government debt? The answer is given by the concept of sustainable debt. The idea underlying this concept is simple. As long as the ratio of debt to gross domestic product is not rising, a moderate level of government debt is likely to be sustainable. On the other hand, a rising ratio is unsustainable because it signals to investors that the government is not able to finance its expenditure program, leading to the likelihood that sooner or later it will be forced to borrow funds from the central bank, that is, print money. That, in turn, is likely to generate more inflation. The expectation of rising inflation is certain to undermine the willingness of the public to voluntarily increase its holdings of government bonds. More accurately, to make the public willing to hold an ever-increasing stock of government bonds relative to gross domestic product, the government would have to offer an ever higher interest rate to offset the expected erosion in the value of government bonds owing to rising inflation. Eventually the crushing burden of rising interest payments on the debt would make it impossible for the government to sustain a rising debt burden.

China has two unusual advantages compared with most states that have gone through systemic bank crises. First, its existing ratio of government debt to output is quite low. Because government bond sales initially were quite modest when they began in 1981 and increased to significant levels starting only in 1994, the total stock outstanding of domestic government debt at year-end 1996 was RMB 426.5 billion, only 6.3 percent of gross domestic output.[112] A hypothetical recapitalization of the banks in 1996 that involved placing government bonds with the banks valued at 25 or 35 percent of gross domestic product, would put the stock of outstanding government debt after the recapitalization at about 30 or 40 percent of output. By comparison in Hungary between 1992 and 1993 the government issued domestic debt equivalent to 9.1 percent of gross domestic product to recapitalize the banking system, increasing the total stock of domestic government debt to an amount equal to 90.2 percent of gross domestic product.[113] Japan's domestic debt was expected to reach 100 percent by year-end 1997.[114] Such high levels of domestic debt inevitably impose substantial constraints on the conduct of fiscal policy. For example, in Japan high domestic debt was a major factor constraining the ability of the government to assist in the rescue of failing financial institutions in the 1990s.

Second, China's economic growth is well above average. If it could sustain growth at a relatively high level after bank recapitalization, it could sell considerable additional debt to finance the interest payments on the bonds injected into the banks. The reason is that if interest payments on the higher stock of government debt were financed by selling even more bonds, the stock of debt would grow at a rate equal to the interest rate on government bonds.[115] For example, if government bonds outstanding were equal to 30 or 40 percent of gross domestic product and the real interest rate was 6 percent, the annual real interest cost of financing the debt would be 1.8 or 2.4 percent of the output of the economy. But if the economy were growing at 6 percent, then the ratio of government debt to output would be constant. More generally, if the economy is growing at a rate at least equal to the real interest rate, the stock of government debt relative to gross domestic product will not rise and the debt is said to be sustainable, even if interest payments on the debt are financed by issuing more debt.

If China is able to sustain a real growth rate of 8 percent and the real interest rate on government bonds were to average 6 percent, it could finance about half of the increased expenditure needs outlined above from the sale of additional debt on an ongoing basis without increasing the ratio of debt to gross domestic product.[116] That means the increased tax revenues needed to finance bank recapitalization and related expenditures would be only 3.0 or 3.6 percentage points of gross domestic product, depending on whether bank recapitalization was the equivalent of 25 or 35 percent of gross domestic product. Of course, if the needed recapitalization was less than 25 or more than 35 percent of gross domestic product, the increase in expenditures financed by tax revenues required to keep the growth of debt at a sustainable level would be lower or higher.

The calculation above does not take into account that the proposed central asset recovery agency will recover some portion of the loans that are written off by the banks. The proceeds from these recoveries could be applied to reducing the stock of government debt associated with the initial write-offs, thus reducing the annual fiscal expenditure on the bank recapitalization program. To the extent the recovery program is successful, the fiscal implications of the bank recapitalization are less onerous than just estimated.

Recapitalization of the major banks, supported by a fiscal reform that provides adequate additional tax revenues, is only one step in creating a viable system of commercial banks. It addresses only the problem of the stock of accumulated nonperforming loans. In and of itself it does not address what is called the flow problem, that is, the extension of new loans not subject to commercial criteria that in the absence of other reform measures almost certainly would become nonperforming loans in the future. Thus bank recapitalization must be accompanied by changes in incentives for banks, especially the punishing taxes they currently face, and in governance structures. Without these additional steps, there is a clear risk that banks will not modify their lending behavior, leading to future demands for additional injections of capital by the government. In short, like enterprises, banks have to be subject to hard budget constraints so they will have an incentive to improve their credit management. These steps should be supplemented with strict enforcement of the provisions of the Central Bank Law and the Commercial Bank Law that make political interference in bank lending decisions a criminal offense.[117] In addition, bank supervision should be strengthened and disclosure of financial information by banks should increase. These and other objectives also will require a substantial increase in the independence of the central bank.

Competition

The most important policy tool to enforce commercial discipline on banks is to increase competition. Despite the growth of new banks, the share of the specialized banks in the financial system remains quite large and in comparative terms China's largest bank controls a huge amount of assets. For example, at year-end 1996 the assets of China's largest bank, the Industrial and Commercial Bank, were RMB 3.6 trillion, an amount equivalent to just over half of China's gross domestic product in the same year. The assets of the China Construction Bank, the second largest, were RMB 2.1 trillion, 30 percent of gross domestic product. Even by the standards of Asia's bank-dominated financial systems, China's largest banks account for an unusually high share of credit creation. Malaysia's biggest lender, Malayan Banking, in 1997 had assets of under 40 percent of gross domestic product. For the biggest Thai bank, Bangkok Bank, the ratio was 25 percent. In contrast, the biggest bank in the United States, Chase Manhattan, controls assets equal to only 4 percent of gross domestic product.[118] Thus China appears to be an extreme example of the Asian pattern where a few banks loom very large on the financial landscape and competition is thus somewhat limited.

All possible steps to increase competition should be pursued. First, the People's Bank of China should allow those banks, created since reform began, that have accumulated sufficient experience in evaluating credit risk to expand their operations more rapidly once the recapitalization of major state banks has created a more level playing field. These banks are more likely to be stronger institutions, such as Everbright Bank, Merchants Bank, Minsheng Bank, Bank of Communications, and CITIC Industrial Bank, rather than weak institutions such as Huaxia Bank. As noted in chapter 3, the People's Bank has restricted the development of these new banks' branch networks, in part to protect the large state-owned banks.

Second, the central bank should allow foreign banks and other foreign financial institutions gradually to expand their domestic currency business by easing the geographic and other constraints it imposed on the handful of foreign banks it allowed to enter the domestic currency business in 1997. The central bank should allow foreign financial institutions broad access to the renminbi lending market by easing the prevailing geographic and client restrictions. Initially the funding of foreign financial institutions could continue to be through the interbank market for shorter-term funds. They should be allowed to sell domestic bonds to Chinese financial institutions to finance longer-term lending. Within a relatively short period of time, perhaps two to three years, the central bank should allow foreign banks to take renminbi deposits directly from Chinese enterprises and institutions as well as the public. This approach, which liberalizes most rapidly on the lending side, takes immediate advantage of the ability of foreign financial institutions to assess credit risk while giving domestic institutions a brief interlude before they would have to compete on the deposit-taking side of the banking business.

Third, the state should allow the creation of genuinely private banks. These new institutions should be subject to an appropriate minimum capital requirement and standards that ensure their independent control and management. This is especially important to avoid the situation emerging in Russia in which many new banks are thinly capitalized and controlled by enterprises with which much of their business is conducted.[119]

Fourth, foreign banks and other institutions should be allowed to buy shares of existing banks, regardless of whether they are publicly or privately owned. The Asian Development Bank's purchase of a small stake in the Everbright Bank in 1997 is a promising precedent. Besides its purchase of shares in Everbright Bank, the Asian Development Bank has launched a technical assistance program "to strengthen the EBBC (Everbright Bank of China) institutionally and operationally so as to provide a role model for the commercial banking sector in general."[120] The program provides equipment and software, consulting services, and staff training.

The resulting substantial increase in competition in the banking industry will place substantial pressure on the largest state-owned banks. As currently configured they probably cannot and almost certainly should not survive. Most important, China's largest banks are grossly overstaffed and, as a result, have unusually low ratios of assets per employee.[121] For example, the Industrial and Commercial Bank at year-end 1996 had assets per employee that were the equivalent of only U.S.$750,000. The similarly sized Hongkong Bank had assets per employee five times that level. The Construction Bank had assets per employee of only one-fifth that of similarly sized BankAmerica. Largely as a result of massive overstaffing, the costs of China's largest state-owned banks in 1996 absorbed an amazing 86 percent of their income. This is the highest ratio of costs to income in 40 countries for which *The Banker* calculated such data.[122]

Regulations should impose no institutional impediments to substantial staff reductions or to reorganizations, including the break-up of the existing large banks, in response to increased competition. The possibilities range from simply accelerating the slight consolidation of subbranches and lower-level bank offices that began in 1996, to the sale of some subbranches or offices to smaller more recently created banks, to even more drastic reorganizations, such as the privatization of state-owned banks.[123]

The experience of eastern Europe again is relevant. Hungary began its transition with insolvent state-owned banks. After banks were recapitalized through a combination of government injections of capital and a modest amount of debt-equity swaps, however, the banks emerged with substantially improved balance sheets, paving the way for their privatization. By the end of 1996 almost the entire banking system had been privatized. Although the state retained a large minority interest in the National Savings Bank, direct state ownership of all banks averaged only 5 percent.[124] Banks have capital adequacy ratios above 8 percent and, with the exception of four small banks, are profitable. The Organization for Economic Cooperation and Development considers Hungary's banking sector to be "among the healthiest in Central and Eastern Europe."[125]

Bank Supervision and Prudential Regulation

Simultaneously, banking supervision must be further strengthened. For example, all banks must be subject to stringent external audits, and criteria for classifying loans as nonperforming must be brought into compliance with international standards. In particular, classification should be based on failure to make interest payments on a timely basis rather than being tied entirely to repayment of principal. China's system of loan loss reserves also needs to be overhauled so that the magnitude of reserves banks are required to set aside is linked directly to the quality of each bank's loan portfolio rather than set at some arbitrary low percent of total loans. The international practice, and the practice in other transition economies, of requiring 20, 50, and 100 percent reserves for past due, doubtful, and bad loans, respectively, should be adopted.[126]

Ultimately a competitive market can provide the most effective discipline of banks. But, as the Bank for International Settlements and others have pointed out, this depends critically on transparency. Most Chinese banks fall short of meeting this standard. For example, among the four largest state-owned banks, only the Bank of China discloses information on the quality of its loan portfolio and the magnitude of nonperforming loans written off annually. And, again except for the Bank of China, the largest state-owned banks do not present their balance sheets on a consolidated basis, allowing them to bury financial losses in their subsidiaries. More generally, both profit and loss statements and the balance sheets of most banks are presented on such an aggregated basis that it is difficult to evaluate their true financial condition.

Interest Rate Liberalization

A key step in the sequence of reforms outlined here is the simultaneous gradual liberalization of interest rates and the eventual complete phasing out of the credit plan. The system prevailing in the first two decades of reform, in which lending rates were fixed by the central bank and adjusted very slowly, guarantees that excess demand for funds emerges strongly whenever inflation rises, causing falling and sometimes even negative real interest rates. That necessitates the administrative allocation of limited credit resources, creating the potential for enormous corruption. Privileged firms, most often state owned, that are allocated funds may find it more profitable to on-lend them at higher interest rates in informal credit markets rather than using the funds themselves. Although the informal credit markets may facilitate the flow of funds to higher-return investments of borrowers who do not have access to bank credit, this has unfortunate side effects. The implicit subsidy to the initial preferred borrower is often converted into illegal private income that accrues to individuals in the borrowing firm who are able to place the funds in the curb or informal credit market. And depositors lose because the artificially low interest rate the banks charge on loans ultimately is financed by unusually low rates of interest that banks offer to households on their savings.

Interest rate liberalization, however, must be carefully coordinated with other elements of the financial reform package. In particular, premature liberalization of deposit rates could undermine the goal of requiring banks to operate on commercial terms. Without a prior or simultaneous freeing of lending rates, freeing deposit rates would result in a substantial squeeze on bank margins, drastically reducing their already low level of profits. Since freeing lending rates on average would raise the rates paid by borrowers, that step cannot be taken prior to the transformation of the relationship between banks and state-owned enterprises.

Ending Confiscatory Taxation of Banks

A successful financial reform package for China must contain several other components. Among the most important is a reduction in the confiscatory taxes that the state currently levies on its largest banks. Historically the Ministry of Finance has fiercely resisted reductions in bank taxation, in part because banks have been such an important source of revenue for the central government. In the mid-1990s about one-sixth of central government revenues was derived from the taxes paid by the four specialized banks.[127] Confiscatory taxation is a function of two features of the tax system. First, reported earnings of banks are vastly overstated. As discussed in chapter 3, taxable income is overstated since the Ministry of Finance does not allow banks to provision sufficiently against nonperforming loans and because it requires banks to accrue interest on nonperforming loans for three years. For any given nominal tax rate, the overstatement results in a higher effective rate of taxation on the "real" income of the banks. Second, as noted in chapter 3, China's largest banks are required to pay significant taxes and surtaxes on their gross income. These business taxes and surtaxes were levied at a combined rate of 5.5 percent through the end of 1996. Since these are levied on gross income from interest and fees, rather than on operating earnings or pre-tax profits, they impose a very heavy tax burden.[128] In most years, the value of these taxes actually exceeds by a substantial margin the amount the banks pay in income taxes, which through 1996 were levied at a 55 percent rate. For example, the Agricultural Bank of China in 1995 paid business taxes that were more than twice their income taxes.[129]

One way of measuring the overall tax burden is to assume the business tax and surtaxes were abolished but that the state collected the same total amount of taxes from banks by levying an appropriately higher rate of income tax on the sum of reported pre-tax profits plus the amount paid in business taxes and surtaxes. The appropriately higher rate is the rate that, when levied on the true pre-tax

Table 4-3. Effective Tax Rates on China's Largest Banks, 1995

Percent of earnings

Industrial and Commercial Bank	83.8
Bank of China	74.1
Agricultural Bank of China	78.7
Construction Bank of China	72.8

Source: *Almanac of China's Finance and Banking 1996*, pp. 482–84.

Note: Effective rates of taxation are calculated as total tax payments divided into pre-tax profits. Total tax payments are the sum of business taxes and income taxes. Pre-tax profits are the sum of reported pre-tax profits and business taxes, which are treated as an above-the-line item in the profit and loss statements of Chinese banks.

income, produces the same tax revenue. These rates, shown in table 4-3, confirm the confiscatory nature of taxes levied on China's largest banks. The rates range from a low of 73 percent, in the case of the Construction Bank of China, to as high as 84 percent, in the case of the Industrial and Commercial Bank. And these rates make no allowance for the fact that part of the income reported by Chinese banks is phantom, owing to the accrual requirement.

In 1997 the Ministry of Finance reduced the income tax rate it levied on China's four largest state-owned banks to 33 percent, seemingly an important step in reducing the confiscatory taxes paid by the Industrial and Commercial Bank and other large banks.[130] Unfortunately, at the same time the Ministry of Finance raised the business tax rate these institutions face to 8 percent, effectively obviating the effect of reducing the income tax rate.[131] Indeed, for financial institutions with relatively low profits, the combination of a lower rate of taxation on profits and a higher rate of taxes on gross business income increased, rather than decreased, their total tax burden.[132]

It is extremely unlikely that China's four major banks, even after they were recapitalized, could operate on a commercial basis if they continued to face these confiscatory rates of taxation; they would be unable to add sufficiently to their capital as their businesses grew. As a result their capital adequacy would shrink and within a few years they would require another injection of fresh capital. If the need for such an injection is only a matter of time, it seriously undercuts incentives for the banks to operate on commercial terms. In short, current rates of taxation are not viable since they are so high that they effectively deplete the capital of the banks.

In addition, it is important that the financial reform package unify the tax rates faced by different categories of banks. In the mid-1990s the tax rates on financial institutions varied considerably. The heavy tax burden borne by the four major state-owned banks has just been analyzed. At the other end of the spectrum the three policy banks created in 1994, which are discussed further below, are entirely exempt from payment of the business tax and have been granted a five-year waiver on the payment of any taxes on their income. In between these two extremes are the banks created since reform began and foreign banks operating in China. The former appear not to pay business taxes and face an income tax rate of 33 percent.[133] The latter face an income tax rate of only 15 percent.[134]

Moving toward an efficient commercial banking system characterized by competitive pricing of loans and deposits requires that all banks face a uniform tax regime. To the extent there is a case for special financial treatment of the policy banks created in 1994, it should be provided through transparent fiscal subsidies, rather than differential rates of taxation.

Independence of the Central Bank

It is difficult to judge the extent to which the People's Bank of China is developing sufficient independence to carry out its role effectively. For the foreseeable future China is unlikely to develop a central bank with the degree of independence of the Federal Reserve in the United States. But considerable autonomy vis à vis other ministerial level units under the State Council in Beijing, as well as vis à vis party and government leaders in the provinces, is essential if the central bank is to exercise effective prudential supervision of banks and other financial institutions. In particular the central bank must have sufficient independence and political power to achieve two objectives. First, it must be able to insulate banks from demands from political leaders to extend loans to projects that do not meet commercial lending standards. Second, it must ensure that any subsidies for policy lending are financed through the budget, rather than borne by the banking system.

What is clear is that at the beginning of the reform process the central bank had little independent power. It had been a separate entity under the State Council, putting it on a par with the Ministry of Finance and the planning agencies, during the First Five-Year Plan (1953–57). But from the beginning of the Great Leap Forward in 1958 through the mid-1970s, the People's Bank of China bureaucratically was subordinate to the Ministry of Finance, reflecting the fact that there was very little separation of banking and fiscal operations of the government during those years. The overriding objective of the bank was to facilitate the production goals that were laid out in annual economic plans. Consequently the People's Bank granted credit virtually automatically to state-owned firms and was little concerned with repayment.[135]

Moreover, the provincial branches of the People's Bank were subordinate to local government and party officials. Provincial Party Committees or, during the Cultural Revolution, Provincial Revolutionary Committees, had the power of appointment, dismissal, transfer, and promotion of personnel of banks operating within their geographic jurisdictions. Not surprisingly, this weakened the ability of the People's Bank headquarters to effectively monitor its branches at the local level.[136] These branches were not selective in the extension of credit but rather were responsive to requests by local Communist Party officials. Because of political interference in lending they were not able to exert much pressure on enterprises that failed to repay their borrowings.[137]

In short, when the People's Bank was separated from the Ministry of Finance in 1976, it was a weak institution. This situation appears to have changed little in the first decade of reform. The People's Bank sought to gain greater control of appointment of personnel in its provincial branches starting in 1979, but in retrospect it appears that little progress was made. In 1988 the People's Bank was formally vested with the power to appoint and remove provincial and lower-level People's Bank managers.[138] However, the People's Bank still was supposed to consult with the localities, which appear to have retained veto power over appointments.

Other aspects of the legal structure vesting more power in the hands of the bank also were slow to take form. The State Council in September 1983 approved in principle the separation of the commercial and central bank functions of the People's Bank. Although the People's Bank assumed the responsibilities of a central bank effective January 1, 1984, it acquired the formal legal authority to exercise these functions only gradually. For example, provisional regulations providing a legal basis for the People's Bank's supervision, regulation, and inspection of banks and other financial institutions were not promulgated until early 1986, two years after the bank began operating.

There is little doubt that the powers of the central bank did increase in the 1990s. First, the appointment of Zhu Rongji as president of the People's Bank of China in July 1993 marked a turning point. Zhu, who already was vice premier, assumed the additional role of president of the People's Bank and thus the responsibility for bringing what was then accelerating inflation back under control. Almost immediately Zhu's position of vice premier and his forceful style gave him the authority to appoint and remove the heads of the People's Bank branches in each province and major municipality. This earned him the enmity of provincial government and party officials, who had previously counted on pliant central bank officials in their jurisdictions to ensure that adequate bank credit was available to fund their favorite enterprises and infrastructure projects.

Second, in an unprecedented move, beginning in 1994 the People's Bank refused to lend money to the Ministry of Finance to cover the state's budget deficit. Initially this refusal was an administrative decision. But it was subsequently embedded in the provisions of the Central Bank Law, passed in 1995.[139] Beginning in 1994 the Ministry of Finance had to increase substantially its sales of bonds to finance the government's budget deficit. The amount of funds required was so large that the ministry was compelled to begin to change its distribution practices. It found that it could no longer rely on coercion to place government bonds and so increasingly was forced to sell the bonds on competitive terms. As a result, it raised interest rates and sanctioned the development of a secondary market in government bonds to increase their liquidity. When the banks introduced inflation indexing on longer-term savings deposits the ministry found it increasingly difficult to sell its own bonds and, after a lag of a few months, was forced to introduce indexing on government bonds.

Third, the head office of the central bank in Beijing gained full control of People's Bank credit extended to financial institutions. Previously, provincial and lower-level branch offices of the People's Bank had discretionary power over 30 percent of central bank lending to the financial system. They were thus vulnerable to importuning by local party officials to extend credit to local branches of state banks that, in turn, would be funneled to support projects sponsored by the officials. After Zhu Rongji took over, the headquarters of People's Bank was able to recentralize authority for all People's Bank of China lending and the allocation of credit quotas.[140]

Despite this progress, the independence of the People's Bank may still fall short of the level necessary to support the transition to a commercial banking system. Although the Central Bank Law states that the People's Bank "shall independently implement monetary policies and be free from any intervention," its exercise of this power is "under the leadership of the State Council." Thus the bank necessarily is not the final authority on many significant matters. Its actions to change interest rates and reserve requirements, for example, must all be referred to the State Council for approval.[141] The bank historically has seemed to be subordinate to other central agencies. The State Planning Commission, for example, appears to have had the critical role in the formulation of the annual credit plan. The Planning Commission regarded the central bank simply as the instrument through which the plan was executed. The elimination of mandatory credit ceilings beginning in 1998 portends a change in this historic relationship but, as just discussed, it remains to be seen whether the central bank will be able to institute the use of indirect instruments of monetary control.

The central bank might be assisted in achieving greater independence through the development of a strong, independent board or policy committee. When the central bank was established in 1983 the principal policy advisory body was the bank's board of directors or council (lishihui). The chair of the board was the governor of the bank.[142] But its members included the presidents of the four large specialized banks as well as a vice minister of the Ministry of Finance.[143] To the extent that the board was a policymaking as opposed to an advisory body, the presence of representatives of these institutions appears to have been a conflict of interest. It did not enhance the ability of the central bank to maintain its independence and regulate and supervise the banking industry.

The 1995 Central Bank law makes no reference to a board of directors but called for the creation of a Monetary Policy Commission (huobi zhengce weiyuanhui) that appears to have assumed some of the functions of the previous board of directors. At its first regular meeting in July 1997 the commission focused primarily on monetary policy issues and "agreed that the country should continue its moderately-tight monetary policy."[144] In short, its functions bear some resemblance to those of the Open Market Committee of the U.S. Federal Reserve Board. The nature of the State Council's appointments to the commission was critical. Among the first appointees was the president of China's largest bank.[145] Although the number of representatives of banks on the Monetary Policy Commission is several fewer than on the old board, the presence of the president of the largest bank on the commission would not appear to contribute to developing the independence of the central bank in matters related to prudential regulation and supervision of banks.

Finally, continued direct lending by the People's Bank to industrial enterprises and other commercial activities also tends to undermine the bank's independence, which ultimately must depend on a complete separation of central and commercial banking functions. In the late 1980s and early 1990s provincial and municipal offices of the People's Bank became shareholders in newly established securities firms. In a few cases these securities firms were owned solely by provincial branches of the central bank. The 1995 Central Bank Law specifically forbids the People's Bank of China from extending credit directly to enterprises and implicitly forbids the central bank from operating stock brokering companies.[146] Although direct lending has been curtailed, at year-end 1997 the central bank still had RMB 17 billion in loans outstanding to enterprises.[147] When the central bank remains responsible for providing directed credit to key enterprises, it undermines its authority to regulate these credits when they are extended by the specialized banks. Similarly, some provincial branches and municipal subbranches of the central bank were involved directly in the securities business as late as December 1997.[148]

Policy Banks

As part of a long-term plan to convert the specialized banks to commercial banks, the State Council in 1994 approved the creation of three new policy banks—the State Development Bank of China, the Import-Export Bank of China, and the Agricultural Development Bank of China. These new institutions were to provide financing for policy-oriented projects identified in the state's development plan or in its industrial policies for specific sectors. Once policy lending was assumed by these new institutions, the four existing large state-owned banks were to become responsible for their own profits and losses. Initially, it was envisaged that this commercialization of the large existing banks would be made possible by transferring existing policy loans to the new policy banks. Although it was never discussed openly, this approach would have required the state to inject other assets into the specialized banks. Otherwise their insolvency would be transparent since their obligations to depositors would remain on their books whereas their principal asset, policy loans outstanding to enterprises, would shrink dramatically. This presumably is one reason that most of these existing policy loans have not been transferred.

The State Development Bank's registered capital of RMB 50 billion is the largest of these new institutions. Its main purpose is to finance long-term infrastructure projects and strategic or "pillar" industries.[149] Particularly for these industries, the expectation was that loans would be extended at below-market interest rates.

Although the Agricultural Development Bank's registered capital is only RMB 20 billion, it quickly became the largest lender of the new policy banks. Its primary role is to provide short-term credit to state agencies responsible for the procurement of agricultural products, but it also provides funds for projects that assist the poor in rural areas as well as general agricultural development projects.

The Import-Export Bank, the smallest of the new institutions, was created primarily to provide export sellers' credit to promote the international sale of Chinese goods, particularly electrical machinery and equipment. But it also provides guarantees of export buyers' credit and export credit insurance. Finally, the bank has assumed the responsibility for handling the concessionary loans that China receives from most industrialized countries and the concessionary loans that China makes, primarily to countries in Africa and Latin America.[150]

The lending of these new policy banks was intended to include the great majority of the policy loans or directed credits that traditionally had been extended by the specialized banks. That was to pave the way for the conversion of the specialized banks to operate on a commercial basis.

At least in the initial stage, however, the new policy banks do not appear to have contributed to the longer-term goal of creating a genuinely commercial banking system in China. One clear precondition for commercialization is the separation of policy from commercial lending. But China's new policy banks have not taken over all of the policy lending responsibilities of the specialized banks. In particular, the large state-owned banks have continued to be the principal source of increased working capital for state-owned enterprises, including those that are losing money. On any reasonable criteria these credits should be considered policy loans. And the State Development Bank has refused to take over the prior outstanding policy loans of the specialized banks. Thus the specialized banks have not been able to improve their balance sheets, an essential precondition to converting them to operate on normal commercial bank principles.

Second, and equally important, the funding for two of the three policy banks comes primarily from existing financial institutions, notably the specialized banks. The policy banks do not take deposits from the public but receive funds through state budgetary appropriations, the sale of financial bonds to other banks and to nonbank financial institutions, loans from international organizations and foreign governments, and borrowing from the central bank.

The sale of financial bonds has been the most important of these sources of funds. The State Development Bank and the Import-Export Bank sold bonds valued at RMB 77.5 billion in 1994 alone.[151] The State Development Bank sold RMB 75.8 billion in three- and five-year bonds. These were sold to the Construction Bank of China, RMB 14.8 billion; the Industrial and Commercial Bank of China, RMB 14.3 billion; the Agricultural Bank of China, RMB 8 billion, and the Bank of China, RMB 5.8 billion. Other banks and nonbank financial institutions purchased an additional RMB 32.9 billion of State Development Bank bonds.[152] The State Development Bank also received an initial RMB 9.86 billion of a five-year planned provision of RMB 50 billion in state budgetary capital, which is to form the bank's own capital;[153] an additional Ministry of Finance budgetary allocation to subsidize certain below-normal interest rate loans; a U.S.$50 million loan from a syndicate of sixteen foreign banks; and RMB 3.7 billion borrowed from the central bank. Thus, bonds were the chief source of funds for the RMB 86.2 billion in loans that the new bank made in 1994, the first year in which it operated.[154] This pattern was repeated in 1995 and 1996 when the State Development Bank sold financial bonds valued at RMB 79.7 billion and RMB 87.1 billion, respectively, all to other financial institutions.[155]

The Import-Export Bank, which has a registered capital of only RMB 3.38 billion, also depends heavily on bonds sold to financial institutions to support its lending. In 1994 it sold RMB 1.7 billion in three- and five-year bonds to the Bank of China in support of its loans of RMB 2 billion. Its only other source of funds was RMB 200 million in loans from the central bank and the provision by the Ministry of Finance of RMB 670 million, a partial payment of the bank's registered capital.[156] It stepped up its bond sales to RMB 5.7 billion in 1995 and RMB 7.0 billion in 1996, about two-thirds of which was purchased by the Bank of China.[157] Bonds remain the principal source of funds for the bank's loan portfolio, which stood at RMB 14.5 billion at year-end 1996.[158]

Only the Agricultural Development Bank does not depend heavily on the sale of bonds to other financial institutions. Although the bank did not open until November 18, 1994, by year-end its total assets had soared to RMB 420 billion, of which loans accounted for RMB 350 billion, making it China's fifth largest financial institution.[159] Its first bond sale of only RMB 10 billion was not until 1996.[160] Instead, it is almost wholly reliant on borrowing from the People's Bank to finance its rapidly growing loan portfolio.[161]

The financial bonds sold by the policy banks were not voluntarily purchased on market terms but were placed by the central bank on an obligatory basis.[162] In other words, the specialized banks were forced to buy the bonds of the policy banks. Voluntary purchases of the bonds were unlikely because the bonds paid interest rates well below the prevailing rate of inflation and, more important, also well below the rates prevailing on state treasury bonds of comparable maturity.[163] In short, the specialized banks were forced to fund the new banks on terms favorable to the latter.

Even if all policy lending had shifted to the new policy banks, this would be of limited significance as long as the specialized banks remain the ultimate source of funds for policy banks for the simple reason that the specialized banks remain exposed to the riskier projects funded by the policy banks.

Rather than relying primarily on credit extended by the People's

Bank, as is so notable in the case of the Agricultural Development Bank, or funds borrowed at artificially low rates from banks that are supposed to begin operating on a commercial basis, policy banks should be financed primarily from the sale of bonds on a voluntary basis at commercial rates. The state should shift all subsidies for policy banks, whether to compensate for loans for high priority state projects financed at below-market interest rates or for losses due to defaults on high risk projects, to state budgetary financing. These subsidies should be managed within a coherent framework for financing the consolidated government deficit through the budget rather than being borne by the central bank or state-owned banks.[164]

The State Development Bank has several other shortcomings. First, initially it had little independent capability to evaluate loan proposals. The staff of the bank came predominantly from six investment corporations of the State Planning Commission, an agency not known for placing a priority on rate of return when evaluating alternative investment projects.[165] Moreover, particularly it its first years, almost all of the lending programs of the Development Bank similarly were transferred from the State Planning Commission and were not subject to review by the Development Bank's credit committee, which nominally is supposed to approve all loans.[166] For example, in 1994 the largest category of loans, RMB 24 billion—or more than one-fourth of all loans—was for electric power projects. The planned level of loans in 1995 for electric power projects was RMB 30.3 billion, including a planned U.S.$845 million to be raised in foreign funds.[167] These projects had all been developed initially by the State Energy Investment Corporation, one of the six State Planning Commission entities absorbed by the new bank.

Conclusion

The Chinese leadership is well aware of the shortcomings of the banking and financial system that evolved in the 1980s and early 1990s. Their concerns were reflected in an important State Council document, "Decision on Reform of the Financial System," promulgated in December 1993.[168] This document was a blueprint for the establishment of a modern commercial banking system. It anticipated the separation of commercial from policy lending, the use of liability:asset ratios in place of lending quotas to regulate the lending of banks, the use of indirect instruments of monetary control, and so forth. In the following two years China adopted the Basle standard of capital adequacy for banks, passed the Central Bank Law that increased substantially the independence of the central bank and a commercial banking law insulating banks at the local level from political interference in lending decisions, and established three new policy banks to take over the policy lending of the four largest state-owned banks.

Although the foundation of a modern commercial banking system reflected in these and many other documents and decisions was well designed and reflected an acute understanding by China's leaders of underlying structural problems in the banking system, much of it has not been put in place or has not been built up to the design standard. The policy banks are thinly capitalized and thus reliant on the existing banks as their principal source of funds, precluding the true separation of policy and commercial lending. The traditional big state banks, while being told to shift their lending operations to a commercial basis, still are required to extend additional working capital loans to money-losing state firms. The headquarters of the central bank remains too weak and frequently appears unable to exercise appropriate control and prudential supervision of banks. One ultimate cause of the gap between design and implementation is the deteriorating financial performance of large parts of the state-owned sector, discussed in chapter 2.

This chapter proposes a series of closely related reforms of state enterprises, the banks, and the tax system. All three components are essential. Recapitalizing the banks will be a waste of fiscal resources if the enterprise sector is not simultaneously subject to hard budget constraints. Enforcing hard budget constraints on enterprises makes little sense if they are not first relieved of the burden of providing a broad range of social services. Subjecting a larger share of tax revenues collected to expenditure controls via the state budget is a prerequisite both for relieving enterprises of their quasi-fiscal burdens and for providing the fiscal resources needed for bank recapitalization.

The proposed reform package takes advantage of one of China's little noted economic advantages—its extraordinarily modest explicit internal debt. The recapitalization of the financial system that is a prerequisite to the true commercialization of the banking system is feasible largely because the existing stock of government debt outstanding is well under 10 percent of gross domestic product. Unless the Chinese Communist Party is willing to default on financial obligations to households, recapitalization, which simply converts an implicit government debt to an explicit one, is the only alternative.

But the reform package entails a real economic cost—paying interest on a vastly expanded stock of government debt. Unless tax revenues are raised relative to expenditures, the reform package ultimately will generate an inflationary spiral. Thus, successfully absorbing the fiscal costs of bank recapitalization necessarily will lead to a somewhat lower rate of economic growth.

The pay-offs to the reform package far outweigh the costs of slower growth during the period in which banks are recapitalized, however, not to mention the even higher ultimate costs of further delay in effectively addressing the problems of the financial sector. It creates the potential for more efficient intermediation of funds, through both a transformed banking system and expanded capital markets that a healthy banking system would facilitate. It also would allow interest rate liberalization, a precondition for the effective use of indirect instruments of monetary control to mitigate the large macroeconomic fluctuations that have marked the reform era. But perhaps most important the reform package enhances the possibility that China will be able to maintain the high rates of household savings that are necessary to sustain robust economic growth in the future.

5

Implications

A M O N G Western observers it is widely believed that the Chinese strategy of gradual economic reform pursued since the late 1970s has been successful. Economic growth has been very strong and broadly shared among all segments of the population. Income inequality has increased since the mid-1980s, but most of those people at the bottom of the income ladder continued to experience significant real income growth. At the same time the economy has been opened up, attracting record amounts of foreign capital and generating unprecedented growth of exports and imports. All of this change has been accomplished without any major sell-off of state firms or any wrenching restructuring of the economy that would have left large portions of the work force unemployed.

Some observers have suggested that this smooth transition is largely explained by China's predominantly agrarian economy. In China on the eve of reform more than 70 percent of the work force was employed in farming and less than a fifth of all workers were employed by the state. In contrast in the former Soviet Union, only an eighth of the work force was employed in farming and nine-tenths of the labor force was employed by the state.[1] Thus China's growth could be fueled in part by shifting workers out of agriculture, where output per worker was relatively low, into manufacturing and services, where output was much higher. Russian reform faced the tougher challenge of generating growth by raising productivity within manufacturing and services. This school of thought attributes China's rapid growth primarily to its initial economic structure.

A second school of thought argues that China's successful transition resulted from its gradualistic reform strategy. Although some observers recognize that state-owned firms constitute a lagging sector of the economy, they argue that China's reform strategy has allowed nonstate firms to flourish. As long as this strategy leads to a continuous decline in the relative contribution of state firms to total output, China ultimately will be transformed into a market-oriented economy capable of sustaining moderately high rates of long-term economic growth. Indeed, some members of this school of thought go further. They imply that given the high social costs and potentially adverse political consequences of rapid privatization and restructuring, the strategy China has followed has in some sense been optimal.

This book, at a minimum, shows that both of these interpretations of China's economic reform contain flaws. First, both schools clearly overstate the success of China's economic transition. This conclusion is not drawn simply because China's real growth appears to be lower than the widely quoted official statistics. More important, the combination of a rising savings rate and significant seignorage have provided the central government with financial resources that it has used to temporarily paper over deeply rooted structural problems. The true success of China's reform cannot be judged until these hidden structural problems have been addressed.

Second, the first school overstates the importance of initial conditions as a variable explaining rapid growth. It is true that part of China's growth is explained by the movement of workers out of agriculture into manufacturing and services where per worker output is higher. But this is not a decisive factor explaining the difference between Chinese and Russian economic performance. As noted in chapter 1, the World Bank estimates that this sectoral transfer of workers accounts for only one-sixth of China's growth in the reform era.[2] This is obviously a very modest factor in explaining the yawning gap between China's growth of about 8 percent a year and the marked, continuous shrinkage of output of the Russian economy since 1990.

Third, this book has shown that the strategy of gradualism has been far from optimal in economic terms. This assessment is not based on a judgment that China should have followed a strategy of rapid privatization of state-owned firms beginning in the late 1970s. Such an approach was not feasible because China lacked the legal, institutional, and governance structures to support a private-property-based economic system. Nor is it meant to suggest that an improved economic outcome required the enforcement of hard budget constraints on state-owned firms from the outset of reform, meaning all unprofitable firms quickly would be forced out of existence. That certainly would have been far from optimal and might not have led to a better economic outcome for the simple reason that some firms were losing money because of the heavy social burdens they financed from their revenues. Rather, the negative assessment of gradualism is based on the belief that resource allocation would have been more efficient if state firms had been relieved of their social burdens, through either the budget or subsidized bank credit, but then were required to compete with all other forms of ownership for fixed investment funds.[3] Under that strategy the more efficient parts of the state sector would have been able to continue to expand. But less efficient firms would not have had access to new capital for fixed investment and would have gradually shrunk as their work forces aged and retired. The state should have accelerated this process by offering generous early retirement to workers in the least efficient firms, those where the value of output sold on the market was less than the value of the inputs used up in the production process. Even if it was not possible to redeploy the physical assets of these value-subtracting firms, society as a whole would have benefited, even if the pensions of workers given early retirement were equal to their preretirement incomes. This strategy could have formed the basis for a more efficient growth path without the abrupt displacement of workers in an environment where the state had not yet developed a social safety net. The alternative growth path almost certainly would have created more new jobs for the simple reason that the systematic underpricing of capital has led to inappropriately high levels of capital intensity in production. The greater efficiency of the alternative strategy means that China could have generated the same high growth rate with a lower rate of savings and investment, thus allowing higher levels of consumption than actually have been achieved.

Given the evidence of deteriorating financial performance of state-owned firms, it seems most improbable that if this strategy had been pursued, the state-owned sector would have increased so dramatically in terms of employment and, even more important, remained a disproportionately large claimant on society's scarce investment resources. Rather than requiring banks to prop up inefficient state-owned firms, the process of commercializing the banking system could have been initiated at the outset of reform rather than in the mid-1990s. That would have allowed a more rapid expansion of private firms, which have not had much access to bank lending over the past twenty years. This strategy would have increased the efficiency of resource use, generated more new jobs, and led to a dramatically smaller state sector as measured by assets and employment. Although economic growth would not necessarily have been higher, it could have been achieved with a smaller sacrifice in terms of forgone consumption. Most important, since policy lending would have been limited, the alternative strategy could have led to a strong and efficient commercial banking system.

At a maximum this book suggests that a significant acceleration of reform will be necessary for China to sustain moderately rapid economic growth. The frequent suggestion of the second school of thought, that a declining relative share of manufacturing output produced in state-owned firms is a sufficient condition to ensure the ultimate success of economic reform, seems mistaken. Most important, that assessment overlooks the huge financial liabilities that have been accumulating since the beginning of reform in the late 1970s. At the enterprise level this problem is reflected in a huge buildup of bank debt relative to assets and in a large accumulation of unfunded pension liabilities. In the financial sector the buildup of a large stock of liabilities to households has occurred. These liabilities vastly exceed the real value of bank assets, which are composed largely of a portfolio of loans of increasingly dubious quality. The rapid parallel increase of liabilities of enterprises relative to their assets and of liabilities of banks relative to their assets are clearly not sustainable. If not curtailed, they have the potential to precipitate a financial crisis. Even if a crisis can be avoided, the failure to address these twin problems will impede the development of a financial system capable of more efficient intermediation. That, in turn, implies that China will not be able to allocate the resources needed to address several critical physical constraints to continued rapid growth.

Physical versus Financial Constraints to Growth

Many studies of China focus on physical rather than financial constraints to sustaining economic growth. These challenges to growth include alleviating environmental deterioration, feeding a growing

population on a small amount of arable land, increasing water shortages, rising infrastructure needs, a rapidly aging population, and
energy shortages.

Environmental Deterioration

Of these challenges environmental degradation is perhaps the
most serious. As a result of rapid industrialization in the past two
decades "particulate and sulfur levels in major Chinese cities are
among the highest in the world, exceeding World Health
Organization and Chinese standards by two to five times."[4] More
than 90 percent of municipal wastewater discharge is untreated, leading to significant deterioration of water quality.[5] Only one-fifth of the
monitored river sections flowing past cities meets China's quality
standards permitting "direct human contact and use as raw water for
potable water systems."[6] Two-fifths do not even meet the lowest
quality standard, allowing use as irrigation water! Children in major
urban centers have blood-lead levels that average 80 percent above
the threshold "considered dangerous to mental development."[7]

The human and economic consequences of this environmental
deterioration are staggering. High levels of air pollution result in an
incidence of chronic obstructive pulmonary disease, China's leading
cause of death, which is twice the average for developing countries.[8]
According to the World Bank, high levels of urban air pollution currently cause 180,000 premature deaths annually, a number that will
rise to 600,000 annually by 2020 if China maintains its current very
modest level of expenditure on pollution abatement. Air pollution
also leads to acid rain, which damages human health, fisheries, and
agriculture.

The World Bank has estimated the economic costs of air and water
pollution. Its estimate takes into account the costs of premature
deaths, increased health care costs, losses owing to physical inactiv-
ity on the part of those suffering from diseases caused by environmental deterioration, the agricultural and fishery losses because of
water pollution, the crop and forest damage because of acid rain, and
so forth.[9]

Depending on the method used to value excess mortality, the
World Bank estimates the total annual economic costs of air and water
pollution in China at from 3.5 to 7.7 percent of its gross domestic prod-

uct.[10] The higher estimate, which the bank characterizes as conservative, implies that the increases in conventionally measured economic output have been largely offset by the cost of premature deaths, increased health care costs, crop damage, and so forth. The lower bound estimate implies that on a proper environmental accounting the real rate of economic growth is only about three-fifths the rate indicated by the official data based on conventional gross national product accounts.[11] If current policies are maintained, the bank estimates that the economic cost of air and water pollution as a percentage of gross domestic product will almost double by the year 2020.[12]

Mitigating the environmental consequences of economic growth will be expensive. The World Bank sketches out two alternative scenarios that China might adopt. The medium-cost scenario, in which China by 2020 would achieve emission standards broadly equivalent to those in the United States and Europe in the early 1990s, would require China to invest about 2 percent of gross domestic product annually in environmental protection. In the high-cost scenario China would invest from 4 to 5 percent of gross domestic product in environmental protection to achieve emissions standards that "correspond to the concept of best available technique." Even the medium-cost scenario requires China to at least double its investment in pollution abatement.[13] But the gains in decreased premature mortality would be substantial—a reduction to 140,000 deaths a year, less than one-fourth the predicted level if current policies are maintained.[14]

Sustaining Agricultural Growth

Other studies point to the increasing difficulty China will have in feeding its population as a significant constraint to its future growth. Water, not arable land, is the biggest constraint to agricultural growth in China.[15] Much of the growth of agriculture in recent decades is explained by more intensive cropping patterns made possible by the green revolution and increased irrigation. In the North China Plain, for example, farmers in the 1960s dug tube wells that allowed them to plant corn as a summer crop. Corn requires significantly more water than the dryland crops it replaced, such as sorghum and millet. This development dramatically increased grain production since irrigated corn yields are much greater than those of the dryland crops it replaced. Farm incomes rose even more rapidly since the unit price of corn is well above that of millet and sorghum. But by the 1970s the water table in the North China Plain began to recede by an average of a meter or more a year, requiring deeper and deeper tube wells.[16] By the mid-1990s the water table had fallen so far that the extra cost of pumping the water began to exceed the extra returns gained from the cultivation of corn. In the summer of 1997, which was drier than usual, farmers in much of the region simply let their corn crop wither and die rather than incur the high costs of pumping water from a depth of more than fifty meters. If this trend continues, in a few years tens of millions of farmers may be forced to revert to a lower-yielding cropping pattern not widely used since the 1950s.

The implication of this and similar developments elsewhere is that sustaining agricultural growth is likely to become more expensive. The state, for example, has approved a long-contemplated massive project that would carry billions of cubic meters of water annually from the Yangzi River in central China to the North China Plain to meet the growing water deficit of the latter region. But the estimated cost of completing the eastern and middle routes is RMB 207.5 billion.[17] Because the returns to water in both agricultural and industrial uses exceed the estimate cost of South-North Water Transfer Project, the World Bank's view is that the project "must rank as a public investment priority."[18] The bank also estimates that to sustain agricultural growth between now and the year 2020 China will have to undertake an additional RMB 325 billion in public investment to improve the distribution of irrigation water. These investments, which include lining irrigation canals and developing pipe and hose systems, would allow the share of water diverted into irrigation canals that is actually delivered to crop root zones to rise above the current level of only 30 percent.[19]

Sustaining agricultural growth and per capita food consumption will require significant additional investments in three other areas. First, it will require "investment and current budgets will need to be increased for agricultural research and extension."[20] Second, China will have to invest RMB 42 billion in increased fertilizer production before the year 2020. Finally, since all of the programs just outlined are likely to leave China sixty million metric tons a year short of its food grain requirements by 2020, it will need to invest an additional RMB 11.5 billion in deep water grain berths, bulk rail wagons, and bulk loading and unloading facilities at railheads, all to move imported grain within China.

Cumulatively, these incremental investments to sustain agricultural production over the next twenty-five years amount to more
than RMB 800 billion. In these projections the World Bank assumes
that China will maintain its current level of expenditures on land
reclamation necessary to ensure that the cultivated area remains
roughly constant, rather than declining in the face of increasing
urban encroachment. By the year 2020 these expenditures would
accumulate to an additional RMB 500 billion.[21]

Infrastructure Needs

Inadequate infrastructure poses yet another physical constraint to
sustaining China's rapid growth. The World Bank estimates that in
1995–2004 China needs to invest U.S.$744 billion, about RMB 6 tril-
lion, in electric power, telecommunications, transportation, and
water and sanitation infrastructure.[22] By 1994 China had stepped up
its annual investment in infrastructure to 7.5 percent of gross domestic product, compared with only 4.4 percent in 1985.[23] There are still
substantial infrastructure projects, however, that would yield large
economic benefits but which cannot be easily financed from higher
user fees or tariffs, as has been done in recent years for electric power.
Perhaps the best example is roads. China's road network lags significantly behind other large countries. The World Bank suggests that
investments in infrastructure should be increased to 8-9 percent of
gross domestic product, primarily by increasing budgetary outlays
for infrastructure projects with public goods characteristics.[24]

Overcoming Physical Constraints to Growth

All of these physical constraints to growth are real, and overcom-
ing each requires significant incremental investment resources. Three
possible means of financing these investments present themselves.
One would be an increase in the rate of domestic saving. This seems
unlikely since China's savings rate is already among the highest in
the world.

A second would be to attract more foreign investment funds in the
form of direct investment, sales of equity in Chinese companies, or by
borrowing. For example, if China liberalized its policies to allow foreign direct investment in telecommunications operating companies,

it is all but certain that tens of billions of dollars of foreign direct investment would be committed. But this possibility needs to be tempered by the fact that, despite unprecedented capital inflows, China has not absorbed any significant foreign savings since reform began in 1978.[25]

Rather than financing increased levels of investment in China, huge capital inflows from foreign direct investment, equity sales, and borrowing have been used, directly or indirectly, for three other purposes. First, large portions of these inflows have been purchased by the central bank and added to official holdings of foreign exchange. In the three years 1994–96 such holdings increased by U.S.$83.8 billion. In 1997 purchases amounted to an additional U.S.$35 billion.[26]

Second, foreign direct investment and other inflows indirectly have financed investment abroad by Chinese firms. Cumulative officially approved foreign direct investment outflows by year-end 1996 totaled U.S.$5.375 billion, a likely significant undercount.[27]

Third, indirectly foreign capital inflows have provided funds for capital flight. The World Bank believes that large unexplained errors and omissions in China's balance of payments, almost U.S.$18 billion in 1995 and almost U.S.$15 billion in 1996, are a sign of large unrecorded capital outflows.[28]

Unless other policy changes are made, there is no reason to believe that increased foreign capital inflows would lead to a net absorption of foreign savings. These policy changes have costs or may not even be feasible. For example, the central authorities could discontinue building up their holdings of foreign exchange. But that would mean that increased foreign direct investment inflows, say from liberalizing the telecommunications sector, would lead to an appreciation of the domestic currency. That likely would cut into export growth, potentially jeopardizing China's ability to service its large outstanding foreign debt.

The authorities could clamp down on approvals of Chinese investment abroad. That would represent a substantial retreat from its course of greater integration with the world economy. More than 4,800 Chinese companies currently operate in more than 180 foreign countries, where they are gaining valuable experience that will help facilitate China's further economic transformation and integration into the world economy. In any case authorized Chinese foreign direct investment abroad is the smallest of the three purposes to which foreign capital flows have been devoted, so eliminating it might not lead to a net absorption of foreign savings.

Alternatively, the authorities could attempt to stem what in recent years has been significant capital flight. But the efficacy of capital controls is limited for any country with an annual trade volume over U.S.$320 billion. A large volume of trade transactions provides ample opportunity for underinvoicing of exports or overinvoicing of imports, with the under or over amounts accruing in overseas bank accounts. This is particularly easy for Chinese companies since a large portion of China's trade with the rest of the world flows through Hong Kong, where Chinese-owned companies handle a large and growing share of these entrepôt transactions. This role gives them the opportunity to control transfer prices so that foreign trade profits accrue in Hong Kong, beyond the reach of Chinese authorities.[29]

Since the prospects for success of any of these three alternative approaches are limited, it appears unlikely that the increased real resources needed for incremental investment to overcome the physical challenges to growth outlined above can come primarily from increased foreign direct investment. The most feasible way of meeting the need is the package of reforms outlined in chapter 4. Financial and related reforms are needed for two reasons. First, as long as the financial system is forced to allocate a disproportionate share of investment resources to state-owned manufacturing firms, there will be insufficient resources for addressing the emerging problems just described. China needs to accelerate the restructuring of its enterprise sector and the commercialization of its banking system. The resulting improvement in the efficiency of resource allocation would free up the funds necessary to solve its long-term environmental, agricultural, and infrastructure problems.

Shortcomings in China's domestic financial system already are reflected in its financing of infrastructure projects. China, with perhaps the highest savings rate of any country in the world except for Singapore, has borrowed or sold bonds totaling several billion dollars on international markets to build roads, bridges, airports, electric power plants, and other infrastructure.[30] These projects have little, if any, import content, so no foreign exchange is needed.[31] Yet these projects are financed offshore largely because the fragility of the banking system effectively has precluded the development of a domestic capital market that could more effectively provide long-term funds for infrastructure.

Since none of these projects generates any foreign exchange earnings, financing these projects with foreign currency loans and other foreign-currency-denominated debt instruments subjects Chinese borrowers to substantial foreign currency risk. Over time, as China continues to reduce tariff and nontariff barriers, domestic demand for foreign exchange is likely to increase relative to supply, much as it did between 1978 and 1994. The decline in the real value of the domestic currency in that period, which amounted to more than 75 percent between 1978 and 1994, is likely to resume.[32] Domestic projects financed with foreign borrowing will face the challenge of the greatly increased domestic currency costs of repaying their foreign currency borrowings.

A second reason the reforms outlined in this book are a prerequisite to addressing the physical constraints to growth is the importance of maintaining a high rate of domestic savings. If China is able to maintain a high rate of savings over the long term, all of the problems discussed, while challenging, are remediable in the long run. If a financial collapse leads to a significantly lower rate of savings, however, not only will the growth rate fall, China will not have the resources to address environmental and other challenges.

China and the Asian Financial Crisis

The conclusion drawn at the outset of this chapter, that the combination of a rapid buildup of bank credit and a significant deterioration of loan quality is unsustainable, is based on four international comparisons. First, the rate of increase in bank credit since reform began in China is similar to that experienced in other countries before the emergence of major banking crises. The Mexican financial debacle, which emerged at the end of 1994, was seen from outside Mexico primarily as a crisis brought on by a large current account deficit financed primarily with short-term external credit. When foreign investor sentiment changed and Mexico could no longer roll over its short-term external debt, a massive international rescue, combined with a major devaluation of the peso, was unavoidable. But the depth of the ensuing crisis, in which real output and living standards fell in the sharpest Mexican recession in the twentieth century, occurred largely because of problems that had accumulated in domestic banks. In the run-up to the crisis, bank credit to the private sector shot from 13 percent of gross domestic product in 1988 to 36 percent in 1994.[33] In large part the decline in domestic output in 1995 occurred because the government was forced to raise interest rates in an effort to defend the value of the peso. This response put a squeeze on borrowers. Many, unable to pay higher rates, defaulted. In what in effect was a bank rescue, the central government in 1995 purchased U.S.$45 billion in bad loans, almost half the loans of the banking system.[34] Even after this rescue, Mexico's major banks were forced to increase their interest rate spreads and further shrink their loan portfolios in an attempt to increase their earnings and restore their financial strength. Although exports grew briskly in response to the devaluation of the peso, the resulting tightening of credit shrank real gross national product more than 6 percent and almost doubled the unemployment rate in the first year after the emergence of the crisis.[35] Similarly, the Thai financial crisis that emerged in the summer of 1997 grew out of a five-year period in which bank lending expanded at an annual rate of 25 percent, three times the rate of real economic growth.[36] The run-up in credit by financial institutions in China, more than 21 percent a year since 1978, has been almost as fast. Moreover, it has been sustained for twenty years, so that by the mid-1990s the level of credit relative to gross domestic product was much higher than in Mexico just prior to the emergence of its crisis.

Similarly, during the second half of the 1980s credit extended by Japanese banks grew much more rapidly than output, fueling a growth of prices of land and financial assets that was not sustainable. The resulting collapse of asset prices has had substantially negative consequences for the health of the banking system and, because Japan postponed addressing these problems in a serious way until 1998, for the pace of economic growth. In early 1998 share prices were more than 50 percent below the peak levels of 1989. Land prices, on average, appear to have fallen by almost as much. In Tokyo and Osaka property prices by mid-1997 had "fallen by at least 70 percent from their peak."[37] Declining asset prices undermined the viability of the projects of many borrowers, especially in the real estate sector, leaving many Japanese banks with huge portfolios of nonperforming loans that they could not liquidate since the collateral of the borrowers, frequently land or stocks, was worth much less than the underlying loans. The weakness of the Japanese economy in the 1990s in part reflects the legacy of the rapid credit buildup of the 1980s.

The second international comparison draws on the experience of the 1980s, when many countries experienced systemic bank problems. The lesson learned was that financial distress is "likely to become systemic when nonperforming loans, net of provisions, reach 15 percent of total loans."[38] As noted in chapter 3, 22 percent of the loans of China's largest banks in 1995 were classified as nonperforming, whereas loan loss reserves were well under 1 percent of loans. Even before making allowances for China's relatively lenient standards for classifying loans, it appears that banks controlling almost half of the assets of China's entire financial system were well beyond the threshold level of 15 percent nonperforming loans, net of provisions.

Third, the excessive reliance on expanding bank credit is reflected in China's unprecedentedly high ratio of incremental bank credit to annual government fiscal revenues. As discussed earlier, by 1995 the annual increase in credit extended through the state-owned banking system was half again as large as the combined annual budgetary expenditures of central, provincial, and local governments. In the mid-1980s this ratio in industrial countries ranged from about 0.15:1 in the United States to as high as 0.55:1 in Great Britain. The ratio in India was about 0.35:1. Japan, with a ratio of increased bank credit to tax revenues of 0.81:1, was an outlier.[39] With the advantage of hindsight, the depths of Japan's banking crisis in the 1990s suggests that this indicator of the relative importance of banks in allocating resources should have received more attention than it did at the time. China's declining fiscal strength, discussed in chapter 1, led the government to finance a larger and larger share of its expenditure program through the quasi-fiscal operations of banks.

Fourth, Chinese banks and other financial institutions appear to be heavily exposed to real estate lending in a market where values, as reflected in rental rates, began to decline sharply as early as the second half of 1995. The cities of Beijing, Shanghai, and Shenzhen seem to have the greatest absolute concentrations of unleased space, but there is a significant problem of overbuilding in many smaller cities, from Haikou on Hainan Island to Beihai in Guangxi, and in county-level towns as well.[40]

Beijing, Shanghai, and Shenzhen have millions of square feet of unoccupied luxury villas and townhouses and even larger amounts of vacant first-class office space. Moreover, the anticipated additions to the stock of space over the next few years exceed by a severalfold multiple the rate at which space has been sold or leased in the past few years. For example, if all projects under construction in 1997 are completed, the additions to new office space in Beijing in the year 2000 would total 14 million square feet, compared with additions that averaged under 1 million square feet between 1990 and 1995.[41] Pudong, designated as Shanghai's new financial and manufacturing center in 1991, is even more overbuilt. The total stock of office space in midyear 1997 stood at 13.5 million square feet, an astounding five times the 2.7 million square feet at year-end 1994. But more than 70 percent of this space in the latter part of 1997 was vacant. If completed, buildings under construction in Pudong in 1997 would take the total available office space to 26 million square feet by year-end 1999. Vacancy rates are not quite as high in other districts of the city, but the anticipated additions to the supply of new office space there in 1998 and 1999 exceed the anticipated additions in Pudong. By the year 2000 total office space in Shanghai, almost entirely built in the 1990s, is expected to match that in Hong Kong, built over four decades.[42]

Vacant office space in Shenzhen in late 1997 was the equivalent of three years of take up. An additional 22.60 million square feet was under construction and scheduled to be completed between 1998 and 2000. Oversupply is expected to last for ten years.[43]

By mid-1997 office rental rates already had declined greatly—by almost 50 percent in downtown Shanghai, over 40 percent in Pudong, and by 40 percent or more in Beijing—and were forecast to fall by as much as 70 percent before bottoming out.[44] In retrospect, the repeated boast of Shanghai's mayor that one-fifth of the world's construction cranes were at work in Shanghai should have been seen as a premonition of overbuilding and a coming collapse of property prices rather than an auspicious sign reflecting the city's economic resurgence following the creation of the Pudong Development Area in 1991.

China's state-owned banks may have significant exposure to property loans but publish no data on this critical variable.[45] Officials frequently assert that their exposure is limited. It is likely, however, that the banks are not fully knowledgeable about the extent of their exposure, partly because a variety of state-owned enterprises have become involved in real estate development projects, sometimes in collaboration with foreign property developers. Loans taken out to finance these companies' traditional lines of business may have been diverted to commercial property development. Additional vulnerability of banks to a collapse of property values stems from the real estate exposure of bank subsidiaries, such as trust and investment companies. Since 1990, these institutions have shifted into riskier property and real estate development lending.[46]

These international comparisons raise several closely related questions. Why hasn't China already experienced a banking crisis? Is a crisis inevitable? If so, what form might it take?

In the short run, China is unlikely to experience a crisis like that of Mexico in 1994–95 or that of several Southeast Asian countries and Korea in 1997 for five reasons. First, and most important, the Chinese currency is not convertible for capital account transactions. As noted in chapter 4, that means that Chinese savers who are concerned about the viability of the country's financial institutions do not have the option of legally converting their renminbi deposits and then purchasing foreign-currency-denominated financial assets. It also means that foreigners are much less likely to open renminbi-denominated bank accounts or purchase renminbi-denominated shares on China's domestic stock exchanges. Indeed, nonresidents legally are precluded from purchasing A shares, the shares bought and sold for local currency on the Shanghai and Shenzhen stock markets. They must buy foreign-currency-denominated B shares that are priced independently from the A shares of the same underlying company. If foreign sentiment on the value of B shares turns negative, there are no adverse consequences for the value of the Chinese currency. Would-be sellers, in effect, cannot exit the market unless they find a foreign buyer who will pay dollars for their shares. This situation contrasts sharply with that of Southeast Asian markets in the summer and fall of 1997. Foreign portfolio managers all rushed for the exits simultaneously, contributing to a sharp decline in local currency share prices. And when they then sold the baht and other local currencies they had gained from the sale of their shares for dollars, they contributed to the plummet of currency values in these countries. Within weeks the foreign currency values of shares listed in these markets had fallen 50 percent or more.

The absence of capital account convertibility also means that speculators, foreign or Chinese, have no way to act on a belief that the renminbi is overvalued and likely to depreciate. Normally these individuals would borrow domestic currency and sell it for foreign exchange with the expectation that they would profit from an ensuing depreciation that would allow them to repurchase the domestic currency at a lower price. These funds would then be used to repay the initial loan, leaving a profit proportionate to the depreciation.[47] Alternatively, they could simply sell domestic currency in the forward market in the expectation that prior to the time the contract matured the currency would have depreciated, again allowing them to buy it more cheaply to deliver when the contract matured.

But China's foreign exchange market is not open to those who wish to purchase foreign exchange for capital account transactions. Only buyers with a demonstrated need related to trade, tourism, repayment of previously approved foreign currency borrowing, or repatriation of profits derived from a prior direct investment are allowed to purchase foreign exchange. That thwarts would-be speculators from buying foreign exchange to sell in the spot market. Similarly, the forward market for foreign exchange in China is extremely limited, so the would-be speculator would not be able to take the short position in Chinese domestic currency just described.[48] Even domestic firms that have foreign-currency-denominated loans are not allowed to purchase foreign exchange to repay their loans until their loan is actually due.[49] That prevents an acceleration of demand for foreign exchange on the part of those that have such loans outstanding.

Second, China's capital inflows predominantly take the form of foreign direct investment. In 1996, for example, China was the recipient of U.S.$56 billion in foreign capital. But the largest component, U.S.$42.5 billion, was direct investment.[50] Cumulatively, by year-end 1997 foreign direct investment in place stood at over U.S.$223 billion, about three-quarters more than the level of China's officially reported external debt.[51] In contrast, in other countries experiencing financial and banking crises, this ratio of direct investment to financial investment is invariably reversed. At year-end 1996 in Korea, for example, cumulative foreign direct investment of U.S.$12.491 billion was only one-ninth the level of officially reported outstanding foreign borrowing of U.S.$110 billion.[52] Even in Thailand, which has a much more open foreign investment climate than Korea, cumulative foreign direct investment at year-end 1996 was only one-fifth of the level of external borrowing.[53] Direct investors differ fundamentally from financial investors since they invest with a long time horizon and their investments are illiquid. Financial investments, such as lending, bank deposits, stocks, and bonds, are frequently of short duration and can be reversed quickly if the investors reevaluate the risk of lending to a particular country. Some financial assets can be sold in the market immediately. Lenders can wind down their exposure over somewhat longer periods by refusing to roll over loans when they come due.

Third, the share of China's borrowing that is short term is somewhat lower than in the countries engulfed in the Asian financial crisis. For example, according to official data, at year-end 1996 almost 90 percent of China's external debt was medium and long term.[54] Independent estimates place short-term debt at 30 percent of a significantly higher total external debt.[55] By contrast, at the time of Korea's financial crisis in late 1997, U.S.$66 billion, or 60 percent of its total external debt of U.S.$110 billion, was short term.[56] When lenders grew reluctant to roll over this short-term lending, a financial crisis was almost inevitable.

Fourth, in contrast to Korea, Thailand, and several other countries in Southeast Asia that experienced currency crises in 1997–98, China in the mid-1990s experienced record trade surpluses. Its trade surpluses were U.S.$16.69 billion, U.S.$12.3 billion, and U.S.$40.2 billion in 1995, 1996, and 1997, respectively.[57] Thus China was not dependent on continued foreign capital inflows to finance a trade deficit.

Finally, at the end of 1997 China had amassed U.S.$139.9 billion in foreign exchange reserves, enough to finance a full year of imports.[58]

In short, the absence of capital account convertibility, the nature of China's capital inflows, and a strong trade and foreign exchange reserve position mean that a banking crisis is unlikely to be precipitated by a change in the sentiment of foreign lenders, foreign or domestic speculators, or domestic firms that have outstanding foreign-currency-denominated liabilities. This does not mean, however, that China is immune to the adverse consequences of a weak financial system characterized by a rapid buildup of nonperforming loans to state-owned enterprises financed largely by household deposits. As explained in chapter 4, the real consequences are the inescapable cost of the poor lending decisions that banks have made and are continuing to make. The cost of these poor decisions ultimately will be borne by depositors or by the government and thus by taxpayers in general.

The limited ability of foreign speculators and lenders to precipitate or even contribute to crises seems, at least superficially, to be to China's advantage compared with countries with capital account convertibility. Particularly in light of the Asian financial contagion of 1997, the insulation provided by China's more closed international financial system seems attractive. In reality it is a two-edged sword. On the one hand, it could work to China's advantage by providing the time necessary to recapitalize and commercialize the banking system and to eliminate the preferred access of state-owned firms to bank loans. As discussed in chapter 4, bank recapitalization will be costly in economic terms because of its fiscal implications. Subjecting state-owned enterprises to hard budget constraints also will be costly politically. But the renewed commitment of the party at the Fifteenth Congress to resolve problems of state-owned enterprises and the urgency with which the highest levels of China's leadership are now addressing the problems of the banking and financial sector provide some grounds for optimism. If the program of reform outlined in chapter 4 is carried out expeditiously, China would emerge with a more efficient financial system and would be more likely to maintain high rates of domestic savings. This combination would sustain China's strong growth performance.

However, if the leadership delays undertaking these fundamental reforms, the possibility of a domestic financial crisis greatly increases for several reasons. First, any growth slowdown is likely to expose dramatically the underlying weakness of the domestic financial system. Slower growth, whether originating from purely domestic sources or from changing relative currency values, would cut into the operating profits of many state-owned companies. Given their extraordinarily high ratio of debt to equity, reduced profitability likely would increase significantly the number of firms unable to amortize their debts, undermining further the financial position of China's major banks.

Second, major currency depreciations in Southeast Asia and Korea in 1997 can be expected simultaneously to reduce the growth of Chinese exports and increase the growth of imports. China's trade surplus may shrink significantly from the historic peak level of 1997. Because China's service account includes increasingly large profit remittances associated with the large stock of foreign direct investment already in place, a shrinking trade surplus could lead to a current account deficit. If strong inflows of foreign direct investment continued, a modest current account deficit would be easily sustainable.

But by 1998 it seemed likely that foreign direct investment inflows would begin to decline, perhaps sharply. Contracts for future foreign direct investment fell sharply in 1996 and 1997, portending a future slowdown in actual foreign direct investment. The likelihood of a decline was reinforced by the Asian currency crisis of 1997. The decline in the value of other Asian currencies vis à vis the renminbi inevitably made China a somewhat less attractive location for export-oriented foreign direct investment. And slower growth in Asia, the source of the lion's share of foreign direct investment inflows into China, is likely to curtail investment by firms in the region, not only in their home countries but in China as well. Finally, foreign direct investment could fall sharply if those Chinese firms and individuals who have been able to avoid currency controls and move tens of billions of dollars offshore annually would elect to keep these funds offshore rather than bringing them back in as "foreign investment."

If a large current account deficit emerged as foreign direct investment declined, China would have to draw down its foreign exchange reserves, step up its external borrowing, or devalue its currency. The first of these alternatives could be used to postpone, but only temporarily, the need to adjust to China's changed international competitive position. Increased borrowing could serve the same function, but again would not provide a permanent solution since it would become increasingly difficult for China to expand its borrowing, given the combination of its already large external debt and heightened lender sensitivity to the risks of lending to countries with a large foreign currency exposure. Devaluation, the last alternative, would pose difficulties for many Chinese banks and firms, given their large foreign-currency-denominated debt.

Even if a crisis could be avoided, delaying fundamental reform would be costly since the longer the banks continue to support money-losing state-owned enterprises, the larger will be the size of the ultimately required bank recapitalization or the financial losses imposed on depositors.

A banking crisis in China is most likely to be precipitated when domestic savers lose confidence in the government's implicit guarantee of the value of their deposits in banks. This loss of confidence could be triggered by a growth slowdown that weakened the domestic banking system or by the prospect of a major devaluation in response to a large emerging current account deficit and a sharp fall in inward foreign direct investment. If households in large number attempt to withdraw their savings, the insolvency problem of several of China's largest banks could become a liquidity problem. At that point the central bank would face two alternatives. It could serve the traditional central bank role of lender of last resort and supply funds to banks to meet the demand for withdrawals. This was not unheard of during the past two decades, when the central bank extended loans to individual provincial branches of state banks to solve liquidity problems.[59] But if the central bank lends money to banks on a large scale to meet a demand for withdrawals throughout China, the resulting burgeoning increase in the money supply could be highly inflationary.

Thus the second, more likely, alternative is that the banks would sharply limit customer withdrawals. That would almost certainly further undermine confidence in the banking system and lead to a dramatic reduction in the flow of funds into savings deposits and to greater capital flight. Anticipating rising inflation, households likely would try to convert part of their increased holdings of currency into goods, again creating an inflationary spiral. In short, a banking crisis in China is most likely to be reflected in an inflationary spiral, whether or not the central bank lends funds to state-owned banks.

China's Response

The Chinese government recognizes the risk associated with delaying further fundamental reforms. On November 17, 1997, China's State Council convened an unusual high-level National Financial Work Conference in Beijing to discuss the problems of China's financial and banking system. The meeting was held against the backdrop of financial crises in three Asian countries—Thailand, Indonesia, and Korea—that had sought massive international financial assistance coordinated by the International Monetary Fund. Indeed, in an unprecedented move, China contributed U.S.$1 billion to the IMF-led bailout of Thailand in 1997. Participants in the Beijing meeting included not only central bank officials at the national and provincial level, officials from the headquarters and major provincial branches of all of China's state-owned banks, insurance companies, and many nonbank financial institutions, but also all provincial governors and provincial-level finance officials. The meeting was addressed by President Jiang Zemin, Premier Li Peng, and Vice Premier Zhu Rongji, the latter widely regarded as China's economic czar. Several other members of the Standing Committee of the Politburo of the Central Committee of the Chinese Communist Party also were present.

The meeting focused on similarities between China's weak financial system and those elsewhere in Asia and steps that should be taken to overhaul the country's financial system. In Thailand, Indonesia, Korea, as well as China, excessive bank lending had financed excess investment across a broad range of industries. In China, for example, these industries ranged from home appliances to beer, property, and automobiles. Firms in these and other sectors have borrowed excessively to finance rates of expansion that are not sustainable. The parallel roles of the governments in Thailand, Indonesia, and Korea, as well as China, in encouraging these lending booms were remarkable, as was the resulting vulnerability of firms that had benefited from the ability to borrow without limit, to a downturn in economic growth. A downturn in economic growth, against the background of massive excess capacity, posed a deflationary threat that would leave highly leveraged firms unable to maintain payments on their massive debts to banks and other financial institutions.

In each of these countries financial systems were heavily bank dominated. The lack of well-developed capital markets made it possible for bank loans to be systematically underpriced over the long run, encouraging excess borrowing and capital formation on the part of companies with preferred access to credit—state-owned firms in China, the chaebol in Korea, those well connected to the government in Indonesia and Thailand—while leaving the rest of the economy starved for funds.

Finally, central banks in these countries are weak and do not exercise adequate prudential supervision over commercial lending. In Korea, for example, the central bank was formally subordinate to the Ministry of Finance. The ministry focused on providing continuous flows of funds to major industrial groups and effectively precluded the central bank from exercising effective supervision. A key condition of the IMF bailout was legislation making the Korean Central Bank an independent entity.

These countries face a shared challenge in their need not only to reform their financial systems but to restructure their productive sectors as well. In Korea increased competition is needed to curb the market power of the chaebol. China's lack of competition is evident not in the domination of the economy by a few large firms, but the birth and survival, through access to bank credit on soft terms, of many small local producers that are grossly inefficient. In the vehicle sector, for example, more than 120 manufacturers were established in the mid- and late-1980s. Production of vehicles of all types tripled, from about a half a million in 1990 to an expected 1.57 million in 1997.[60] Most of the 120 manufacturers, however, have production levels that are too low to be efficient. The top 13 firms produce 91 percent of the vehicles, meaning that the average number of vehicles produced by the remaining firms in 1997 was only 1,300. Capital invested per vehicle produced by the large number of small producers was three times the average of the top 13 producers.[61] Undoubtedly, labor and other noncapital costs per vehicle also were much higher than costs sustained by the larger producers.

The government has sought, since at least 1994 when it promulgated an automotive industrial policy, to engineer a consolidation in the industry.[62] But dozens of provincial and local governments have resisted fiercely, each determined to maintain a presence in what the central government has identified as a pillar industry. Some of these localities have fostered their own producers by imposing restrictions within their jurisdictions on the sale and licensing of vehicles produced elsewhere. They have been abetted by a highly restrictive national auto import policy. After several cuts, tariff rates on imported sedans are still as high as 100 percent and imports are also subject to quotas and other restrictions.[63] In a more market-oriented economy, with more efficient intermediation of capital and less restrictive trade practices, it is highly unlikely that 120 vehicle producers could have been established over a period of almost a decade. If they somehow had been created, it is even more unlikely that they would have had ongoing access to funds, not only to cover their operating losses and thus sustain their existence, but even to continue to expand their fixed assets.

In Thailand, Indonesia, and Korea, the IMF is providing the incentive for needed restructuring—both financial and real. Insolvent financial institutions have been closed—dozens of finance companies in Thailand; 16 of 240 banks in Indonesia, including several owned by relatives or close associates of President Suharto; and many merchant banks in Korea. The IMF-led bailout in Korea is conditioned on substantial long-term financial reform undergirded by a requirement to open up its financial sector to external competition. That is likely to ensure that domestic institutions will pay more attention to the quality of their borrowers' projects and less to government signals on whom to lend to. Otherwise these institutions would be unable to compete with new foreign financial institutions that would be able to offer higher rates to depositors because they earned more on their outstanding loan portfolios. In Thailand the reforms allow foreign financial institutions to buy majority stakes in domestic banks for the first time.

Because China's currency is not convertible for capital account transactions and because its trade account is at least temporarily quite strong, China has been insulated from a currency crisis and is not subject to an IMF-imposed restructuring program. There can be little doubt, however, that Premier Zhu Rongji believes that a restructuring program for banks and their principal borrowers, state-owned enterprises, is urgently needed. The share of nonperforming loans in bank lending portfolios in China was higher than in Korea or Thailand just before the onset of their financial crises.[64] Moreover, the share of nonperforming loans of China's major banks has continued to grow in recent years, despite the program of reform and commercialization of the banking system initiated in late 1993. In November 1997 the new president of the Agricultural Bank of China, in a remarkable interview published in English on the opening day of the high-level financial meeting, explicitly acknowledged that the portion of bad loans in the bank's total portfolio was continuing to rise, despite the best efforts of the bank in recent years to be more selective in its lending.[65] Commentary in China's leading financial newspaper, published jointly by the central bank and several of China's largest financial institutions immediately after the financial conference, suggested that the problem of an increasing share of nonperforming loans was not restricted to the Agricultural Bank. According to the paper, "A considerable amount of loans extended by banks are disappearing like stones dropped into the sea; principal and interest are difficult to recover; thus the non-performing assets of these banks is increasing."[66] Two months later central bank Governor Dai Xianglong, in early 1998, confirmed that the ratio of nonperforming loans in the banking system was rising. He said that the share of non-performing loans at year-end 1997 stood at 25 percent and implied that a larger share of the total than in earlier years fell in more impaired subcategories.[67]

The increase in lending by banks and other financial institutions in 1997 was 17 percent, twice the rate of nominal growth of gross domestic product.[68] The continued increase in the ratio of loans outstanding to gross domestic product strongly suggests a further expansion of enterprise losses and inventories.[69] Some Chinese manufacturers are sitting on mountains of unsold inventories.[70] The exposure of Chinese banks to a rapidly weakening property sector is on a par with Thailand.

Finally, losses caused by fraud, corruption, and other lending irregularities in Chinese banks may be similar to those associated with crony capitalism in Indonesia or by corrupt Korean bank lending practices that were used to channel hundreds of millions of U.S. dollars into the pockets of Korea's highest leaders. The People's Bank of China in 1996 acknowledged that some banks had lent funds "without recording them in their account books," and that some non-bank financial institutions created "false assets" to cover up the "black holes" in their balance sheets caused by large financial losses. Ominously, the bank admitted that the number of serious financial crimes was on the rise and that the manner in which such crimes were committed was making them more and more difficult to detect.[71] Since these astonishing admissions, the situation seems to have worsened. The editorial appearing in *People's Daily*, the Chinese Communist Party newspaper, at the conclusion of the November 1997 financial conference, admitted that "criminal activities in banking and finance are rampant."[72] Whether in China or elsewhere in the region, the common element leading to fraud and corruption in lending is inadequate regulation and supervision of banks by central banks and the lack of sufficient central bank independence. In large measure that, in turn, reflects the extreme reluctance of political leaders, especially at the provincial and local level, to relinquish their power to direct loans funds to certain industries and firms.

In the wake of the November 1997 financial conference, the government announced important steps to reduce the risks that the Asian financial contagion would spread to China. Among the most important was a reorganization of the local branches of the People's Bank along regional lines in order to reduce political interference in lending decisions at the local level. The initial experiment in creating new supraprovincial branches of the People's Bank is under way in south China where previous provincial branches in Guangdong, Jiangxi, Guangxi, and Hainan are being consolidated to form a single regional office in Guangdong's provincial capital, Guangzhou. The goal of the reorganization remains the same as that of several earlier reforms promoted by Vice Premier Zhu Rongji—finally ending the common practice of provincial governors and party officials influencing the flow of lending in their regions. Zhu has been widely quoted as stating, "The power of provincial governors and mayors to command local bank presidents is abolished as of 1998."[73]

A second major step is a planned capital injection of RMB 270 billion into the four largest state-owned banks. This injection, which will basically double the capital of the four largest banks, is a prerequisite to the commercialization of the banking system. Its relatively large size is perhaps a reflection that the leadership believes that the process of commercialization is well begun.

The central government also has committed substantially more funds to finance the write-off of enterprise bad debts. As noted in chapter 2, this program began in 1996 with an allocation of RMB 20 billion to write off bad debts to banks of enterprises that were being restructured. In 1997 the funds earmarked for this purpose were RMB 30 billion. In 1998 the amount was increased to RMB 40 billion with further increases to follow in 1999 and 2000.[74] These funds are generally allocated to assist in the merger of two or more state-owned firms, thus their use is tied to enterprise restructurings.

Besides stepped up write-offs of bad debt, the authorities announced several other steps designed to encourage banks to operate on a more commercial basis. Perhaps the most important is that the central bank is to encourage banks to take risk into account when they set interest rates for specific borrowers.[75] The practice of the central bank setting uniform lending rates for each loan category historically has precluded banks from pricing loans according to risk.[76] To further encourage commercial banking behavior, reportedly the heads of bank branches and subbranches where nonperforming assets increase will be fired. The system of mandatory lending quotas, which has placed a ceiling on total lending and required loans to specific projects, is also to be phased out in 1998. Instead, the central bank will regulate the lending of banks primarily through specifying certain asset-to-liability ratios, as the State Council originally called for in 1993.[77] The precise implications of this remain to be seen since a system of "guidance quotas for lending" is to remain in place.

In the wake of the meeting the Chinese central bank also tightened supervision and regulation of both banks and nonbank financial institutions. The central bank has closed dozens of unauthorized financial institutions, in some cases providing billions of RMB to prevent individual depositors from losing their savings.[78] One element of the enhanced supervision and regulation of banks is a new scheme for classifying nonperforming loans.[79] It is already in use by the State Development Bank and will be more broadly adopted by the end of 1998.[80] The new system will move China from its rather lax system of loan classification, analyzed in chapter 3, to a system more closely aligned with international standards. Most important, classification will be based partly on risk rather than exclusively on payment status. At the same time the system of setting aside provisions for nonperforming loans is to be overhauled.[81]

Finally, the State Administration of Exchange Control has been charged with the responsibility of ensuring both that all international commercial borrowing by domestic institutions is approved in advance and that borrowed amounts do not exceed certain multiples of the borrowers' net assets and foreign exchange earnings. These new regulations severely limit the ability of nonfinancial firms to incur foreign exchange risk.[82] The regulations also limit the magnitude of foreign exchange borrowing that banks may undertake.[83] These provisions are far more restrictive than those they replace.

The new regulations also are designed to measure more accurately and to discourage off-shore borrowing by subsidiaries or affiliates of Chinese firms and financial institutions operating abroad. This reflects a growing recognition on the part of the central bank that China has a large "hidden foreign debt," that China's official foreign debt statistics are inaccurate, and that the central bank runs the risk of losing control of the country's total exposure to foreign currency debt.[84] The People's Bank of China wants to avoid the Korean experience in which, after the financial crisis began, the country's actual foreign debt was discovered to be far in excess of the officially reported total, largely because of borrowing by subsidiaries of Korean companies operating abroad.[85] In the past some of the proceeds from commercial borrowing and the issuance of bonds by foreign subsidiaries of Chinese companies has entered China as the "foreign" contribution to a joint venture. Thus these capital inflows are reported in Chinese statistics as foreign direct investment, whereas they are actually foreign-currency-denominated debt. To reduce this problem the new regulations prohibit transferring for use in China proceeds from foreign-currency-denominated bonds issued by foreign subsidiaries of Chinese financial institutions.[86] Foreign currency commercial borrowing by the same subsidiaries must be approved in advance if the amount is U.S.$50 million or more, and these funds may not be transferred into China without the approval of the State Administration of Foreign Exchange.[87]

The new regulations also require that foreign exchange deposits in Chinese banks by institutions and individuals outside China be "considered and managed as international commercial loans."[88] The significance of this latter rule may be small since the flow of "hot money" into Chinese banks from abroad has abated considerably since the mid-1990s. At that time Chinese inflation and nominal interest rates were both high. For example, from July 1993 through April 1996 the rate on one-year time deposits was 10.98 percent, substantially higher than interest rates elsewhere. China's fixed exchange rate system appeared to offer a risk-free method of capturing this higher return on renminbi deposits.

Implications for China's Integration into the World Economy

China's pace in restructuring its enterprises, commercializing its banking system, and consolidating its fiscal reform will have important implications for the global and Asian regional economy as well as for China. If these reforms, including the initiatives undertaken in late 1997 and early 1998, proceed slowly or in fits and starts, China could be dragged into and contribute to a further episode of the Asian financial crisis. Slow implementation also would mean that

China would be unlikely to comply with the conditions the international community has laid down for entry into the World Trade Organization. These expectations include not only a substantial further reduction of tariffs and a specific schedule for eliminating non-tariff barriers such as quotas, licensing, and tendering requirements, but also phasing out of price controls and subsidies and liberalization of telecommunications, financial, legal, accounting, and other services markets.

One lesson of the Asian financial crisis of 1997 is that a financial sector problem in a comparatively small economy, like Thailand, can have relatively wide-ranging effects. Because China's economy is several times larger and its foreign trade almost three times that of Thailand, its potential involvement in the Asian financial crisis carries enormous financial consequences. Although China is less well integrated into the international economy, especially financially, than some of its Asian neighbors, there are indirect ways in which China is vulnerable to and could exacerbate Asia's financial problems. The most obvious and important indirect linkage, of course, is through Hong Kong. Hong Kong banks in late 1997 were already suffering from the effects of the higher interest rates necessary to maintain the peg of the Hong Kong dollar to the U.S. dollar. In part the adverse consequences for banks stemmed from declining local property values, which weakened the balance sheets of the local property developers, who were among the biggest borrowers from Hong Kong banks.

Hong Kong banks also have exposure to the property bubble in China because of their acknowledged cross-border lending. In addition, in Hong Kong banks lend to Hong Kong companies that are China majority owned, including companies that are known as "Red Chips." As just noted, these companies often use these loans to finance their property and other projects in China. The Bank of China and its affiliated institutions, which account for about one-fourth of all deposit taking and lending activity in Hong Kong, are active participants in lending to Red Chip companies.[89] Other Chinese-owned banks presumably also lend to Red Chip companies.[90] These exposures might lead to such a severe attack on the Hong Kong dollar peg that China might make good on its pledge to use its foreign exchange reserves to contribute to the defense of the value of the Hong Kong dollar. That, in turn, might lead to a weakening of the ability of the

Chinese authorities to maintain the fixed exchange rate of its own currency. As noted, China is vulnerable to capital flight, and its short-term external debt is much higher than indicated by official data. A significant drop in the value of the renminbi could lead to further depreciation in the value of other currencies in the region.

If China vigorously implements Premier Zhu Rongji's reform agenda for state-owned banks and state-owned enterprises, it will dramatically reduce the risk that China might be dragged into or con-tribute to an exacerbation of the Asian financial contagion. It would signal to markets that China was effectively addressing its financial problems, reducing the risk of a domestic banking crisis. It would restore China's very favorable access to international capital markets and indirectly contribute importantly to the viability of the Hong Kong dollar peg to the U.S. dollar.

The constraint that China's partially completed economic reforms have imposed on China's integration into the world economy is reflected in the limited participation of the state-owned sector in China's rapidly expanding external trade. Put simply, state-owned firms have been the least successful in competing in international markets. The growth of exports from the state-owned sector has lagged far behind that of joint ventures and other nonstate firms. Not only do state-owned firms exhibit lagging export performance, but in some sectors high tariff and nontariff barriers have insulated them from competition from foreign firms, even on their own home turf.

Lagging export performance is easiest to document. At the outset of reform most of China's exports were produced by state-owned firms. But over time firms with other forms of ownership have been far more successful in competing in international markets. By 1996, for example, 44 percent of all exports were produced by joint venture companies. Put alternatively, between 1978 and 1996 China's total exports grew from U.S.$9.75 billion to U.S.$151.1 billion, a fifteenfold increase. But over half the growth was accounted for by a category of firm ownership, joint ventures, which did not exist until the reform era. Furthermore, a substantial portion of the balance of China's exports is produced under processing contracts, mostly involving township and village enterprises or other nonstate firms. In process-ing, foreign firms agree to purchase output assembled from compo-nents or assemblies, which the foreign firm provides. But because there is no foreign equity position in the firms engaged in the assembly activity, these exports do not get reported as joint venture exports. The sum of joint venture exports and processing undertaken by indigenous firms constitutes about two-thirds of China's total exports.

State-owned manufacturing firms in some sectors also have been largely protected from competition with foreign firms within China by relatively high tariff and nontariff barriers, which drastically limit foreign imports. China has reduced its average tariff level signifi-cantly in recent years, from 43.2 percent in 1992 to 17 percent as of October 1, 1997.[91] The present level of tariffs is not high compared with many developing countries. Tariff protection in India, for exam-ple, averages about twice that in China.[92] China also has maintained an array of nontariff barriers. These include well-known forms of protection, such as import licensing and quotas, as well as less com-monly used restrictive practices, such as state trading and designated trading.[93] Nontariff barriers in 1996 applied to about one-third of all imports. The World Bank estimates that the tariff equivalent of these nontariff barriers averages 9 percent.[94] Again this figure is not high compared with India, which has used nontariff barriers for decades to effectively preclude imports of almost all consumer goods. Nonetheless, because of the way that Chinese tariff and nontariff bar-riers are structured, some sectors remain highly protected. The World Bank, for example, estimates that effective rates of protection on machinery and equipment exceed 100 percent and on transport equipment, 500 percent.[95]

The same protection of state-owned firms is evident in the service sector. Only a handful of foreign banks with branches in Pudong are able to take renminbi deposits and offer renminbi-denominated loans. And, as explained in chapter 4, these banks are subject to numerous restrictions that effectively preclude them from competing with domestic banks. Much the same is true in the insurance indus-try. Foreign firms were kept out of the domestic market for more than a decade after reform began. In 1992 the People's Bank of China licensed the first foreign firm, American International Group, to sell insurance in China. But the license allowed AIG to operate in one city—Shanghai—and only to sell life and property insurance. Since then Tokio Marine and Fire Insurance Company of Japan, Manulife of Canada, Winterthur Swiss Insurance, and a few other foreign firms have been allowed to enter the market. But some of them were required to take on Chinese partners as a condition for receiving a license. They also are restricted to sell insurance only in Shanghai and in Guangzhou and are limited to selling only one or two types of insurance products. Although these firms have begun to compete effectively in Shanghai and Guangzhou for the limited range of insurance products they are licensed to sell, their share of premium income in 1996 was only 0.74 percent.[96] The People's Insurance Company, a state-owned company, continues to be the dominant player in China's insurance market.

The difficulties China will face in meeting the expectations of the international community in the absence of fundamental domestic reform is especially obvious in services. The international community expects China to provide national treatment for foreign financial institutions, meaning that the latter would have the opportunity to engage in the same lines of business as domestic financial institutions. Thus foreign insurance companies would be able to offer a full range of insurance products throughout China; foreign accounting firms would be able to provide services to domestic firms; foreign securities firms would be able to open local branches or subsidiaries and to trade B shares for their customers without sharing commissions with Chinese brokers; and foreign banks would be able to offer a full range of banking services, including taking RMB-denominated deposits and making RMB-denominated loans, to foreign and domestic customers. Foreign law firms would be able to open offices in more than one city, hire Chinese nationals, represent foreign and Chinese clients in court proceedings, and form joint ventures with Chinese law firms.

The need for domestic reform to precede or at least go hand in hand with the further opening of the domestic banking market follows from the discussion in chapter 4. Given the current fragility of domestic banks, they would be unable to compete successfully against foreign banks. Foreign banks would be able to simultaneously offer higher rates on deposits and lower rates on loans than would state-owned banks. In the absence of interest rate liberalization, foreign banks would be more profitable and would be able to offer depositors and lenders more services than do Chinese banks. Thus with or without interest rate liberalization, allowing foreign banks unrestricted access to the domestic market would lead to a large outflow of deposits from domestic banks into foreign banks.

Because the assets of Chinese banks are tied up in nonperforming loans, these institutions would be unable to meet the demands of depositors, exposing the underlying insolvency of China's largest state-owned banks. Premature liberalization thus would set off the type of domestic financial crisis discussed above.

Again, if China can implement Premier Zhu Rongji's aggressive reform schedule, which calls for completing reforms of both state-owned banks and state-owned enterprises within three years, the stage will be set for China's accession to the World Trade Organization. Even if China is not able to come into compliance with all of the provisions of the World Trade Organization on the date of its entry, developing a strong and credible reform in these difficult areas is likely to lead members of the working party to take a more positive view toward China's accession. Reasonable phase-in periods for some requirements will be politically more palatable if there is a strong forward momentum of domestic reforms in China.

Implications for the United States

Many analyses of China's future role in the world, particularly the likely course of relations between China and the United States, take China's continued rapid economic growth as a given.[97] Richard Bernstein and Ross H. Munro go further, asserting that China's rising economic strength already has contributed to more aggressive behavior, will give China the basis for a world-class military and technological capability, and is likely to lead to conflict.[98] They believe that China is on the verge of becoming an economic and military superpower and argue that the primary U.S. policy objective in Asia "must be to prevent China's size, power, and ambition from making it a regional hegemon."[99] They further argue that "the United States cannot block Chinese hegemony in Asia unless Japan is an equal and willing partner."[100]

Yet this study suggests that an extrapolation of past growth into the indefinite future is highly problematic. External observers have placed far too much weight on indicators suggesting the success of China's economic transition, while ignoring deep structural problems that have not been resolved. These structural problems mean that China's sustained and rapid growth is far from assured. Even if

China's leaders have the political will and power to implement fully Premier Zhu Rongji's ambitious reform program, the pace of economic growth is almost certain to decline somewhat as fiscal resources are devoted to bank recapitalization and enterprise restructuring.

Apart from the cost of bank recapitalization, the World Bank has forecast that even if deepening reforms are successful, the pace of growth in China is likely to fall by about half from its current level, to 5 percent by 2020. The decline is the consequence of several factors. The first is China's aging population. By "2020 the labor force will essentially have stopped growing."[101] Second, they forecast that because of the law of diminishing returns, each additional unit of capital will contribute less to output. Third, structural change, such as shifting labor from agriculture to manufacturing and services, will no longer be a significant source of growth. Finally, the technology gap with other countries will be smaller, diminishing the impetus for technical change. Because of China's huge population, even a slower growth path will propel China's economy to become the second largest in the world by 2020. But in 2020 China's per capita income would be less than that of Portugal today and less than half of that of the United States.[102]

Of course, if Premier Zhu Rongji's program of accelerated reform is unsuccessful, future growth could be even lower than the forecast just summarized. Such a slowdown could trigger a domestic banking crisis and an ensuing inflationary spiral. At a minimum that would reduce the rate of savings, further undermining the prospect that China will be able to sustain reasonably rapid growth. Failed reforms and slower growth also increase the likelihood that China could become enmeshed in and exacerbate the Asian financial crisis.

Assisting China's Economic Transition

Rather than recruiting Japan to join the United States in blocking an emerging hegemon in Asia, the United States should be playing a more active role in assisting China in its economic transition. This goal would serve U.S. economic and noneconomic interests. In the 1990s up to the eve of the Asian financial crisis, as Japan's economy has stagnated, China has emerged as the principal engine of economic growth in Asia. Asia, in turn, has been the largest source of growth of the world economy in the 1990s and is the destination for fully one-third of U.S. exports. China alone has emerged since 1990 as the fastest-growing large export market for U.S. firms.[103] Sustaining this growth not only would serve U.S. commercial interests but likely would contribute importantly to the recovery from the Asian financial crisis. The U.S. government has placed enormous emphasis on the role that Japan could play in encouraging economic recovery in the region, through a combination of fiscal stimulus and further deregulation. This approach overlooks the fact that in 1990–97 while Japan's global imports rose by $103 billion, China's rose almost as much, $90 billion.

Since 1992 the United States has spent hundreds of millions of U.S. dollars in economic assistance for Russia under Title II of the Freedom Support Act.[104] About one-third of these funds has gone to support economic restructuring in three programmatic areas. In finance and banking the programs include commercial bank reform, enhanced banking supervision, and capital market development. In the fiscal area the program focuses on improving tax administration and creating a more efficient fiscal system. Programs to promote private enterprise focus on creating a regulatory framework favorable to private ownership and entrepreneurship and the commitment of U.S.$400 million to the U.S.-Russia Investment Fund, which makes equity investments and lends to support private sector growth. Although U.S. firms export far more products and invest more funds in China than in Russia, the United States has no comparable program to assist in China's enterprise and bank restructuring program.

In the long run a program of assisting China in its economic transition is likely to lead to a more pluralistic political system and to other changes that are desirable from the U.S. perspective. Historical experience elsewhere in East Asia, particularly in Taiwan, suggests that an economy that is market oriented and open to the outside world will eventually stimulate a demand for choice in governance and political leadership. Moreover, if China's reform program falters, it will retard China's further integration into the world economy. If China has a diminishing stake in the world economy, it is less likely to take cooperative steps on issues ranging from human rights to nonproliferation.

Both the World Bank and the International Monetary Fund have provided technical assistance to Chinese financial institutions, but the amounts are modest. The IMF since 1990 has run dozens of small seminars and workshops on monetary, budgetary, and tax reform as well as on statistics. These programs, however, have only occasionally addressed such important topics as central bank supervision of financial institutions or the development of the skills necessary to run true commercial banks. Many seminars have focused on rather technical issues, such as balance of payments accounting, in order to develop the accounting systems necessary to compile accurately the data that China has committed to report periodically to the IMF. More of the World Bank's technical assistance program deals directly with the health of the domestic banking system. World Bank funds have been used to hire major international accounting firms to assess the risks in the banking system and to provide training. For example, Price Waterhouse is engaged in a three-year program to train Chinese bankers in modern systems for classifying loans.[105]

The Hong Kong Monetary Authority and the Hong Kong Securities and Futures Commission are training Chinese officials in bank supervision and capital market development and regulation. But these Hong Kong organizations have not had firsthand experience in restructuring failing financial institutions. The U.S. government should launch a program to assist in China's economic transition, focusing on the lessons learned from the painful restructuring of the U.S. savings and loan industry in the first half of the 1990s.

China's Accession to the World Trade Organization

Besides initiating a significant program of technical assistance to China's financial system, if China does implement Premier Zhu Rongji's reform program, the United States should recalibrate its historic position on China's accession to the World Trade Organization. In the past the United States has demanded that China dismantle most of its trade barriers and come into compliance with WTO standards as a precondition for membership. Given the weak condition of China's state-owned sector, especially its banking system, however, immediate dismantling of all trade barriers could cause a collapse of significant parts of the economy. China would be forced to absorb all of the costs of restructuring in a compressed period of time, which is neither economically desirable nor politically feasible.

The U.S. negotiating position fails to take into account that China already enjoys the major benefits of WTO membership even though it is not a member. Most important, it already enjoys permanent most-favored-nation (MFN) treatment from every major country in the world. Only the United States grants this status on a year-by-year basis. The U.S. negotiating position on China's entry into the WTO is further weakened because even if China were to meet all of the demands of the United States and other members of the Working Party negotiating the terms of its entry into the WTO, China is not assured of receiving permanent MFN status in the U.S. market. Under conditions imposed by the Jackson-Vanik amendment to the Trade Act of 1974, the United States is precluded from extending MFN to China. Until the Jackson-Vanik amendment is suspended with respect to China, the United States will be forced to invoke the nonapplication provision of the Uruguay Round Treaty establishing the World Trade Organization, meaning that the United States will not recognize China's accession and will not provide permanent MFN treatment to Chinese goods entering the U.S. market. The United States thus will have to continue to renew China's MFN status on an annual basis until U.S. trade law is amended. Given the high level of congressional criticism of China, particularly in the U.S. House of Representatives, the ability of the Clinton administration to secure the necessary amendment of U.S. trade law is uncertain, further undermining China's incentives to undertake the commitments the United States and other industrialized countries seek from China. From the Chinese perspective, the question is why agree to a painful restructuring if attaining the most significant gain from WTO membership is uncertain?

Not only has the U.S. negotiating stance tended to ignore that in China's calculation the relative cost of entry into the WTO far outweighs the benefit, it also appears to undervalue the extent to which China's accession would serve U.S. interests. First, membership in the WTO would lock in the many market-opening measures that the Chinese have already taken. Quotas, licensing requirements, and other nontariff barriers have been eliminated on more than one thousand imports in recent years and, as noted, tariff levels have been reduced significantly.[106] China's trade negotiators in Geneva have pledged to what is called a stand-still posture, meaning that they will not pull back from liberalizing measures already put forward in their WTO accession negotiations. But this stance is not a binding agreement. If its economic growth should decline markedly or its trade balance deteriorate, China could raise tariffs and nontariff barriers with impunity. By contrast, once the country is in the WTO, any increase in trade protection would be subject to careful international monitoring and would have to be phased out as soon as possible.

Second, China's entry would lock it into a transparent, time-certain schedule of future reforms and opening-up measures, thus giving important information to U.S. and other foreign firms that would like to penetrate China's more closed sectors but now have no idea about when they should launch their marketing efforts. Finally, China's membership in the WTO would serve U.S. interests by providing a mechanism for dealing with inevitable trade frictions on a multilateral rather than a purely bilateral basis.

Licensing Chinese Banks in the United States

The U.S. regulatory agencies should continue to take a very cautious approach to licensing additional branches of China's largest state-owned banks to operate in the United States. Beginning in late 1992 and continuing through 1995 the Agricultural Bank of China, the Industrial and Commercial Bank, the Construction Bank of China, and the Bank of China, successively, applied to open branch banks in the United States.[107] Because they were unable to meet the capital adequacy standard set forth in U.S. law and because the People's Bank had not demonstrated that it exercised prudential supervision of state-owned banks on a consolidated basis, the U.S. Federal Reserve Board did not approve these applications.[108] Subsequently, three of these institutions withdrew their applications and resubmitted applications to open representative offices. Since representative offices are limited to general marketing and promotional activities and are not allowed to conduct banking business, the criteria for approval of representative offices are far less stringent than those for branches. As a result, the U.S. Federal Reserve in 1996 and 1997 approved the applications of the China Construction Bank, the Industrial and Commercial Bank, and the Agricultural Bank of China to open representative offices in New York.[109]

When these institutions failed to receive licenses to open branches in the United States, the People's Bank stepped up its prudential supervision of state banks. Notably, in 1996 it conducted an audit of the Bank of China Hong Kong branch, its first surveillance action on an overseas China-funded financial institution.[110] Given the fact that the Bank of China by international standards does an extraordinarily high portion of its business overseas, this action is most welcome.[111]

Except for the Bank of China, however, China's four largest banks do not publish their financial results on a consolidated basis. Furthermore, the capital of these banks relative to their assets is well below the Basle standard; indeed, it is likely to be negative on a realistic accounting basis. Thus branch licenses for these institutions would not be warranted until well after China launches the reform program outlined in chapter 4.

Conclusion

It is important to recognize that, unlike most of the countries in eastern and central Europe, most of the nonperforming loans of Chinese banks were not inherited from the prereform era. They mostly were created after reform began, as a by-product of the strategy of gradualism. Indeed, they were mostly created in the 1990s. Rather than subject state-owned firms to hard budget constraints and accept the short-term increase in unemployment and the transitional decline in output associated with the ensuing restructuring, under the strategy of gradualism the state provided subsidies of various kinds to keep virtually all existing firms going. Chinese reform mainly took the form of easing constraints that had precluded the development of a large and dynamic nonstate sector, rather than imposing market discipline on existing state-owned firms.

In part the rapid buildup of nonperforming loans in the financial system in the 1990s reflects the success of economic reforms in other areas. At the outset of reform state-owned enterprises benefited from a variety of implicit and explicit subsidies. Reforms gradually have closed off most of these subsidies, leaving preferential access to credit as the major policy instrument for supporting state-owned enterprises. By the early 1990s, for example, price reforms had virtually eliminated subsidies via access to underpriced agricultural and other raw materials. Reforms of the foreign exchange system, particularly the elimination of the two-tier pricing of foreign exchange at the beginning of 1994, largely eliminated the value of the implicit subsidy once provided to state-owned firms by preferential access to foreign exchange. Similarly the number of commodities requiring import licenses, another mechanism once used to support preferred state end users of scarce commodities, has been reduced in response to international pressure for China to conform to WTO trade standards. Finally, as shown earlier in table 2-4, by 1996 fiscal subsidies to loss-making state-owned enterprises measured as a percentage of gross domestic product were less than one-tenth the level of 1985.

The current stage of reform is in many ways more difficult than earlier stages of reform. Economically it is more complex since it requires closely coordinated reforms of state enterprises, the financial system, and tax administration. Politically it is extremely challenging for two reasons. First, the required closure of insolvent firms and the recapitalization and associated restructuring of the financial system is leading to rates of unemployment far higher than China has experienced since the economic depression in the early 1960s, in the wake of the catastrophic Great Leap Forward.[112] In contrast to the first two decades of reform, in which almost everyone shared to some degree in the gains from growth, the current phase will reduce the real incomes of a significant portion of the population, at least on a transitory basis. This outcome is certain to stress the political system far beyond the experience of recent decades.

Second, the restructuring of the banking system, particularly eventually allowing the emergence of private banks through the sale of shares of existing banks to individual investors or by the licensing of new private institutions and expanding the role of foreign financial institutions, will require the state and the party to surrender a great deal of economic and political power. Since the financial system in particular is the last remaining powerful instrument through which the state and party directly influence resource allocation, they are naturally reluctant to give up this power.

Despite these difficulties, it seems likely that the leadership will continue to push its current reform agenda aggressively. However painful the process of closing insolvent firms, recapitalizing and commercializing the banking system, and relinquishing the power to direct loans, these reforms will in the end lead to a more efficient system of resource allocation and utilization. That, in turn, is most likely to ensure the growth of jobs and output that the party views as essential for political stability. The alternative of delaying or slowing the current reforms in the short run might mitigate some of the adverse

Statistical Appendix

Table A-1. Assets of Chinese Financial Institutions, 1986, 1994, 1995

Renminbi billions

Financial institution	1986	1994	1995
Central bank	334.5	1,758.8	2,062.4
State banks	1,231.1	7,635.7	8,803.6
Policy banks	0	513.3	747.3
State Development Bank of China	0	90.8	194.6
Agricultural Development Bank of China	0	420.0	542.5
Import-Export Bank of China	0	2.5	10.2
Specialized banks	1,231.1	7,122.4	8,056.3
Industrial and Commercial Bank of China	419.5	2,633.9	3,107.5
Bank of China	345.0	1,837.9	1,995.1
Agricultural Bank of China	236.9	1,253.1	1,231.0
Construction Bank of China	229.7	1,397.5	1,722.7
Commercial Banks	2.6	590.0	758.7
National Commercial Banks	0	401.8	494.4
Bank of Communications	0	305.0	362.0
CITIC Industrial Bank	0	70.7	86.5
China Everbright Bank	0	20.3	33.7
Huaxia Bank	0	5.8	12.2
Regional Commercial Banks	2.6	188.2	264.3
Merchants Bank	0	44.7	64.8
China Investment Bank	2.6	44.5	52.7
Guangdong Development Bank	0	43.1	54.7
Fujian Industrial Bank	0	19.8	19.7
Pudong Development Bank	0	17.8	48.0
Shenzhen Development Bank	0	15.4	20.3
Yentai Housing Bank	0	2.5	3.6
Bengbu Housing Bank	0	0.4	0.5
Nonbank Financial Institutions	161.6	1,214.2	1,584.7
Rural Credit Cooperatives	122.5	505.3	679.1
Trust and Investment Companies	29.3	390.6	458.6
Urban Credit Cooperatives	3.2	214.8	303.9
Finance Companies	0	27.6	49.0

Table A-1. (continued)

Renminbi billions

Financial institution	1986	1994	1995
People's Insurance Company	6.6	66.1	78.1
China Pacific Insurance Company	0	4.2	8.4
China Ping-an Insurance Company	0	5.6	7.6
Total assets (excluding foreign)	1,729.8	11,198.7	13,209.4
Memo: Foreign banks and finance companies	*	101.7	159.8
Foreign insurance companies	0	n.a.	0.5

Sources: *Almanac of China's Finance and Banking 1989* (Beijing: China Financial Publishing House, 1989), pp. 70–71; *Almanac 1991*, pp. 121, 125; *Almanac 1992*, pp. 517–18, 520–21, 540, 546; *Almanac 1996*, pp. 108, 122; *Almanac 1997*, p. 499. People's Bank of China, *China Financial Outlook '96* (Beijing: China Financial Publishing House, 1996), pp. 67–68; World Bank, *The Chinese Economy: Fighting Inflation, Deepening Reform* (Washington, 1996), p. 26; Anjali Kumar and others, *China's Non-Bank Financial Institutions: Trust and Investment Companies*, Discussion Paper 358 (Washington: World Bank, 1997), p. 10.

n.a. Not available.

* Negligible.

Note: Data for leasing, securities, and mutual fund companies are not available.

Table A-2. Regional Distribution of Loans and Deposits by Chinese State Banks

RMB billions

	Deposits						Loans[a]						Loan-to-deposit ratio					
	1988	1989	1990	1991	1992	1993	1988	1989	1990	1991	1992	1993	1988	1989	1990	1991	1992	1993
National	742.60	901.44	1166.32	1487.91	1889.11	2323.03	1055.15	1240.97	1516.65	1804.42	2161.55	2646.12	1.42	1.38	1.30	1.21	1.14	1.14
Beijing	58.09	67.81	84.59	108.10	135.55	164.58	41.57	48.01	55.22	63.27	76.94	97.16	0.72	0.71	0.65	0.59	0.57	0.59
Tianjin	15.66	17.88	23.54	29.61	37.44	45.96	27.63	31.91	38.91	45.00	53.95	65.60	1.76	1.78	1.65	1.52	1.44	1.43
Hebei	34.67	43.52	55.54	69.87	87.96	107.27	45.04	52.48	63.17	74.01	89.19	108.60	1.30	1.21	1.14	1.06	1.01	1.01
Shanxi	19.39	24.91	31.43	38.14	46.95	56.83	23.83	28.10	35.73	42.75	51.42	62.97	1.23	1.13	1.14	1.12	1.10	1.11
Inner Mongolia	11.99	13.62	16.98	20.57	26.28	30.89	18.02	21.27	27.29	32.68	39.52	49.20	1.50	1.56	1.61	1.59	1.50	1.59
Liaoning	41.52	50.71	63.01	77.60	104.50	125.26	62.08	74.22	92.91	112.35	136.33	164.13	1.50	1.46	1.47	1.45	1.30	1.31
Jilin	17.76	20.45	25.25	31.67	40.90	49.56	33.43	38.48	50.70	62.91	76.14	93.55	1.88	1.88	2.01	1.99	1.86	1.89
Heilongjiang	29.08	34.84	43.63	53.83	69.01	79.85	45.51	52.59	65.17	79.89	94.81	115.41	1.56	1.51	1.49	1.48	1.37	1.45
Shanghai	39.53	45.09	57.18	71.17	108.92	146.84	54.77	65.69	80.48	94.95	123.99	155.02	1.39	1.46	1.41	1.33	1.14	1.06
Jiangsu	38.73	48.15	64.72	84.11	114.00	145.69	60.98	68.90	82.32	97.83	123.01	145.95	1.57	1.43	1.27	1.16	1.08	1.00
Zhejiang	27.58	33.60	45.78	58.62	75.85	95.11	34.69	40.04	48.17	56.65	70.54	87.19	1.26	1.19	1.05	0.97	0.93	0.92
Anhui	16.56	19.88	25.02	33.09	41.03	51.44	28.32	32.47	40.08	49.51	59.95	72.98	1.71	1.63	1.60	1.50	1.46	1.42
Fujian	18.36	22.67	29.80	38.92	53.33	62.91	22.62	26.81	32.01	37.24[b]	46.96	59.90	1.23	1.18	1.07	0.96	0.88	0.95
Jiangxi	14.40	16.73	21.75	26.93	34.83	45.08	22.95	27.39	33.91	41.91	51.72	61.72	1.59	1.64	1.56	1.56	1.48	1.37
Shandong	45.09	53.14	68.72	84.51	107.30	133.12	66.51	76.48	93.63	111.34	132.43	157.74	1.48	1.44	1.36	1.32	1.23	1.18
Henan	30.27	36.06	46.73	60.37	73.01	92.46	44.93	51.15	63.51	77.20	90.98	110.68	1.48	1.42	1.36	1.28	1.25	1.20
Hubei	28.27	32.72	40.15	49.76	62.23	79.89	51.39	59.35	72.38	83.90	98.15	116.05	1.82	1.81	1.80	1.69	1.58	1.45
Hunan	18.84	23.87	31.98	41.34	52.73	63.69	32.87	38.46	45.77	54.97	66.48	79.80	1.74	1.61	1.43	1.33	1.26	1.25
Guandong	72.61	86.29	114.16	156.62	244.62	282.24	97.57	109.02	127.51	147.02	186.00	230.70	1.34	1.26	1.12	0.94	0.76	0.82
Guangxi	14.62	17.40	23.50	29.85	41.84	55.25	21.06	23.77	27.82	32.90	41.12	51.19	1.44	1.37	1.18	1.10	0.98	0.93
Hainan	5.64	6.40	8.75	11.31	27.58	33.96	8.56	9.70	11.99	14.51	21.00	28.66	1.52	1.52	1.37	1.28	0.76	0.84
Sichuan	36.87	44.28	56.61	72.72	92.46	109.96	53.58	62.69	77.18	96.50	119.28	146.12	1.45	1.42	1.36	1.33	1.29	1.33
Guizhou	9.08	10.75	13.48	17.45	21.01	25.37	12.54	14.23	17.31	21.82	26.52	32.37	1.38	1.32	1.28	1.25	1.26	1.28
Yunnan	15.96	19.85	26.56	32.65	42.35	51.97	18.43	21.25	25.11	29.54	37.32	46.83	1.15	1.07	0.95	0.90	0.88	0.90
Tibet	1.76	1.96	2.01	2.44	2.49	2.88	0.92	1.39	1.67	1.61	1.63	2.77	0.52	0.71	0.83	0.66	0.65	0.96
Shaanxi	17.55	21.41	27.93	34.93	43.70	53.70	25.43	30.57	38.57	46.26	56.12	67.40	1.45	1.43	1.38	1.32	1.28	1.26
Gansu	10.55	12.38	15.92	20.01	25.72	30.34	13.99	16.21	20.21	25.09	30.21	36.78	1.33	1.31	1.27	1.25	1.17	1.21
Qinghai	4.22	4.57	5.61	6.47	7.24	8.53	4.88	5.89	7.22	8.75	10.51	13.42	1.16	1.29	1.29	1.35	1.45	1.57
Ningxia	3.22	3.83	4.85	5.98	7.33	8.87	4.70	5.50	6.95	8.38	9.89	12.09	1.46	1.44	1.43	1.40	1.35	1.36
Xinjiang	14.18	16.76	22.33	28.42	33.87	40.63	13.99	17.37	23.44	30.04	38.12	46.77	0.99	1.04	1.05	1.06	1.13	1.15

	Loan-to-deposit ratio, national avg. = 1.00						'Excess loans' and 'loan shortfalls' to provinces (actual loans − expected loans)						'Excess' or 'shortfall' as percentage of provincial GDP				
	1988	1989	1990	1991	1992	1993	1988	1989	1990	1991	1992	1993	1989c	1990	1991c	1992	1993
National	1.00	1.00	1.00	1.00	1.00	1.00	—	—	—	—	—	—	-99.48	-109.38	-113.25	-110.22	-104.59
Beijing	0.52	0.51	0.50	0.48	0.50	0.52	-40.97	-45.34	-54.78	-67.83	-78.16	-90.31	25.75	26.69	26.52	27.02	24.71
Tianjin	1.28	1.30	1.27	1.25	1.26	1.25	5.38	7.30	8.30	9.09	11.11	13.25	-9.92	-10.83	-11.17	-9.92	-8.67
Hebei	0.94	0.88	0.87	0.87	0.89	0.89	-4.22	-7.43	-9.05	-10.72	-11.46	-13.59	-17.69	-12.85	-8.12	-4.43	-2.73
Shanxi	0.89	0.82	0.87	0.92	0.96	0.97	-3.72	-6.19	-5.14	-3.50	-2.30	-1.76	9.80	18.17	24.09	24.96	28.80
Inner Mongolia	1.09	1.13	1.24	1.31	1.31	1.40	0.98	2.52	5.21	7.73	9.45	14.01					
Liaoning	1.09	1.06	1.13	1.19	1.14	1.15	3.08	4.41	10.97	18.24	16.76	21.45	4.78	11.36	17.00	12.91	11.86
Jilin	1.37	1.37	1.54	1.64	1.63	1.66	8.20	10.33	17.87	24.50	29.34	37.10	28.58	45.34	57.79	57.02	55.20
Heilongjiang	1.14	1.10	1.15	1.22	1.20	1.27	4.19	4.63	8.43	14.61	15.85	24.45	7.94	12.80	19.88	18.52	22.71
Shanghai	1.01	1.06	1.08	1.10	0.99	0.93	-1.40	3.62	6.12	8.64	-0.64	-12.24	5.19	8.22	10.07	-0.57	-8.10
Jiangsu	1.14	1.04	0.98	0.96	0.94	0.88	5.95	2.61	-1.84	-4.17	-7.43	-20.00	2.13	-1.40	-2.84	-3.77	-7.26
Zhejiang	0.91	0.87	0.81	0.80	0.81	0.80	-4.50	-6.22	-11.36	-14.44	-16.68	-21.15	-7.87	-13.58	-14.68	-13.67	-12.45
Anhui	1.24	1.19	1.23	1.23	1.28	1.25	4.79	5.10	7.54	9.38	13.00	14.39	8.92	12.44	15.63	17.81	14.69
Fujian	0.89	0.86	0.83	0.79	0.77	0.84	-3.47	-4.40	-6.74	-9.96	-14.06	-11.76	-10.56	-14.67	-18.19	-20.24	-11.44
Jiangxi	1.16	1.19	1.20	1.28	1.30	1.20	2.49	4.36	5.63	9.25	11.87	10.37	11.99	13.41	20.28	21.21	14.77
Shandong	1.07	1.05	1.05	1.09	1.08	1.04	2.44	3.32	4.27	8.85	9.66	6.11	2.77	3.20	5.54	4.87	2.26
Henan	1.08	1.03	1.05	1.05	1.09	1.05	1.92	1.51	2.74	3.99	7.44	5.36	1.83	3.21	4.02	6.13	3.39
Hubei	1.32	1.32	1.39	1.39	1.38	1.28	11.22	14.31	20.17	23.55	26.95	25.05	20.41	25.50	27.49	26.91	19.29
Hunan	1.27	1.17	1.10	1.10	1.10	1.10	6.10	5.60	4.18	4.84	6.15	7.25	8.74	5.96	6.15	6.68	6.08
Guandong	0.98	0.92	0.86	0.77	0.66	0.72	-5.60	-9.77	-20.94	-42.92	-93.90	-90.79	-7.45	-14.23	-24.10	-40.94	-28.15
Guangxi	1.05	0.99	0.91	0.91	0.86	0.81	0.29	-0.18	-2.74	-3.30	-6.75	-11.74	-0.53	-6.97	-7.28	-11.80	-14.90
Hainan	1.10	1.10	1.05	1.06	0.67	0.74	0.55	0.89	0.61	0.79	-10.56	-10.02	10.23	6.44	7.36	-74.51	-44.51
Sichuan	1.06	1.03	1.05	1.09	1.13	1.17	1.19	1.73	3.57	8.31	13.49	20.87	1.73	3.11	6.49	9.10	10.65
Guizhou	1.00	0.96	0.99	1.03	1.10	1.12	-0.36	-0.57	-0.22	0.66	2.48	3.47	-2.42	-0.86	2.27	7.48	8.50
Yunnan	0.84	0.78	0.73	0.75	0.77	0.79	-4.25	-6.08	-9.43	-10.06	-11.14	-12.37	-19.26	-23.81	-23.23	-21.84	-18.68
Tibet	0.38	0.52	0.64	0.54	0.57	0.84	-1.58	-1.31	-0.94	-1.35	-1.22	-0.51	-59.74	-38.52	-44.23	-36.61	-13.69
Shaanxi	1.05	1.04	1.06	1.09	1.12	1.10	0.49	1.10	2.25	3.90	6.12	6.23	3.23	6.02	9.11	12.42	10.14
Gansu	0.96	0.95	0.98	1.03	1.03	1.06	-1.00	-0.83	-0.49	0.82	0.78	2.22	-3.84	-2.10	3.22	2.59	6.20
Qinghai	0.84	0.94	0.99	1.12	1.27	1.38	-1.12	-0.40	-0.08	0.90	2.23	3.70	-6.64	-1.13	12.45	26.40	35.04
Ningxia	1.06	1.04	1.10	1.16	1.18	1.20	0.12	0.23	0.64	1.13	1.50	1.99	4.08	10.53	16.47	19.12	20.19
Xinjiang	0.72	0.75	0.81	0.87	0.98	1.01	-6.16	-5.70	-5.60	-4.43	-0.63	0.49	-26.23	-22.22	-14.20	-1.66	1.01

Sources: Almanac of China's Finance and Banking 1991 (Beijing: China's Financial Publishing House, 1992), pp. 45–46; Almanac 1993, pp. 360–61; Almanac 1994, pp. 439–40; and national and provincial data on GDP from State Statistical Bureau, China Statistical Yearbook, 1990–1994.

a. The data on deposits and loans are the amounts outstanding at the end of the period.

b. Fujian's 1991 loan amount appears to have been a typographical error in original (27.24).

c. Calculated on the basis of GNP rather than GDP.

Table A-3. Bank of China, Estimated Average Cost of Funds, 1989

| | Amount | | | Contribution |
| | RMB | | Interest | to weighted |
Source of funds	billions	Percent	rate	interest rate
Borrowing from central bank	96.3	65.6	10.44	0.0685
Deposits by households	17.6	12.0	14.75	0.0177
Deposits by enterprises	32.8	22.4	4.8	0.0108
All	146.7	100.0	9.69	1.0000

Sources: *Almanac of China's Finance and Banking 1990* (Beijing: China Financial Publishing House, 1990), p. 169; *Almanac 1991*, p. 156. Interest rate on household and enterprise deposits estimated in tables A-5 and A-6.

Table A-4. Bank of China, Maturity Structure of Renminbi Savings Deposits, 1987–94

RMB billions and (percent)

Year	Total deposits	Sight deposits	<3 year deposits[a]	Indexed deposits
1987	2.273	(23)	(77)	0.000 (0)
1988	6.928	(25)	(53)	1.537 (22)
1989	17.597	2.798 (16)	9.201 (52)	5.598 (32)
1990	31.210	4.697 (15)	17.998 (58)	8.515 (27)
1991	47.197	7.987 (17)	26.905 (57)	12.305 (26)
1992	74.705	18.160 (24)	48.456 (65)	8.089 (11)
1993	108.129	27.120 (25)	68.249 (63)	12.760 (12)
1994	164.827	39.422 (24)	125.405 (76)	

Sources: *Almanac of China's Finance and Banking 1991*, p. 48; *Almanac 1992*, p. 533; *Almanac 1994*, p. 526; *Almanac 1995*, p. 535; People's Bank of China, *Financial Outlook '94* (Beijing: China Financial Publishing House, 1994), p. 95; *Financial Outlook '96*, p. 96

a. The 1994 data for < 3-year deposits are inclusive of indexed deposits, data for prior years are not. The share of sight deposits for the Bank of China in 1987 and 1988 is assumed to be equal to that for all financial institutions. The < 3 year deposit share is calculated as a residual.

Table A-5. Bank of China, Estimated Cost of Funds from Savings Deposits

	Sight deposits		<3 Year deposits		Indexed deposits		Estimated cost of funds
	Percent[a]	r[b]	Percent[a]	r[b]	Percent[a]	r[b]	
1987	23	2.88	77	7.9	0	0.00	6.745
				8.1			6.90
1988	25	2.88	53	7.7	22	18.35	8.84
1989 Q3	16	2.88	52	11.0	32	28.64	15.35
1989	16	2.88	52	11.0	32	26.82	14.77
1992	24	1.80	65	7.0	11	9.18	5.99
1994	24	3.15	76	0.5		18.49	

Sources: Tables 3-9, A-4.

a. Percent is the share of deposits of each type. For 1994 the share for < 3-year deposits includes indexed deposits, for prior years it does not.

b. r is the estimated interest rate prevailing for each category of deposit, taken from or estimated from data in table 3-9.

Table A-6. Bank of China, Estimated Cost of Enterprise Deposits

	Sight deposits		<3 Year deposits		Indexed deposits		Estimated cost of funds, r[a]
Period	Percent	r[a]	Percent	r[a]	Percent	r[a]	
1989	88	2.88	6	11.0	6	26.8	4.80

Sources: World Bank, *Financial Sector Policies and Institutional Development* (Washington, 1990), p. 8, table 1-2, and table 3-9 in this book. Table 1-2 gives the sight deposit share of enterprise deposits in all banks in 1989 as 88 percent as derived from 89 percent and 86 percent in 1988 and 1990, respectively. I assume that the average applies to the Bank of China in 1989 and that the rest of the bank's enterprise deposits were evenly split between < 3-year deposits and indexed deposits.

a. See table A-5.

Table A-7. Supplementary Interest Paid on Indexed Time Deposits, 1988–91, 1993–97

Year	Month(s)	Supplementary interest
1988	October-December	7.28
1989	January-March	12.71
...	April-June	12.59
...	July-September	13.64
...	October-November	8.36
...	December	...
1990	January	.89
...	February	1.46
...	March	0
...	April	1.42
...	May	1.38
...	June-December	0
1991	January-November	0
1993	July-December	0
1994	January-February	0
...	March	1.19
...	April	1.50
...	May	2.70
...	June	3.38
...	July	4.58
...	August	4.27
...	September	4.96
...	October	5.62
...	November	6.57
...	December	8.79
1995	January	9.84
...	February	10.38
...	March	11.87
...	April	11.47
...	May	12.27
...	June	12.92
...	July	13.01
...	August	12.99
...	September	12.64
...	October	12.07
...	November	12.07
...	December	13.24
1996	January	11.31
...	February	10.83
...	March	11.29
...	April	9.00

Table A-7. (continued)

Year	Month(s)	Supplementary interest
...	May	7.61
...	June	7.23
...	July	6.24
...	August	4.75
...	September	3.61
...	October	3.62
...	November	4.04
...	December	3.72
1997	January	2.87
...	February	2.09
...	March	0.94
...	April	0.17
...	May	0

Source: *Almanac of China's Finance and Banking 1990*, p. 187; *Almanac 1991*, p. 85; *Almanac 1995*, p. 513; *Almanac 1996*, p. 468; and *Jinrong shibao* (Financial News), various issues.

Notes

Notes to Chapter 1

1. On declining disparities in the regional distribution of output in the first decade of reform see David L. Denny, "Provincial Economic Differences Diminished in the Decade of Economic Reform," in *China's Economic Dilemmas in the 1990s: The Problems of Reforms, Modernization, and Interdependence,* Committee Print, Joint Economic Committee, 102 Cong. 1 sess. (Government Printing Office, April 1991) vol. 1, pp. 186–208; and Huo Shitao, "Regional Inequality Variations and Central Government Policy, 1978–1988," in Jia Hao and Lin Zhimin, eds., *Changing Central-Local Relations in China: Reform and State Capacity* (Westview Press, 1994), pp. 181–206. On urban-rural inequality see Zhao Renwei, "Three Features of the Distribution of Income during the Transition to Reform," in Keith Griffin and Zhao Renwei, eds., *The Distribution of Income in China* (St. Martin's Press, 1993), pp. 74–92. Zhao shows that rural incomes as a percent of urban incomes rose from 1978 through the mid-1980s and then began to fall. By 1990, the last year for which he presents data, the degree of income disparity prevailing in 1978 had been almost exactly restored. According to the World Bank, inequality in the distribution of income within rural China declined in the early years of economic reform. The gini coefficient fell from 0.257 in 1979 to 0.225 percent in 1982. World Bank, *China: Long Term Issues and Options* (Washington, 1985), p. 29.

2. The poverty line is defined as the income level required to purchase a 2,150-calorie-a-day food consumption basket that supplies adequate nutrients for normal human functioning plus a sum for expenditures on nonfood commodities and services based on the average expenditure pattern of the poor. World Bank, *China: Strategies for Reducing Poverty in the 1990s* (Washington, 1992), pp. ix, 22.

3. Carol Graham, *Safety Nets, Politics, and the Poor: Transitions to Market Economies* (Brookings, 1994); and Susan Shirk, *The Political Logic of Economic Reform in China* (University of California Press, 1993).

4. Nicholas R. Lardy, *China in the World Economy* (Washington: Institute for International Economics, 1994), pp. 58–63.

5. Thomas G. Rawski, "Progress Without Privatization," Research Paper Series CH 17, Policy Research Department (Washington: World Bank, October 1992).

6. William A. Byrd, "The Impact of the Two-Tier Plan/Market System in Chinese Industry," *Journal of Comparative Economics*, vol. 11 (September 1987), pp. 295–308; and Wu Jinglian and Zhao Renwei, "The Dual Pricing System in China's Industry," *Journal of Comparative Economics*, vol. 11 (September 1987), pp. 309–18.

7. Lawrence J. Lau, Yingyi Qian, and Gerard Roland, "Reform without Losers: An Interpretation of China's Dual-Track Approach to Transition," unpublished manuscript, November 1997.

8. Nicholas R. Lardy, *Foreign Trade and Economic Reform in China, 1978-1991* (Cambridge University Press, 1992).

9. The literature is voluminous. See, for example, Peter Murrell, "The Transition According to Cambridge, Mass.," *Journal of Economic Literature*, vol. 33 (March 1995), pp. 164–78. Andrew G. Walder, ed., "China's Transitional Economy: Interpreting Its Significance," in *China's Transitional Economy* (Oxford University Press, 1996), pp. 1–17; John McMillan and Barry Naughton, "How to Reform a Planned Economy: Lessons from China," *Oxford Review of Economic Policy*, vol. 8 (Spring 1992), pp. 130–43; Barry Naughton, *Growing Out of the Plan: Chinese Economic Reform 1978-1993* (Cambridge University Press, 1995); and Thomas G. Rawski, "Implications of China's Reform Experience," in *China's Transitional Economy*, pp. 188–211.

10. Jeffrey D. Sachs and Wing Thye Woo, "Structural Factors in the Economic Reforms of China, Eastern Europe, and the Former Soviet Union," *Economic Policy*, vol. 18 (April 1994), pp. 102–45; and Wing Thye Woo, "The Art of Reforming Centrally Planned Economies: Comparing China, Poland, and Russia," *Journal of Comparative Economics*, vol. 18 (June 1994), pp. 276–308.

11. This estimate of subsidies to state-owned enterprises is inclusive of explicit fiscal subsidies paid from the central government budget to offset financial losses; implicit fiscal subsides in the form of interest rate subsidies on funds borrowed from the Construction Bank, plus funds provided directly by the State Planning Commission, both to cover capital construction expenditures; and quasi-fiscal subsidies, the amount of lending by the central bank to the financial system for policy loans to meet the working capital needs of state enterprises. Harry G. Broadman, *Meeting the Challenge of Chinese Enterprise Reform*, Discussion Paper 283 (Washington: World Bank, 1995), p. 15. These subsidies to state-owned enterprises form a very large share of the state public sector deficit.

12. Many of these firms thus appear to be value subtractors, that is, the value of the output they produce is less than the value of the inputs into the production process. For a discussion of this phenomenon in transition economies, see Ronald I. McKinnon, *The Order of Economic Liberalization: Financial Control in the Transition to a Market Economy*, 2d ed. (Johns Hopkins University Press, 1993), pp. 162–86.

13. Unfunded pension liabilities are analyzed in chapter 2. Only a portion of interenterprise arrears, what the Chinese call triangular debt, is included in the calculation of the relative value of assets and liabilities. Unlike taxes, which are entirely liabilities to the state; loans, which are entirely liabilities to banks; or pensions, which are entirely liabilities to workers, interenterprise arrears are partly debts within the state-owned enterprise sector. Although these interenterprise debts are large in gross terms, the net debt of state firms to nonstate firms composed only about two-thirds of total triangular debt at year-end 1994. See the discussion of asset-to-liability ratios of state-owned firms in chapter 2.

14. The concept of money here is M2, that is, currency in circulation plus demand and time deposits of households, enterprises, and institutions. "Materials on Financial Statistics for the Fourth Quarter of 1996," *Jinrong shibao (Financial News)*, January 21, 1997, p. 1; State Statistical Bureau, "Statistical Communiqué on Socio-Economic Development in 1996," *Beijing Review*, March 10-16, 1997, p. 23; and Morris Goldstein and Philip Turner, *Banking Crises in Emerging Economies: Origins and Policy Options*, Economic Papers 46 (Basle: Bank for International Settlements, 1996), p. 14.

15. An article based on an interview with Dai Xianglong, then vice governor of the central bank, states that the proportion of nonperforming loans of China's large state-owned banks "has been rising by 2 percentage points per annum in recent years." Zhao Yining, "The Financial Situation and Financial Reform," *Liaowang* (Outlook), May 15, 1995, pp. 12–13. As discussed in detail in chapter 3, for China's four largest banks the magnitude of nonperforming loans stood at 20, 22, and 25 percent of all loans outstanding at year-end 1994, 1995, and 1997, respectively.

16. Bank insolvency occurs when the value of a bank's assets is less than the value of its liabilities.

17. Total government revenues relative to gross domestic product fell from 31.2 percent in 1978 to 10.7 percent in 1995. State Statistical Bureau, *China Statistical Yearbook 1996* (Beijing: China Statistical Publishing House, 1996), p. 223. Because some revenue and expenditure items have been reclassified over time, the 1978 and 1995 revenue data are not exactly comparable. For example, subsidies for losses of state-owned enterprises beginning in 1986 were treated as a negative revenue item. Adjusting the 1995 data to make it comparable to that for 1978 would add RMB 32.8 billion or 0.6 percent of gross domestic product (see table 2-4). However, price subsidies financed from the state budget were treated as a reduction in revenue until 1986 when they were changed to a budgetary expenditure. Adjusting the 1978 revenue figure to make it comparable to that for 1995 adds approximately 1 percentage point.

18. The concept of the public sector deficit is explained at the outset of the next section of this chapter. World Bank, *The Chinese Economy: Fighting Inflation, Deepening Reform* (Washington, 1996), p. 66; and World Bank, *Economic Note* (Beijing: World Bank Resident Mission, February 1997), p. 14. See also Christine P. W. Wong, Christopher Heady, and Wing T. Woo, *Fiscal Management and Economic Reform in the People's Republic of China* (Oxford University Press, 1995), pp. 27–29. They estimate China's "consolidated deficit," a concept similar to the public sector nonfinancial deficit.

19. World Bank, *The Chinese Economy: Fighting Inflation, Deepening Reform*, p. 65.

20. Ibid., p. 10.

21. As discussed in chapter 4, the U.S. government in the savings and loan crisis committed significant federal budget resources to limit the financial losses of depositors in failed institutions.

22. Thomas G. Rawski, "How Fast Has Chinese Industry Grown?" unpublished manuscript, March 1991; Robert Michael Field, "China's Industrial Performance Since 1978," *China Quarterly*, no. 131 (September 1992), p. 588; Gary Jefferson, "Growth and Productivity Change in Chinese Industry: Problems of Measurement," in Manoranjan J. Dutta, ed., *Asian Economic Regimes: An Adaptive Innovation Paradigm*, Research in Asian Economic Studies, vol. 4B (JAI Press, 1992), pp. 427–42, cited and summarized in Peter Harrold, "China: Enterprise Reform Strategy," unpublished manuscript, August 27, 1993, p. 49; Jeffrey D. Sachs and Wing Thye Woo, "Chinese Economic Growth: Explanations and the Tasks Ahead," in *China's Economic Future: Challenges to U.S. Policy*, Committee Print, Joint Economic Committee, 104 Cong. 2 sess. (GPO, August 1996), p. 75; and Ren Ruoen, *China's Economic Performance in an International Perspective* (Paris: Organization for Economic Cooperation and Development, 1997).

23. For example, the deflator that the State Statistical Bureau uses to calculate the rate of growth of industrial output shows that prices doubled between 1978 and 1995. However, the bureau's separately published index of producer goods shows that prices tripled over the same period. State Statistical Bureau, *China Statistical Yearbook 1996*, pp. 42, 271.

24. Official data show the output of collectively owned firms grew in real terms at 16.1 percent a year between 1980 and 1992. The independent estimate suggests a growth rate of 12.4 percent. Gary H. Jefferson, Thomas G. Rawski, and Yuxin Zheng, "Chinese Industrial Productivity: Trends, Measurement Issues, and Recent Developments," *Journal of Comparative Economics*, vol. 23 (October 1996), p. 165.

25. The overstatement of the rate of economic growth is an issue separate from the question of whether Chinese data understate the level of economic output. On the latter question see World Bank, *China: GNP Per Capita* (Washington, 1994).

26. World Bank, *China 2020: Development Challenges in the New Century* (Washington, 1997), p. 3.

27. World Bank, *The Chinese Economy: Fighting Inflation, Deepening Reform*, p. 13.

28. Ibid., p. 72.

29. That is about one-sixth of the average annual rate of growth of 9.4 percent between 1978 and 1995. World Bank, *China 2020*, p. 5.

30. World Bank, *The Chinese Economy: Fighting Inflation, Deepening Reform*, p. 13.

31. Ibid., p. 14, estimates that improvements in total factor productivity account for 2.2 percentage points a year or 22 percent of the growth rate of 10.2 percent a year between 1985 and 1994. World Bank, *China 2020*, p. 5, puts the factor productivity gain at 2.7 percentage points or 29 percent of the growth rate of 9.4 percent a year between 1978 and 1995.

32. A 1 percentage point reduction in the rate of economic growth does not necessarily imply a 1 percentage point reduction in the estimated gains in factor productivity. The reason is that if the real rate of growth of output is less than that given by official Chinese data, that also implies that the official data overstate the rate of growth of capital. The precise effect of a 1 percentage point reduction in the rate of economic growth on estimated gains in factor productivity depends on the extent to which overstatement of output is concentrated in the producer goods sector and the assumed elasticity of output with respect to capital.

33. Richard Cookson, "A Survey of Japanese Finance," *Economist*, June 28, 1997, p. 56.

34. Seignorage arises when the nominal value of money issued exceeds the cost of issuance and management. For paper money the costs of management, which include note security, distribution, and reissuance owing to wear, can be significant. Seignorage increases tax revenues of the Chinese government because it increases the profits of the central bank. The mechanism through which seignorage accrued to the government changed over time. Initially the profits of the central bank were remitted in their entirety to the Ministry of Finance. Subsequently the central bank was subject to tax on its profits but was allowed to retain the balance. Thus only part of the increased profits associated with seignorage now flow directly to the treasury. The rest are reflected on the balance sheet of the central bank. Seignorage can also be extracted by requiring banks to maintain noninterest-bearing reserves at the central bank. In China, however, the central bank pays interest on these reserves. Since the interest rate the central bank pays is roughly comparable to the rate that banks charge on their loans, seignorage in China is raised only through increases in currency in circulation. The government also benefits from fixing the interest rate on sight deposits at a level that has usually been below the rate of inflation. This inflation tax, which can also be considered a form of seignorage, is discussed and estimated in chapter 4. For further discussion of these issues see Maxwell J. Fry, "Can Seignorage Revenue Keep China's Financial System Afloat?" in Donald J.S. Brean, ed., *Taxation in Modern China*, (Routledge, forthcoming 1998).

35. Nicholas R. Lardy, *Agriculture in China's Modern Economic Development* (Cambridge University Press, 1978), p. 161. The conversion to U.S. currency is at the average official exchange rate prevailing during 1978, RMB 1.68 per U.S. dollar.

36. In the first five years of reform the number of rural markets expanded by more than one-fourth and the annual value of transactions on these markets increased 130 percent. State Statistical Bureau, *Statistical Yearbook of China 1993* (Beijing: China Statistical Publishing House, 1993), p. 386.

37. Lardy, *Agriculture in China's Modern Economic Development*, pp. 66–74.

38. At the end of 1995 the value of U.S. currency outstanding was $375 billion. Of this $200–$250 billion was abroad. Thus currency in circulation within the United States was $125 to $175 billion or roughly 2 percent of gross domestic product of $7,253 billion. Richard D. Porter and Ruth A. Judson, "The Location of U.S. Currency: How Much Is Abroad?" *Federal Reserve Bulletin*, October 1996, p. 883. By contrast, in China, currency in circulation at year-end 1996, RMB 880.2 billion, was 13 percent of gross domestic product of RMB 6,780 billion.

39. Ronald I. McKinnon, *The Order of Economic Liberalization*, p. 206.

40. World Bank, *The Chinese Economy: Fighting Inflation, Deepening Reform*, p. 14.

41. In addition to several World Bank books cited throughout this study see the following: William A. Byrd, *China's Financial System: The Changing Role of Banks* (Westview Press, 1983); Carsten Holz, *The Role of Central Banking in China's Economic Reforms* (Cornell University, East Asia Program, 1992); Paul Bowles and Gordon White, *The Political Economy of China's Financial Reforms: Finance in Late Development* (Westview Press, 1993); Leroy Jin, *Monetary Policy and the Design of Financial Institutions in China, 1978-1990* (St. Martin's Press 1994); Gang Yi, *Money, Banking, and Financial Markets in China* (Westview Press, 1994); On Kit Tam, ed., *Financial Reform in China* (London and New York: Routledge, 1995); Brian W. Semkow, gen. ed., *China Finance Manual* (Hong Kong: Asia Law and Practice Ltd., 1995); Eric Girardin, *Banking Sector Reform and Credit Control in China* (Paris: Development Center of the Organization for Economic Cooperation and Development, 1997); and I. A. Tokley and Tina Ravn, *Banking Law in China*, China Law Series (Hong Kong and London: Sweet & Maxwell, 1997).

42. According to official data the growth rate was somewhat higher, between 5 and 6 percent a year. It is widely accepted among Western scholars that the officially reported growth rate for the 1960s and 70s is biased upward, in large part because it is based on output measured in 1957 prices, which overvalue industry and undervalue agriculture. Recalculated based on the more market-oriented prices of the 1980s, the growth rate between 1957 and 1976 has been estimated to be just under 4 percent. Dwight H. Perkins, "Reforming China's Economic System," *Journal of Economic Literature*, vol. 26 (June 1988), p. 628.

43. Argentina, Brazil, and Venezuela have financial systems in which banks control an even higher share of all financial assets than in China. Colombia and Mexico have financial systems in which banks control a portion of all financial assets comparable to that in China. Morris Goldstein and Philip Turner, *Banking Crises in Emerging Economies: Origins and Policy Options*, BIS Economic Papers 46 (Basle: Bank for International Settlements, 1996), p. 19; and Bank for International Settlements, *66th Annual Report* (Basle, 1996), pp. 120, 126.

44. Morris Goldstein, *The Case for an International Banking Standard*, Policy Analyses in International Economics 47 (Washington: Institute for International Economics, 1997), pp. 3–5.

45. In 1996, for example, increased lending by banks and other financial institutions was RMB 1.08 trillion. See table 3-1. That was equal to 40 percent of gross domestic capital formation of RMB 2.69 trillion. This is an upward biased estimate of the share of fixed asset and working capital investment financed by borrowing if financial losses of firms exceed those associated with the buildup of inventories, which are financed from increased working capital investment. See discussion in chapter 2. For the state industrial sector the role of retained profits in financing fixed and working capital investment is extremely modest. In 1996, for example, after-tax profits of state owned industrial enterprises were RMB 149 billion, only 11 percent of the combined value of fixed asset investment of RMB 703 billion and increased working capital investment of RMB 604 billion. State Statistical Bureau, *China Statistical Yearbook 1996*, pp. 411–12; and *Statistical Yearbook 1997*, pp. 421–22.

46. See Steven Mufson, "China's Economic 'Boss': Zhu Rongji to Take Over as Premier," *Washington Post,* March 5, 1998, p. A1; Xinhua (New China News Agency), "Zhu Inspects Tianjin Reemployment Work," February 15, 1998, in Foreign Broadcast Information Service, *China,* 98-051, February 20, 1998; and "Financial System to Undergo Five Major Changes," *China Daily,* February 28, 1998, p. 4.

Notes to Chapter 2

1. The concept of state ownership used here is "ownership by the whole people" (quanmin suoyou zhi) and is inclusive of state ownership at the central, provincial, and local level.

2. Barry Naughton, *Growing Out of the Plan: Chinese Economic Reform 1978-1993* (Cambridge University Press, 1995), p. 97.

3. Ibid., pp. 27–30, 177.

4. Ibid., pp. 262–63.

5. Ibid., pp. 228–33.

6. "Decision of the CPC Central Committee on Some Issues Concerning the Establishment of a Socialist Market Economic Structure," *Renmin ribao* (People's Daily), November 17, 1993, pp. 1–2, in Foreign Broadcast Information Service, *Daily Report: China,* 1993, 93-220, November 17, 1993, pp. 22-35. (Hereafter FBIS, *China.* No page numbers are provided for the online version of Foreign Broadcast Information Service, which replaced the hard copy edition in July 1996.)

7. Harry Broadman, *Meeting the Challenge of Enterprise Reform,* Discussion Paper 283 (Washington: World Bank, 1995), pp. xiv, 25.

8. Yuanzheng Cao, Yingyi Qian, and Barry R. Weingast, "From Federalism, Chinese Style, to Privatization, Chinese Style," unpublished manuscript, December 1997.

9. Xinhua (New China News Agency), "The Company Law of the People's Republic of China" (adopted at the fifth session of the Standing Committee of the Eighth National People's Congress, December 29, 1993), December 30, 1993, in FBIS, *China,* 94-017, January 26, 1994, pp. 26–48. The law provides for two basic types of shareholding companies: limited liability companies and limited liability stock companies. The former can be established when there are from two to fifty shareholders, except that an authorized government department may be the sole investor, in which case the entity is a wholly state-owned limited liability company. Limited liability stock companies may, but are not required to, sell shares to the public. These shares may or may not be listed, that is, traded on the Shanghai or Shenzhen stock markets.

10. World Bank, *China's Management of Enterprise Assets: The State as Shareholder* (Washington, 1997), p. 11.

11. World Bank, *China's Management of Enterprise Assets,* p. 4.

12. The balance was produced by firms classified as collectively owned, a category that includes small-scale rural industry under the management of people's communes.

13. State Statistical Bureau, *Statistical Yearbook of China 1986* (Oxford University Press, 1986), pp. 95, 97, 189, 224.

14. Reliable data on the share of assets in industry in state-owned enterprises before 1985 are not readily available. However, in 1985, when state-owned industrial enterprises accounted for only 20 percent of all industrial enterprises, they owned 74.6 percent of total industrial assets. State Statistical Bureau, *Communiqué of the State Statistical Bureau of the People's Republic of China and the Third National Industrial Census Office on the Third National Industrial Census* (Beijing: China Statistical Publishing House, February 1997), p. 15.

15. State Statistical Bureau, *China Statistical Yearbook 1996* (Beijing: China Statistical Publishing House, 1996), p. 457. Data on these variables for 1978, the formal beginning of the economic reform program, do not appear to be available.

16. State Statistical Bureau, *Statistical Yearbook of China 1981* (Hong Kong: Economic Information and Agency, 1982), pp. 290–91.

17. State Statistical Bureau, *Statistical Yearbook of China 1986*, pp. 414, 445–46.

18. Budgetary expenditures in 1978 were RMB 112 billion, gross domestic product was RMB 362 billion. State Statistical Bureau, *Statistical Yearbook of China 1986*, p. 509; and *China Statistical Yearbook 1996* (Beijing: China Statistical Publishing House, 1996), p. 42.

19. State Statistical Bureau, *Statistical Yearbook of China 1983* (Beijing: China Statistical Publishing House, 1983), p. 215; and State Statistical Bureau, *China Statistical Yearbook 1996*, p. 401. The figure for 1995 excludes output valued at RMB 460 billion produced by former state-owned firms that have been corporatized and are now classified as shareholding firms. This is equal to 5.0 percent of industrial output. See discussion in notes 23 and 31.

20. Naughton, *Growing Out of the Plan*.

21. State Statistical Bureau, *China Statistical Yearbook 1996*, p. 457. This figure probably overstates the role of state-owned construction firms since increasingly they subcontract work to nonstate firms. This probably is not reflected in the official data.

22. State Statistical Bureau, *China Statistical Yearbook 1996*, p. 543.

23. Corporatization involves a change to a shareholding form of ownership. But the shares usually are not listed on the Shanghai or Shenzhen stock markets, and in almost all cases the state retains more than half of the shares in the "new" corporatized firm. This dominant ownership position means that there is little change in corporate governance in the firms that have been corporatized. Nonetheless, once this change takes place, the firms are no longer classified in China's statistical system as state owned but rather as shareholding units. Employment in shareholding firms was first reported in 1993 at 1.6 million employees. By 1996 the number had risen to 3.63 million. This new form of ownership accounts for most of the decline in the share of employment in state-owned firms since 1992.

24. State Statistical Bureau, *China Statistical Yearbook 1997*, p. 93.

25. State Statistical Bureau, *China Statistical Yearbook 1996*, p. 91.

26. The 62 million figure is the sum of what the Chinese report as private enterprise and individual employment, in both urban and rural areas. State Statistical Bureau, *China Statistical Yearbook 1997*, p. 97.

27. The balance of new jobs was created in the intermediate collective sector and in joint venture firms. State Statistical Bureau, *China Statistical Yearbook 1996*, p. 90.

28. The new classification system was first used in the *China Statistical Yearbook 1995*, which presents data for both 1993 and 1994.

29. The category of foreign-funded firms includes joint ventures and wholly foreign-owned firms. The Chinese government does retain a majority ownership in some joint ventures, which might be a reason to continue to regard them as state owned. However, even when the state retains a majority ownership, it appears that the governance of the firms changes sufficiently that they should no longer be regarded as state-owned firms of the traditional type. But the shareholding firms are a different matter. For reasons explained in notes 23 and 31, I believe they should continue to be regarded as state owned.

30. Two sources report that the share of assets in the state sector in 1995 exceeded 65 percent. New China News Agency, "PRC: State Sector Holds 'Monopoly' in Key Industries," May 8, 1996, in FBIS, *China*, 96-091, May 9, 1996, p. 23; and Liu Yuping, "The State-Owned Economy Occupies the Leading Position of the National Economy," *Jinrong shibao* (Financial News), May 10, 1996, p. 8. Another author, presumably rounding up the true figure, reported a share of 70 percent. Wang Yantian, "How Much Do You Know About 'Resources' of the State?" *Renmin ribao* (People's Daily), July 14, 1997, pp. 1, 4, in FBIS, *China*, 97-203, July 22, 1997.

31. The state share of industrial output fell from 61.9 percent in 1985 to 29.0 percent in 1995, a decline of more than half. The share of industrial assets owned by state firms declined by less than three-fifths. Interestingly, in table 12-1 of the *China Statistical Yearbook 1996*, p. 401, the footnote that gives the value of output of shareholding companies describes these companies as "state-owned holding companies," supporting the view that for all practical purposes limited liability and limited liability stock companies remain state-owned companies. See note 23.

32. New China News Agency, " PRC: State Sector Holds 'Monopoly' in Key Industries," May 8, 1996, in FBIS, *China*, 96-091, May 9, 1996, p. 23.

33. At the end of 1995 private firms owned less than a fifth and less than a tenth of the haulage capacity of motorized vessels and barges, respectively. State Statistical Bureau, *China Statistical Yearbook 1996*, pp. 515, 518.

34. State Statistical Bureau, *Communiqué of the State Statistical Bureau of People's Republic of China and the Third National Industrial Census Office on the Third National Industrial Census*, p. 21; and "State Statistical Bureau Director Liu Hong Expresses View on China's Economic Situation," *Jingji ribao (Economic Daily)*, September 15, 1997, p. 5, in FBIS, *China*, 97-281, October 18, 1997.

35. For a useful survey of more than a dozen such studies see Peter Harrold, "China: Enterprise Reform Strategy," annex 1, unpublished manuscript, August 1993.

36. Chen Kuan and others, "Productivity Change in Chinese Industry: 1953-1985," *Journal of Comparative Economics*, vol. 12 (December 1988), p. 585; and Gary Jefferson, Thomas G. Rawski, and Yuxin Zheng, "Chinese Industrial

Productivity: Trends, Measurement Issues, and Recent Developments," *Journal of Comparative Economics*, vol. 23 (October 1996), p. 155.

37. Gary Jefferson, Thomas G. Rawski, and Yuxin Zheng, "Chinese Industrial Productivity: Trends, Measurement Issues, and Recent Developments," p. 170.

38. Chong-en Bai, David D. Li, and Yijiang Wang, "Enterprise Productivity and Efficiency: When Is Up Really Down?" *Journal of Comparative Economics*, vol. 24 (June 1997), pp. 269– 71.

39. World Bank, *China: Reform of State-Owned Enterprises* (Washington, 1996), p. 4.

40. Zhongguo Xinwen She (China News Service), "State Planning Commission on State Enterprise Losses," July 2, 1996, in FBIS, *China*, 96-132, July 9, 1996, p. 26.

41. World Bank, *China's Management of Enterprise Assets*, p. 1.

42. World Bank, *China: Reform of State-Owned Enterprises*, p. 3. Though not stated, these numbers were calculated by dividing post-tax profits by the net value of fixed assets. An alternative measure of financial performance, pre-tax profits as a percent of total assets, or the rate of return on assets, is presented later in this chapter.

43. At the end of 1995 there were 118,000 state-owned industrial enterprises. Of these, 87,905 practiced independent financial accounting. These firms accounted for just over four-fifths of the output of state-owned industrial firms. State Statistical Bureau, *China Statistical Yearbook 1996*, p. 401. In the same year there were 38,200 state-owned industrial enterprises under the budget. They all practice independent financial accounting and have received capital or financial subsidies from the central government. Harry Broadman, *Meeting the Challenge*, p. 12.

44. New China News Agency, "Statistical Communiqué of the PRC State Statistics Bureau on National Economic and Social Development in 1997," March 4, 1998, in FBIS, *China*, 98-071, March 12, 1998.

45. Calculated from the data on losses of state-owned firms with independent financial accounting in table 2-3 and a reported RMB 134.1 billion and RMB 64.8 billion in combined losses of state- and nonstate-owned firms in 1997 and 1985, respectively. Wu Yunhe, "Reform Targets State-owned industrial firms," *China Daily Business Weekly*, August 26, 1996, p. 1; and "Statistical Communiqué of the PRC State Statistics Bureau on National Economic and Social Development in 1997."

46. This has been a theme of several World Bank reports. See, for example, World Bank, *The Chinese Economy: Fighting Inflation, Deepening Reform* (Washington, 1996), p. 15.

47. The prevalence of this practice is discussed in greater detail in chapter 3.

48. Zhou Tianyong, "The Feasibility of Debt Restructuring during the Ninth Five-Year Plan," *Gaige (Reform)*, no. 5 (September 1995), pp. 30-36, in FBIS, *China*, 95-236, December 8, 1995, p. 58.

49. RMB 1,215 billion is 5.9 times and 4.5 times the cumulative financial losses through 1994 of state-owned industrial enterprises under the budget and state-owned industrial enterprises practicing independent financial accounting, respectively. Part of the discrepancy is that Zhou's estimate of needed write-offs

of state-owned enterprise debt to banks includes commercial as well as industrial state-owned firms.

50. For example, of 24,000 state enterprises running at a loss, 19,700, or 82.1 percent of the total, were classified as small. The source does not specify the year for this observation but presumably it is for 1994. "Small State Enterprises Are Not a Trivial Matter," *Jingji ribao* (Economic Daily), November 7, 1995, p. 1, in FBIS, *China*, 95-227, November 27, 1995, p. 34.

51. That was the share in 1992. State Statistical Bureau, *Statistical Yearbook of China 1993*, p. 417.

52. Wang Lihong, "Trial Project Targets Debt," *China Daily Business Weekly*, October 7, 1996, p. 1.

53. Zhou Tianyong, "The Feasibility of Debt Restructuring during the Ninth Five-Year Plan."

54. World Bank, *China: Reform of State-Owned Enterprises*, p. 4.

55. See chapter 1, note 45.

56. State Council, "Notice Approving and Promulgating the Report of the People's Bank Concerning Changing the Provision of Working Capital to State-Managed Enterprises to be Under the Unified Management of the People's Bank," in National People's Congress Standing Committee Legislative Affairs Work Committee, *Zhonghua renmin gongheguo falu fenlei zonglan, jingji fajuan (Zhongshou)* (A classified compendium of laws of the People's Republic of China, economic laws), vol. 2 (Beijing: Legal Publishing House, 1994), pp. 68–72; State Planning Commission, Ministry of Finance, and People's Construction Bank of China, "Interim Regulations Converting All State Budgetary Capital Construction Investment from Appropriations to Loans" (in Chinese), *Almanac of China's Finance and Banking 1986* (Beijing: China Financial Publishing House, 1986), pp. VI-79–VI-82.

57. In 1994, 85 percent of the liabilities of state-owned enterprise were loans from banks. Yu Jian, "The Predicament and the Solution for State-Owned Enterprises," *Jinrong shibao* (Financial News), January 29, 1996, p. 3. Presumably the balance of the liabilities consisted of bonds that some enterprises have sold to the public, unpaid taxes, and unpaid levies to social insurance and unemployment funds. The rise in the liability ratio occurred despite the fact that between 1984 and 1988 loans to enterprises valued at RMB 66 billion were converted into state investment in enterprises. A Ming, "State-Owned Enterprises: How to Confront the Debt Ratio?" *Jinrong shibao* (Financial News), October 7, 1995, p. 1.

58. Yu Jian, "The Predicament and the Solution for State-Owned Enterprises," *Jinrong shibao* (Financial News), January 29, 1996, p. 3.

59. This is initially puzzling, since according to articles 27 and 36 of Accounting Standards for Enterprises promulgated by the Ministry of Finance in late 1992, which was to take effect beginning July 1, 1993, accounts payable should be included as a liability in the balance sheets of all firms. *China Laws for Foreign Business—Taxation and Customs* (North Ryde, Australia: CCH International, 1993), pp. 44371–395. It appears that the industrial census that produced the data on enterprise asset-to-liability ratios excluded both payables and receivables because for the economy as a whole they are fully offsetting items.

60. World Bank, *China: GNP per Capita* (Washington, 1994), p. 13.

61. Edward Steinfeld, *Forging Reform in China: From Party Line to Bottom Line in the State-Owned Enterprises* (Cambridge University Press, forthcoming), chapters 4,6.

62. Li Chiliang, "Realignment of Enterprise Debt," *Jingji cankao bao* (Economic Reference News), August 8, 1996, p. 1, in FBIS, *China*, 96-187, August 8, 1996.

63. Su Ning and Lu Zhongyuan, "State-Owned Enterprises Financial Problems and Their Remedies," *Caimao jingji* (Finance and Trade Economics), no. 8 (August 1994), in Joint Publications Research Service, *China Report*, 94-055 (Washington, August 11, 1994).

64. Qiu Mingchen, "Concerning the Way to Advance the Transformation of the Method of Managing Credit Funds," *Jinrong shibao* (Financial News), May 18, 1996, p. 5.

65. The precise share in each of these two categories was 27.6 percent and 21.5 percent, respectively. A Ming, "State-Owned Enterprises: How to Confront the Debt Ratio?" *Jinrong shibao* (Financial News), October 7, 1995, p. 1.

66. Dai Jianming, "Enterprises Cannot Rely on Loosening the Money Supply to Solve Their Problems," *Jinrong shibao* (Financial News), September 6, 1996, p. 1.

67. See chapter 1, note 12.

68. The top five chaebol at year-end 1996 had debt-to-equity ratios that ranged from Samsung at 473 percent to Sunkyong's 262 percent. John Burton, "Seoul Fires Warning Shot over Chaebol," *Financial Times*, January 22, 1998, p. 6.

69. World Bank, *China: Pension System Reform* (Washington, 1996), p. 26.

70. As discussed below, the bank recommends termination of the present pension system. It thus is interested in estimating the present value of current pension obligations, exclusive of the additional benefits current workers would accrue prior to their retirement if the current system remained in place.

71. Thus the 50 percent figure should not be compared with estimates of unfunded pension liabilities for other countries.

72. World Bank, *China: Pension System Reform* (Washington, 1996), p. ix.

73. Henry Aaron, "The Myths of Social Security Crisis: Behind the Privatization Push," *Washington Post*, July 21, 1996, p. C1.

74. World Bank, *China: Pension System Reform*, p. 2.

75. State Statistical Bureau, *China Statistical Yearbook 1996*, p. 6; and World Bank, *China Pension System Reform*, p. 15.

76. The Board of Trustees, Federal Old-Age and Survivors Insurance and Disability Insurance Trust Funds, *The 1996 Annual Report of the Board of Trustees of the Federal Old-Age and Survivors Insurance and Disability Insurance Trust Funds* (Washington, 1996), p. 105; and *Survey of Current Business*, vol. 76 (December 1996), p. D-2.

77. Department of Population and Employment Statistics, State Statistical Bureau and Department of Overall Planning and Wages, Ministry of Labor, *China Labor Statistical Yearbook 1996* (Beijing: China Statistical Publishing House, 1996), p. 441.

78. World Bank, *China: Pension System Reform*, p. xiv.

79. Ibid., pp. xiii, 20.

80. Ibid., p. 23.

81. Pension contributions exceeded payments to retirees in the 1950s, and the system built up significant reserves. These reportedly were used for purposes other than paying pensions during the Cultural Revolution. Ibid., pp. 3–4.

82. Ibid., pp. 10- 11.

83. Virginia Marsh, "Hungary Spreads the Pension Load: Looming Contribution Crisis Is Forcing Painful Adjustment," *Financial Times*, January 22, 1997, p. 2.

84. World Bank, *China: Pension System Reform*, pp. 36–37.

85. Ibid., pp. xvii–xviii.

86. Ibid., p. 54.

87. Naughton, *Growing Out of the Plan*, pp. 236–40.

88. Nicholas Lardy, *Agriculture in China's Modern Economic Development* (Cambridge University Press, 1983).

89. Calculated using Naughton's approach, which is pre-tax profits divided by the sum of depreciated fixed capital plus working capital.

90. Calculated as pre-tax profits relative to total assets. Total assets is the sum of the net value of fixed assets, working capital, and intangible assets. State Statistical Bureau, *China Statistical Yearbook 1997*, pp. 428–31, 464.

91. Ministry of Finance, "Accounting Standards for Enterprises," *China Laws for Foreign Business—Taxation and Customs*, Document 35-536, pp. 44368–395. In one survey almost all state-owned enterprises reported that they were in compliance with the new accounting standards. However, these firms were not a random sample but chosen because of their advanced status. Moreover, "Application of the accounts produced to reach a commercially meaningful assessment of SOEs (state-owned enterprises) assets and net worth—consistent with international standards—is still problematic." World Bank, *China's Management of State-Owned Enterprises*, pp. 57, 67.

92. Yuan Zheng Cao, Gang Fan, Wing Thye Woo, "Chinese Economic Reforms: Past Successes and Future Challenges," in Wing Thye Woo, Stephen Parker, and Jeffrey D. Sachs, eds., *Economies in Transition: Comparing Asia and Eastern Europe* (MIT Press, 1997), p. 36.

93. State Statistical Bureau, *China Statistical Yearbook 1997*, pp. 122, 267.

94. Barry Naughton, *Growing Out of the Plan*, p. 208.

95. "State-Owned Enterprise Law," in National People's Congress Standing Committee Legislative Affairs Work Committee, *A Classified Compendium of Laws* (in Chinese), vol. 2, pp. 1029–34.

96. World Bank, *China: Reform of State-Owned Enterprises*, p. 19.

97. For example, Gao Shangquan places the surplus at 24 million, about a fifth of the workers in the state sector. "Innovation of the State Enterprise System and Development of the Capital Market," *Jingji cankao bao* (Economic Reference News), September 30, 1997, pp. 1, 2, in FBIS, *China*, 97-325, November 21, 1997.

98. The percentage calculation assumes that housing of state-owned units is built exclusively in urban areas. Although this is not strictly true, for example, a state oil drilling company may build housing for its workers who live in remote

areas far from any city, it is a close approximation of reality. State Statistical Bureau, *China Statistical Yearbook 1996*, pp. 143, 312.

99. Yu Jian, "The Predicament and the Solution for State-Owned Enterprises," *Jinrong shibao* (Financial News), January 29, 1996, p. 1.

100. World Bank, *China: Reform of State-Owned Enterprises*, p. 16.

101. Dian Jianming, "Enterprises Cannot Rely on Loosening the Money Supply to Solve Their Problems," *Jinrong shibao* (Financial News), September 6, 1996, p. 1.

102. The People's Bank in the spring of 1997 issued an urgent nationwide notice requiring enterprises and organizations to end this practice. New China News Agency, "Public Funds in Savings Accounts Forbidden," March 19, 1997, in FBIS, *China*, 97-078, March 19, 1997.

103. Enterprises, of course, are free to deposit funds in interest-bearing bank accounts. But the interest would be an income item for the firm and would, if the firm were profitable, lead to an increase in the firm's tax liability. Chinese workers generally pay no taxes on interest income since their incomes are below the threshold level above which taxes must be paid on personal income, including interest income. The state has sought to limit this practice by forbidding enterprises and government institutions from depositing public funds under private names. People's Bank of China, "Notice Forbidding Turning Public Funds into Private Deposits," cited in Wang Baoqing, "Strengthen the Management of Deposits, Prohibit Public Funds into Private Deposits," *Jinrong shibao* (Financial News), May 1, 1997, p. 1.

104. Yu Jian, "The Predicament and Solution for State-Owned Enterprises," *Jinrong shibao* (Financial News), January 29, 1996, p. 3.

105. Fan Bi, "Current Situation, Mechanism, and Countermeasures for Losses of State Assets," *Jingji guanli* (Economic Management), no. 2 (March 1996), pp. 86–93, in FBIS, *China*, 96-133, July 10, 1996, pp. 55, 58.

106. Jen Hui-wen, "Zhu Rongji Presides over Work of Screening State-Owned Assets Erosion," *Hong Kong Hsin Pao* (Hong Kong Economic Journal), January 10, 1997, p. 22, in FBIS, *China*, 97-014, January 10, 1997; and World Bank, *China's Management of Enterprise Assets*, p. 53.

107. Alan Gelb, "China's Reforms in the Wider Context of Transition," in *China's Economic Future: Challenges to U.S. Policy*, Joint Committee Print, Joint Economic Committee, 104 Cong. 2 sess. (Government Printing Office, August 1996), pp. 96–97.

108. Terry Sicular, "Going on the Dole: Why China's State Enterprises Choose to Lose," unpublished manuscript, May 1994.

109. Sicular, "Going on the Dole."

110. Yuanzheng Cao, Yingyi Qian, and Barry R. Weingast, "From Federalism, Chinese Style, to Privatization, Chinese Style," unpublished manuscript, December 1997. Many township and village enterprises and urban collectives also are being transformed into joint stock companies, effectively privatizing them. By year-end 1995 there were more than 3 million stock cooperative enterprises in rural areas and more than 140,000 in urban areas. Zhu Jianhong, "Stock

Cooperative System Should Be Promoted," *Renmin ribao* (People's Daily) August 8, 1997, p. 2, in FBIS, *China*, 97-289, October 16, 1997. Zhu is deputy minister of the State Commission for Restructuring the Economy.

111. Karby Leggett, "China Requires Stock Purchases to Be Voluntary," *Asian Wall Street Journal*, February 20–21, 1998, p. 17.

112. Dai Yulin, "Financial Creativity: Ways to Solve the Problem of Bad Debts between Banks and Enterprises," *Caijing wenti yanjiu* (Research in Financial and Economic Issues), August, 1997, pp. 14-18, in FBIS, *China*, 97-294, October 21, 1997.

113. "New Progress in Restructuring Economy," *Beijing Review*, June 2–8, 1997, p. 5.

114. World Bank, *China's Management of Enterprise Assets*, p. xii.

115. Ibid., p. 4. By the end of 1997, 69 of 73 companies that had completed the transformation of their ownership had become wholly state-owned corporations. Sun Shangwei, "State Firms' Reform Going Successfully," *China Daily*, December 16, 1997, p. 1.

116. Although state-owned companies are subject to provisions set forth in the Company Law, traditional state-owned enterprises are governed by the 1988 "State-Owned Enterprise Law of the People's Republic of China," in National People's Congress Standing Committee Legislative Affairs Work Committee, *A Classified Compendium of Laws* (in Chinese), vol. 2, pp. 1029–34.

117. "Company Law of the People's Republic of China," article 66.

118. World Bank, *China's Management of Enterprise Assets*, p. 39.

119. Ibid., p. 51. See also World Bank, *From Plan to Market* (Oxford University Press, 1996), p. 55.

120. At year-end 1996, 514 companies were listed on either the Shanghai or the Shenzhen stock exchanges.

121. World Bank, *China's Management of Enterprise Assets*, p. 39.

122. See discussion in chapter 4.

123. At year-end 1996 of the companies listed on the Shanghai Stock exchange the state held 43.9 percent of the shares and companies held 27.3 percent. These shares are not traded on the market. See discussion in chapter 4 and notes to table 4-1.

124. World Bank, *China's Management of Enterprise Assets*, p. 40.

125. Seth Faison, "Seeking a Remedy for Its Industrial Woes, the Chinese Think Big," *International Herald Tribune*, February 21-22, 1998, pp. 1, 5.

126. New China News Agency, "Circular Issued on Debts of Merged Enterprises," June 21, 1995, in FBIS, *China*, 95-128, July 5, 1995, p. 48.

127. Faison, "Seeking a Remedy for Its Industrial Woes, pp. 1, 5.

128. "State Council Outlines State Enterprise Reform Plan," China News Agency, December 1, 1996, in *FBIS, China*, 96-234, December 1, 1996; and New China News Agency, "$3.65 b Goes into Special State Fund," *China Daily*, March 4, 1997, p. 2.

129. World Bank, *China's Management of Enterprise Assets*, p. 4.

130. This proposal is discussed in detail in chapter 4.

Notes to Chapter 3

1. For the best accounts of the role of banks and financial institutions in the pre-reform era see Katharine Huang Hsiao, *Money and Monetary Policy in Communist China* (Columbia University Press, 1971); and Tadao Miyashita, *The Currency and Financial System of Mainland China* (University of Washington Press, 1966).

2. Households are the source of from 40 to 60 percent of domestic savings in most low- and middle-income countries. World Bank, *China: Finance and Investment* (Washington, 1988), p. 19.

3. *Almanac of China's Finance and Banking 1990* (Beijing: China Financial Publishing House, 1990), p. 60; and State Statistical Bureau, *Statistical Yearbook of China 1992* (Beijing: China Statistical Publishing House, 1992), p. 31.

4. Government savings is equal to the difference between tax revenues and current (that is, noninvestment) expenditures.

5. The role of funds retained by enterprises grew over time, even in the years before 1978. For example, in the First Five-Year Plan (1953–57) while enterprises were not allowed to retain their depreciation funds, they were allowed to retain a share of their above-plan profits. Nicholas R. Lardy, *Economic Growth and Distribution in China* (Cambridge University Press, 1978), pp. 50–52. On the eve of reform retained depreciation funds, mostly of state-owned enterprises, and profits, mainly of rural enterprises, funded almost a third of total investment. Profit retention was introduced for state-owned firms in the late 1970s, and the share of profits retained rose in the 1980s. Barry Naughton, *Growing Out of the Plan: Chinese Economic Reform 1978–1993* (Cambridge University Press, 1995), pp. 99–101, 106, 122–25.

6. In most of the First Five-Year Plan (1953–57) the state budget was the source of permanent or "quota" working capital, and banks were the source for "over-quota" working capital of enterprises. Hsiao, *Money and Monetary Policy in Communist China*, p. 125, reports that at year-end 1957, 45 percent of the working capital of the state sector was provided through budgetary grants. Annual state budgetary appropriations for working capital averaged RMB 5.5 billion in 1975–78, more than 2.5 times the level of the first plan. State Statistical Bureau, *Statistical Yearbook of China 1993*, p. 222.

7. Before March 26, 1996, the Construction Bank of China was named the People's Construction Bank of China. All references to this bank in the text use the new name. However, in citations of documents that predate the name change, when the People's Construction Bank of China is the originator of a document or referred to in the title of a document, that name is used.

8. Between 1958 and 1962 and again between 1970 and 1972 the Construction Bank did not exist as a separate, independent financial institution. During the first period its tasks were subsumed within the Capital Construction Financial Affairs Office of the Ministry of Finance. In the second period it was part of the People's Bank. *Almanac of China's Finance and Banking 1986*, p. II-13.

9. Nicholas R. Lardy, *Agriculture in China's Modern Economic Development* (Cambridge University Press, 1983), p. 240.

10. William A. Byrd, *China's Financial System: The Changing Role of Banks* (Westview Press, 1983), p. 10.

11. The total deposits and loans of the entire financial system in 1978 were RMB 113.5 billion and RMB 190 billion, respectively. I estimate the deposits and loans of the People's Bank by subtracting known or estimated deposits and loans of other financial institutions, that is, the systems of rural and urban credit cooperatives and the Bank of China. Deposits in rural credit cooperatives in 1978 were RMB 16.60 billion. Loans were RMB 4.51 billion. *Almanac of China's Finance and Banking 1990*, p. 65. Deposits and loans in urban credit cooperatives in 1978 must have been zero since the first experimental urban credit cooperative was not established until 1979. I estimate Bank of China RMB deposits and loans at RMB 2 billion and RMB 8 billion, respectively, based on reported data for 1985 and the assumption that loans and deposits each grew sevenfold between 1978 and 1985, the same as the reported rate of expansion of the total assets of the bank. *Almanac 1986*, pp. II-11, III-62. Thus estimated lending of the People's Bank is RMB 177.49 billion out of total lending of RMB 190 billion. *Almanac 1988*, p. 58, table 3-1.

12. World Bank, *China: Finance and Investment*, pp. 244–45.

13. The Agricultural Bank of China previously had existed as an independent bank during 1951, from March 1953 until April 1957, and from October 1963 through November 1965. In the periods in which the bank (or its predecessor, the Agricultural Cooperative Bank) did not formally exist as an independent financial institution, its operations were subsumed within the Rural Bank Management Bureau of the People's Bank.

14. Lardy, *Agriculture in China's Modern Economic Development*, pp. 140–41.

15. Table A-1.

16. *Almanac of China's Finance and Banking 1986*, p. II-10.

17. Table A-1.

18. *Almanac of China's Finance and Banking 1986*, p.II-13.

19. Ibid., p. II-14.

20. The World Bank approved its first loans to China in June 1981. However, no significant disbursements of these funds occurred until after June 1982.

21. The Construction Bank, because of its role in financing state investment projects, was the source of most of the domestic currency funds. The China Investment Bank was owned by the Construction Bank, presumably because of this close financial relationship.

22. China Investment Bank, *1994 Annual Report* (Beijing, 1995), pp. 5, 16. The State Administration of Exchange Control was first created in 1979. Its name and administrative subordination have undergone several changes in the ensuing years. The translation of its name into English changed to the State Administration of Foreign Exchange (SAFE) in early 1998.

23. *Almanac of China's Finance and Banking 1995*, pp. 114–15; and China Investment Bank, *1995 Annual Report*, p. 3.

24. State Council, "Decision to Have the Specialized Bank the People's Bank of China Serve the Function of the Central Bank of China," in National People's Congress Standing Committee Legislative Affairs Work Committee, compiler, *Zhonghua renmin gongheguo falu fenlei zonglan; jingji fajuan shangshou* (A classified

compendium of laws of the People's Republic of China; economic law volume), vol. 1 (Beijing: Legal Publishing House, 1994), pp. 17–18.

25. World Bank, *China: Finance and Investment*, pp. 246, 298–99.

26. *Almanac of China's Finance and Banking 1986*, p. II-18.

27. State Council, "Provisional Regulations of the People's Republic of China on the Control of Banks," in *China Laws for Foreign Business* (North Ryde, Australia: CCH International, 1993), Document 8-690, pp. 10651–677.

28. The bank's total loans outstanding at the end of 1985 were RMB 300.8 billion. *Almanac of China's Finance and Banking 1986*, p. III-28. That was 51 percent of total bank lending of RMB 591 billion (see table 3-1).

29. *Almanac of Chinese Finance and Banking 1986*, p. II-46.

30. Table A-1.

31. *Almanac of China's Finance and Banking 1986*, p. III-9.

32. Nonbank financial institutions are discussed later in this chapter.

33. *Almanac of China's Finance and Banking 1988*, p. 141.

34. *Almanac of China's Finance and Banking 1993*, p. 50.

35. The Bank of China in 1996 handled nearly U.S.$120 billion in import and export settlement, 41 percent of China's total trade volume. Zhongguo Xinwen She (China News Service), "Report on Total 1996 Revenues for Bank of China," January 13, 1997 in Foreign Broadcast Information Service, *China*, 97-008, January 13, 1997. (Hereafter FBIS, *China*.)

36. The Bank of Communications was founded in Shanghai in 1908. After 1949 the bank became a public-private jointly operated bank. But in 1958 its banking business was taken over by the People's Bank and the Bank of Construction. Its Hong Kong branch, however, continued to operate under the supervision of the Bank of China. Ruan Hong, "The Bank of Communications— The Rise of a National Shareholding Commercial Bank," *Zhongguo jinrong* (Chinese Banking), no. 10 (October 1993), p. 19. The Hong Kong–based Bank of Communications continued to operate under the Bank of China, even after the Bank of Communications was reestablished in China as a separate entity. The State Council approved the reestablishment of the Bank of Communications as a national bank on July 24, 1986. The bank opened its Shanghai headquarters for business in April 1987. The State Council approved the establishment of the CITIC Industrial Bank in April 1987, and it opened for business in August of the same year.

37. The interim charter of the bank specified that half its shares should be owned by the state. Presumably this half of the initial share capital came primarily from the central government. Since, until the bank's ownership structure was revised in 1994, each branch of the bank had a separate and unique capital structure, after 1987 local governments provided much of the increased capital necessary for the bank to expand its branch network. By the end of 1992 the central government held 23 percent of the bank's shares; local governments in cities where branches had been established owned 42 percent of the shares, and the remaining 35 percent was held by enterprises. Thus in the first five years of the bank's existence the combined ownership share of the central government and local governments rose. Ruan Hong, "The Bank of Communications," p. 19. Over the next six-

teen months enterprises must have provided a significant portion of the increased capital since at the end of April 1994 the central government and local governments combined held 53 percent of the outstanding shares, whereas enterprises held 47 percent. *Almanac of China's Finance and Banking 1995*, p. 105. The revised charter of 1994, which specifies a fivefold increase in the registered capital of the bank, does not restrict the proportion of the bank's shares to be held by the state. By the end of 1995 the value of paid-in capital reached RMB 11.1 billion.

38. The provision for individual ownership was contained in the Interim Charter of the bank, issued in March 1987. "Charter of the Bank of Communications (Interim)," in *Almanac of China's Finance and Banking 1988*, pp. 467–68. Since the bank's shares are not traded publicly, it is not clear by what mechanism individuals would be able to acquire shares in the bank. The 1994 revisions of the charter, which provides for a substantial increase in the bank's registered capital, continues to allow individual shareholders as a class to own up to 10 percent of the bank's shares. However, a new proviso restricts the number of shares a single individual can own to no more than 10,000. With 12 billion shares, each valued at RMB 1, no individual could own more than 0.00008 percent of the bank. "Charter of the Bank of Communications (revised)," *Almanac of China's Finance and Banking 1995*, pp. 426–28. Although the People's Bank of China approved the clauses in the 1987 and 1994 charters allowing individual shareholders in principle, it has not yet approved implementing this provision.

39. For example, loans were limited to an amount no more than 70 percent of deposits. Wang Mingquan, "Several Issues in the Reform and Development of the Bank of Communications," *Jinrong shibao* (Financial News), September 20, 1995, p. 3. For the specialized banks the ratio was set somewhat higher, 75 percent, and they were given a number of years to come into compliance.

40. See detailed discussion of the performance of the Bank of Communications at the end of the chapter.

41. Table A-1.

42. Table A-1.

43. The bank spun off its securities business into a newly established independent Everbright Securities Company Ltd. The new company also took over the securities business of the Everbright International Trust and Investment Corporation. "Bright and Secure," *China Daily*, May 27, 1996, p. 5.

44. Everbright Bank of China, *Documents on the Restructuring and Increased Capital in 1996* (in Chinese) (Beijing, 1996), pp. 9–10. Subsequently a 20 percent ownership was injected into China Everbright Holdings Co. Limited, a Hong Kong affiliate of China Everbright Group Limited. China Everbright Holdings Company Limited subsequently sold these shares to China Everbright-IHD Pacific limited, a Hong Kong–listed arm of China Everbright Holdings Company Limited. After this transaction was completed China Everbright Group Limited directly owned 31 percent of the shares of Everbright Bank. China Everbright-IHD Pacific Limited, *Annual Report 1996/97* (Hong Kong, 1997), pp. 14–16. China Everbright IHD-Pacific subsequently was renamed China Everbright Ltd. It is considered the flagship listed company of the group. The other listed companies of the group are China Everbright Technology and China Everbright International.

45. Wang Xiangwei, "ADB Set to Invest in Mainland Bank," *South China Morning Post International Weekly* (Business Post), October 26, 1996, p. 3; and Tong Xu, "Move Bolsters Bank Reform: ADB Buys Stake in Everbright," *China Daily Business Weekly*, November 18, 1996, p. 3. The Asian Development Bank purchased 92.22 million shares or 3.3 percent of the bank's total shares. Everbright Bank of China, *Annual Report 1996* (Beijing, 1997), p. 16.

46. "ADB Buys Stake of China's Everbright Bank," Cbnet database, January 29, 1997.

47. *Almanac of China's Finance and Banking 1995*, p. 110; and Huaxia Bank Co., Ltd., *1995 Annual Report* (Beijing, 1996), p. 16.

48. This judgment is based on indirect evidence, and the drop by half between 1994 and 1995 in the ratio of the bank's own capital to total assets. Huaxia Bank Co., Ltd., *1995 Annual Report*, pp. 16–17.

49. Xiang Xiaofang, "Win Early in the Battle: A Short Note on Huaxia Bank's Corporatization System Reform," *Jinrong shibao* (Financial News), September 6, 1996, p. 1.

50. Formal criminal charges were filed against Zhou in September 1996 in the Beijing People's Intermediate Court. Jane Macartney, "China Charges Disgraced Princeling with Corruption," Reuters, October 18, 1996, as found at Clarinet newsgroup. Zhou was found guilty and sentenced to death with a two-year reprieve in October 1996 for offering and taking bribes involving more than nine million renminbi. He has since been given a suspended death sentence, which will result in a life sentence after a two-year reprieve. Chen Chiu, "Court Says Zhou Beifang Not Given Death Sentence on Account of His Pleading Guilty in Answer to Questions at Home, Abroad," *Sing Tao Jih Pao*, March 27, 1997, p. A7, in FBIS, *China*, 97-094, April 4, 1997.

51. Liang Guoren, "Shougang Undergoes Reorganization, Abandons Projects," *Ming Pao*, April 5, 1995, p. A2, in FBIS, *China*, 95-070, April 12, 1995.

52. It appears that the selection of firms to purchase shares of the bank was based at least partly on their profitability. Yuxi cigarette factory was the second most profitable firm in China, racking up profits of almost RMB 15 billion in 1995. "China Appraises 500 Largest Enterprises in 1995," *Beijing Review*, February 12-18, 1996, p. 22.

53. Article 28 of the Commercial Bank Law, adopted at the Thirteenth Session of the Eighth National People's Congress Standing Committee on May 10, 1995, requires the prior approval of the People's Bank of China of any unit or individual that purchases more than 10 percent of the total amount of shares of any bank, in *China Law and Practice*, June 27, 1995, p. 7.

54. Xu Fei, "The Tide of Commercial Bank Shares," *Jinrong shibao* (Financial News), August 28, 1996, p. 5. The parent company, Shougang Group, also received a massive injection of equity in 1995 to stave off the financial collapse of the firm's steel producing operations. Edward Steinfeld, *Forging Reform in China: From Party Line to Bottom Line in the State-Owned Enterprises* (Cambridge University Press, forthcoming), chapter 6.

55. "Minsheng Names U.S. Auditor," *China Daily*, January 22, 1997, p. 5.

56. John Ridding, Peter Montagnon, and Tony Walker, "Nimble Newcomer Appears on China's Banking Scene," *Financial Times*, May 18, 1996, p. 4.

57. Xiao Xu, "World Bank Continues Minsheng Discussions," *China Daily Business Weekly,* July 7, 1997, p. 1; and "IFC Confident of Approval to take Minsheng Stake," *South China Morning Post,* December 4, 1997. The IFC also expects approval for its purchase of a minority ownership in Xiamen International Bank, a small Sino-foreign joint venture bank.

58. In most financial systems development banks are government funded and do not take deposits from the public. However, in China all of the development banks do take deposits.

59. Xu Fei, " The Development Road of Commercial Banks," *Jinrong shibao* (Financial News) March 12, 1997, p. 4.

60. Tang Xian, "The Yantai Housing Savings Bank," *Jinrong shibao* (Financial News), April 15, 1996, p. 6.

61. China Merchants Bank, *1995 Annual Report* (Shenzhen, 1996), p. 5.

62. Cheung Lai-kuen, "Shanghai Bank Aims for Listing by 2000," *South China Morning Post,* September 25, 1997.

63. *Almanac of China's Finance and Banking 1988,* p. 234.

64. Ibid.; and People's Bank of China, *China Financial Outlook '96* (Beijing: China Financial Publishing House, 1996), p. 100.

65. *Almanac of China's Finance and Banking 1992* (Beijing: China Financial Publishing House, 1992), p. 549; and People's Bank of China, *China Financial Outlook '95* (Beijing: China Financial Publishing House, 1995), p. 94.

66. People's Bank of China, *China Financial Outlook '96,* p. 94.

67. State Council, "Notice Concerning the Creation of Urban Cooperative Banks," *Zhonghua renmin gongheguo guowuyuan gongbao* (Bulletin of the State Council of the People's Republic of China), October 5, 1995, pp. 949–51.

68. China News Service, "Urban Cooperative Bank Opens in Beijing," January 8, 1996, in FBIS, *China,* 96-008, January 11, 1996, p. 57.

69. Shanghai City United Bank, *Shanghai City United Bank,* 3 undated reports of the same title published in 1996.

70. People's Bank of China, *China Financial Outlook '97* (Beijing: China Financial Publishing House, 1997), p. 38.

71. State Council, "Charter of the China International Trust and Investment Company," in National People's Congress Standing Committee Legislative Affairs Work Committee, *A Classified Compendium of Laws* (in Chinese), vol. 2, pp. 4–5.

72. Almanacs of finance and banking beginning in the mid-1980s include both narrative histories, as well as balance sheets and profit and loss statements, of some of these trust and investment companies.

73. People's Bank of China, "Notice Concerning Actively Establishing Trust Business," cited in *Jinrong shibao* (Financial News), April 21, 1996, p. 5.

74. People's Bank of China, "Provisional Regulations on the Management of Trust and Investment Corporations," in Gong Sun Zhi Yuan, chief ed., *Zhongguo jinrong falu shiwu quanshu* (The complete book of China's financial laws) (Beijing: China Economic Publishing House, 1994), pp. 124–26.

75. Seemingly identical companies established by the Bank of China are called trust and consultancy companies (xintuo zixun gongsi) rather than trust and investment companies (xintuo touzi gongsi).

76. "The Situation with Regard to the Credit Income and Expenditure of Trust and Investment Companies," *Jinrong shibao* (Financial News), February 1, 1996, p. 1. See table A-1.

77. Table A-1.

78. The central bank initiated a campaign to reregister existing trust and investment corporations in 1995. By year-end 1995 the number of these institutions dropped to 332, compared with 393 at year-end 1994. People's Bank of China, *China Financial Outlook '96*, p. 35. By the end of 1996 the number had fallen to 244. People's Bank of China, *China Financial Outlook '97*, p. 39.

79. *Almanac of China's Finance and Banking 1993*, p. 104.

80. Nicholas R. Lardy, *China in the World Economy* (Washington: Institute for International Economics, 1994), pp. 56–57.

81. The Overseas Economic Cooperation Fund, *OECF Annual Report 1996* (Tokyo, 1996), p. 35.

82. *Almanac of China's Finance and Banking 1993*, p. 503.

83. *Almanac of China's Finance and Banking 1988*, pp. 235–36.

84. *Almanac of China's Finance and Banking 1995*, p. 573

85. People's Bank of China, *China Financial Outlook '97*, p. 39.

86. Ren Kan, "Finance Firms Seek Role," *China Daily Business Weekly*, April 15, 1996, p. 1.

87. Francis A. Lees and K. Thomas Liaw, *Foreign Participation in China's Banking and Securities Markets* (Westport, Conn.: Quorom Books, 1996), p. 109.

88. Leases also apparently were a mechanism for foreign financial institutions to avoid the restrictions that then applied to the operation of foreign banks in China. By the mid-1990s joint venture leasing companies were involved in a number of lawsuits over the alleged nonpayment of lease fees. By 1994 the lease payments in dispute reached about $600 million. In September 1996 the State Council directed the Bank of China to lend $200 million to help settle outstanding debts to foreign leasing companies. "China to Settle Debts to Foreign Leasing Companies," BT Online: News-China/HK/Taiwan, September 23, 1996; "China to Repay Debts to Foreign Leasing Companies," BT Online: News-China/HK/Taiwan, October 18, 1996.

89. *Almanac of China's Finance and Banking 1988*, p. 142.

90. *Almanac of China's Finance and Banking 1993*, p. 109.

91. Ouyang Weimin, "The Development and Management of Nonbank Financial Institutions," *Caimao jingji* (Finance and Trade Economics), no. 1 (January 1996), p. 32.

92. *Almanac of China's Finance and Banking 1988*, p. 142

93. Cecil R. Dipchand, Zhang Yichun, and Ma Mingjia, *The Chinese Financial System* (Westport, Conn., and London: Greenwood Press, 1994), p. 149.

94. Liu Yuanda, "A Great Endeavor Brings a Major Success—A Brief Exploration of China's Capital Market," *Jingji cankao bao* (Economic Reference News), July 15, 1996, p. 2, in FBIS, *China*, 96-192, July 15, 1996.

95. *Almanac of China's Finance and Banking 1988*, p. 142.

96 State Statistical Bureau, *Statistical Yearbook of China 1986* (Oxford University Press, 1987), p. 509; and table 3-1.

97. State Statistical Bureau, *China Statistical Yearbook 1995,* p. 215; and table 3-1.

98. Liu Zhongli, "Report on the Implementation of the Central and Local Budgets for 1996 and on the Draft Central and Local Budgets for 1997," *Beijing Review,* April 7-13, 1997, p. 28; and table 3-1.

99. *Almanac of China's Finance and Banking 1993,* p. 400; and *Almanac 1996,* p. 473.

100. Although they are not treated as loans, funds in these categories are carried on the published balance sheets of financial institutions.

101. *Almanac of China's Finance and Banking 1996,* pp. 472–73; and *Almanac 1993,* pp. 398–401.

102. *Almanac of China's Finance and Banking 1990,* pp. 73, 77, 79–82; *Almanac 1993,* pp. 398–401; and *Almanac 1997,* pp. 502–03.

103. See chapter 4.

104. Xie Ping, "On the Reform of State-Owned Specialized Banks," *Jingji yanjiu* (Economic Research), no. 2 (February 1994), pp. 25, 26.

105. "Top 50 by Total Assets," *The Banker,* July 1997, p. 141.

106. Xu Binglan, "BOC Beijing Branch Launches Personal Cheque Service," *China Daily Business Weekly,* April 8, 1996, p. 3.

107. By the end of June 1996 MasterCard had issued 11 million of the 14 million credit cards outstanding. Virtually all of the cards issued by MasterCard were corporate cards. Its consumer credit card was not rolled out until September 1996. Xu Binglan, "Maestro Credit Card Issued in 12 Cities," *China Daily,* September 9, 1996, p. 5.

108. Martin Mayer, *The Bankers: The Next Generation, The New Worlds of Money, Credit and Banking in An Electronic Age* (New York: Truman Talley Books/Dutton, 1997) pp. 109, 140. Interestingly, the claim by MasterCard International that its credit card volume is the largest in China is hotly contested by Visa. Visa cards in China can only be used to make retail purchases and Visa argues only these retail transactions, not fund and cash transfers which are offered by MasterCard, should be used to determine market rankings. Trish Saywell, "Credit Crunch: Visa and MasterCard dogfight over China," *Far Eastern Economic Review,* November 28, 1996, p. 71.

109. Almost all of the articles in the Chinese financial press, notably *Jinrong shibao* (Financial News), describing the growth of the credit card business of banks discuss the volume of savings deposits that the card business has generated; none discuss the volume of credit outstanding. This is because banks require customers to open savings accounts prior to issuing cards. The value of purchases is deducted from the saving account at the time of the transaction. A very small number of these cards offer overdraft privileges. None appear to offer revolving credit based on a preapproved line of credit.

110. New China News Agency, "Bank Offers Loans to Private Buyers for Car Purchases," July 22, 1996 in FBIS, *China,* 96-145, July 26, 1996, p. 42.

111. Chang Weimin, "Survive the Drive—Car Makers Face Chilly Winter," *China Daily Business Weekly,* October 14, 1996, pp. 1–2.

112. *Almanac of China's Finance and Banking 1996,* pp. 68, 472; New China News Agency, "Bank to Offer Mortgages for 'Genuine' Home Owners," in FBIS,

China, 96-059, March 26, 1996, p. 48; and "ICBC to Release More Funding for House Purchases," in FBIS, *China*, 97- 139, May 19, 1997.

113. *Almanac of China's Finance and Banking 1996*, p. 64.

114. Xu Binglan, "Mortgage Loans Find Maturity," *China Daily Business Weekly*, April 22, 1996, p. 3.

115. Nie Shui, "Mortgage Loans for Housing Come True," *China Economic News*, May 26, 1997, pp. 2–3. Nie cites People's Bank of China, "Provisional Procedures on Administration of Individual Housing Mortgage Loans," as the source for the terms under which loans will be offered.

116. Wang Lihong, "Trial Project Targets Debt, *China Daily Business Weekly*, October 7, 1996, p. 1.

117. Jin Rong, "State Enterprise Investment Occupies Nine-Tenths," *Jinrong shibao* (Financial News), May 29, 1996, p. 1.

118. World Bank, *The Chinese Economy: Fighting Inflation, Deepening Reform*, p. 86. These numbers exclude direct People's Bank of China lending to enterprises. In 1988 and 1989 the central bank lent funds directly to 180 and 600 key enterprises. This practice was supposed to be discontinued in 1990, but in fact the central bank continued to lend directly to 236 key enterprises. World Bank, *China: Financial Sector Policies and Institutional Development* (Washington, 1990), pp. 32, 121. Direct central bank lending to enterprises, identified in the bank's balance sheet as "other lending" and beginning in 1995 as "loans to non-financial departments," rose continuously from RMB 9 billion in 1985 to RMB 72.8 billion in 1994 and then fell for the first time to RMB 68 billion by year-end 1995. *Almanac of China's Finance and Banking 1995*, p. 464; and *Almanac of China's Finance and Banking 1996*, p. 412.

119. Calculated on the basis of data in table 3-1.

120. *Almanac of China's Finance and Banking 1994*, p. 508; and People's Bank of China, *China Financial Outlook '94*, p. 90.

121. The World Bank in a calculation of China's public sector deficit in 1994 estimated, based on interviews with the People's Bank and other government agencies, that from 60 to 80 percent of the central bank lending was used for "policy purposes" and thus should be included in the consolidated government deficit. World Bank, *China: Macroeconomic Stability in a Decentralized Economy* (Washington, 1994), p. 27.

122. *Almanac of China's Finance and Banking 1993*, pp. 398–401, 414. For the Bank of China the numbers are for domestic currency business only.

123. Lou Jiwei, "Financial System and Policy," paper presented to the Harvard Institute of International Development, Workshop on China's Economic Reforms, 1993, p. 1.

124. As discussed in chapter 5, beginning in 1998 the central bank no longer set a mandatory credit ceiling for each of the large state-owned banks. The central bank was to continue, however, to issue "guidance" lending quotas that were to require each of the major state banks to support the "state's regional development policy and credit principles" in order "to meet the rational credit needs of central and western regions where deposits are insufficient." New China News Agency, "The Elimination of Credit Quota Controls on State Commercial Banks," *Renmin ribao* (Haiwai ban) (People's Daily) (overseas edition), December 26, 1997, p. 1.

125. Hassanali Mehran and others, *Monetary and Exchange System Reform in*

China: An Experiment in Gradualism, Occasional Paper 141 (Washington: International Monetary Fund, September 1996), p. 42.

126. Banks with surplus funds also might have lent them in the interbank market, which was first created in the mid-1990s. However, as late as the mid-1990s this market was regionally oriented, making it unsuitable for large interprovincial transfers of funds. Mehran and others, *Monetary and Exchange System Reforms in China,* pp. 24–27.

127. In some years this linkage was even more evident since the interest rate the central bank charged on lending to specialized banks to fund the lending of the latter within the credit plan was much more favorable than the interest rate charged for loans beyond the credit plan. World Bank, *China: Finance and Investment,* p. 298.

128. I have excluded both Beijing and Tibet from the analysis. Although they have the lowest ratios of loans to deposits it appears that they are special cases. Beijing has very high deposits because the Ministry of Finance and many other central organizations maintain large amounts of funds on deposit in banks in the capital. Tibet also appears to be a special case because the Autonomous Region, relative to its local population, has a large garrison of People's Liberation Army soldiers as well as centrally dispatched administrative units. These units presumably maintain deposits in banks in Tibet that are large relative to other deposits. Thus the ratio of loans to deposits in both these regions appears to be relatively low for special reasons.

129. It might seem natural to think of "excess loans" and "loan shortfalls" as inward fiscal transfers and tax surcharges, respectively. I have avoided the analogy with taxes for two reasons. First, the redistribution of lendable funds is not quite parallel with redistributive expenditure and tax payments since banks in provinces with excess loans must pay interest on the funds they borrow from the central bank to finance the excess loans and banks in provinces with loan shortfalls receive interest on the excess reserves they maintain with the central bank. Second, at least in principle, these are not permanent transfers since when banks are fully commercialized and the credit plan is phased out the redistributive flows could be reversed. Provinces previously constrained in their lending presumably would be able to withdraw their excess reserves and increase their lending when credit quotas eventually are phased out.

130. There is a statistically significant relationship between the ratio of loans to deposits, on the one hand, and the share of state-owned firms on the other. Other variables, such as provincial per capita gross domestic product, were not significant in explaining the pattern of loans to deposits. That suggests that regional equity was not a significant criteria in fixing provincial lending quotas.

131. Tianjin Municipality, which has provincial-level administrative status, was tied with Heilongjiang for this dubious distinction. Each experienced an average annual growth of provincial gross domestic product of 6.96 percent.

132. State Statistical Bureau, *China Statistical Yearbook 1995,* p. 249.

133. See table 3-9.

134. Morris Goldstein and Philip Turner, *Banking Crises in Emerging Economies: Origin and Policy Options,* Economic Papers 46 (Basle: Bank for International Settlements, 1996), p. 25.

135. *Almanac of China's Finance and Banking 1986*, p. II-28.

136. *Ibid*. The 1996 data are from the annual reports of the four banks.

137. People's Bank of China, "Notice Concerning Carrying Out Asset:Liability Ratio Management by Commercial Banks" (February 18, 1994), cited by Liu Tiancai, "An Analysis of and Suggestions Regarding the Capital Adequacy Rates of China's Commercial Banks," *Guoji jinrong yanjiu* (International Banking Research), no. 11 (November 1995), p. 37. This commitment was reaffirmed by embedding it in article 39 of the Commercial Bank Law. However, the fifth clause of article 39 stipulated that banks established before the enactment of the law and whose balance sheets did not meet the capital adequacy standard or other specified asset:liability ratios, would be required to meet the standards within a time limit to be separately specified by the State Council. *Zhonghua renmin gongheguo shangye yinghang fa* (Commercial Banking Law of the People's Republic of China) (Beijing: China Legal Publishing House, 1995), p. 13. The law was passed by the Thirteenth Session of the Eighth National People's Congress Standing Committee on May 10, 1995, and took effect July 1, 1995.

138. Core or tier-one capital was defined by the Basle agreement to include equity capital and disclosed reserves from post-tax retained profits; tier-two capital adds to this sum undisclosed reserves from post-tax retained profits, loan loss reserves that are not ascribed to particular assets, up to 45 percent of the unrealized gain on marketable securities, hybrid debt/equity capital instruments and subordinated term debt that meets certain specifications. Risk weighting effectively requires banks to hold more capital against assets that are riskier. For example, cash balances held with the central bank and short-term government securities are assigned a weight of zero, meaning that no capital has to be held in support of these assets. Other assets are assigned weights that start at 10 percent and range up to 100 percent as risk increases. For example, loans for owner-occupied housing fully secured by mortgages are assigned a risk weight of 50 percent, whereas most loans (except those fully collateralized by cash) carry a weight of 100 percent. Basle Committee on Banking Regulations and Supervisory Practices, *International Convergence of Capital Measurement and Capital Standards* (Basle: Bank for International Settlements, 1988), pp. 16, 20–25. Ethan B. Kapstein, *Supervising International Banks: Origins and Implications of the Basle Accord*, Essays in International Finance 185 (Princeton: Department of Economics, International Finance Section, 1991), pp. 19–24.

139. "Standard Raisers," *Economist*, November 30, 1996, pp. 77–78; and Morris Goldstein and Philip Turner, *Banking Crises in Emerging Economies: Origin and Policy Options*, p. 26.

140. Although some Chinese banks report ratios that meet or exceed the Basle standard, they appear to be based on an undervaluation of the riskiness of bank assets. Interestingly, the failure of Chinese banks to meet the Basle standard on capital adequacy is conceded by some Chinese publications. See, for example, Zheng Genwen, "An Examination of the Problem of Credit Fund Losses during the Process of Transforming Banks," *Jingji guanli* (Economic Management), no. 5 (May 1995), p. 22.

141. Jiang Zuqi, "The Progress and Future of China's State Specialized Banks'

Commercialization Reform," *Guoji jinrong yanjiu* (International Banking Research), no. 1 (January 1996), p. 8.

142. Wang Xiyi, "Manage Bank Asset Risk in an All-Around Way; Further Perfect the Special Zone's Financial Regulatory System," *Zhongguo jinrong* (Chinese Banking), no. 11, (November 1994), p. 10.

143. Bank recapitalization is discussed in detail in chapter 4.

144. Liu Tiancai, "An Analysis of and Suggestions Regarding the Capital Adequacy Rates of China's Commercial Banks," p. 39.

145. *Almanac of Finance and Banking 1995*, p. 75.

146. Liu Tiancai, "An Analysis of and Suggestions Regarding the Capital Adequacy Rates of China's Commercial Banks," pp. 38–39. Since Chinese banks have not fully disclosed their investments in subsidiary financial institutions, it is unlikely that the data in table 3-5 have been adjusted to take this factor into account.

147. The largest institution to fail was the Agricultural Development Trust and Investment Company, which was closed in early 1997. At year-end 1995 its assets were RMB 29.9 billion. *Almanac of China's Finance and Banking 1996*, p. 518. Other failing financial institutions taken over by the People's Bank of China include the Zhongyin Trust and Investment Company and the China Financial Trust and Investment Company. Subsequently, the Guangdong Development Bank acquired the Zhongyin Trust and Investment Company and the China Financial Trust and Investment Company. People's Bank of China, *China Financial Outlook '97*, p. 44; and Zhan Lisheng, "Merger Spurs Guangzhou Bank's Development," *China Daily*, September 8, 1997, p. 5.

148. See note 138 for an explanation of risk weighting.

149. For example, according to the provisions the Chinese use to calculate risk-weighted capital adequacy, loans to central government public utility enterprises, such as those for the development of telecommunications, water supply, transportation and other infrastructure, carry only a 10 percent weight rather than the 100 percent weight required by the Basle agreement. Mao Hongjun, *Zhongguo jinrong tizhi gaige xin jucuo* (New measures in the financial system reform in China) (Beijing: Beijing University Press, 1994), p. 118. This criticism does not apply to table 3-5 which, to the extent underlying data allowed, were calculated on the Basle risk-weighting criteria.

150. Moody's Investors Service, *China Construction Bank* (New York, October 1996), p. 9.

151. Zhao Wenjie and Wang Jianxin, "A Discussion of Central Bank Supervision of Bank Asset Risk," *Zhongguo jinrong* (Chinese Banking), no. 10 (October 1994), p. 30.

152. Zhang Qingshou, "Concentrate Funds, Promote Economic Development," *Zhongguo jinrong* (Chinese Banking), no. 9 (September 1994), p. 10.

153. Goldstein and Turner, *Banking Crises in Emerging Economies: Origin and Policy Options*, p. 21.

154. Mao, *New Measures in the Financial System Reform in China*, p. 119.

155. "Commercial Banking Law" *China Law and Practice*, June 27, 1995, p. 13.

Ten percent is also the maximum ratio specified in U.S. regulations of commercial banks. World Bank, *China: Finance and Development*, p. 309.

156. As discussed in chapter 3, in some other banking systems nonperforming loans are divided into three categories. Typically banks must set aside, within thirty days, an amount equal to 20 percent, 50 percent, and 100 percent of any loan classified, respectively, overdue, doubtful, and bad.

157. In normal banking practice provisions are a deduction from income so any provisioning, no matter how small, would reduce a bank's income taxes. However, in China banks allocate their pre-tax profits to income taxes, provisioning, and retained earnings. Thus modest amounts of provisions would not reduce taxes paid by Chinese banks. The key interest of the Ministry of Finance is to ensure that provisioning is limited to an amount that will not impair the ability of the banks to pay 55 percent of profits in the form of income tax.

158. Zhang Fenwen, "An Examination of the Problem of Credit Fund Losses during the Process of Transforming Banks," *Jingji guanli* (Economic Management), no. 5 (May 1995), p. 22. Ministry of Finance, "Provisional Regulations concerning the Establishment of Bad Debt Reserve Funds by the Specialized Banks," cited in Liu Tiancai, "An Analysis of and Suggestions Regarding the Capital Adequacy Rates of China's Commercial Banks," p. 38. Xie Ping, *Financial Services in China* (Geneva: UN Commission on Trade and Development, 1995), p. 30.

159. Moody's Investors Service, *China Construction Bank*, p. 7.

160. *Almanac of China's Finance and Banking 1995*, p. 517. It appears that these reserves were accumulated over a period of years. Presumably before 1994 loan loss reserves were buried in other items in the bank's balance sheet.

161. The Construction Bank of China did not announce any write-offs in 1992. But the data in table 3-6 imply that the bank wrote off RMB 944 million in bad loans that year.

162. In normal practice banks report the magnitude of reserves at the beginning of the year, the amount of provisions (that is, additions to reserves) during the year, the quantity of loans written off during the year, and the resulting magnitude of reserves at the end of the year. The Agricultural Bank of China, however, reports only its year-end reserve position. Without information on provisions made during the year it is not possible to estimate the magnitude of loans written off during 1996. All that can be said with certainty is that the write-offs were equal to RMB 127 million (the difference between the two year-end numbers) plus whatever provisions were made that year.

163. See "Nonperforming Loans" in this chapter.

164. Because Chinese banks have very little capital, their rate of return on capital is biased upward. Comparing returns on capital of Chinese banks with banks in other countries would be misleading.

165. Declining profitability could reflect loan write-offs charged against profits. Thus declining profitability in the short run could be a good sign, reflecting the determination of a bank to aggressively write off bad debt. But, under accounting practices prevailing in China this is unlikely. As explained in note 157, additions to reserves are distributions from after-tax profits, that is, they are a below-the-line item rather than an above-the-line expense. There is no evidence

of write-offs of nonperforming loans except against reserves, so declining profitability is not likely to reflect a more aggressive writing off of loans than can be financed from reserves.

166. "Banking Boredom," *Economist*, November 30, 1996, p. 75.

167. The rate of return on assets of international banks in this paragraph is taken from "The Top 1000 World Banks," *The Banker*, vol. 146 (July 1996), p. 144. According to *The Banker* the rate of return on assets of the Industrial and Commercial Bank of China was only 0.15 percent. I have not used this number because China's large banks pay business taxes and surtaxes of 5.5 percent of their gross interest income. These business taxes are treated as an operating expense and deducted from revenues prior to calculating pre-tax profit. In short pre-tax profit for Chinese banks means profit after business taxes and surtaxes but before income taxes. To make the data on the Industrial and Commercial Bank comparable to that for other international banks, I have added business taxes of RMB 8.319 billion to reported pre-tax profits.

168. This procedure may be followed in part because banks have to declare as income interest on their entire portfolio of loans outstanding, regardless of whether interest is actually paid by the borrower. Then the banks must pay income taxes at 55 percent on these reported "profits." Sun Shuangrui, "Subordinate Specialized Bank Commercialization to Enterprise Reform," *Caimao jingji* (Finance and Trade Economics), no. 3 (March 1995), in FBIS, *China*, 96-048, March 11, 1996.

169. Andrew Sheng, ed., *Bank Restructuring: Lessons from the 1980s* (Washington: World Bank, 1996), p. 10; and Goldstein and Turner, *Banking Crises in Emerging Economies: Origin and Policy Options*, p. 23.

170. *Almanac of China's Finance and Banking 1993*, pp. 403–04.

171. Yang Jisheng, "The Economic 'Big Triangle' in Perspective," *Jingji cankao bao* (Economic Reference News), August 6, 1997, p. 1, in FBIS, *China*, 97-253, September 10, 1997.

172. Moody's Investors Service, *Effects of Recent Reforms on the Credit Quality of China's Specialized Banks* (New York, 1995), p. 7.

173. Although there is a long menu of interest rates that banks charge on various types of loans, the variation in the rates is quite small. This allows one to estimate the average interest rate with some confidence. For example in 1992 the central bank authorized the specialized banks to levy the following basic rates: working capital loans of six months, 8.10 percent; working capital loans of one year, 8.64 percent; loans for technical renovation, 8.46 percent; and loans of three to five years for capital construction, 9.54 percent. There were also a variety of preferential interest rates for specific purposes. Based on the composition of the loan portfolio of the Industrial and Commercial Bank in 1992 (85 percent of its loans outstanding were for working capital, 14 percent for fixed asset investment, and 1 percent were special purpose loans), the average interest rate can be estimated (assuming half of the working capital loans were for six months, half for one year) as 8.47 percent. The bank's reported interest income of RMB 72,661 million falls only 8 percent short of estimated total interest income of RMB 79,101 million (= 0.0847 x RMB 933,709 million in loans outstanding).

174. World Bank, *China: Financial Policies and Institutional Development* (Washington, October 1990), pp. 61–62, 65.

175. See note 232 for details.

176. Calculated on the basis of data in tables 3-2 and 3-7 following the standard practice of treating such provisions as a deduction from income. As discussed in note 157, because Chinese banks finance provisions as a distribution from profits, a marginal increase in provisions would not lead to a reduction in the rate of return on assets as calculated by the Chinese.

177. China is hardly unique in this respect. More than seventy countries, all but one from the developing world, offer no formal deposit insurance scheme. Goldstein and Turner, *Banking Crises in Emerging Economies: Origins and Policy Options*, p. 30.

178. Gerard Baker, "Insurance Fees to Leap for Banks in Japan," *Financial Times*, December 23, 1995, p. 1.

179. John R. Wilke, "FDIC Premiums for Most Banks Eliminated in 1996," *Wall Street Journal*, November 15, 1995, p. A4.

180. Deposits of the four specialized banks at year-end 1993 stood at RMB 2,140 billion. People's Bank of China, *China's Financial Outlook 1994*, p. 90. 0.2 percent of this amount equals 18 percent of reported profits of RMB 23,354 million (table 3-8).

181. Deposits of the four specialized banks at year-end 1995 (excluding interbank transactions) were RMB 4,053 billion. *Almanac of China's Finance and Banking 1996*, pp. 472–73. 0.2 percent of this amount is RMB 8.1 billion, which is equal to 31.7 percent of pre-tax profits of RMB 25.544 billion (table 3-8)

182. World Bank, *China: Financial Sector Policies and Institutional Development*, p. 28.

183. Of course, the lack of any compounding significantly reduces the real return on longer- term deposits.

184. Beginning in July 1993 China's specialized banks, along with all other enterprises, were to begin adopting accrual based accounting. That means interest costs would have to be reflected in profit and loss statements as they were accrued, even if the interest actually had not yet been paid. Ministry of Finance, "Accounting Standards for Enterprises," in *China Laws for Foreign Business—Taxation and Customs* (North Ryde, Australia: CCH International, 1993), Document 35-536, pp. 44372–373.

185. People's Bank of China, "Opinion on the Divesture of the Trust and Investment Companies that Are Subordinate to the Industrial and Commercial Bank and China's Three Other Specialized Banks," *Zhonghua renmin gongheguo guowuyuan gongbao* (Bulletin of the State Council of the People's Republic of China), no. 14 (June 13, 1995), pp. 568–71. The State Council endorsed this opinion in August 1995. New China News Agency, "Circular Ordering Specialized Banks to Disaffiliate Themselves from Trust and Investment Operations," August 2, 1995, in FBIS, *China*, 95-149, August 3, 1995, p. 27.

186. People's Bank of China, *China Financial Outlook '96*, p. 34.

187. In its report covering 1996 the central bank reported that it "would fully accomplish the segregation of banking and trust and investment industry in 1997

on the basis of careful examination, asset evaluation and checking up claims and liabilities." People's Bank of China, *China Financial Outlook '97*, p. 41.

188. "Call to End Subsidies on Long-Term Deposits," *Hong Kong Standard*, March 29, 1996.

189. Ye Guiguang, "Bank of Agriculture: Profit Increased Twofold," *Jingji cankao bao* (Economic Reference News), January 14, 1996, p. 1, in FBIS, *China*, 96-036, February 22, 1996, pp. 56–57. Ye's article quotes He Linxiang, who at that time was vice president of the Agriculture Bank, as the source of this information. He was promoted to president of the bank in late 1997.

190. The Ministry of Finance provides these transfers by reducing the income taxes that these banks are required to pay. Thus these subsidies do not appear in the published annual reports on government expenditures. The same procedure was followed in the late 1980s when value-guarantee deposits were first used. World Bank, *China: Financial Policies and Institutional Development*, p. 53.

191. The People's Construction Bank, *1995 Annual Report* (Beijing, 1996), p. 6.

192. This calculation assumes that the total subsidies received were simply four times those received by the Construction Bank. However, because it is dwarfed in size by the Industrial and Commercial Bank and is significantly smaller than the Agricultural Bank, the Construction Bank accounts for just under a fifth of the savings deposits of the four banks as a group. Since the subsidies were used to offset the higher interest cost on savings deposits, an alternative assumption is that RMB 2.92 billion would account for just under a fifth of the total subsidies. On this alternative assumption the total subsidy would be RMB 16.2 billion or 63 percent of reported pre-tax profits in 1995.

193. The treatment of subsidies received from the Ministry of Finance in the 1996 annual reports of the four largest banks is sufficiently opaque that it is not possible to estimate profits net of such subsidies.

194. As already noted, in 1996 RMB 334 billion in interest was not actually paid. Loan volume outstanding in 1995 was 20 percent less than in 1996. If the portion of unpaid interest was the same, it would have amounted to RMB 280 billion. China's four biggest banks accounted for about three-quarters of all loans outstanding. If unpaid interest was evenly distributed across all financial institutions, the amount unpaid at the four biggest banks in 1995 would have been RMB 210 billion.

195. World Bank, *China: Macroeconomic Stability in a Decentralized Economy* (Washington, 1994), p. 9.

196. Table A-2.

197. The supplementary interest rates that banks paid are shown in table A-7.

198. Three, five, and eight-year deposits were eligible for the indexing to offset inflation. For three-year deposits the combined interest rate was to be set to fully offset inflation. For five- and eight-year deposits the combined interest rate was supposed to more than offset inflation. People's Bank of China, "Announcement Concerning Initiating Long-Term Value-Guarantee *Renminbi* Deposits," in *Almanac of China's Finance and Banking 1989*, p. 526.

199. Although the announcement of the program's formal termination, as of December 1, 1991, was not made until November 1991, as a practical matter after

May 1990 long-term time deposits no longer benefited from the program since the supplementary interest rate for maturing deposits was set at zero for eighteen consecutive months beginning in June 1990 (table A-7). *Almanac of China's Finance and Banking 1992*, p. 34. The zero rates were a consequence of the dramatic decline in the inflation rate in 1990, particularly in the second half. Inflation was almost as low in 1991. See World Bank, *The Chinese Economy: Fighting Inflation, Deepening Reform* (Washington, 1996), p. 104, for the monthly rates of inflation during this period.

200. New China News Agency, "PBC Halts Interest Rate Subsidies on Fixed Deposits," *China Daily*, April 2, 1996, p. 5. Long-term deposits made before April 1, maturing after April 1, continued to be eligible for the subsidy payments and continued to receive such payments through April 1997. Beginning in May 1997 the subsidy rate fell to zero, so long-term deposits maturing after April received no subsidy. See table A-7.

201. State Statistical Bureau, *China Statistical Yearbook 1995*, p. 233; and table 3-1.

202. The marginal cost of funds is the cost of the last dollar of funds attracted, that is, the most expensive funds.

203. Eight-year fixed-term savings deposits were first offered on April 1, 1982. Since none of these deposits would have matured during the 1988–89 inflation, the marginal cost of funds was the interest rate paid on five-year fixed-term deposits. The base rate on five-year deposits rose by 5.58 percentage points, that is, from 9.36 percent a year in 1987 to 14.94 percent a year by February 1989. In addition the supplementary interest rate peaked at 13.64 percent in the third quarter of 1989. Since banks at that time were required to pay the rising base rate even on old deposits, the increase in the marginal cost of funds to the banks is the sum of the increase in the base rate plus the subsidy rate. Thus the marginal cost of funds to banks peaked in the third quarter of 1989 when they had to pay interest on maturing five-year deposits at the rate of 28.58 percent a year. Over the longer run the increase was somewhat higher since there had been modest increases in the base rate for long-term deposits in years before 1987. Take, for example, a bank accepting a five-year fixed term deposit on September 1, 1984. It expected to pay interest of 7.92 percent a year, the rate prevailing at that time. But because of three subsequent increases in the base rate and the introduction of indexing, by the final quarter that the funds were on deposit the bank had to pay a total annual interest rate almost four times that prevailing when it accepted the deposit.

204. In 1993 the People's Bank announced that after March 1 any change in base interest rates on long-term deposits occurring would apply only to new deposits, not to those funds already on deposit. Thus, unlike in the late 1980s when the increase in base rates and the supplement were additive, when indexing was reintroduced after March 1, 1993, the increase in the marginal cost of funds to the banks was simply the amount of the interest supplement. People's Bank of China, "Regulations on Managing Savings," cited in Xing Benxiu and Yi Xiao, "Several Issues Concerning the Calculation of Interest Rates on Savings Deposits after an Adjustment of Interest Rates," *Zhongguo jinrong* (Chinese Banking), no. 9 (September 1993), pp. 27–28.

205. The cost of funds peaked in December 1995 when banks had to pay an interest rate supplement for maturing deposits of 13.24 percent. Among the deposits maturing at that time, eight-year deposits paid the highest interest rate and thus represent the marginal cost of funds to the banks. The base rate was the 10.44 percent rate in effect when the deposit would have been placed in the bank in December 1987.

206. Recall that one reason individuals held such a high portion of their savings in sight deposits is that banks did not offer checking accounts to individuals.

207. *Almanac of China's Finance and Banking 1993*, pp. 364, 549.

208. Naturally, the reversal was slower since depositors could not withdraw funds in longer-term deposits until they matured. But as these deposits matured, they were partially deposited in sight accounts, rather than entirely rolled over.

209. The bank's domestic currency deposits shot up from a little over RMB 2 billion at year-end 1987 to almost RMB 110 billion at year-end 1993. *Almanac of China's Finance and Banking 1989*, p. 248; *Almanac 1990*, p. 242; *Almanac 1992*, p. 533; and *Almanac 1994*, p. 526.

210. The value-guarantee program was discontinued for new deposits at the end of 1991. The RMB 8 billion in value-guarantee deposits listed by the Bank of China in 1992 represents those longer-term deposits made before that time, on which the bank was obligated to pay supplementary interest if a supplementary interest rate was still being offered when the deposits matured. For example, a five-year certificate taken out on October 1, 1989, would have been still been included in the reported magnitude of value-guarantee deposits outstanding at the end of 1992.

211. See tables A-3 through A-6. This is substantially higher than a reported 8 percent average nominal cost of bank funds reported by the World Bank for the same year. The bank does not report how its estimate was derived. World Bank, *China: Financial Sector Policies and Institutional Development*, p. 27.

212. Estimated based on data in table 3-9 and the fact that nine-tenths of the bank's domestic currency loans were for working capital. *Almanac of China's Finance and Banking 1992*, p. 533.

213. In 1987 only 11.5 percent of the deposits of enterprises in the four specialized banks, the CITIC Industrial Bank, and the Bank of Communications were term deposits. In 1989 at the end of the second quarter, despite the huge run-up in inflation, this share had increased to only 12.2 percent. World Bank, *China: Financial Sector Policies and Institutional Development*, p. 8.

214. This was the rate in 1989 both for one-year loans and for capital construction loans. Central bank interest rates on shorter-term loans, probably less common, were somewhat lower. *Almanac of China's Finance and Banking 1990*, p. 169.

215. *Almanac of China's Finance and Banking 1992*, p. 533.

216. *Almanac of China's Finance and Banking 1990*, pp. 79–80, 239.

217. Based on the assumption that the noninterest costs per unit of domestic currency lending is the same as that for the bank's total lending, including foreign-currency-denominated loans. In 1989 the bank reported RMB 159 billion in domestic currency lending, an amount equal to 64 percent of its total reported lending of RMB 247.5 billion. *Almanac of China's Finance and Banking 1992*, p. 533.

218. *Almanac of China's Finance and Banking 1991* (Beijing: China Financial Publishing House, 1992), pp. 129, 156. Because the bank's profit and loss state-

ment does not report on interest earnings and interest expenditures for domestic and foreign currency business separately, there is no way to confirm that margins are higher on the bank's foreign currency business. However, this seems likely since most of the bank's foreign currency business is carried out by branches abroad where interest rates are not regulated by the People's Bank.

219. This is borne out by the high portion of indexed deposits at these institutions. At mid-year 1989 indexed deposits accounted for 40 percent of all deposits at the Agricultural Bank of China and at the largest urban branches of the Industrial and Commercial Bank as well. World Bank, *China: Financial Policies and Institutional Development*, p. 8. Based on data in tables A-3 through A-6 the share of indexed deposits at the Bank of China can be calculated to have been only 15.2 percent.

220. *Almanac of China's Finance and Banking 1993*, p. 398.

221. *Almanac of China's Finance and Banking 1992*, p. 521.

222. Foreign currency lending was based on one-month, three-month, and six-month floating rates.

223. For example, the interest rate banks paid on one-year dollar-denominated deposits made by individuals in 1990 was only 6.9375 percent. That was actually less than the 7.25 percent rate prevailing in 1985. For dollar-denominated sight deposits the rate went from 2.5 percent to 2.0 percent. Over the same period the rate on one-year domestic currency deposits rose from 6.84 percent to 11.34 percent and the rate on sight deposits was static (table 3-9).

224. James Harding, Peter Montagnon, and Tony Walker, "Command Performance by Bank of China Chief," *Financial Times*, June 6, 1997, p. 23.

225. As in the earlier program, all term deposits of three years or more, including the longest deposits of eight years, were indexed.

226. In 1994 fixed-term deposits absorbed 77 percent of incremental savings deposits. People's Bank of China, *China Financial Outlook '95*, p. 96. In 1995 this share increased to 85 percent. People's Bank of China, *China Financial Outlook '96*, p. 96

227. However, as discussed in note 204, the effect of increasing inflation on banks' cost of funds was mitigated by a change in the method of calculating the interest to be paid on longer-term deposits already in banks. All existing long-term deposits were eligible for indexing when it was reintroduced. But unlike in the earlier inflationary period, deposits made after March 1, 1993, were not eligible for any subsequent increases in the base interest rate.

228. Zhao Minshan and Zhou Xuewen, "Causes of the Difficulties of State-Owned Enterprises," *Qiye guanli* (Enterprise Management), no. 8 (August 1995), in FBIS, *China*, 95-229, November 29, 1995, p. 72.

229. Ni Xiaolin," Walk Out of the Odd Circle," *Jingji cankao bao* (Economic Reference News), May 14, 1995, p. 1.

230. Moody's Investors Service, *Effects of Recent Reforms on the Credit Quality of China's Specialized Banks*, p. 9.

231. People's Bank of China, "General Rules on Loans (for trial implementation)," *Jinrong shibao* (Financial News), August 23, 1995, p. 2. These provisions were carried over to "General Rules on Loans," chapter 7, articles 33–37, *Jinrong shibao* (Financial News), June 29, 1996, p. 2. These rules took effect August 1, 1996.

232. The "General Rules on Loans" governs the possibilities for extending the original maturity of any loan. Loans of less than one-year duration are not supposed to be extended; medium-term loans, those of from one to less than five years duration, can be extended for a period of no more than one-half their initial length; long-term loans, those of five years or more, can not be extended by more than three years.

233. For example, HSBC Holdings increased its provisions for bad and doubtful debts 60 percent in 1997, to £615 million. This included a special general provision of £175 million reflecting emerging credit difficulties in Asia, primarily in HSBC's Hongkong Bank Group. Nicholas Reynolds, Peter Chan, and Sheel Kohli, "HSBC Braces for Wave of Bad Debt," *South China Morning Post* (Business Post) February 24, 1998, p. 1.

234. This is because Chinese borrowers generally are allowed to use loan proceeds to make interest payments or their interest payments are built into the principal (capitalized) when loans are rolled over. Thus it would be uncommon for a borrower to be behind on interest payments. On multiple-year loans used to finance investment projects, construction proceeds in stages, and the borrower draws down the loan periodically to finance all ongoing expenditures, including quarterly or semiannual interest payments. Since interest payments are a legitimate use of loan proceeds, the size of the loan at the outset is based on the expectation that it will need to finance not only the costs of construction, new machinery, and so forth, but also the interest that will be paid on the loan before the time the project enters production. One-year working capital loans frequently do not have periodic interest payments but rather payment of interest at the end of the term. Most of these loans are rolled over, and the interest on the prior loan is built into the new loan, allowing the borrower to "pay" the interest on the old loan at the time it is rolled over.

235. International practice varies between 90 and 180 days. In the United States the norm is 90 days. Sheng, *Bank Restructuring*, p. 10.

236. World Bank, *China: Financial Sector Policies and Institutional Development*, p. 72.

237. Only loans that are 100 percent collateralized with cash would not be classified.

238. Moody's Investors Service, *Effects of Recent Reforms on the Credit Quality of China's Specialized Banks*, p. 7.

239. China's first bankruptcy law was passed in 1986. However, it contained a provision that it would not be implemented until after the law on state-owned enterprises took effect. The latter law was passed by the National People's Congress on April 13, 1988, and went into effect on August 1 of the same year.

240. World Bank, *China: Financial Sector Policies and Institutional Development*, pp. 94–95.

241. Moody's Investors Service, *Bank of China* (New York, October 1996), pp. 7, 15.

242. World Bank, *China: Financial Sector Policies and Institutional Development*, p. 68.

243. Wang Xiaozhong, "Bold, New Moves Needed to Make Headway," *China Daily*, January 9, 1995, p. 4.

244. Tang Xiong, "How to Regard the Bank's Non-Performing Assets," *Jinrong shibao* (Financial News), April 21, 1996, p. 5.

245. The sum of loans outstanding of the four largest banks at year-end 1995 was RMB 3,908 billion according to the data given in these banks' balance sheets. *Almanac of China's Finance and Banking 1996*, pp. 472–73.

246. *Almanac of China's Finance and Banking 1996*, pp. 472–73.

247. In 1995 and the first three quarters of 1996 the Industrial and Commercial Bank recovered about 15 percent of its outstanding loans to more than 5,000 enterprises that went bankrupt and were liquidated. See chapter 4, note 51.

248. Bank of China, *Annual Report 1996*, p. 43. The Bank of China's financial statements, like those of other banks, are also subject to review by the Ministry of Finance and the State Auditing Administration.

249. Moody's Investors Service, *China Construction Bank* (New York, October 1996), pp. 6, 9. More generally, see World Bank, *China: Financial Sector Policies and Institutional Development*, p. 59.

250. Anjali Kumar and others, *China's Non-Bank Financial Institutions: Trust and Investment Companies*, Discussion Paper 358 (Washington: World Bank, 1997), p. 12.

251. "Enterprises Need Personal Savings," *China Daily*, May 23, 1995, p. 4. The article in *China Daily* draws on an interview with Dai Xianglong published in *Liaowang* (Outlook). At the time he was the vice governor of the bank. The English-language article states that the portion of "bad loans" has been rising by 2 percent a year. In the original article the language used by Dai is not "daizhang daikuan," the term for bad loans, but "buliang daikuan." Buliang daikuan is a generic term that corresponds to what would usually be called nonperforming loans. It is inclusive of all three types of classified loans. The original article states that the share of nonperforming loans is rising by 2 percentage points a year. Zhao Yining, "The Financial Situation and Financial Reform," *Liaowang* (Outlook), May 15, 1995, pp. 12–13.

252. Sun Shangrui, "An Investigation of a Number of Issues in the Commercialization Reform of the Specialized Banks," *Caimao jingji* (Finance and Trade Economics), no. 3 (March 1996), p. 8.

253. Hu Chushou, "The Causes and Solutions to the Financial Risk of China's Agricultural Policy Bank," *Jingjixue dongtai* (Economic Dynamics) October 18, 1997, pp. 22–25 in FBIS, *China*, 97-350, December 16, 1997.

254. The pre-tax profit comparison is based on profits before both income and business taxes. This is an important adjustment since the Bank of Communications is not required to pay the latter, whereas the Industrial and Commercial bank is. *Almanac of Finance and Banking 1996*, pp. 472, 474, 482, and 484. Bank of Communications, *1995 Annual Report* (Shanghai, 1996), pp. 26–28.

255. *Almanac of China's Finance and Banking 1988*, p. 72. Bank of Communications, *1995 Annual Report*, p. 27.

256. At year-end 1993 the bank's capital adequacy was reported to be 14.18 percent. *Almanac of China's Finance and Banking 1994*, p. 88; and *Almanac 1995*, p. 519. Neither the bank's annual report nor the *Almanac of China's Finance and Banking* provides information on the bank's capital adequacy for the years after

1993. It is likely that the bank overstates its capital adequacy since, as discussed earlier, the risk-weighting procedures do not fully conform to international standards.

257. The failure of the Bank of Communications to publish data on the quality of its loan portfolio after 1994 may mean that the bank's financial position has worsened in more recent years.

258. *Almanac of China's Finance and Banking 1996*, pp. 472–74.

259. Bank of Communications, *1995 Annual Report* (Beijing, 1996), pp. 26–27. The China Construction Bank was the only other bank to report allowances for potential losses on receivables. In 1995 these stood at 0.37 percent of receivables, about one-sixteenth the ratio of allowances of the Bank of Communications. *Almanac of China's Finance and Banking 1996*, p. 473.

260. Harding, Montagnon, and Walker, "Command Performance by Bank of China Chief," p. 23.

261. Bank of China, *Annual Report 1996*, p. 45. Wang, in his interview in the *Financial Times*, asserted that only 3 percent of the loans made by the bank since 1994 are nonperforming. That suggests that the performance of the bank has improved considerably since Wang became president in late 1993.

262. *Almanac of China's Finance and Banking 1995*, p. 41.

263. Ibid., p. 578.

264. John P. Bonin and Bozena Leven, "Polish Bank Consolidation and Foreign Competition: Creating a Market-Oriented Banking Sector," *Journal of Comparative Economics*, vol. 23 (August 1996), p. 53.

265. Wei Min, "Int'l Banking Institutions Pour into China," *Beijing Review*, June 17–23, 1996, p. 4. This information is attributed by the author to Xiao Yunquan of the Foreign Financial Institutions Management Department of the People's Bank of China. Wang Lihong, "Growth in Finance Institutions," *China Daily Business Weekly*, October 28, 1996, p. 3.

266. Table A-1. Data on the assets of foreign-funded financial institutions have been converted from U.S.$ to RMB based on the average exchange rate prevailing during the year.

267. Wang Lihong, "A More Open Finance Sector in '97," *China Daily Business Weekly*, January 6, 1997, p. 1.

268. Anatol Lieven, "Hungarian Banks Stronger after Braving Pain of Reform," *Financial Times*, September 11, 1997, p. 2.

269. Bonin and Leven, "Polish Bank Consolidation and Foreign Competition," p. 59.

270. Christopher Bobinski, "Polish Banking Sales Advance on Two Fronts," *Financial Times*, May 22, 1997, p. 3.

271. If the informal credit market represents an equilibrium, all those willing to pay the going rate will have their projects funded. But the limited supply of credit on the informal market creates a large gap between the official and informal interest rates. Many borrowers without access to loans from state banks may have projects with a rate of return greater than the low interest rate changed by state banks but below the very high rates prevailing in the informal market. Because the shortage of funds in the informal market drives up the informal interest rate to such a high level, these projects will go unfunded.

272. "Banks Closed," *Far Eastern Economic Review*, June 1, 1995, p. 1
273. AsiaOne/BT Online July 16, 1996.
274. New China News Agency, "State Eliminates Illegal Banking," *China Daily*, November 25, 1996, p. 5.

Notes to Chapter 4

1. In the words of a senior partner in Price Waterhouse, "China's bankers are still ill-equipped to evaluate the quality of new loans." "Long and Slow Road Ahead for Banking System Reform," *Hong Kong Standard*, January 31, 1997. This assessment was offered after Price Waterhouse completed a three-year World Bank project to strengthen the supervisory controls of the central bank.

2. Moody's Investors Service, *Bank of China* (New York, October 1996), p. 5.

3. Beginning in April 1996 the central bank instituted a system of loan certificates to eliminate the practice of firms borrowing simultaneously from several banks and to provide lenders with information on the borrowers' credit history and other financial information. These certificates are to be issued by the People's Bank, and firms must present them when opening accounts or borrowing money. "Loan Certificate Management Procedure," *Jinrong shibao* (Financial News), March 31, 1996, p. 1.

4. Robert G. King and Ross Levine, "Finance and Growth: Schumpeter Might Be Right," *Quarterly Journal of Economics*, vol. 53 (August 1993), pp. 715–37.

5. Marco Pagano, "Financial Markets and Growth: An Overview," *European Economic Review*, vol. 37 (April 1993), pp. 613–22. Of these three effects only the last is ambiguous.

6. King and Levine, "Finance and Growth: Schumpeter Might Be Right."

7. Joseph E. Stiglitz, "Financial Markets and Development," *Oxford Review of Economic Policy*, vol. 5 (Winter 1989), p. 61.

8. In Asia, for example, in Hong Kong, Malaysia, the Philippines, Singapore, and Thailand the market capitalization of stocks in the mid-1990s exceeded the total domestic currency assets of the banking system. Andrew Sheng, *Bank Restructuring: Lessons from the 1980s* (Washington: World Bank, 1996), p. 176.

9. World Bank, *From Plan to Market* (Oxford University Press, 1996), p. 100.

10. The People's Bank has closed many unauthorized private banks, including some in financial distress. It is not clear whether depositors lost money in these cases. The People's Bank of China has closed three failed trust and investment companies: the Zhongyin Trust and Investment Company in 1995, the China Finance Trust and Investment Company in 1996, and the China Agricultural Development Trust and Investment Company in 1997. However, trust and investment companies are not authorized to take deposits from the public. A number of securities firms also have failed. It is not clear whether individuals that did business with these firms lost money.

11. Household hard currency deposits in the Bank of China began to grow rapidly in the mid-1980s and reached U.S.$1.21 billion by year-end 1988. *Almanac*

of China's Finance and Banking 1989 (Beijing: China Financial Publishing House, 1989), p. 249. At the end of 1997 individual foreign exchange deposits in the bank reached U.S.$17.5 billion. Ren Kan, "Banks Fight for Hard Currency Deposit Business," *China Daily Business Weekly*, February 15-21, 1998, p. 3. At mid-year 1997 individual hard currency deposits in all domestic banks exceeded U.S.$30 billion. Yang Jisheng, "The Economic 'Big Triangle' in Perspective," *Jingji cankao bao* (Economic Reference News), August 6, 1997, p. 1 in Foreign Broadcast Information Service, *China*, 97-253, September 10, 1997 (Hereafter FBIS, *China*.)

12. China also has a postal savings system, but the deposits in the system are extremely small. For example, at year-end 1989 total deposits were RMB 10.1 billion, about 2 percent of total household savings. *Almanac of China's Finance and Banking 1990*, pp. 60, 285. By year-end 1996 deposits had increased to RMB 215 billion, under 6 percent of total savings. *Almanac 1997*, pp. 466, 581.

13. This figure includes treasury bills, treasury bonds, state construction bonds, key state construction bonds, special bonds, index linked bonds, and special purchase bonds. *Almanac of China's Finance and Banking 1996*, p. 436. The estimate of the share of these bonds held by households is based on annual data on the percent of government debt purchased by households. Anjali Kumar and others, *China's Emerging Capital Markets* (Hong Kong: FT Financial Publishing Asia Pacific, 1997), p. 93.

14. *Almanac of China's Finance and Banking 1996*, p. 436. The figure for enterprise bonds and short-term commercial paper appears to exclude central government enterprise bonds and housing construction bonds, both of which are classified as enterprise bonds. At year-end 1994 there was RMB 7.41 billion and RMB 643 million outstanding of these bonds, respectively. *China Securities Market Yearbook 1995* (Beijing: Chinese Legal Publishing House, 1996), p. 27.

15. Liu Yuanda, "A Great Endeavor Brings a Major Success–A Brief Exploration of China's Capital Market," *Jingji cankao bao* (Economic Reference News), July 15, 1996, p. 2, FBIS, *China*, 96-192, July 15, 1996.

16. One estimate is that the value of internal enterprise stock and unauthorized securities issued outside the plan amounted to about RMB 122 billion in 1992. It is not clear what portion of these securities were purchased by individuals. Most of the internal enterprise stock was presumably purchased by individual workers, but the magnitude of enterprise stock, as opposed to other unauthorized securities, is not specified. Xie Ping, "On the Reform of the State-Owned Specialized Banks," *Jingji yanjiu* (Economic Research), no. 2 (February 1994), p. 25. Presumably the purchase of shares in unlisted companies grew as the de facto privatization of small state-owned companies at the county level accelerated in the mid-1990s. See discussion in chapter 2.

17. These calculations do not take into account the value of shares in nonlisted joint stock companies owned by households. The number of firms in this category is several times the number of listed companies, but little information is available on the share price or the number of shares of these nonlisted companies. See previous note.

18. Wang Lihong, "Steady Advance Predicted for 1997," *China Daily*, January 6, 1997, p. 3; and Xu Binglan, "$421m in Bonds Ready to Go to Market Next

Week," *China Daily*, January 9, 1997, p. 5. The numbers for corporate debt and government debt are gross. The value of these assets outstanding rose by less than these amounts because some previously issued debt matured and was redeemed.

19. In 1996 the average stock price rose 65 percent in Shanghai and 226 percent in Shenzhen. "Stocks Turnover up Four Times to Record $2,000b," *Hong Kong Standard*, January 3, 1997.

20. Liu Weiling, "The Doors to Open Wider," *China Daily*, January 22, 1994, p. 1.

21 "Foreign Banks in China to Deal in RMB," *Beijing Review*, January 30-February 5, 1995, p. 6.

22. The authorities allowed these banks to continue to operate their original banks in Shanghai proper as subbranches of their Pudong branches. The subbranches are not authorized to carry out domestic currency banking.

23. Ren Kan, "Foreign Banks to Use RMB," *China Daily*, February 1, 1996, p. 1.

24. Pamela Yatsko, "Strings Attached: Foreigners Get Limited Entry into Renminbi Banking," *Far Eastern Economic Review*, January 16, 1997, p. 52.

25. Foreign banks operating in China pay a 15 percent tax on their profits as well as a business tax of 8 percent of gross business income. Banks licensed to carry out domestic currency business pay a 33 percent tax on profit, the same as that paid by Chinese state-owned banks. However, the higher rate applies only to profits earned on their domestic currency business. Their profits from foreign currency business continue to be taxed at the lower rate. Tong Ting, "Overseas RMB Banks Face 33% Tax," *China Daily Business Weekly*, June 2, 1997, p. 1.

26. The nine were Citibank, Hongkong and Shanghai Banking Corp, Bank of Tokyo-Mitsubishi, Industrial Bank of Japan, Daichi Kangyo Bank, Sanwa Bank, Standard Chartered Bank, International Bank of Paris and Shanghai, and Banque Indosuez. A number of other foreign banks have applied for licenses to do domestic currency business. Some of them already have moved their existing Shanghai branches to Pudong in anticipation of central bank approval of their applications.

27. Table 3-9.

28. Based on the assumption that the spread between the deposit and lending rate would be about 4 percent. The World Bank estimated that the intermediation costs of commercial banks in industrialized countries is from 3 to 5 percent of assets. The bank reported slightly higher margins in a small sample of developing countries. World Bank, *China: Finance and Investment* (Washington, 1988), pp. 265–66.

29. RMB 530 billion is the average magnitude of household sight deposits at year-end 1994 and year-end 1995.

30. This advice appears to have been first made in 1990 when the World Bank recommended moving toward market determination of interest rates over the medium term. World Bank, *China: Finance and Investment*, p. 50. This advice has been reiterated since, although with cautions attached. For example, see World Bank, *China: Macroeconomic Stability in a Decentralized Economy* (Washington, 1994), pp. 83–84; and World Bank, *The Chinese Economy: Fighting Inflation, Deepening Reform* (Washington, 1996), pp. 30–31.

31. World Bank, *The Chinese Economy: Fighting Inflation, Deepening Reform*, pp. 13–14.

32. World Bank, *China: Financial Sector Policies and Institutional Development* (Washington, 1990), p. 121.

33. Ibid., p. 31.

34. World Bank, *China: Financial Policies and Institutional Development* (Washington, October 1990), p. 121.

35. Hassanali Mehran and others, *Monetary and Exchange System Reforms in China: An Experiment in Gradualism*, Occasional Paper 141 (Washington: International Monetary Fund, 1996), pp. 47–48.

36. "People's Bank Law of China," article 22.

37. Ding Jianming, "Elimination of State-Owned Commercial Bank Lending Quota Controls," *Renmin ribao* (Haiwai ban) (People's Daily) (overseas edition), December 26, 1997, p. 1

38. Peter J. Quirk and Owen Evans, *Capital Account Convertibility: Review of Experience and Implications for IMF Policies*, Occasional Paper 131 (Washington: International Monetary Fund, 1995), p. 3.

39. State Council, "Decision on Establishing a Unified Basic Pension Insurance Scheme for Enterprise Staff and Workers," cited by New China News Agency, August 26, 1997, in FBIS, *China*, 97-247, September 4, 1997. The decision was taken on July 16, 1997.

40. World Bank, *China: Pension System Reform* (Washington, 1996), p. xvi.

41. Ibid., p. 15.

42. Ibid., p. 63.

43. Wu Jinglian and others, *The Road to a Market Economy: A Comprehensive Framework and Working Proposals* (Beijing: Party Central Translation Publishing House, 1995). See also the important speech given by Wu Jinglian at the Central Party School on April 13, 1994, "From 'Increasing Quantity Reform' to the 'Integrated Advance' Strategy of Reform," in Wu Jinglian, *The Basic Structure of Constructing a Market Economy* (Beijing: China Economic Publishing House, 1997), pp. 44–56.

44. "Redundancy Twice Official Jobless Rate," Reuters, September 17, 1997, as found at Clarinet newsgroup. Although some Western press reports suggested that the number of furloughed workers rose sharply in 1997, 15 million workers were reported to be on furlough as early as the end of 1993. Wei Jie and Dong Jingyi, "Evidence-Supported Analysis of Risk Expectations of the State-Owned Economic Sector," *Jingji cankao bao* (Economic Reference News), March 18, 1997, p. 4, in FBIS, *China*, 97-112, March 18, 1997.

45. "China Loan Quota," February 10, 1998, via *Wall Street Journal*, interactive edition.

46. Tsao Hsiao, "Jiang, Li and Zhu's New Ideas for Banking Reform," *Ching Pao* (Mirror), January 1, 1998, pp. 32–36 in FBIS, *China*, 98-015, January 15, 1998.

47. In 1996, 6,232 firms declared bankruptcy compared with 2,385 in 1995. That represents a bankruptcy rate of 0.06 percent in 1996. Jane Macartney, "China Sharply Accelerates Bankruptcies in 1996," Reuters, as found at Clarinet newsgroup, January 28, 1997. The source of the information given in this article is Cao Siyuan, China's leading authority on bankruptcy.

48. Matt Forney, "We Want to Eat," *Far Eastern Economic Review,* June 26, 1997, pp. 14–16; and Kan Ke, "Inside Story of Large-Scale Sit-in Heilongjiang on New Year's Day," *Hong Kong Hsin Pao* (Hong Kong Economic Journal), January 21, 1997, in FBIS, *China,* 97-015, January 21, 1997.

49. Donald Clarke, "State Council Notice Nullifies Statutory Rights of Creditors," *East Asian Executive Reports,* April 15, 1997, p. 10.

50. "People's Republic of China Security Law," in *Almanac of Chinese Finance and Banking 1996,* pp. 312–17.

51. In 1995, for example, 1,920 firms, which owed RMB 8.84 billion in principal and interest to the Industrial and Commercial Bank, went through bankruptcy. The bank recovered RMB 1.45 billion or 16 percent of the principal and interest outstanding. In the first nine months of 1996 the recovery rate was 15 percent on RMB 19.22 billion in principal and interest outstanding to 3,208 firms that went through bankruptcy. China Industrial and Commercial Bank Enterprise Bankruptcy Issues Group, "An Investigation Report on Issues in Enterprise Bankruptcy," *Jingji yanjiu* (Economic Research), no. 4 (April 1997), p. 15.

52. In 1995 only 47 of 2,385 bankruptcies were initiated by banks. In 1996 it was 72 of 6,232 bankruptcies. Macartney, "China Sharply Accelerates Bankruptcies in 1996."

53. See, for example, State Economic and Trade Commission and People's Bank of China, "Notice Concerning Several Issues in Carrying Out Mergers and Bankruptcy of State-Owned Enterprises on a Trial Basis," *Jingji gongzuo tongxun* (Economic Work Bulletin), August 31, 1996, pp. 14,13, in FBIS, *China,* 96-212, August 31, 1996.

54. World Bank, *From Plan to Market,* p. 101.

55. Tong Ting, "Citizens Maintain Focus on Savings," *China Daily Business Weekly,* February 15-21, 1998, p. 3. Gross domestic product in 1997 was RMB 7,477 billion.

56. World Bank, *From Plan to Market,* p. 101.

57. Sheng also includes other bankers in his list, between shareholders and employees. Regulatory authorities may force healthy banks to absorb part of the cost of rescuing a single failing institution. This is not relevant in China since the healthy banks are recently created and thus far too small to absorb a significant share of the losses of the largest state-owned banks. Sheng, *Bank Restructuring,* p. 32.

58. A formal law establishing the legal principles governing the use of collateral was not passed by the Standing Committee of the National People's Congress until October 1995. "Security Law of the People's Republic of China," in *Almanac of China's Finance and Banking 1996,* pp. 312–17.

59. At year-end 1997 there were 745 listed companies on the Shanghai and Shenzhen stock exchanges. Karby Leggett, "China Cos Raised CNY44.12B on Shanghai Stk Exchange in '97," *Wall Street Journal,* interactive edition, January 7, 1998.

60. Article 43 precludes commercial banks from investing in nonbank financial institutions or in enterprises. Article 43 does allow banks to hold real estate or stock in companies but only when these assets have been pledged as collateral

on loans. If the borrower fails to repay the principal and interest on the loan, the bank may obtain ownership of these pledged assets by foreclosing on the borrower. Banks, however, are required to sell such assets within one year. "Commercial Banking Law," *China Law and Practice*, June 27, 1995, p. 40. The restriction in investing in nonbank financial institutions or in enterprises, however, does not apply to the policy banks. By mid-1996, for example, the State Development Bank had swapped RMB 24.2 billion of debt of state-owned enterprises into equity. These swaps were in key industries such as coal, hydroelectric power, and the military sector. International Monetary Fund, *People's Republic of China–Selected Issues*, Staff Country Report 97/72 (Washington, 1997), p. 27. Trust and investment companies have also undertaken some swaps of this nature.

61. Michael S. Borish, Millard F. Long, and Michel Noel, *Restructuring Banks and Enterprises: Recent Lessons from Transition Countries*, Discussion Paper 279 (Washington: World Bank, 1995), pp. 21–23.

62. There is some indication that the state is preparing to reorganize the four largest state-owned banks into shareholding companies. That could be an initial step in preparing for public listings of these institutions.

63. Data on the high operating costs of China's major banks are presented in the section on competition.

64. Sheng, *Bank Restructuring*, p. 34.

65. David Begg and Richard Portes, "Enterprise Debt and Financial Restructuring in Central and Eastern Europe," *European Economic Review*, vol. 37 (April 1993), p. 400.

66. In addition to household and enterprise deposits, the other sources of bank deposits were treasury deposits (1.8 percent), government departments (1.7 percent), and an unidentified "other deposits" (7.3 percent). People's Bank of China, *China Financial Outlook '96* (Beijing: China Financial Publishing House, 1996), p. 95.

67. Liu Yuanda, "A Great Endeavor Brings a Major Success—A Brief Exploration of China's Capital Market."

68. In some cases borrowers are required, as a condition for receiving a loan, to maintain a certain minimum level of so-called compensating balances in their account at the bank that extends the loan. This was particularly prevalent in periods of inflation when banks were able to raise interest rates they charged borrowers by only a small fraction of the increase in prices. Requiring borrowers to maintain compensating balances raised the effective interest rate borrowers paid on the funds they were actually able to use. For example, if as a condition for extending a one-year working capital loan of RMB 1 million carrying a nominal interest rate of 10.98 percent, the bank required the borrower to maintain RMB 500,000 in its account at the bank, the effective interest rate on the RMB 500,000 the borrower would be able to use would be 21.96 percent.

69. Shan Li and Daoqui Li, "How to Reform a State Enterprise," *Asian Wall Street Journal*, December 26, 1995, p. 12.

70. Household savings deposits at year-end 1995 were RMB 2,966 million. Gross domestic product in the same year was RMB 5.8 trillion. People's Bank of China, *China Financial Outlook '96*, pp. 96, 89.

71. World Bank, *From Plan to Market*, p. 101. The bank's analysis fails to note that the main reason that these recapitalizations were not successful may have been that they were too partial. Since they did not fulfill the condition necessary to allow the banks to operate on commercial criterion, it is perhaps not surprising that the behavior of banks did not change and that the government was forced to inject additional capital.

72. World Bank, *From Plan to Market*, p. 103.

73. Sheng, *Bank Restructuring*, p. 41.

74. World Bank, *From Plan to Market*, p. 103.

75. Sheng, *Bank Restructuring*, p. 77.

76. Ibid., p. 79.

77. *Sheng, Bank Restructuring*, p. 83.

78. General Accounting Office, *Financial Audit: Resolution Trust Corporation's 1995 and 1994 Financial Statements* (Washington, July 1996), p. 13.

79. Zhou Zhengqing, "Actively, Steadily Develop Stock Market, Further Improve Shares Issuance, Listing," *Renmin ribao* (People's Daily), October 15, 1997, p. 1, in FBIS, *China,* 97-301, October 29, 1997. This amount excludes money raised through the sale of "Red Chips," Hong Kong companies that control assets in China.

80. Calculated based on data in table 3-1 and a figure of total loans outstanding at the end of the third quarter of 1997 of RMB 7.056 trillion. "Materials on Chinese Financial Statistics for the Third Quarter of 1997," *Jinrong shibao* (Financial News), October 24, 1997, p. 2.

81. Zhou Zhengqing, "Actively, Steadily Develop Stock Market, Further Improve Shares Issuance, Listing," October 15, 1997, p. 1, in FBIS, *China,* 97-301, October 29, 1997; Li Xin, "US$ 13 Billion in China's Stock Market from Overseas," *China Economic News*, November 10, 1997, p. 3; and New China News Agency, "Shanghai Paper Reports 'Successful' PRC Share Issue," August 21, 1997, in FBIS, *China,* 97-232, August 20, 1997.

82. All information on China Telecom (Hong Kong) Limited comes from the prospectus offering the Company's American Depository Shares, dated September 19, 1997.

83. Financial data presented in the offering prospectus are constructed as if the business activities of the company's predecessor operations had been conducted by the company throughout the relevant periods.

84. Net worth or owners' equity is equal to total assets less total liabilities. China Telecom (Hong Kong) Limited, prospectus offering of American Depository Shares, September 19, 1997, p. 3.

85. It is not clear if its pledge means that the MPT, which has a monopoly on wired telephone service in all of China, will not provide interconnections for any cellular services that are competitive with China Telecom. If that were to be the case, any new entrants into the mobile phone market would not have access to MPT-provided interconnections to fixed-line subscribers. Thus subscribers to any new competitive mobile service would not be able to receive calls from or place calls to subscribers to the MPT's fixed line services.

86. China Telecom (Hong Kong) Limited, prospectus offering of American Depository Shares, September 19, 1997, p. 3.

87. World Bank, *China: Pension System Reform* (Washington, 1996).

88. World Bank, *China: Urban Land Management in an Emerging Market Economy* (Washington, 1993).

89. The value of household financial assets at year-end 1995 was RMB 3.8 trillion (table 4-1). In 1995 enterprise deposits in the banks and nonbank financial institutions, which except for receivables is their only significant financial asset, was RMB 1.7 trillion. *Almanac of China's Finance and Banking 1996*, p. 428. The combined amount of RMB 5.5 trillion is in some sense an overstatement since the source of almost all of the enterprise deposits is borrowing.

90. Earlier proposals for bank recapitalization have been presented by Lawrence J. Lau and Yingyi Qian, "A Proposal for Financial Reorganization of Banks and Enterprises in China," *Gaige (Reform)*, no. 6 (November 1994), pp. 25–38; Wu Xiaoling and Xie Ping, "Envisaging the Restructuring of the Debts of China's State-Owned Banks and Enterprises," *Caimao jingji* (Finance and Trade Economics), no. 12 (December 1994), pp. 13–17; and Wu Xiaoling, ed. *Research Report on Restructuring the Debt of State-Owned Enterprises in China* (Beijing: China Financial Publishing House, 1997).

91. Sheng, *Bank Restructuring*, p. 34.

92. People's Bank of China, *China Financial Outlook '97* (Beijing: China Financial Publishing House, 1997), p. 95.

93. In most financial systems excess reserves are reserves placed in the central bank voluntarily by financial institutions. In China, however, banks are mandated to maintain both required reserves (*zhunbei jin*) and excess reserves (*chaoe chubei*). In the mid-1990s the mandated ratios were 13 percent and 5 to 7 percent of each bank's total deposits, for required and excess reserves, respectively. In practice the quantity of excess reserves commercial banks as a group placed in the central bank exceeded the 5 to 7 percent mandated level. As explained in chapter 3, this phenomenon is likely to reflect the effect of the credit plan of the People's Bank.

94. Although the central bank could discontinue paying interest on such deposits, there would be no net gain in the strength of the financial system since the gain of the central bank would be fully offset by the reduction of the interest income of the commercial banks.

95. Fiscal revenues at all levels of government in 1996 were RMB 736.661 billion; gross domestic product was RMB 6,779.5 billion. Liu Zhongli, "Report on the Implementation of the Central and Local Budgets for 1996 and on the Draft Central and Local Budgets for 1997," *Beijing Review*, April 7-13, 1997, p. 30; and State Statistical Bureau, "Statistical Communiqué on Socio-Economic Development in 1996," *Beijing Review*, March 10-16, 1997, p. 23.

96. On this assumption the nonperforming loans of these other financial institutions would be RMB 95 billion or about 8 percent of their loans outstanding.

97. Minxin Pei, "Banking Reforms in China in 1993–96," unpublished manuscript. Measured by the share of loans that are "past due," the quality of township and village enterprise borrowing, mostly from rural credit cooperatives, is the lowest of any single category of loans. Xu Yuyun, "Earnestly Resolve the New Problems in the Management of Credit to Township and Village Enterprises," *Jinrong shibao* (Financial News), November 26, 1998, p. 5.

98. Thirty-five percent of gross domestic product in 1995 is equivalent to 15 percent of the assets of all domestic financial institutions. See table A-1.

99. Sheng, *Bank Restructuring*, p. 54.

100. David K. H. Begg, *Monetary Policy in Central and Eastern Europe: Lessons after Half a Decade of Transition*, Working Paper 108 (Washington: International Monetary Fund, 1996), p. 37.

101. Sheng, *Bank Restructuring*, p. 41.

102. Payments at a below-market interest rate, which reduced the real value of the bonds injected into Hungarian banks to a level less than the face value of the bonds, was a factor contributing to inadequate recapitalization.

103. Nan Ke, "The Sale by a Syndicate of This Year's Ten-Year State Bond Has Been Satisfactorily Completed," *Jinrong shibao* (Financial News), June 13, 1996, p. 8. The Ministry of Finance did not offer indexing on the interest rate on this bond to protect investors from inflation.

104. Qian Jin, "The Ten-Year Government Bond Enters the Market with a Sparkle," *Jinrong shibao* (Financial News), July 13, 1996, p. 8.

105. Peter Dittus, "Bank Reform and Behavior in Central Europe," *Journal of Comparative Economics*, vol. 19 (December 1994), pp. 342–43.

106. World Bank, *China: Reform of State-Owned Enterprises* (Washington, 1996), p. 13 reports the 7.6 per cent figure for 67 profitable enterprises found in a sample of 156 enterprises. In the sample the ratio of value added to sales is 0.32. In 1995 state-owned enterprises produced about one-third of industrial output, and industry accounted for 42 percent of gross domestic product. Thus the social expenditures of state-owned manufacturing firms can be estimated as 3.3 percent of gross domestic product (= $(0.076/.32) \times 0.33 \times 0.42$).

107. If other sectors provide social services directly to their employees that are comparable to those provided by state-owned industrial enterprises, the total amount of such expenditures would be 10 percent of gross domestic product. I assume that one-third is expenditure on day care, lounges, athletic facilities and other amenities for workers that are treated as a normal cost of doing business by firms in most market economies; one-third is expenditure to cover the difference between nominal rental payments and the cost of providing housing to workers that should be paid for by workers from their wages; and one-third is for schools, hospitals, and other expenditures that should be financed from the state budget.

108. World Bank, *China 2020: Development Challenges in the New Century* (Washington, 1997), p. 143.

109. In 1994 budgetary revenue in China was 14.1 percent of gross national product. The average for all developing countries was 31.7 percent. World Bank, *The Chinese Economy: Fighting Inflation, Deepening Reforms*, p. 39.

110. In 1996 taxes as a share of gross domestic product rose to 10.9 percent, compared with 10.7 percent in 1995. Liu Zhongli, "Report on the Implementation of the Central and Local Budgets for 1996 and on the Draft Central and Local Budgets for 1997," *Beijing Review*, April 7–13, 1997, p. 30; and State Statistical Bureau, "Statistical Communiqué on Socio-Economic Development in 1996," *Beijing Review*, March 10-16, 1997, p. 23. Revenue from the industrial and com-

mercial tax, the value-added tax, and the consumption tax grew by 15 percent in 1997, roughly twice the rate of growth of nominal output. These taxes account for a relatively large share of government revenue. If the remaining taxes grew by the same proportion, the tax share of gross domestic product rose by more than 0.5 percentage point in 1997.

111. State Statistical Bureau, *China Statistical Yearbook 1995*, pp. 32, 222.

112. Xinhua (New China News Agency), "Vice-Minister on Issuing Treasury Bonds," February 26, 1997 in FBIS, *China*, 97-039, February 26, 1997.

113. James A. Daniel, *Fiscal Aspects of Bank Restructuring*, Working Paper 52 (Washington: International Monetary Fund, 1997), p. 27. This figure subsequently fell when the government allocated substantial privatization revenues in the mid-1990s to the repayment of debt. Gross debt stood at 75 percent of gross domestic product in 1996 and was expected to fall to 70 percent in 1997. Organization for Economic Cooperation and Development, *Hungary* (Paris, 1997), p. 6.

114. Richard Cookson, "A Survey of Japanese Finance," *Economist*, June 28, 1997, p. 3.

115. Two technical modifications to this statement are required. First, it assumes that the government cannot finance part of the deficit from seignorage. As discussed in chapter 1, seignorage was large in the past but has declined dramatically since 1993 and is likely to continue to remain low. Second, it assumes that there is no primary government deficit that also needs to be financed. The primary deficit is the government deficit net of interest expenditures to finance the existing stock of government debt. For example, as noted, in 1995 the government deficit was 1.7 percent of gross domestic product or RMB 98 billion. But interest paid from the budget on the existing stock of government debt outstanding was RMB 35 billion. Thus the primary deficit was 1.1 percent of gross domestic product.

116. The total increase in expenditures needed to finance the program is the sum of 1.8 or 2.4 percent of gross domestic product to finance the total stock of debt after recapitalization (= 30 or 40 percent x 0.06), 3.3 percent to move quasi-fiscal social expenditures to the budget, and 1.1 percent to finance the primary government deficit (see previous note) for a total of 6.2 or 6.8 percent of gross domestic product. If real growth is 8 percent then 3.2 percentage points or about one-half of the total increase in expenditure needed could be financed by increased issue of debt. The balance of 3.0 or 3.6 percentage points of gross domestic product, about half of the total, would have to be financed by increased tax revenue.

117. Article 48 of the central bank law prohibits a local government, government departments at all levels, social organizations, and individuals from forcing the People's Bank to make a loan to a local government, a government department, a nonbank financial institution, work unit, or individual. "People's Bank of China Law," *China Law and Practice*, June 27, 1995, pp. 23–31. Article 41 of the commercial bank law prohibits units or individuals from compelling a commercial bank to extend a loan or provide guarantees for a loan. New China News Agency, "Commercial Bank Law of the People's Republic of China," May 11, 1995, in FBIS, *China*, 95-094, May 16, 1995, pp. 27–35.

118. *Almanac of China's Finance and Banking 1997*, pp. 3, 502–04; and Henry Sender, "Money Isn't Everything," *Far Eastern Economic Review*, February 12, 1998, p. 58.

119. Article 13 of the 1995 Commercial Bank Law specifies RMB 1 billion, approximately U.S.$120 million, as the minimum capital requirement for forming a new bank. This is more than adequate. In fact it is so high that it may constitute a significant barrier to the entry of new banks.

120. Asian Development Bank, *Report and Recommendation of the President to the Board of Directors on a Proposed Loan to the People's Republic of China for the Everbright Bank of China Project and a Proposed Equity Investment in the Everbright Bank of China* (Manila, 1996), p. 12.

121. The countries are a mix of high-income industrialized countries, transition economies, and emerging market economies. "Strength, Jobs and Employee Performance," *The Banker*, vol. 147 (July 1997), p. 142.

122. "Efficiency Figures in the List," *The Banker*, vol. 147 (July 1997), p. 140.

123. In 1996 the largest four state-owned banks as a group shuttered 2,138 of their offices. Although this was a reduction of only about 2 percent, it is nonetheless significant since it marks the first time in the reform period that these banks as a group have reduced their network of offices. *Almanac of China's Finance and Banking 1996*, p. 542; and *Almanac 1997*, p. 592; and Kathy Chen, "China to Restructure Central Bank, Plans Panel to Guide Finance Policy," *Wall Street Journal*, interactive edition, April 7, 1998.

124. Organization for Economic Cooperation and Development, *Hungary*, pp. 46–47.

125. Ibid., p. 54.

126. Begg, *Monetary Policy in Central and Eastern Europe*, p. 40.

127. Xie Ping, "On the Reform of the State-Owned Specialized Banks," *Jingji yanjiu* (Economic Research), no. 2 (February 1994), p. 23.

128. Interest earned on government bonds and bonds issued by financial institutions, such as the policy banks, is exempt from the business tax and surtax.

129. The bank paid RMB 4.789 billion in business taxes and surtaxes and RMB 2.367 billion in income taxes. *Almanac of China's Finance and Banking 1996*, p. 483.

130. Tony Walker, "China Reduces Bank Taxes," *Financial Times*, March 3, 1997, p. 4; and Li Zhiqiang, "Background and Possible Effects of Tax Policy Adjustment for Financial and Insurance Sectors," *Zhongguo shuiwu bao* (China Tax Bulletin), May 23, 1997, in FBIS, *China*, 97-223, August 11, 1997.

131. Tong Ting, "Overseas RMB Banks Face 33% Tax," *China Daily Business Weekly*, June 2, 1997, p. 1. It appears that the Ministry of Finance wanted to respond to the longstanding suggestion of the World Bank that China unify the tax rates faced by different categories of financial institutions but was unwilling to countenance the reduction in revenues caused by reducing the rate on China's four largest banks from the previous level of 55 percent to 33 percent, the rate faced by other banks.

132. Li, "Background and Possible Effects of Tax Policy Adjustment for Financial and Insurance Sectors."

133. The sole exception is the China Investment Bank, which was created in

1981. Since it became a subsidiary of the Construction Bank of China in 1994, its income tax rate has been 55 percent.

134. Foreign banks that have been licensed to conduct domestic currency business have had their income tax rates raised to 33 percent (30 percent is an enterprise income tax, 3 percent is a local income tax). But the higher rate will be paid only on the income from the domestic currency business earned by their branches located in Pudong.

135. Paul Bowles and Gordon White, *The Political Economy of China's Financial Reforms* (Westview Press, 1993), pp. 58–62.

136. Recall from chapter 3 that at that time China had a monobanking system in which the People's Bank served simultaneously as the central bank and the country's only bank. Thus the branches of the People's Bank were the source of most loans.

137. William A. Byrd, *China's Financial System: The Changing Role of Banks* (Westview Press, 1983), p. 12.

138. World Bank, *China: Financial Sector Policies and Institutional Development*, p. 5; and World Bank, *China: Macroeconomic Stability in a Decentralized Economy*, pp. 43–44.

139. National People's Congress, People's Bank of China Law, adopted on March 18, 1995. A bilingual text of the law is available in *China Law and Practice*, June 27, 1995, pp. 23–30. The prohibition on government borrowing from the central bank is contained in article 28. For a detailed analysis of the law see Lester Ross and Mitchell A. Silk, "Banking on Change," *China Business Review*, vol. 22 (November-December 1995), pp. 35–39.

140. World Bank, *China: Macroeconomic Stability in a Decentralized Economy*, pp. 44, 73; and Minxin Pei, "Banking Reforms in China 1993–96," unpublished manuscript.

141. People's Bank of China Law, article 7.

142. State Council, "Decision to Have the Specialized Bank, the People's Bank of China, Serve as the Central Bank of China"; and "Provisional Regulations of the People's Republic of China on the Control of Banks," in *China Laws for Foreign Business* (Hong Kong: CCH Australia Limited), pp. 10652–653.

143. The other members of the board of directors stipulated in the 1983 regulations were a few advisers and specialists of the People's Bank, the deputy governor of the People's Bank, a vice minister of the State Planning Commission, a vice minister of the State Economic Commission, and the head of the People's Insurance Company of China. By the late 1980s, the composition of the board was little changed except that a vice minister of the State Economic Reform Commission had replaced the vice minister of the State Economic Commission, presumably because the State Council abolished the later organization in 1988. World Bank, *China: Financial Policies and Institutional Development*, p. 5.

144. New China News Agency, "State Council Appoints First Currency Policy Committee," August 1, 1997, in FBIS, *China*, 97-213, August 1, 1997.

145. At the first meeting of the Monetary Policy Commission, People's Bank of China Governor Dai Xianglong was identified as chairman of the commission and People's Bank Vice Governor Chen Yuan was identified as vice chairman. Members

identified were vice minister for the State Planning Commission, Wang Chunzheng; vice minister of the State Economic and Trade Commission, Chen Qingtai; vice minister of finance, Xie Xuren; director of the State Administration of Foreign Exchange, Zhou Xiaochuan; vice chairman of the State Securities Regulatory Commission, Chen Yaoxian; president of the Industrial and Commercial Bank of China, Shi Jiliang; and the former president of People's University, Huang Da.

146. People's Bank of China Law, article 29, forbids the bank from making loans to financial institutions other than banks, except when a specific exception is authorized by the State Council. Article 4 authorizes the central bank to carry out financial business only as part of its implementation of monetary policy. Thus it can require banks to deposit reserves, buy and sell state bonds and foreign exchange in the open market, and so forth. This authority obviously would not extend to running a stock brokerage business for individual or institutional clients.

147. People's Bank of China, *People's Bank of China Quarterly Statistical Bulletin*, vol. 9, no. 1 (1998), p. 10. Central bank lending to nonfinancial institutions peaked at RMB 74.4 billion at mid-year 1996. Outstanding lending was RMB 68.6 billion at year-end 1996. Thus the big drop in such lending occurred largely in 1997.

148. In December 1997 the Liaoning Provincial branch of the central bank divested itself of the Liaoning Securities Company. The company was originally established by the provincial branch of the central bank in 1988, and it subsequently absorbed twenty-four securities firms owned by municipal subbranches of the central bank. Karby Leggett, "China: Liaoning Securities Cos Spun Off from PBOC," *Wall Street Journal* interactive edition, December 8, 1997. The identity of the new owners of Liaoning Securities Company was not disclosed.

149. State Council, "Notice Concerning the Establishment of the State Development Bank," *Zhonghua renmin gongheguo guowuyuan gongbao* (Bulletin of the State Council of the People's Republic of China), no. 10 (June 1994), pp. 393–96.

150. Tong Ting, "Eximbank's Functions Strengthened," *China Daily Business Weekly*, June 1, 1995, p.3. This responsibility was previously handled by the China Trust and Investment Corporation for Foreign Economic Relations and Trade, a nonbank financial institution established in 1987. The China Trust and Investment Corporation for Foreign Economic Relations and Trade subsequently became the finance arm of the China National Chemicals Import and Export Corporation, one of China's largest trading companies. After the merger the government loans it previously held were transferred to the China Import-Export Bank.

151. Mou Ling, "Stride Toward a Completely New System," *Jinrong shibao* (Financial News), June 14, 1995, p. 1.

152. Dai Gang, "The Deep Footprint of China's Financial Reform," *Renmin ribao* (People's Daily), January 12, 1995, pp. 1–2; and *Almanac of China's Finance and Banking 1995* (Beijing: China Financial Publishing House, 1995), p. 67. "President on Work of the State Development Bank," *China Economic News*, April 3, 1995, p. 7.

153. *Almanac of China's Finance and Banking 1995*, p. 67.

154. Dai Gang, "The Deep Footprint of China's Financial Reform," *Renmin ribao* (People's Daily), January 12, 1995, p. 1; and *Almanac of China's Finance and Banking 1995*, pp. 65, 516.

155. *Almanac of China's Finance and Banking 1996*, p. 437; and *Almanac 1997*, p. 474.

156. Liu Weiling, "Export-Import Business Tries to Feed Fund Hunger," *China Daily*, January 23, 1995, p. 1; and *Almanac of China's Finance and Banking 1995*, p. 516.

157. *Almanac of China's Finance and Banking 1997*, p. 474.

158. Ibid., p. 474.

159. Ibid., p. 501.

160. New China News Agency, "Agricultural Development Bank to Issue Bonds," March 18, 1996, in FBIS, *China*, 96-055, March 20, 1996, p. 31.

161. At year-end 1996 the Agricultural Development Bank had 610 billion in loans outstanding from the central bank, an amount equal to 98 percent of the bank's outstanding loans of RMB 624.8 billion. *Almanac of China's Finance and Banking 1997*, p. 502.

162. World Bank, *The Chinese Economy: Fighting Inflation, Deepening Reforms*, p. 31.

163. In 1994 the State Development Bank and the Import-Export Bank each issued three-year bonds that paid 12.5 percent and five-year bonds that paid 14.0 percent. By contrast three-year treasury bonds paid 13.96 percent and five-year treasuries paid 15.86 percent. Moreover, state treasury bonds also paid supplementary interest designed to insulate purchasers from the effects of inflation. The supplement was not offered on the bonds of either the State Development Bank or the Import-Export Bank. *Almanac of China's Finance and Banking 1995*, pp. 485, 513. The same pattern was evident in 1995. For example, the banks' three-year bonds paid 11.2 percent, 2.3 percentage points less than three-year treasury bonds. *Almanac of China's Finance and Banking 1996*, pp. 437, 468.

164. World Bank, *China: Macroeconomic Stability in a Decentralized Economy*, p. 79; and World Bank, *The Chinese Economy: Fighting Inflation, Deepening Reform*, pp. 35–36.

165. *Almanac of China's Finance and Banking 1995*, p. 65.

166. World Bank, *China: Macroeconomic Stability in a Decentralized Economy*, p. 142. The transferred amount was RMB 65 billion.

167. Liu Weiling, "Bank Support to Power Projects," *China Daily Business Weekly*, May 8, 1995, p. 3.

168. This is State Council Document 91. *Zhonghua renmin gongheguo guowuyuan gongbao* (Bulletin of the State Council of the People's Republic of China) no. 31, 1993 (January 29, 1994), pp. 1488–496.

Notes to Chapter 5

1. World Bank, *From Plan to Market* (Oxford University Press, 1996), p. 21.

2. According to the World Bank, 1.5 percentage points of the 9.4 percent aver-

age annual real growth between 1978 and 1995 equals one-sixth. World Bank, *China 2020: Development Challenges in the New Century* (Washington, 1997), p. 5.

3. Money losing firms, under this scheme, would have been allowed to borrow to finance operating losses but would not have been allowed to purchase new fixed assets or to hire any new workers.

4. World Bank, *Clear Water, Blue Skies: China's Environment in the New Century* (Washington, 1997), p. 1.

5. Ibid., p. 12.

6. Ibid., p. 91.

7. Ibid., p. 2.

8. Ibid., p. 17.

9. The study does not estimate the economic losses from climate change induced by the increasing concentration of carbon dioxide in the atmosphere. Although the resulting greenhouse effect damages "agricultural production, terrestrial and aquatic ecosystems, human settlement, and human health," the World Bank did not attempt to quantify these costs. In part this was because of complications of valuation and in part because "most of the effects of climate change are expected to occur beyond the time frame of this study (that is, after 2020)." Ibid., pp. 22–23.

10. The two methodologies differ in their approach to valuing human life. The higher number is based on an estimated value of a human life in China of U.S.$60,000 in urban areas and U.S.$31,800 in rural areas. These numbers set the value of a life in China at 2 percent of the value of a life in the United States, the latter derived from the standard methodology for evaluating environmental impacts in industrial countries. The lower number is based only on the wages lost owing to a premature death, U.S.$9,000 in urban areas, U.S.$4,800 in rural areas. Ibid., p. 23.

11. Ibid., p. 38.

12. Ibid., p. 37.

13. Ibid., p. 38.

14. World Bank, *China 2020*, p. 75.

15. Ibid., p. 65.

16. Vaclav Smil, *Environmental Problems in China: Estimates of Economic Costs*, Special Reports 5 (Honolulu: East-West Center, 1996), p. 51.

17. World Bank, *At China's Table: Food Security Options* (Washington, 1997), pp. 20, 36.

18. World Bank, *China 2020*, p. 66.

19. World Bank, *At China's Table*, pp. 19, 38.

20. Ibid., p. 38.

21. The bank estimates the cost of reclamation as ranging from RMB 15,000 to RMB 150,000 per hectare. If the midpoint of this range represents the average cost of reclamation per hectare, annual expenditure for reclaiming 245,000 hectares, the average annual amount reclaimed between 1988 and 1995, can be estimated at RMB 20.2 billion. The bank recommends that China award long-term leases for reclaimed land, so that reclamation expenditures would no longer be borne by the state.

22. World Bank, *Infrastructure Development in East Asia and Pacific: Towards a New Public-Private Partnership* (Washington, 1995), p. 4.

23. World Bank, *The Chinese Economy: Fighting Inflation, Deepening Reform* (Washington, 1996), p. 56.

24. Ibid.

25. For more details on the analytical framework used in the analysis and a discussion of the data through 1994, see Nicholas R. Lardy, "The Role of Foreign Trade and Investment in China's Economic Transformation," *China Quarterly*, no. 144 (December 1995), pp. 1065–82.

26. Tian Li, "Another Steadily Evolving Year: A Review of the Financial Situation in 1997," *Renmin ribao* (Haiwai ban) (People's Daily) (overseas edition), January 13, 1998, p. 2.

27. Lin Ying, "Chinese Enterprises' Investments Abroad Have Reached a Certain Preliminary Scale," Hong Kong Zhongguo Tongxun she (Hong Kong China News Agency), October 30, 1997, in Foreign Broadcast Information Service, *China*, 97-310, November 6, 1997. (Hereafter, FBIS, *China*.) The United Nations estimates that China's cumulative foreign direct investment outflows by year-end 1996 were U.S.$18.002 billion. UN Conference on Trade and Development, *World Investment Report 1997: Transnational Corporations, Market Structure and Competition Policy* (New York: United Nations, 1997), p. 322. See also David Wall, *Outflows of Capital from China*, Technical Papers 123 (Paris: Organization for Economic Cooperation and Development Development Center, March 1997).

28. World Bank, *China 2020*, pp. 92, 125. Alternative explanations for the large magnitude of the error and omissions term include the failure of China's balance of payments accounting system to capture all of the reinvested profits of foreign-funded enterprises and the remittances of expatriate managers of foreign-funded enterprises in China.

29. Chinese enterprises account for 22 percent of Hong Kong's total trade volume and 24 percent of all the entrepôt trade into China. Gu Yongjiang, "Chinese Enterprises Become Hong Kong's Important Economic Force," *Ta Kung Pao*, October 21, 1997, p. 1, in FBIS, *China*, 97-307, November 3, 1997.

30. Nonsovereign bonds issued internationally in 1997 for road building included the U.S.$200 million Zhuhai Highway, the U.S.$280 million Greater Beijing Regional Expressway, and the U.S.$600 million Guangzhou Superhighway. Many other highway bond issues were in the pipeline in late 1997. How many will ultimately reach the market remains to be seen. Dehong Wang, "Highways-High Yields and High Hopes," *South China Morning Post, China Business Review–Transportation*, February 12, 1998, p. 1. In addition, there are several mainland China toll-road stocks listed on the Hong Kong Stock Exchange, including Zhejiang, Anhui, Jiangsu, Shenzhen, and Sichuan Expressway Companies. Of course, the flotation of these companies in Hong Kong does not involve any foreign exchange risk since the investment by foreigners is in the form of equity rather than debt.

31. An obvious exception is nuclear power plants, for which China relies primarily on imported equipment. Imported turbines are frequently used in conventional electric power plants too.

32. World Bank, *China 2020*, p. 11.

33. Stephen Fidler, "More Time and Money Needed," Mexico Survey, *Financial Times*, October 28, 1996, p. 3.

34. Leslie Crawford and Stephen Fidler, "Mexico Seeks to Sell $45 Billion Bad Loans Back to Banks," *Financial Times*, December 6, 1997, p. 4.

35. International Monetary Fund, *International Financial Statistics* (Washington, August 1997), p. 474.

36. Jathon Sapsford, " The Outlook: What Asia May Need Is Far Slower Growth," *Wall Street Journal*, November 3, 1997, p. A1.

37. Richard Cookson, "A Survey of Japanese Finance," *Economist*, June 28, 1997, p. 9.

38. Andrew Sheng, *Bank Restructuring: Lessons from the 1980s* (Washington: World Bank, 1996), pp. 10–11.

39. Huang Da, "On Financial and Monetary Reforms," *Caimao jingji* (Finance and Trade Economics) no. 8 (August 1994), cited in An Tifu and Liang Peng, "China's State Finance: Current Situation, Problems, and Remedies," *Caizheng yanjiu* (Financial Research), no. 7 (August 1996), pp. 15-19, in FBIS, *China*, 96-207, July 5, 1996.

40. In numerous small county-level towns it is very common "for just one small real estate company to hold non-performing loans worth tens of millions of yuan." Jasper Becker, "Crisis Feared in Property Sector," *South China Morning Post*, December 3, 1997. Becker's source is a lengthy article in the Chinese newspaper *Economic Information Daily*. In 1996 China had 18,200 towns that were designated as county level.

41. Peter Churchouse, "China: Property," Asia/Pacific Investment Research (Hong Kong: Morgan Stanley Dean Witter, 1997), pp.1, 3.

42. Yu Wong, "Shanghai Faces a Towering Overcapacity of Office Space," *Asian Wall Street Journal*, weekly edition, October 3, 1997, p. 6.

43. Jasper Becker, "Crisis Feared in Property Sector," *South China Morning Post*, December 3, 1997.

44. Peter Churchouse, "China: Property," p. 3. James Harding, "Shanghai Real Estate Market Down 50%," *Financial Times*, October 7, 1997, p. 6. For example, in Beijing the average rent for prime office space fell from U.S.$70 to U.S.$75 per square meter per month in 1995 to as low as U.S.$25 to U.S.$35 in late 1997. Yu Wong, "Developers Build in Beijing, Vying for 'Downtown' Mantle," *Wall Street Journal*, interactive edition, December 5, 1997.

45. An investment banker based in Singapore estimates that real estate loans account for 20 to 25 percent of total domestic credit. There is no indication how this estimate was derived. Chi Lo, "Despite Big Bad Loans, China Can Avert a Financial Crisis," *Asian Wall Street Journal*, weekly edition, January 5, 1998, p. 16.

46. Anjali Kumar and others, *China's Non-Bank Financial Institutions: Trust and Investment Companies*, Discussion Paper 358 (Washington: World Bank, 1997), pp. 15–16.

47. Profit would be reduced by any interest premium they had to pay to borrow the domestic currency compared with the interest they earned on their temporary holdings of foreign exchange.

48. Beginning in mid-1997 the Bank of China began offering forward foreign currency contracts of up to six months. But the bank will only enter into these contracts with firms that can demonstrate a contractual trade-related commitment to pay dollars in the future. Thus a Chinese company with a contract to pay U.S. dollars for imports to be delivered in three months could purchase U.S. dollars for forward delivery. Illegal forward trading by unauthorized financial institutions frequently is reported, but the magnitude of this trading is likely to be limited.

49. The purchase of foreign exchange by Chinese firms and institutions to repay foreign loans requires the approval of the State Administration of Exchange Control. People's Bank of China, "Regulations on Forex Sale, Purchase, and Payment," part 2, June 20, 1996, *China Economic News*, September 9, 1996, p. 7.

50. International Monetary Fund, *People's Republic of China–Recent Economic Developments*, Country Report 97/21 (Washington, 1997), pp. 88–89.

51. As of August 1997 cumulative actually utilized foreign direct investment stood at U.S. $204.4 billion. Guo Xin, "China's Foreign Trade Blossoms," *China Daily*, November 4, 1997, p. 4. Officially reported external debt at mid-year 1997 was U.S.$118.64 billion.

52. UN Conference on Trade and Development, *World Investment Report 1997: Transnational Corporations, Market Structure and Competition Policy*, p. 316. Note that the external debt figure excludes in excess of $50 billion borrowed by Korean subsidiaries operating abroad. If this borrowing is included in external borrowing, the borrowing is thirteen times foreign direct investment.

53. Cumulative foreign direct investment stood at U.S.$19.589 billion. UN Conference on Trade and Development, *World Investment Report 1997*, p. 316. External borrowing stood at U.S.$98.368 billion. J. P. Morgan, *Emerging Markets: Economic Indicators* (New York, November 7, 1997), p. 18.

54. International Monetary Fund, *People's Republic of China—Recent Economic Developments*, p. 91.

55. Moody's Investors Service, *China* (New York, September 1997), p. 10, places China's short-term debt at $40 billion of a total debt at year-end 1996 of $138. 5 billion.

56. Andrew Pollack, "Package of Loans Worth $55 billion Is Set for Korea," *New York Times*, December 4, 1997, pp. A1, A4.

57. State Statistical Bureau, *A Statistical Abstract of China 1996* (Beijing: Statistical Publishing House, 1996), p. 105.

58. Tian Li, "Another Steadily Evolving Year: A Review of the Financial Situation in 1997," *Renmin ribao* (Haiwai ban) (People's Daily) (overseas edition), January 13, 1998, p. 2.

59. Paul Bowles and Gordon White, "Contradictions in China's Financial Reform: The Relationship between Banks and Enterprises," *Cambridge Journal of Economics*, vol. 13 (December 1989), p. 489.

60. Xinhua (New China News Agency), "Vice Minister on Making Auto Industry More Competitive," November 28, 1997, in FBIS, *China*, 97-334, November 30, 1997.

61. Capital invested per vehicle produced is calculated based on data on investment in fixed assets between 1990 and 1995. Ibid.

62. State Planning Commission, "Auto Industry Policy," *Renmin ribao* (People's Daily), July 4, 1994, p. 2, in FBIS, *China*, 94-136, July 15, 1994, p. 26.

63. As of October 1, 1997, tariff rates on sedans were reduced from an initial level of 120 percent to 100 percent or from an initial level of 100 percent to 80 percent, depending on engine size. Shen Bin, "Car Sales Slack Despite Interest and Tariff Cuts," *China Daily Business Weekly*, December 22, 1997, p. 2. Prior to the tariff cuts that began in the mid-1990s, tariff rates on imported autos were as high as 200 percent.

64. As discussed in chapter 3, officially acknowledged nonperforming loans of the largest state- owned banks in China constituted 22 percent of their loan portfolios at year-end 1995. In Korea the level of nonperforming loans officially acknowledged by the Ministry of Finance in November 1997 constituted 18.5 percent of total loans outstanding. Peter Montagnon and John Ridding, "Banks 'Face Years of Losses and Cuts,'" *Financial Times*, November 25, 1997, p. 10. Actual losses could ultimately be higher in both countries. Note that the ratio of domestic credit to gross domestic product in Korea is 120 percent, about a third more than the ratio in China while the ratio of nonperforming loans in China is about a fourth greater than in Korea. Thus the costs of resolving financial problems in the two countries may be roughly similar.

65. Wang Lihong, "Bank Works on Improving Efficiency," *China Daily Business Weekly*, November 17, 1997, p. 1.

66. Ye Yaozhong, "Raise Credit Quality by Deepening Reform," *Jinrong shibao* (Financial News), November 20, 1997, p. 2.

67. Ye Hongyan, "Recognizing the Current Crisis of Bad Loans in China's Financial Structure," *Ta Kung Pao*, January 20, 1998. Governor Dai explained that 25 percent was the sum of past due, doubtful, and bad loans, the three-tier structure explained in chapter 3. Of the 25 percent nonperforming loans, only 2 percentage points was acknowledged to be "bad," the same percent previously announced for year-end 1995. Of the remainder, the majority was said to be doubtful, indicating a further deterioration in the quality of loan portfolios as compared with year-end 1995 when the ratio of doubtful to past due was 2:3. From the context of Governor Dai's remarks it appears that the numbers apply to the loans of the four largest state-owned banks.

68. Loans outstanding grew from RMB 6.4 trillion to RMB 7.5 trillion in 1997, an increase of 16.7 percent. See table 3-1, including notes. Gross domestic product grew at the rate of 8.8 percent in 1997 according to statistics released by the State Statistical Bureau. New China News Agency, "Statistical Communiqué of the PRC State Statistics Bureau on National Economic and Social Development in 1997," March 4, 1998, in FBIS, *China*, 98-071, March 12, 1998.

69. The alternative hypothesis is that state banks in 1997 finally succeeded in directing a dramatically higher share of their loans to more creditworthy borrowers. Presumably many of these would be in the nonstate sector and would use such funds for investment. But for the first time in a decade the rate of investment in the first eight months of 1997 in nonstate industry fell below that of state-

owned industry. That is not consistent with the hypothesis. Tony Walker, "The Economy: A New and Testing Phase," *Financial Times, China Survey*, December 8, 1997, p. II.

70. Craig S. Smith, "Asia's Vast Inventories Threaten to Make Downturn More Painful," *Wall Street Journal*, November 26, 1997, pp. A9, A11. Smith presents data for seven Chinese companies that in 1996 had ratios of unsold inventory to sales of from 9.3 percent to 80.6 percent. For these firms the average ratio of inventory to sales in 1996 almost doubled compared with the figures for 1995.

71. *Almanac of China's Finance and Banking 1996* (Beijing: China Financial Publishing House, 1996), p. 30.

72. Editorial, "Strive to Usher In Financial Reform and Development," *Renmin ribao* (People's Daily), November 21, 1997, in FBIS, *China*, 93-327, November 23, 1997.

73. "Central Authorities Forbid Local Governments to Interfere in Banks' Loan-Granting Power," *Ming Pao*, January 11, 1998, p. A8, in FBIS, *China*, 98-012, January 12, 1998; and Tsao Hsiao, "Jiang, Li, and Zhu's New Ideas for Banking Reform," *Ching Pao* (Mirror), January 1, 1998, pp. 32–36, in FBIS, 98-015, January 15, 1998.

74. Wang Lihong, "Bad Loans Only 5% of Bank Credits," *China Daily*, January 17, 1998, p. 3; and Ye Hongyan, "Recognizing the Current Crisis of Bad Debt in China's Financial Structure," *Ta Kung Pao*, January 20, 1998.

75. Craig S. Smith, "China Banks Get Freer Hand," *Asian Wall Street Journal*, weekly edition, February 5, 1998, p. 6; and Sun Shangwu, "Financial Reform Outlined," *China Daily*, February 23, 1998, p. 1.

76. The central bank for most of the reform period has allowed some modest adjustment above or below the posted rates for each loan category. But banks were not encouraged to adjust from the posted rate on the basis of risk. More commonly, when inflation was high and posted lending rates declined in real terms, banks moved their actual rates upward by the full amount of the allowed adjustment. This points out that unless banks have considerable discretion in setting nominal interest rates, it may be impossible for them to fully take into account the variation in risk associated with different borrowers.

77. State Council, "Decision on the Reform of the Financial System," *Zhonghua renmin gongheguo guowuyuan gongbao* (Bulletin of the State Council of the People's Republic of China), 1993, no. 3 (January 29, 1994), p. 1489.

78. Mark O'Neill, "Funny Money Leaves Central Bank Feeling Distinctly Unamused," *South China Morning Post* (Business Post), February 8, 1998, p. 3.

79. Wang Wei, "Five-Grade Credit System to Come Into Force Late This Year, Zhu Rongji Says No To Double-Track System and Transition," *Sing Tao Jih Pao*, February 26, 1998, p. B5 in FBIS, *China*, 98-057, February 26, 1998. "China Increases Control over Central Bank Branches amidst Asia Crisis," Agence France-Presse, as found at Clarinet newsgroup, January 21, 1998.

80. Cheng Ruihua, "The Method for Carrying Out Credit and Asset Quality According to Five Categories," *Jinrong shibao* (Financial News), March 13, 1998, p. 1.

81. Shen Haixiong and Zhang Jinsheng, "Central Bank Governor Briefs

Reporters," New China News Agency, March 7, 1998 in FBIS, *China*, 98-068, March 9, 1998.

82. New China News Agency, "Procedures for International Borrowing Implemented," January 3, 1998, in FBIS, *China*, 98-008, January 8, 1998. For example, the procedures limit the sum of borrowing and foreign exchange guarantees extended by a nonfinancial firm to an amount not to exceed their foreign exchange earnings of the previous year. "Administrative Procedures for Borrowing International Commercial Loans by Institutions in China," *Jinrong shibao* (Financial News), December 16, 1997, p. 2, translated in *China Economic News*, January 19, 1998, pp. 8–10, and January 26, 1998, pp. 7–10.

83. The total value of guarantees overseas, guarantees of foreign exchange within China, and all foreign-exchange-denominated debt of a bank or other financial institution cannot exceed twenty times the value of its own foreign-currency-denominated capital. State Administration of Foreign Exchange, "Detailed Rules for the Implementation of the Procedures for the Administration of Guarantees Overseas by Institutions in China," article 21, *Jinrong shibao* (Financial News) January 13, 1998, p. 2, translated in *China Economic News*, March 9, 1998, pp. 8–10, and March 16, 1998, pp. 6–9.

84. "Place 'Hidden Foreign Debt' under Foreign Debt Control," *Jingji daobao* (Economic Reporter), December 1, 1997, p. 37, in FBIS, *China*, 97-346, December 12, 1997.

85. This borrowing is called nonresident borrowing from nonresident institutions.

86. "Administrative Procedures for the Issuances of Foreign Currency Bonds by Institutions in China," *Jinrong shibao* (Financial News), December 16, 1997, p. 2, translated in *China Economic News*, February 9, 1998, pp. 7–9, and February 16, 1998, pp. 7–9.

87. "Procedures on the Administration of Borrowing of International Commercial Loans by Institutions in China," articles 30, 31.

88. Ibid, article 2.

89. In addition to two branches in Hong Kong the Bank of China also controls, directly or indirectly, Nanyang Commercial Bank, Hua Chiao Commercial Bank, Po Sang Bank, Kuangtung Provincial Bank, Sin Hua Bank, China and South Sea Bank, Kincheng Banking Corporation, China State Bank, National Commercial Bank, and Yien Yeh Commercial Bank. These banks as a group had deposits of HK$560 billion at year-end 1995, 25.36 percent of all bank deposits in Hong Kong. Noel Fung and Cheung Lai-Kuen, "BOC Boasts 21pc Rise," *South China Morning Post International Weekly* (Business Post), March 9, 1996, p. 1.

90. For example, Ka Wah Bank Limited is 61 percent owned by China International Trust and Investment Corporation. Bruce Gilley, "More Read Than Red," *Far Eastern Economic Review*, August 28, 1997, pp. 50–52. The bank announced in early 1998 that it was changing its name to CITIC Ka Wah Bank.

91. Zhong Bian, "Foreign Investors Increase Actual Funds," *China Daily*, November 20, 1997, p. 4; and World Bank, *China 2020*, p. 85.

92. World Bank, *China Engaged: Integration with the World Economy* (Washington, 1997), p. 14.

93. State trading is the term applied when only a single national-level state-

owned foreign trade company is authorized to import or export a specific good. The China National Cereals Import-Export Corporation, for example, is the sole authorized company to handle international trade in wheat and rice. Designated trading is the term used when authority to trade has been given to one or a small number of provincial or local state trading companies.

94. World Bank, *China Engaged*, p. 14.

95. World Bank, *China 2020*, p. 88.

96. Yuan Guanhua, "Insurance Market's Paced Opening Works," *China Daily*, December 18, 1997, p. 6.

97. Denny Roy, "Hegemony on the Horizon," in Michael E. Brown, Sean M. Lynn-Jones, and Steven E. Miller, eds., *East Asian Security* (MIT Press, 1996).

98. Richard Bernstein and Ross H. Munro, "The Coming Conflict with America," *Foreign Affairs*, vol. 76 (March-April 1997), pp. 18–32.

99. Ibid., p. 31.

100. Ibid., p. 32.

101. World Bank, *China 2020*, p. 21.

102. The World Bank projects that China's annual growth will decline gradually to 5 percent by 2020. The projected rates are 8.4 percent for 1996–00; 6.9 percent for 2001–10; and 5.5 percent for 2011–20.

103. Nicholas R. Lardy, "Normalizing Economic Relations with China," in *Promoting U.S. Interests in China: Alternatives to the Annual MFN Review*, NBR Analysis, vol. 8 (July 1997), p. 15.

104. In fiscal year 1997 expenditure was U.S.$173 million. Of this amount $66.8 million was for economic restructuring. In fiscal year 1998 the proposed authorization was U.S.$241.5 million of which U.S.$122.8 million was for economic restructuring. *USAID Congressional Presentation*, fiscal year 1997, vol. 2, p. 877, and *USAID Congressional Presentation*, fiscal year 1998 (Washington). The formal name of this act is the Freedom for Russia and Emerging Eurasian Democracies and Open Markets Support Act of 1992.

105. Peter Wonacott, "China Terms for Bad Loans," *Wall Street Journal*, interactive edition, February 25, 1998.

106. Susan G. Esserman, U.S. Trade Representative General Counsel, testimony, Hearings before the Ways and Means Committee, Subcommittee on Trade, November 4, 1997.

107. In the case of the Bank of China the application was for a Limited Federal Branch in San Francisco. At the time of that application, June 1995, the Bank of China was already operating two branches in New York and one in Los Angeles. The Bank of Communications was licensed to open a branch in New York in 1991.

108. The requirement that a country's central bank exercise effective prudential supervision on a consolidated basis prior to allowing banks from a foreign country to open branches in the United States was established by the Foreign Bank Supervision Enhancement Act of 1991. This requirement does not apply retroactively. Thus although the Federal Reserve has not approved new applications by the Bank of China to open additional branches, it has not required the closure of branches that already existed in the United States at the time the law took effect.

109. The dates on which the approvals were given were September 23, 1996; January 27, 1997; and May 14, 1997, according to Federal Reserve Press releases of those dates. Only the Bank of China has not withdrawn its application to open an additional branch. According to Wang Xuebing, the bank's president, the bank's application to open a branch was still pending as of mid-December 1997. "Bank of China Hopes to Open New Foreign Branches," Agence France-Presse, as found at Clarinet newsgroup, December 13, 1997.

110. People's Bank of China, *China Financial Outlook '97* (Beijing: China Financial Publishing House, 1997), p. 44.

111. Ranked by assets, the Bank of China in 1995 was the thirtieth largest bank in the world. Ranked by the ratio of its foreign currency income to its total income, the Bank of China in 1995 ranked fifth in the world. *Almanac of China's Finance and Banking 1996*, p. 78.

112. Nicholas R. Lardy, "The Chinese Economy under Stress," in Roderick MacFarquhar and John K. Fairbank, eds., *The Cambridge History of China, Volume 14, The People's Republic, Part I: The Emergence of Revolutionary China 1949–1965* (Cambridge University Press, 1987), pp. 360–97.

Index

Accounting: cash *versus* accrual, 38, 104; reforming, 48–49, 129, 168; weak environment of, 49, 69, 105–06, 119–20

Agricultural Bank of China, 62, 65, 81, 85–86, 99, 105, 114, 122, 156, 205, 219; tax rate of, 170–71

Agricultural Development Bank of China, 156, 176–80

Agricultural sector: moving beyond reform, 22; raising prices in, 48; research needed, 189; sustaining growth in, 188–90; unique role in China, 3, 183; workers moving out of, 184

All-China Federation of Industry and Commerce, 69

Anhui Province, 70

Asia, U.S. exports to, 215–16

Asian banking, 166

Asian Development Bank (ADB), 67, 167

Asian financial crisis, 116, 193–209; China's vulnerability to, 18–19, 199–201, 207–9, 215; lessons of, 210

Assembly activity. *See* Manufacturing sector

Assets: false, 206; household, 132; liquidity of, 105, 199; rate of return on, 33–34

Asset stripping of state-owned enter-

prises, 51–52

Asset-to-liability ratios, 186, 208; managing, 66; in state sector, 39–43

Automotive industry: consolidation needed, 204; lending for, 82–83

Bad debts, 115–16, 119, 207. *See also* Bond-bad debt swaps

Balance sheets, black holes in, 206; consolidated, 169, 220

Bangkok Bank, 166

BankAmerica, 167

The Banker, 167

Bank for International Settlements, 168

Banking system: in China's economic transition, 15–20; commercializing, 185–86, 192, 207; confidence in, 131, 146; evolving, 59–61; imperative for modernizing, 140, 143, 165, 181–82, 200; quality of data on, 15, 99; state ownership of, 16–17; widespread insolvency of, 5–6

Bank of China, 61–62, 65, 81, 85–86, 102, 119–20, 168–69, 210, 219–20; dollar-denominated lending by, 114; losses, calculating, 112–15; superior performance of, 124; tax rate of, 171; Trust and Consultancy Corporation, 75

Bank of Communications, 66–67, 70,